GERMAN-SPEAKING EX[ILES IN] GREAT BRITAIN

3 0116 00427 6117

This book is due for return not later than the
last date stamped below, unless recalled sooner.

THE YEARBOOK OF THE RESEARCH CENTRE FOR GERMAN AND AUSTRIAN EXILE STUDIES

1

Amsterdam - Atlanta, GA 1999

GERMAN-SPEAKING EXILES IN GREAT BRITAIN

Edited by

Ian Wallace

♾ The paper on which this book is printed meets the requirements of "ISO 9706:1994, Information and documentation - Paper for documents - Requirements for permanence".

ISSN: 1388-3720
ISBN: 90-420-0415-0
©Editions Rodopi B.V., Amsterdam - Atlanta, GA 1999
Printed in The Netherlands

Table of Contents

Preface
Ian Wallace

The Integration of Aliens: 1
The Early Years of the *Association*
of Jewish Refugees Information, 1946-1950
Anthony Grenville

A Tale of One Institute and Two Cities: 25
The Warburg Institute
Dorothea McEwan

The 'Endsieg' as Ever-Receding Goal.   43
Literary Propaganda by Bruno Adler and
Robert Lucas for BBC Radio
Jennifer Taylor

The *Thomas Mann Newsletter* in London   59
1940-1942
J. M. Ritchie

'Characterology', not 'Ideology':   75
Sebastian Haffner's Refutation of Daniel Goldhagen
in *Germany: Jekyll and Hyde* (1940)
Jörg Thunecke

'Grenzüberschreitungen'. The Life and Works   95
of Werner Ilberg (1896-1978)
Jonathan Ross

'Im politischen Niemandsland der Heimatlosen,   117
Staatenlosen, Konfessionslosen, Portemonnaielosen...':
Otto Lehmann-Russbueldt in British Exile
Charmian Brinson / N. A. Furness†

Erich Fried — Language and *Heimat*   145
Steven W. Lawrie

'Eine Synthese deutscher und englischer   163
Dichtungstraditionen': Erich Fried and
Michael Hamburger as translators and poets
Axel Goodbody

Wo andere Leute wohnen. Kinder- und Jugend-   199
literatur des österreichischen Exils in Großbritannien
Ursula Seeber

Free Austrian Books: The Austrian Centre   219
and its Publications 1939-1946
Charmian Brinson and Richard Dove

'Mit freundlichen Grüßen aus der Ferne':   251
Exile Holdings at the Institute of Germanic Studies
William Abbey

The Research Centre   261
for German and Austrian Exile Studies
J. M. Ritchie, Richard Dove, Marian Malet

Index   265

Preface

Recent years have witnessed a remarkable growth of interest among academic researchers in the experiences and achievements of the German and Austrian refugees who came to Britain after the rise of fascism in the 1930s. It was this which led in 1995 to the setting up of the Research Centre for German and Austrian Exile Studies at the Institute of Germanic Studies, University of London. The publication, four years later, of the first volume of this Yearbook represents an important new milestone in the Centre's development and demonstrates too the continuing vitality of German and Austrian Exile Studies as a field of research.

The first three of the articles assembled here explore the significance of particular British institutions which in various ways offered support and encouragement to those who had fled from Germany and Austria - the Association of Jewish Refugees, the Warburg Institute, and the BBC -, while a fourth analyses the *Thomas Mann Newsletter*, one of the most significant publications produced by the refugees themselves as a means of keeping in touch with each other about their shared situation. A second group of articles deals with a number of individual refugees - Sebastian Haffner, Werner Ilberg, Otto Lehmann-Russbueldt, Erich Fried, Michael Hamburger -, men of varying fame and achievement but all of them important contributors to the story of exile in Britain. Erich Fried also forms part of a third section of the volume. This focuses on the specifically Austrian aspect of exile in Britain, with particular emphasis both on literature intended for Austrian children and adolescents and on the importance of the Austrian Centre. The volume concludes with an introduction to the exile holdings at the Institute of Germanic Studies and a brief account of the Research Centre's history and of the two major research projects in which it is currently involved.

Volumes 2 and 3 of the Yearbook, edited by Anthony Grenville and J. M. Ritchie respectively, are already in preparation. In all future volumes it is intended to focus particularly on German and Austrian exile in Great Britain while reflecting other aspects of exile studies where appropriate. The editors also intend to include some of the distinguished work being produced by the many international scholars who are now active in this important field of research.

Ian Wallace

Anthony Grenville

The Integration of Aliens: The Early Years of the *Association of Jewish Refugees Information*, 1946-50

This article analyses the first five post-war years of the *Association of Jewish Refugees Information* (1946-50), the monthly journal of the Association of Jewish Refugees, the representative organisation of the German-speaking Jewish refugees from Hitler in Britain. It examines the earliest stages of the refugees' integration, as reflected in the journal's reports on the process of naturalization, and the factors influencing them to settle in Britain, as reflected in their sense of profound alienation from their former homelands and in their sense of distance from other potential lands of settlement, principally Palestine/Israel.

The importance of Great Britain as a country of refuge and later of settlement for Jews fleeing first Germany, then Austria and Czechoslovakia in the years before the Second World War has long been insufficiently recognized. The most reliable recent estimates state that over 70,000 refugees from Hitler's pre-war Reich, the vast majority of them Jewish, reached safety in Britain,[1] of whom some 50,000 settled permanently, allowing a vigorous and readily identifiable community life with its own distinctive Central European culture to spring up, concentrated especially in North-West London. In relation to its size, population and absorptive capacity, Britain arguably took in more Jewish refugees before the war than any other country; only the USA took in more, but in terms of absolute numbers alone, while British policy severely restricted emigration to Palestine.

Whereas the refugee communities in other European countries were destroyed by the Nazis, that in Britain was able to survive and flourish, overcoming every obstacle to become, on the whole, a settled, stable and prosperous community, integrated by and large successfully into the society of its adopted homeland, which it has rewarded with cultural, commercial, intellectual and economic contributions out of all proportion to its numbers. It is the prime example of a Central European, German-speaking, Jewish refugee community taking root and thriving amidst an alien host society; this is the case neither with the Jewish refugees from Hitler in Palestine/Israel, where they were self-evidently not an alien group, nor with those in the USA, who found themselves to be but one small community among a host of immigrant groups, not a minority confronted by a broadly homogeneous majority.

The Association of Jewish Refugees is the principal organization that represents the former Jewish refugees from the Reich who settled in Britain; founded in 1941, the Association continues to this day to promote their interests and to act as a focal point for the development of a sense of community life and identity among the refugees and their descendants. The principal means by which it communicates with its members and through which it communicates the public image of the community it represents to society at large is its monthly journal, the *Association of Jewish Refugees Information*, which began life in the summer of 1941 as a circular sent to members of the Association and appeared irregularly every few months during the war in a small-scale format.

In January 1946 the *AJR Information* commenced publication as a regular monthly journal, initially eight full-size pages in length, and it continues to appear to this day. In 1946 its co-editors were Werner Rosenstock, for many years also General Secretary of the Association, and Herbert Freeden (Friedenthal), who left for Israel in 1950. From its inception, the journal acquired a special place in the hearts and loyalties of its readers — it has a circulation of over 3,500, spread over many countries — and it also reached an enviable level in its coverage of cultural, political and social matters relevant to the readership, an intellectual standard that has been maintained by Rosenstock's successors, including Richard Grunberger, editor for the past ten years and himself a boyhood refugee from Vienna.

Scholarly research came late to the German-speaking refugees from Hitler in Britain. Only in the 1980s did academic studies of the community that had developed in Britain after 1945 start to appear in any number, and almost all of these were studies of particular sections or aspects of the community and its development: the areas of public life where refugees made a notable contribution to British society, the economy or the arts and sciences, the field that has attracted the most attention; particular groups like the Kindertransportees; exceptional experiences like the mass internment of 1940; local groups; or relations with the host society and British government policy as it affected the refugees in the earlier years of their exile.[2]

Modern academic studies of the refugee community as a whole are remarkable by their paucity. Marion Berghahn's study *Continental Britons* stands almost alone as an attempt to present an overview of the community; based on some 180 interviews with former refugees and their children, it uses detailed information about their experiences and daily lives to build up a picture of the ordinary, 'average' refugees, as opposed to the *Prominenz*, and thereby to analyse the character and development of the community. However, as Berghahn readily admits, her interviewees are not a scientifically selected sample of the former refugees, nor indeed was it possible as late as the 1980s to arrive at such a statistically representative sample.[3]

Given the shortage of source materials which has contributed to this lack of general studies of the Jewish refugees from the German-speaking lands, it is all the more surprising that no systematic scholarly research has been carried out on the *AJR Information*, the principal publication over more than half a century of the refugees' representative organization.[4] Its pages are a mine of information about their activities, problems, achievements and experiences, their sense of identity and self-perception, as well as their interaction with British society and with the Anglo-Jewish community that existed prior to their arrival. Exploiting that wealth of material, this article, the first in its field, aims to make an initial assessment of the process by which the refugees began to attain a settled life in post-war Britain, and, proceeding largely empirically at this stage, to investigate the extent and manner of their initial integration into British society and the first stages in the definition of their own distinct and recognisable community identity, as reflected through the pages of 'their' journal.[5]

At the outset one must recognize that there were several alternatives open to the refugees after 1945 other than that of remaining in Britain and forming there a distinct group defined by the culture of its Central European origins. Most obviously, it might have been expected that a community of deracinated Jews might prefer to settle in Palestine, especially once it became the new Jewish state of Israel, rather than in solidly gentile Britain; indeed, two of the twelve members of the Association's Executive listed in June 1943,[6] A. P. Michaelis, the Vice-Chairman, and S. Adler-Rudel, both leading figures in the Association, emigrated there, as did Herbert Freeden. Another possibility open to the refugees was to return to their countries of origin, as most of the other European émigrés exiled in Britain for the duration of the war hastened to do. Even given the terrible rift that the period of Nazi rule had created between the refugees and their homelands in Germany and Austria (and the

effective elimination of German-speaking elements in the case of
Czechoslovakia), there were those, like the Executive member and
journalist Ernst Löwenthal, who went back.

Another attractive alternative to the drab, impoverished life of post-
war Britain was further emigration, most commonly to the USA, where
economic and professional opportunities beckoned; another leading figure
in the Association, Kurt Alexander, founder member of its Executive and
its General Secretary since 1943, left for America in 1949.[7] However,
although the *AJR Information* published prominent front-page articles on
conditions in America, such as those by the visiting Rabbi Joachim Prinz in
August 1946 and by Kurt Alexander in December 1948, the attraction of
the USA remained largely limited to those who wished to rejoin family
members there and those who had affidavits. The reluctance of many
refugees to undertake a second emigration so soon after resettling in
Britain was compounded by the difficulties of entry posed by the American
immigration quota system, while some would have been deterred by the
materialism and competitiveness of American society, captured in Kurt
Alexander's image of the 'wild race for the dollar which dominates
everything in the States'. America consequently appears in the journal as a
foreign country with a substantial refugee community, not as a prospective
homeland.

Finally, there was the option of absorption into existing Anglo-
Jewry, which must have had a strong appeal to a relatively small group of
Jewish refugees, embattled and uprooted in a new and strange post-war
world where their ties with their past lives, their communities and all too
often their families at home had been brutally destroyed. In 1941 the
founding objectives of the AJR had included the entry of the refugees into
the communal life of Anglo-Jewry: 'It is our aim to enable Jewish refugees
to take part in the activities of the Anglo-Jewish Community so that they
may share the life and fate of British Jewry in all respects.' It was the sole
aim to remain unattained, though the reasons for that lie beyond the scope
of this article.

The German-speaking Jews in Britain thus found themselves after
1945 at a cross-roads, where several avenues of opportunity led forward
into the future. The pages of the *AJR Information* throw crucial light on
the process by which the great bulk of the refugees opted to remain in
Britain, though a considerable number did not, and the reasons why they
did so; it also shows why relations between Anglo-Jewry and the majority,

though by no means all, of the refugees from Central Europe remained somewhat distant, never approaching the embrace of total amalgamation. The result of this opting for Britain was the development in this country of a distinct and discrete community of erstwhile refugees from the German-speaking lands, held together primarily by the culture and language of their homelands and by their common fate as Jewish victims of Nazi persecution who had survived the wartime years on British soil. The *AJR Information* itself bears eloquent testimony to the level of culture maintained by the refugees, a key constituent element of the identity that they created for themselves in their new homeland.

The first barrier to be surmounted on the road to integration in Britain was the bureaucratic but essential process of naturalization, which gave the former refugees formal equality of status with British-born citizens. Not surprisingly, naturalization is one of the dominant topics in the early years of the *AJR Information*, and the manner in which it is discussed is so instructive about refugees' attitudes to the new homeland and perceptions of the British authorities that it forms a natural starting point for detailed analysis. In an editorial article[8] on the first page of the issue of May 1949, securing 'the right of permanent residence in Great Britain for all those who wished to stay here after the war' is unambiguously declared to have been 'the first central task for whose accomplishment the AJR had been founded'. That right, which would have been guaranteed by naturalization, remained out of reach during the war, when Home Secretary Herbert Morrison refused to commit himself to any post-war naturalization of refugees, even those serving in H.M. Forces. The acquisition of British citizenship would not only have relieved the refugees of the disabilities of their status as stateless aliens; it would also have removed the lingering threat of the reimposition on them of German or Austrian nationality, opening the way to their compulsory repatriation to their countries of origin.

The end of the war and the replacement of Morrison by Chuter Ede as Home Secretary in the Labour Government marked the opening of a new chapter. The first issue of the full-size, monthly journal that appeared in January 1946 quotes at length from the Home Secretary's announcement in Parliament on 15 November 1945 of the setting up of procedures to resume naturalization after the wartime halt, beginning with certain priority categories of refugees. In the same issue, the very first published letter from a reader proceeds from the assumption that naturalization for all refugees was imminent; and 'What the Press Says', a column devoted to press coverage of issues relevant to the readership, quotes a favourable commentary from the *New Statesman* on the procedures adopted, on the Home Secretary's tone and manner, 'which should entirely allay the [refugees'] widespread fears' of expulsion, adding that 'we shall accept as citizens men and women who can adapt themselves to our way of life', a broad but vague assimilationist requirement that many refugees were only too happy to fulfil.

The Home Office opted for the customary process of checking each application for naturalization individually, which, slow and time-consuming as it was, resulted in considerable initial anxiety and frustration. Commenting on the priority categories for naturalization set out elsewhere in the journal of April 1946, an editorial recognizes that those many refugees not included in these categories would naturally feel disappointed; by referring to the efforts that had been needed to have naturalization resumed in the first place, it hints at the existence of residual opposition to it in influential quarters. Its expression of hope that non-priority cases will attain naturalization 'in due course' scarcely conceals its concern to the contrary. Detailed evidence of the slow progress of the naturalization process, and hence of what could be interpreted as official obstructionism similar to that practised over the issue of immigration before the war, is noted several times. In March 1946, a report on government action makes dismal reading: a mere 220 certificates of naturalization had been granted, of the pre-war applications only 300 were under examination, and the other priority categories could only be promised that plans for dealing 'expeditiously' with their applications were 'in an advanced state'. In July 1946, the journal contrasted the Home Secretary's statement of 30 May that 250 certificates of naturalization had been granted with the 22,000 applications awaiting decision.

But a key factor on the positive side of the balance was the government's preservation of the requirement of five years' Crown service or residence in Britain or the dominions as the central condition for naturalization, as detailed in the section 'In Parliament' in the issue of September 1947. This was a condition that the refugees who had come before September 1939 could hardly fail to satisfy, thanks to the war, which had stopped most civilians from leaving the country. As is well known, the abandonment of the almost automatic granting of citizenship to those who had resided here for five years marked a crucial step in the restriction of government policy on immigrant settlement in later decades; it is profoundly significant that no such removal of the effective right to citizenship from the Jewish refugees from Hitler long resident in Britain was invoked. The cautiously qualified optimism expressed on the front page of the *AJR Information* of May 1946, on the occasion of the fifth Annual General Meeting of the Association since its foundation, was to prove justified:

> The outstanding event for refugees in Great Britain during the year under review was the resumption of naturalization. Even if many will have to wait a considerable time until they will become British subjects, the barriers which have hitherto blocked the way to legal absorption are removed.

1947 did indeed see a dramatic speeding up of naturalization. AJR members could read that more cases were dealt with in the first three months of that year than in the whole of 1946; and that the total for the year was five times more than in 1946. By September 1947, the journal could report that 1,600 cases — a case would often be an entire family, with the wife and minor children covered by the husband's application — were being dealt with per month, and that 13,415 certificates had been granted, over one third of the total, leaving 23,070 outstanding; confidence in the procedures would have been boosted by the tiny number of applications rejected, only 160, or just over 1% of those processed. As the only alien immigrant minority resident since pre-war days, applicants of German and Austrian origin made up by far the largest group of candidates for naturalization and continued to do so until 1950, by which time their naturalization was largely complete. The final statistics published by the journal in July 1950 tell their own story: 407 certificates of naturalization were granted in 1945 (May-December), 3,630 in 1946, 17,742 in 1947, 15,108 in 1948, 9,593 in 1949, and 3,582 in January-May 1950. By January 1950 the journal's regular and authoritative feature on legal matters, 'Law and Life', could state with some finality that 'every refugee who applied for it and had not made himself personally objectionable to the authorities has become a British subject' (p. 4).

A new tone of relaxed confidence made itself felt. An editorial article entitled 'The Third Volume' stated with evident satisfaction in January 1948 that it might well be only 'one or two years until the whole problem of naturalization has been settled'. By March 1949, the column 'From My Diary', written by the editors under the pseudonym 'Narrator', could afford to treat the subject with humour, a sure sign of anxieties

defused. Surveying the register of aliens naturalized in 1947, the authors
came across not only celebrities like Adolf Wohlbrück, 'known as Anton
Walbrook', but also a battery of aristocratic 'vons', Bethmann-Hollweg,
Neurath, Etzdorf, Westarp, and even, lurking 'von'-less among the
commoners, a grandson of Kaiser Wilhelm II, Friedrich Georg Wilhelm
Christoph Hohenzollern, 'known as George Mansfield'. Commenting on the
changes of name that often accompanied the acquisition of British
citizenship, the article, tongue-in-cheek, chided those who took the process
of anglicization to extremes:

> Without wishing to hurt anybody's sentiments, one feels tempted to ask, whether
> people do not overdo the expression of their gratitude to their new country if they
> adopt names like Eden or Kipling, and whether names starting with 'Mac' should
> not rather be left to Members of the Scottish Clans. (p. 6)

It concludes with an altogether serious assessment of the importance of
the register for future historians: 'It vividly illustrates the legal absorption
of thousands of individuals who, in times of their greatest peril, found
refuge in this island.' This type of discourse is often seized on by
commentators as evidence of an excessive desire to express loyalty and
gratitude to Britain, arising out of the perceived need to propitiate potential
or actual anti-Semitism or anti-alienism among the host population. The
AJR Information, however, seldom reads in that ingratiating way. A
defensive tone does sometimes appear, as in an editorial article on
naturalization in December 1946, which is evidently concerned to damp
down criticism of the authorities and to display an attitude of loyal
appreciation of the efforts of the Home Office. It is at pains to point out the
scale and complexity of the task confronting the Home Office and attributes
the slowness of the naturalization process to 'the limitation of man-power
with which the Home Office, no less than any other public or private body,
has to contend', while assuring readers that 'no doubt, every effort is being
made to tackle the many thousands of applications'.

While recognizing its readers' 'ardent' desire to acquire the status of
'citizens of a country in which they and their children want to live', the
article goes on to urge them not to give voice to their dissatisfaction, nor to
spread 'rumours' critical of the government, and to contain their
impatience, in the interest of 'see[ing] things in their right perspective' and
avoiding friction with their hosts. Such protestations of well-ordered
loyalty can indeed be seen as evidence of an excessive concern not to 'rock
the boat', itself the product of an uneasy awareness of the hostile reaction

that an over-vocal insistence on their rights by the refugees might provoke among the host population.[9] The issue of discourse has taken us to the central question of relations between refugees and native British, as defined by the interplay between friendly acceptance and hostile rejection, between harmonious integration and anti-Semitic prejudice, between trust and fear.

The discourse of fear, driven by a consciousness of the threat of anti-Semitism, is uncommon in the *AJR Information*, and is certainly not the rule. Thus another major article entitled 'A Mirror of Our Time' (January 1947, p. 3) describes the machinery set up to deal with naturalization and the progress made in an even and matter-of-fact tone wholly lacking the between-the-lines anxiety discernible in the previous article, then abandons all defensiveness in favour of a confidently optimistic prediction: 'A liberal principle has been evolved and the technical apparatus to carry it out is gradually gathering speed. No doubt, in the coming year, the number of naturalization certificates granted will greatly exceed last year's figure.' As indeed it did.

A striking example of the exhortatory rhetoric that enjoined the refugees to act as loyal citizens, to be duly grateful for their good fortune in being allowed to settle in Britain, and above all to behave in a manner that would give no occasion for outbreaks of anti-Semitism occurs in the issue of January 1947, but it comes from a prominent outsider, not from among the refugees. In his message of congratulation to the *AJR Information* on its first anniversary, the Jewish peer Lord Reading highlights the progress made in the naturalization process, adding: 'I am sure that those whose applications are granted will show their gratitude and prove their worthiness by accepting not only the privileges but also the responsibilities of British citizenship.' (p. 1) It is significant that this statement, whose routine sentiments barely conceal the standard Jewish fear that recently arrived co-religionists might behave in such a manner as to attract the hostility of the native population, should come from a prominent member of Anglo-Jewry. One might argue that the discourse of fear, designed to appease and propitiate the ubiquitous threat of perceived anti-Semitism, was perhaps more characteristic of existing Anglo-Jewry in the years of immigration and settlement of the Jews from Germany and Austria than it was of the refugees themselves.

One of the most frequently cited examples of such discourse aimed at the refugees, the pamphlet 'Helpful Information and Guidance for Every Refugee', published in 1939, emanated from the highest echelons of Anglo-

Jewry, the German Jewish Aid Committee in conjunction with the Board of Deputies of British Jews itself. The pamphlet, which would be comic if it were not so demeaning, urges the refugees to adopt British customs in dress, speech and manner, to refrain from political activity and from criticism of all things British, to show loyalty to 'England, your host', and generally exhibits a timid pettiness that betrays Anglo-Jewry's overriding fear of anything that might conceivably incite anti-Semitism.[10] A further excellent example of this discourse of fear, right down to the imagery of Jews being forced to slink along by the side of the highway, is given by a German-speaking Jewish refugee from Prague, quoting the accusation levelled at her by a British Jew that the new arrivals from Central Europe threatened the tenuous security painstakingly achieved over many years by Anglo-Jewry:

> I remember in Anson Road there was a house next to us which belonged to some English Jewish people [...] They had some friends in one evening and we were also invited, Andrew and I, and we had a rather unpleasant conversation because they told us they didn't want us. They, the Jews, didn't want us to come in here [...] So he said, he explained to me. My family came from Poland or Russia, I don't know, at the beginning of the century. He described it rather sort of picturesquely, he had to go in the street quite by the wall [...] slink along by the wall, and then as he grew up and made his way, he was by now proudly walking in the middle of the road. Now we came and pushed them back to the wall. That was their explanation [...] Because we didn't speak English, we were not English [...] our habits [...] That's how we pushed them back to the wall and they held this against us.[11]

The difference in culture revealed here between the community of 'British' Jews who had come here between 1880 and 1914 to escape the pogroms in Tsarist Russia and the later wave of Jewish immigrants from Central Europe is also reflected in the degree of their integration into British society. Whereas the former created their own institutions and separate social culture largely derived from religious custom and practice, the later refugees, already far more assimilated and secularized in their home countries, were keener to integrate themselves more fully. The eagerness with which they seized the chance to become British citizens was proof of this, and their embrace of Britishness did not end there. By the end of the post-war years, those refugees who had not availed themselves of the chance to become British subjects almost took on the role of relics from a bygone age, a species so rare that it deserved to be exhibited in museums, as in the humorous reminiscence that 'Narrator' shared with his readers in March 1950: 'Do you still remember the joke about the two refugees who were exhibited at Madame Tussaud's, because they had not applied for naturalization under one of the priority categories?' (p. 6)

The other main factor in this equation was the degree of willingness of the British to accept the refugees into British society and to allow them to integrate. Space does not permit an analysis of the great mass of evidence on this subject available in the pages of the *AJR Information*, some of it pointing to the prevalence of native anti-Semitism and other forms of hostility to the newcomers, but much of it casting their reception in the more positive light of acceptance, mutual respect and tolerance. On the specific subject of naturalization, the balance of the journal's coverage indisputably lies on the positive side, with little mention of opposition to the process of the granting of citizenship.

A particularly striking example of this occurs in the issue of October 1946, when naturalization was entering its phase of decisive acceleration and, as a highly topical issue, came under discussion in that venerable forum of intellectual and moral guidance to middle Britain, the BBC Home Service's 'Brains Trust'. The published extracts from the debate on the question 'Is Naturalization Good for this Country?' occupy nearly a page of the journal, and the responses of the panellists are remarkable for their unanimity. The political scientist Sir Ernest Barker, the editor of the *New Statesman* Kingsley Martin, the conductor Malcom Sargent and the scientist Julian Huxley, leaders of British thought and opinion for millions of listeners, were instinctively and spontaneously at one in their approval of the proposition that naturalization brought the greatest benefits to the country and in their abhorrence of any discrimination on grounds of race or national origin that undermined the principle of the equality of all British citizens.

But it was the novelist and broadcaster E. Arnot Robertson whose heated response to the premises underlying the question took even the question master John Gloag by surprise:

> This is the sort of subject that brings the hair up on the back of my neck and I think on a lot of other people. Does the writer of the question really feel that he has distinguished — I presume that he is English [...] that he has really distinguished himself by being in the right bedroom of the right parents — therefore he deserves automatically the honour of being what he considers the member of a good race — why should people who have come over to our country because they preferred it

and have perhaps given the whole of their lives to work in this country, be regarded
as any more undesirable than people who just happen to be born here. Surely, one
of the first things is to admit your indebtedness to other great races [...] I don't feel
that a refugee should in any way distinguish himself for his being allowed to
become an English citizen if he has lived over here for some considerable time. (p.
3)

It is of course one thing for privileged intellectuals to express such
admirable sentiments in the rarefied surroundings of BBC radio, and
another thing entirely for a Jewish refugee to experience in everyday life
the petty prejudices and animosities that beset post-war British society.
Nevertheless, the published extracts, which would have been unimaginable
on a comparable radio programme in the refugees' countries of origin even
before Hitler, would have brought cheer to their hearts, and it says much
about the journal's perceptions of the values and attitudes of British society
that it chose to present the extracts as it did.

An essential precondition of the integration of the Jewish refugees
from Hitler into British society and their establishment of a new communal
identity in their adopted homeland was their separation from their former
identity in their countries of origin. The latter had largely been achieved
by the Nazis, who had driven them from their homes, stripped them of
their citizenship and destroyed their communities. This separation was
cemented for the great majority by post-war developments in Germany and
Austria: the failure of denazification, the continuing anti-Semitism, the
often shamefully lenient treatment of Nazis by the courts, the reluctance to
make restitution to the victims, and above all the refusal to confront the
guilt and crimes of the Nazi past and to assume moral responsibility for
what had been done in the name of the German people — all this is
reflected in great and frequently depressing detail in the *AJR Information*'s
many reports from Germany and Austria. The dismal failure of Germans
and Austrians, with honourable exceptions, to seize the chance of making a
fresh start morally after 1945, by making the necessary change of attitude
that would have allowed their former fellow citizens of Jewish extraction
to feel at home again in their native lands, effectively destroyed the
possibility of the refugees' re-adoption of a sense of German or Austrian
identity. They were left with little option but to become British citizens,
for all their distinctive Central European culture, a crucial development
that Berghahn, for example, underestimates.[12]

That so few refugees chose to return is irrefutable evidence of the
break with the former homelands. As late as September 1950, an article on

'Jews in Austria' reported that just 603 Austrian Jews had returned (p. 3), of the very substantial number, predominantly Viennese, settled in Britain. In June 1946, an item in the regular feature 'In Parliament' reported a statement by the Chancellor of the Duchy of Lancaster that the Control Office had received a mere 197 written applications for repatriation, adding rather vaguely that 'many thousands' had applied 'in various ways' to return to Germany and Austria (p. 6); presumably many of these progressed no further than registering their applications. In May 1946, the *Zionist Review*, quoted in 'What the Press Says' (p. 3), found that the Communist-controlled Free German Movement, which was encouraging refugees to return 'home', had received 600 applications from an estimated 26,000 German refugees in Britain, to which were added 500-600 applications made directly to the Foreign Office; the Austrian equivalent, the Austrian Centre, had registered 1,600 applications for return from some 13,000 Austrians in Britain (a figure that probably understates the Austrian Jewish immigration).

Both Austrian and German Jews, the extract decisively concludes, rejected overwhelmingly 'the idea of going back to a country which has murdered their families and where the poison of Anti-Semitism is as virulent as ever'. Unlike the 'political fugitives who had sought temporary shelter from Hitler's storm', the Jewish refugees were not eager to return, and their reluctance could only have been strengthened by regular warning voices exhorting them not to do so. An early letter to the editor, published in April 1947, asks bluntly:

> who can expect that a self-conscious Jew would or should return to a country which has inflicted upon him and his community sufferings unparalleled in history [...] He is bound to meet people in Germany who either have taken part in the atrocities or have profiteered by them and with whom he naturally would not have any contact. But he will also meet people who had not the courage and strength [...] to make a stand against the disgraceful actions and who now ought to blush with shame and penitence. Every Jew who wants to be respected must avoid such encounters for psychological or ideological reasons. All the more so as the poison of Nazism has not been eliminated and may become effective at any time. (p. 5)

Many refugees would have taken to heart the warning expressed by a former welfare worker for the Jewish Relief Unit from Britain about conditions in Vienna, in an article extending over the first two pages of the journal in November 1948: 'Jews are coming back — and bitterly regretting it.' His condemnation of the left-wingers who returned is unambiguous:

> To me it is simply impossible to understand the mentality of young persons who willingly come back to a city where their families underwent every humiliation and insult a bare few years ago, and which sent amidst the plaudits of the Viennese many thousands of their own parents, relatives and friends to a nameless end in the death camps.

In March 1949, C. C. Aronsfeld, one of the intellectual stars writing for the journal, expertly analysed the strange phenomenon whereby Jews had returned time and again over the centuries to the places where persecution had been visited upon them. Counselling insistently against repeating this historical pattern, Aronsfeld nevertheless saw the reasons behind it, quoting the Jewish historian Adolph Kohut: 'It is almost impossible to understand, and only to be explained by the Jews' deep-felt attachment to their homesteads, that in spite of the sad experiences and terrible catastrophes, they yet again returned to the old places.' (p. 5) Unable to return to the physical environment of their native towns and cities after the Holocaust, the Jewish refugees from Central Europe were yet deeply attached to the culture, customs and spiritual values in which they had grown up, and it was above all through the German-language culture that they had brought with them that they created and retained a sense of their own distinct identity in their adopted country.

A poem entitled 'Der Flüchtling', published in January 1948 under the pseudonym 'Inquit', catches this combination of rejection and attachment, the painful pairing of an abhorrence of the Nazi past of Germany and Austria with a continued longing for what was valued in the lost 'Heimat'. The poem's first stanza expresses a strong revulsion against the besmirched homeland:

> Kehr nicht zurück in das verfluchte Land,
> Den Unterschlupf der abgefeimten Horde.
> Um seine Trümmer wittert noch gebannt
> Der Blutgeruch der Schlachten und der Morde.

But the final stanza evokes by contrast the lonely refugee's despairing longing for that part of the once beloved homeland which lives on in memory alone, the values and community of a past long buried:

> Bleib, wo du bist, vereinsamt und verkannt.
> Wach auf aus deinen Träumen sehnsuchttrunken.
> Kehr nicht zurück in das geliebte Land.

Was Heimat war, ist ach so tief versunken. (p. 6)

The refugees were mostly able to salvage enough of their intellectual, cultural and social heritage to build from it a new identity and existence that would draw both on the lost homeland and on the new country of refuge.

The countries of origin were now alien territory, separated by a psychological chasm that could not be bridged by the post-war resumption of transport and communications. Returning to Berlin after a gap of eight years, as Adolf Schoyer, Chairman of the Association, told readers in a front-page article in November 1946, had been like 'travelling into an unknown and uncannily foreign land'; and a German Jew who returned to Germany with the British occupying forces was unable to feel 'any connection' between pre- and post-war Germany (March 1946, p. 2). Reflecting in the same month on his disappointment on seeing the German film *Maskerade* again after an interval of seven years, 'Narrator' conveys a similar sense of the gulf between his German-Jewish past and the present: 'Sometimes it is as if the films, books, streets, towns and people we remember existed only in our memory'. (p. 4)

The German-speaking Jewish refugees had suffered not only the material loss of their homes and familiar surroundings in the war; by destroying the entire communities in which they had lived, the Holocaust had also robbed them of the possibility of re-establishing emotional and spiritual contact with the past. The refugees' pre-war lives had been irreparably severed from the post-war present, and the realization of this was often traumatic, as in the case of Werner Rosenstock, who received 'the shock of my life' on returning to his native district of Berlin, the badly bombed Hansa-Viertel:

> Before 1933 there was hardly a house in which one did not know at least one family. Jews in the Hansa-Viertel formed a closely knit community. First, when Hitler came, the Jews had to go, partly to strange countries, partly to the extermination camps. Now their dwellings have also ceased to exist. A centre of Jewish life has been erased entirely. What is left is the memory of the happy days which many of us once spent in Berlin's Hampstead. (October 1950, p. 6)

The positive note on which this piece closes, implying that the refugees had perhaps found an alternative to the Tiergarten in Hampstead Heath, is not maintained in its sequel, where Rosenstock describes his visit to the Jewish cemetery at Weissensee:

> The cemetery is again as peaceful and dignified as it was before the war [...] There is only one difference: you do not meet a single person when wandering around.

> What struck me most were the tombstones whose inscriptions were unfinished.
> Half of the space had been left blank for the husband or wife until his or her turn
> would have come. Now we know that this space will remain blank for ever.
> (November 1950, p. 6)

Small wonder that refugees like Rosenstock preferred to live out their lives
in North-West London rather than amidst the ghosts of their vanished
native communities.

In June 1950 a major front-page article, tellingly entitled 'Beginning
or End?', discussed the future, if any, of the Jewish community in post-war
Germany, which by then consisted mainly of displaced refugees from other
countries and of Jewish partners in mixed marriages. The number of
German Jews remaining is described as 'infinitesimally small'; those
returning to Germany from all allied countries are estimated at 'no more
than three to four hundred'. The survey reaches the sombre conclusion that
German Jewry, once one of the jewels in the crown of Judaism, has
disappeared:

> Community life cannot be compared with that in the former Jewish communities
> [...] There are no central institutions, no teachers and theological seminaries and it
> is not to be expected that such institutions will be established. All this cannot be
> taken as a continuation of the history of German Jewry, which has come to an end
> once and for all.

But the spirit of German Jewry, though extinguished in Germany and
Austria, was not dead. Indeed, a frequent theme in the *Association of
Jewish Refugees Information* is the survival of precious parts of the
German-Jewish heritage in the alien, but not entirely unwelcoming
environment of Britain. An important front-page article in September 1947
by a leader of Berlin's Jews, Hans-Erich Fabian, makes this point
powerfully; it is the more convincing as it is written by an outsider with no
interest in lauding the settled conditions enjoyed by the Jewish refugees in
Britain. Viewed from post-Hitler Berlin, Britain offered conditions
enviably favourable to the recreation of a form of German-Jewish culture,
albeit adapted to its new setting as well as sadly truncated by the Nazi
terror:

> No doubt in Great Britain, too, the Jews originating from Germany lived through
> difficult times, being subjected to the 'Blitz' and internment, yet they never ceased
> to enjoy a certain measure of security. The world around them was by no means
> hostile; on the contrary, in many cases distinctly friendly even. Despite all the
> hardships that were occasioned by the war, they were able to proceed with their
> plans for settlement and had, at the same time, an opportunity for reconstructing

Jewish life, as they had known it in Germany. In short, they were able to adjust themselves to their new surroundings.

Fabian foresaw a transplantation of German-Jewish culture to Britain, a combination of the heritage of the past with the demands of the present, which meant both that the refugees must 'remain conscious of their origin' and that they must 'take root' in their new homeland, becoming 'integrated into the world around them' as 'British citizens in the full meaning of the term'. But this is not a straightforward statement of the old assimilationist agenda, modified into a demand for total integration into British society. Far from it: Fabian exhorts the refugees to preserve those parts of their communal identity which had historically given German Jewry its lustre, to carry their culture on into the future:

> Such a policy does obviously not mean that the refugees should deny their origin or write off their past. On the contrary, German Jewry can be proud of its history. It can, indeed, it should build on its meritorious achievements. Yet we must not be content with retrospection.

Thus a leader of Germany's principal surviving Jewish community entrusted the continuation of the traditions and values particular to the German-speaking Jews of Central Europe in large measure to those of them who had settled in Britain, where they would preserve their own heritage, at least for the lifetime of the German-speaking generations. Furthermore, an article entitled 'Trustees of an Heritage' occupies almost the entire front page of the journal in July 1947, quoting a phrase from Leo Baeck's speech opening the first plenary session of the 'Council for the Protection of the Rights and Interests of Jews from Germany', the international organization representing the dispersed remnants of German Jewry. Fittingly, this body was based in London, then the key bridgehead between the continent of Europe and the Jews overseas, and, again fittingly, its president was Rabbi Dr Baeck, the spiritual leader of the German Jews in Britain. In a sombre address, he declared the history of the Jews in Germany to be at an end, but went on to proclaim the London-based Council 'the trustee of [their] spiritual heritage'; the refugees in Britain would play a leading part in ensuring that their creative legacy passed on into the future.

That legacy, emancipated and secular in its subordination of fidelity to traditional religious practices and beliefs to the goal of assimilation into the German-speaking *Bildungsbürgertum*, the educated middle class, set its refugee heirs in Britain apart from many other Jewries, including Anglo-Jewry. This emerges clearly in the *AJR Information*'s attitude to

Palestine/Israel, which, though overwhelmingly positive and supportive, was plainly neither Zionist, in that it notably refrained from encouraging its readers to emigrate there, nor influenced by traditional religious considerations. The journal was often severely critical of British policy in Palestine, especially of the inhumanity of the restrictions on immigration that left Jews to rot in thousands in D.P. camps in Europe.[13] But at the same time it condemned unreservedly the use of terrorist violence in the struggle for independence against the British mandatory authority. This reflected a deeper ambiguity towards the concept of a Jewish homeland: before 1948 the journal did not endorse the principle of the establishment of a Jewish state, stopping short at the humanitarian demand that homeless Jews be admitted to Palestine in the framework of a peaceful compromise accord. Clearly, the establishment of a Jewish state claiming to represent all Jews would pose a serious problem for those Jews whose loyalties lay elsewhere and who had opted to settle in host countries like Britain and to integrate into British society.

The editorial front-page column of the journal's January 1947 issue contains two contrasting items. The first, resoundingly entitled 'Testimony of Faith', quotes from Chaim Weizmann's proud account to the Zionist Congress in Basle of the progress made towards the establishment of a free Jewish state; the second records that the Pioneer Corps had been granted the privilege of the title 'Royal' in recognition of its war service, a distinction that would gratify the many refugees who had served in its 'Alien Companies'. Together, these items neatly encapsulate what Herbert Freeden termed 'the intricate problem of "double loyalty"' (July 1947, p. 4), the divide between pride in the nascent Jewish state on the one hand and the refugees' pleasure in official recognition and acceptance by Britain on the other. Loyalty to Britain proved the stronger, at least for the majority whose natural enthusiasm for Israel did not extend to resettling there. Lutz Weltmann, a gifted reviewer who contributed articles of outstanding erudition to the journal, recognized the pull of conflicting loyalties: 'The Zionists have achieved their chief aim with Israel's statehood. But for the greater number of Jews in the Diaspora the problem of a dual loyalty still exists'. (October 1950, p. 6) He went on stoutly to defend the 'healthy middle course', midway between Zionism and total assimilation, taken by the German-speaking Jews concerned to preserve their own culture and identity both in Central Europe and in Britain.

Reports from Palestine/Israel in the *AJR Information* are outnumbered only by those from Germany, not least because of the obvious impact on Jews world-wide of the creation of the Jewish state. As an editorial article in October 1948 makes clear, its impact on the refugees from Hitler in Britain was twofold and potentially divisive. On the one hand, some welcomed the establishment of Israel unreservedly as 'the fulfilment of dreams they have cherished throughout their lives'. But for others, who 'react to the new situation with qualified rejoicing', Israel also represented a threat to the security of their identity as Jews settled in the Diaspora, since it called into question the claim to full Jewishness of those communities that remained outside the Jewish state; they must 'hope that the conception of a Jewish State may not impair the position of the majority of Jews outside Israel, who feel themselves politically integrated into their countries of residence'. These included the heirs to the German-Jewish tradition, who arguably had by now too little in common with the core values of the Jewish state to be easily transplanted there from Britain, though they supported it warmly.

It is readily understandable that statements emphasizing the role of Israel as the sole true homeland to which all Jews should return, such as Weizmann's impassioned appeal for a massive 'ingathering of the exiles' in his first address to the Knesset as President of Israel (March 1949, p. 1), or the celebration of the feast of Passover in April 1949 as 'the passing over of innumerable homeless Jews from the insecurity of their existence into the security and freedom of Israeli citizenship' (p. 1), should be counterbalanced by reassuring statements of the continuing validity of community life in Britain. Thus in March 1949 the column 'Anglo-Judaica', which appeared regularly on the third page and was intended to inform readers about events in Anglo-Jewry, quoted at some length from a speech by Maurice Edelman, M.P., about divided loyalties: 'Emotionally, Jews could feel sympathy and, indeed, affection for the State of Israel. Politically, the Jew had a single allegiance and that was to the country of which he was a citizen.' The Chief Rabbi, quoted in 'Anglo-Judaica' of February 1950, defended Diaspora Jewry, while appealing strongly to traditional religious sentiments:

> Jews outside the land of Israel will continue to exist; they will be regarded as Jews and will feel far from being cut off from the Land of Israel; they will still form the people designed by God Himself to fulfil a purpose for Mankind.[14]

To judge by the journal's reports, the Jews from Central Europe were both less emotionally committed to Israel and less confident of their identity as a traditionally Jewish community than was established Anglo-Jewry. It is, for example, hard to imagine a leading figure among the refugees declaring his belief, as did Professor Selig Brodetsky, President of the Board of Deputies of British Jews, that 'Jewish education in this country should be associated with Jewish life in Palestine and that the Jewish child should be made to feel that he is a part of the unity of the Jewish people' (April 1948, p. 3). It is also unlikely that the Board of the Association of Jewish Refugees would, as the Board of Deputies did, have burst spontaneously into a rendition of the Hatikvah to welcome the proclamation of the Jewish state. Nor that the violent argument, also reported in July 1948 in 'Events in Anglo Jewry' (the forerunner of 'Anglo-Judaica'), which broke out at the Council of the United Synagogue about the suitability of sending a message of congratulation to the Yishuv would have been repeated among the refugees, the bulk of whom did not share the sensitivity of the religious factions to the inclusion of political matters in synagogue business. The development of the collective identity of the refugees from Hitler kept them at arm's length from Israel, and the relative weakness of their allegiance to traditional Jewish religious and social practices was also to distance them from Anglo-Jewry.

As long as immigration to Palestine was made problematical by restrictions on entry and by the general uncertainty of life there, the Jewish refugees in Britain were under little immediate pressure to opt for settlement in the Jewish homeland. But by 1948, when an independent Jewish state became a reality, they had to choose between their attachment to Britain, their country of residence, and the appeal of Israel to all Jews in the name of their common heritage and as the land of their historic ingathering. In a major front-page article in January 1948, Robert Weltsch, distinguished editor of the *Jüdische Rundschau* in pre-Hitler Germany, struggled to find a form of words that celebrated the 'birth of the Jewish State' while justifying the continued existence of Jewish communities elsewhere. His key sentence, awkwardly phrased, is hedged about with reservations that convey this uncomfortable dilemma: '[The UN decision] means the official recognition of the legitimate right of — not the Jewish people as a whole, but — a certain Jewish community on ancient Jewish soil to free national life in its own state.'

When Weltsch returned to the subject some two years later, in a lecture entitled 'Zweierlei Judentum — Israel und Diaspora', he saw the division between Diaspora and Israeli Jews as an established fact. The challenge posed by the establishment of the Jewish state had, according to the report of his lecture in April 1950, led some Jews in Britain to emphasize the independence of their community and to regard Israel as a separate entity, which they supported in a spirit of philanthropy, but which could not match 'the sole political allegiance to the country of residence' (p. 7). Significantly for the refugees, he added that the problem of dual loyalty 'was eased by the very undogmatic conception held in English speaking countries of the relationship between the State and the individual', one of many tributes from refugees weaned on German authoritarianism to easy-going British pragmatism as a factor smoothing the path to integration.

The early post-war years saw the community of German-speaking Jewish refugees in Britain struggling to create its own identity amidst the conflicting claims to its allegiance from Britain, from the countries of origin and from the new Jewish state. This article has examined some of the preconditions for the development of that identity; by investigating the refugees' perceptions of the naturalization process and their attitudes to alternative countries of settlement, as reflected through the pages of the *AJR Information*, it has aimed to initiate analysis of the early, defining stages of their settlement and integration.

Notes

[1] See the detailed discussion of immigration figures in Charmian Brinson, *The Strange Case of Dora Fabian and Mathilde Wurm* (Berne: Lang, 1997), pp. 24ff.

[2] On groups that contributed prominently to British society, see *Second Chance: Two Centuries of German-speaking Jews in the United Kingdom*, ed. by Werner E. Mosse (Tübingen: Mohr, 1991), and *Exile in Great Britain: Refugees from Hitler's Germany*, ed. by Gerhard Hirschfeld (Leamington Spa: Berg, 1984); on the Kindertransports, see *I Came Alone: The Stories of the Kindertransports*, ed. by Bertha Leverton and Shmuel Lowensohn (Lewes: The Book Guild, 1990), and Barry Turner, *... And the Policeman Smiled* (London: Bloomsbury, 1990); on internment, see François Lafitte, *The Internment of Aliens* (Harmondsworth: Penguin, 1940), and Peter and Leni Gillman, *'Collar the Lot!': How Britain Interned and Expelled its Wartime Refugees* (London: Quartet, 1980); a good study of a local community is Zoe Josephs, *Survivors: Jewish Refugees in Birmingham 1933-1945* (Warley: Meridian Books, 1988); two essential studies of British government policy towards the refugees are Bernard Wasserstein, *Britain and the Jews of Europe 1939-*

1945 (Oxford: Oxford University Press, 1979), and A. J. Sherman, *Island Refuge: Britain and Refugees from the Third Reich 1933-1939*, 2nd edn (Ilford: Cass, 1994).

[3] Marion Berghahn, *Continental Britons: German-Jewish Refugees from Nazi Germany* (Oxford: Berg, 1988). For her remarks on the impossibility of achieving an 'objective sample', see p. 2. The book was originally published as *German-Jewish Refugees in England: The Ambiguities of Assimilation* (London: Macmillan, 1984).

[4] Berghahn frequently refers to the journal, but the main focus of her study lies elsewhere. Other scholars have dipped into it for references to specific topics.

[5] A comparable study in a related field is Richard Bolchover, *British Jewry and the Holocaust* (Cambridge: Cambridge University Press, 1993), a study of a chapter in the history of Anglo-Jewry drawing largely on the *Jewish Chronicle*.

[6] *Association of Jewish Refugees Information*, June 1943, p. 6. Before January 1946 the individual issues of the journal were not numbered. In 1946 the journal was paginated consecutively for the whole year, but this practice was not continued thereafter.

[7] Government figures on the emigration of aliens from the United Kingdom show how many refugees went to the United States. In a careful analysis of refugee re-emigration in the June 1946 issue of the *AJR Information* (p. 3), Ernst Löwenthal gives the total number of Jewish refugees who had left Britain for the USA since 1933 at 13,000, with a further 500 leaving monthly. This amounted to nearly 60% of total re-emigration, and also represented some 16% of the Jewish refugees from Germany and Austria who came to Britain before the war.

[8] The first page of the journal in these years usually consisted of a left-hand column written by the editor(s) and two more columns devoted to a major article on an important subject. The former were the nearest thing to an editorial in the journal, and will be referred to as such.

[9] One example among many is the accusation that by 1960 the *AJR Information* had 'sanitized' the mass internment of aliens in 1940 'into a jolly jape', discouraging those refugees with a critical perspective from airing their views, out of a misplaced desire not to appear ungrateful to Britain and a sense of the continuing vulnerability of the former refugees' position. See Tony Kushner and David Cesarani, 'Alien Internment in Britain During the Twentieth Century: An Introduction', in *The Internment of Aliens in Twentieth Century Britain*, ed. by David Cesarani and Tony Kushner (London: Cass, 1993), pp. 1-22 (p. 7).

[10] See the discussion of this in Bolchover, p. 50.

[11] Interview conducted with Eva Sommerfreund on 16 February 1996 for the Oral History Project of the Research Centre for German and Austrian Exile Studies, Institute of Germanic Studies, University of London.

[12] Berghahn proceeds from the questionable assumption that in the fullness of time the refugees could make their peace ('resume their ties') with Germany, while at the same time over-emphasizing the barriers to their integration in Britain, to the extent of claiming that anti-Semitism in Britain was equal to that in Germany — no comparison with Austria is attempted.

[13] See for example the front-page article 'The Hamburg Tragedy' in October 1947, one of several searing denunciations of the mistreatment of the would-be immigrants to Palestine

aboard the ship *Exodus 1947*; also the dramatic report in the same issue of the appalling conditions under which other would-be immigrants were held in refugee camps in Cyprus (p. 3).

14 The Chief Rabbi was responding to the idea, advanced prominently by Arthur Koestler, that the foundation of the state of Israel meant that Diaspora Jews had either to emigrate there or to throw in their lot with their fellow citizens in their country of residence; the Galut no longer had any claim to a valid existence. Koestler's book *Promise and Fulfilment*, in which he sets out these notions, was the subject of a hostile review by Herbert Freeden in the *AJR Information*, December 1949, p. 4.

Dorothea McEwan

A Tale of One Institute and Two Cities: The Warburg Institute

Research in the 'Kulturwissenschaftliche Bibliothek Warburg', founded by Aby Warburg (1866-1929), the son of a banker in Hamburg, focused on the 'Wanderwege des Geistes' from antiquity to Renaissance Europe and modern times. The political situation in Germany at the beginning of the 1930s, however, forced the KBW into exile. In 1933 the stock of 55,000 books together with the photographic collection, library furniture and bindery equipment was transported to London, where the KBW became the Warburg Institute, offering help to fellow academics, friends, and friends of friends forced to leave Germany and Austria for political reasons. In 1944 the Institute was incorporated into the University of London.

Aby Warburg, eldest of seven children of the Hamburg banker Moritz Warburg and Charlotte, née Oppenheim, gave his name first to a library, the 'Kulturwissenschaftliche Bibliothek Warburg' in Hamburg, and then to an Institute, the Warburg Institute in London. If people in Hamburg in the 1920s were not too clear what sort of books to look for in a Kulturwissenschaftliche Bibliothek, people in London today also find it hard to imagine what the Warburg Institute does. Interestingly, there is no precise word in the English language with which to translate 'Kulturwissenschaft'; and so the term is rendered as intellectual history or the history of ideas encompassing research in the continuity of ideas and metamorphoses of ideas from antiquity to Renaissance Europe and modern times or, to use Warburg's phrase 'Das Nachleben der Antike', the survival of classical antiquity.

Research interests in the library in Hamburg as well as in the Institute in London are wide, and cannot easily be brought down to one common denominator. Broadly speaking they span and yoke the history of religion and the history of art, exploring the interface between the world of ideas and the world of images. The Warburg Institute is concerned with all research loosely called humanities, but not excluding the sciences. Tellingly, the Oxford English Dictionary has accepted the adjective warburgian in connection with method, meaning a very broad approach to investigation and research or, as Ernst Gombrich put it, Warburg could not

> conceive of an approach to art which disregarded the moral emotions. His concern [...] is not with the identification of pictorial content but with mental images and

their emotional aura. [...] a separation between form and subject matter was [...] out of the question.[1]

Gertrud Bing, Director of The Warburg Institute in the 1950s, explained 'Warburgian studies' as a term representing 'the achievements of a group of scholars rather than those of the person whose name served them as a descriptive label'.[2]

Aby Warburg, born in 1866, precocious and intelligent, is said to have been interested in books from a tender age. The story of relinquishing his birthright is a case in point. Aby, as the eldest of the five brothers, was destined to enter the family firm. His brother Max Moritz, one year younger, 'rather too immature to reflect' in his own words, agreed to purchase the birthright for the promise that Max M. would always buy Aby all the books he wanted. After a brief pause for reflection, Max M. consented. He told himself

> that when I was in the business I could, after all, always find the money to pay for the works of Schiller, Goethe, Lessing and perhaps also Klopstock, and so, unsuspecting, I gave him what I must now admit was a very large blank cheque.[3]

Max M. went on to become the head of the bank and a leading German banker. He was also a member of the German delegation at the negotiations at Versailles in 1919. He never treated his bank only as a financial institution, but was actively engaged in supporting humanitarian causes, relief work, struggling artists etc. and, of course, his brother's library.

Aby Warburg chose to study history of art and went to the universities of Bonn, Munich and Strasbourg. He enjoyed living away from family restrictions. When he was reprimanded by his father for ceasing to patronize the kosher restaurant Rothschild in Bonn because it was not up to his standard, he quipped that he could not choose the universities by the quality of the kosher restaurants.[4]

In his doctoral thesis on Botticelli's two mythological masterpieces 'The Birth of Venus' and 'Primavera'[5] Warburg sought to find out how Botticelli and his patrons imagined antiquity, what ideas were evoked in their minds by the stories they read in Ovid and in Ovid's Renaissance imitators. Both paintings embodied to the late nineteenth century the very essence of the Florentine Renaissance. The dawning of a new era, of awakening paganism, found expression in art. Warburg investigated the mythical figure of the winged woman with her clothes fluttering in the wind, the figure of the Ninfa, in which he saw the apollonic element and its opposite, the river god, in which he saw the dionysic element; both of which were to exert a lifelong fascination on his mind.

After his marriage to the painter and sculptor Mary Hertz in 1897, he set up residence with her in Florence among a cosmopolitan group of scholars. He stayed there for the best part of five years, thereafter making Hamburg his home for the rest of his life. In Florence he worked in archives and libraries, viewed collections, wrote, concerned himself with art as an expression of vital human issues. These were important years for Warburg as he made contacts and forged lifelong friendships with a group of scholars from many countries in Europe and the US. The large collection of correspondence still kept in the Warburg Institute, estimated at some 25,000 letters and postcards from and to Warburg, shows the extent of these contacts. As a banker's son he knew about the value of meticulously kept files, particularly the need for keeping copies of outgoing correspondence, something which proves extremely useful to students of intellectual history today.

When Warburg returned to Hamburg in 1902 he started giving lectures in various scholarly societies which were the forerunners of Hamburg University. In time offers of university posts in Bonn, Greifswald und Halle were made to him, but he did not take them up. When he turned down the offer of Halle University in 1912, the Hamburg city fathers honoured his wish to stay in Hamburg by awarding him the title professor. He could not envisage uprooting his library, his very own creation, and having to set it up elsewhere.

In his student days he started to collect books. Although he was not a trained librarian, he ran the library, his 'laboratory',[6] in a professional way. He catalogued accessions, kept correspondence ledgers, accounts for book purchases and library expenditure such as bookbinding. He had embarked on a library system which contrasted markedly with the tendencies of the time of alphabetization and arithmetic arrangements. Most libraries did not allow open access, the book-title in the catalogue indices replaced in most cases that other, and much more scholarly, familiarity which is gained by browsing. Warburg spoke of the 'law of the good neighbour':

> The book of which one knew was in most cases not the book which one needed. The unknown neighbour on the shelf contained the vital information, although from its title one might not have guessed this. The overriding idea was that the books together — each containing its larger or smaller bit of information and being supplemented by its neighbours — should by their titles guide the student to perceive the essential forces of the human mind and its history. Books were for

Warburg more than instruments of research. Assembled and grouped, they
expressed the thought of mankind in its constant and in its changing aspects.[7]

He employed both men and women as secretarial staff and cataloguers,
because librarianship, like school teaching, provided a new professional
opportunity for women.[8] They were also trained to work on the
'Zettelkasten', his very own subject catalogue, a method of yoking ideas in
a way similar to his method of shelving books in the library. He jotted
down ideas, quotes from literature and bibliographical references,
sometimes augmented by postcards and letters from friends with relevant
information on particular aspects of their research work. He then put these
slips of paper into boxes according to topics, arranged them and re-
arranged them as and when a new topic necessitated a new synopsis, thus
creating the so-called 'Zettelkasten' which grew to more than one hundred
boxes. The slips of papers, bibliographical references, pieces of
correspondence, newspaper cuttings, jottings, notes etc. held the clues to
particular questions of research he was engaged in, they formed the links
uniting various branches of the history of humanity. It grew out of a very
practical understanding of turning clues into links.

> Warburg, in his burning desire to unriddle the mystery of the pictures, went from
> one of these seminar libraries [in Strasbourg] to another, pursuing his clues from
> art to religion, from religion to literature, from literature to philosophy. To give the
> student a library uniting the various branches of the history of human civilization
> where he could wander from shelf to shelf was his resolve. The Government
> would, in his opinion, never be willing to create such an instrument.

This is how his successor as director of the library in Hamburg and first
director of the Institute in London, Fritz Saxl, explained the thinking
behind the creation of the library.[9]

By 1914 Warburg and Saxl, then his young library assistant, were
thinking of the next step, to turn the library into an institute. The
progression from intuition to institution can be traced in the many letters
they exchanged about this project, of creating scholarships for young
scholars from Germany and abroad which would enable them to come to
the library in Hamburg and pursue their studies.

However, World War I stopped all such projects. When it was finally
over, Warburg's health was broken and he was to spend the years until
1924 in sanatoria. His assistant from the pre-war days, the young Viennese
scholar Fritz Saxl, who had by then became a trusted friend, was appointed
by the family to run the library in Warburg's absence.[10] With the
establishment of the University of Hamburg after World War I, the library

became a venue for seminars of the newly established Department of Art History. Saxl, as acting director during Warburg's absence from Hamburg, undertook the formidable managerial and intellectual task of transforming the private library of one scholar into a library at the disposal of a group of scholars. And as Saxl had instituted a series of around eight lectures per year and started two publication projects, the series called 'Vorträge' and the 'Studien', the library had its own lecture and publication programme. He invited teachers from Hamburg and other universities in Germany as well as independent scholars to give lectures in the library offering — through the financial support of the Warburg family — reimbursement for travel expenditure, accommodation and a lecture fee. Printing and publication costs were also provided.

In December 1927, the family, which had supported Aby Warburg for so many years, had declared their willingness to support his library by establishing the foundation 'Kulturwissenschaftliche Bibliothek Warburg' [KBW]. By the time of Warburg's death on 26 October 1929, the library had grown to 50,000 books. It was Carl Georg Heise, Warburg's pupil and friend, who in his memories of Warburg repeated Warburg's point of view: 'Other wealthy familes own race horses, you own my library — which is more valuable.'[11] But the sinister signs of the coming storm soon became visible: the international bank crisis in 1929, its economic and political consequences and political developments in Germany in 1933 created conditions in which it was difficult to see how a cross-cultural pluri-disciplinary institute could flourish. From 1932 onwards Saxl had come to the conclusion that it would be impossible to continue the work of the KBW in Germany.

The family backed the efforts of Fritz Saxl and his colleagues, notably Edgar Wind, to find a suitable alternative home for the library to continue its work. No effort was spared to find a country which would welcome such a library. The University of Leiden in The Netherlands would have liked to accommodate it, but did not have the necessary funds. There were talks about moving it to Rome,[12] but again, Italy would not have been able to support it financially. In July 1933, W. G. Constable, first Director of the Courtauld Institute, and C. S. Gibson, of Guy's Hospital, were alerted to the plight of the KBW by the Academic Assistance Council in England. They decided to travel to Hamburg to see for themselves. In their report to Sir Denison Ross, then Director of The School of Oriental and African Studies of the University of London, they

strongly advocated a move to London. Saxl went to London to liaise with
institutes and individuals and to seek academic opportunities for the staff
from Hamburg. In a very short time, the US Consul General in Berlin,
George Messersmith, procured a document which declared that part of the
Foundation was to be considered US property, as it was partly supported
by the members of the Warburg bank in the US. This was done in order to
forestall any manoeuvres by the German authorities to stop the removal of
the library. Gertrud Bing wrote to Erich Warburg, son of Max M.
Warburg, in September 1933 that there were employment possibilities for
some of the collaborators of the KBW, Professor Ernst Cassirer in Oxford,
Edgar Wind in Cambridge, Erwin Panofsky in Edinburgh.[13] A committee
was formed, premises were found in Thames House, Millbank, London,
and financial support was pledged for three years by Samuel Courtauld and
the Warburg family.

The task of uprooting such a large library was initiated and ably
overseen by Saxl, who was director of the KBW from 1929 onwards and
director of The Warburg Institute from 1933 to his death in 1948. In
December 1933, two little steamers brought 55,000 books, thousands of
slides, photographs, letters and heavy furniture to London.

From Thames House the library moved to rooms in the Imperial
Institute Buildings, by courtesy of the University of London authorities. In
the months immediately following the reopening of the library as The
Warburg Institute in May 1934, some informal lectures were held in
German, attended mostly by Germans. That autumn, however, a very
ambitious programme of nineteen lectures was inaugurated, attracting a
large audience of roughly equal numbers of English and German speakers.
Ernst Cassirer, Robin E. W. Flower, Roger Hinks, Fritz Saxl, Jean Seznec
and Edgar Wind gave lectures on Renaissance topics, Richard Salomon on
palaeography, Gabriel Théry on the activities of Greek monks in ninth
century Paris and Adolph Goldschmidt on the influence of English art on
the continent in the Middle Ages.

At the end of July 1934 a special photographic exhibition, the first of
many, was arranged for the International Congress of Anthropological and
Ethnological Sciences, intended to demonstrate the connection between
anthropological and historical studies.

To begin with, there were very few contacts with scholars in Great
Britain; the move to London was an adventure for everybody aggravated
by the need to speak and write in English, a not inconsiderable hurdle. Saxl

deplored the language 'which it was quite impossible ever to learn!'[14] In
Britain, there were two currents in the discipline of art history — art
appreciation and scholarly history of art. The staff of The Warburg
Institute looked for opportunities to continue their work in England and
thereby prove to their new colleagues the usefulness of their method of
historical enquiry, juxtaposing texts and images, posing new questions,
examining the unfamiliar. In time, The Warburg Institute successfully
established 'a wider conception of art-historical studies, extending beyond
the traditional confines of connoisseurship to the study of images in their
cultural context'.[15]

The English world of learning responded well to the newcomer, the
Institute, and the six members of staff who had come from Nazi Germany,
Gertrud Bing, Eva von Eckardt, Otto Fein, Hans Meier, Fritz Saxl and
Edgar Wind. Technically, the staff were not asylum-seekers or people who
had gone into exile. It was only natural that very soon they were sought out
by people who did have to leave their country, which meant for them, as a
matter of course, loss of livelihood and research facilities. The Warburg
Institute was also sought out to supply information on matters of German
scholarship, language, the world of learning. Esther Simpson, then
Assistant Secretary of the Academic Assistance Council, handed on a
request to Saxl: the Library Association had contacted her to say that they
were printing in the January issue of the *Library Association Record* a list
of modern German literature 'for the use of Public Librarians in this
country who may wish to build up their sections of German books'.
However since the editor of the *Record* was doubtful whether the list was
'sufficiently balanced', he had asked her if she could let him have a
supplementary list including 'the chief books by the principal authors no
longer resident in Germany who are not represented on this list'. They
would wish to publish such a supplementary list of authors and books on
art history in the February issue of the *Record*.[16]

In due course Simpson forwarded five and a half pages, the printer's
proof of the list for the January issue of the *Record*, ranged into sections
'History, General', 'The New Germany', 'Biographies', 'Art', 'Music',
'History of Literature', 'Novels'.[17] It was Bing who undertook to check the
list and who then felt stirred to write the following letter:

'Dear Miss Simpson,

I am sending you the list of books for the Library Association Record with
our corrections. I am sorry they seem so many. Some of them are due to mistakes

made on our part, for which I apologize. We only corrected the list compiled by us, but out of interest we, of course, also looked through the other parts, and I must ask your pardon for taking a great liberty. I want to draw your attention to a fact which we discussed amongst ourselves when we first saw this new list and which is confirmed, in a not quite pleasant way, by yesterday's issue of the Neue Züricher [sic] Zeitung: The new list of novels contains almost entirely works of jewish [sic] authors, who have left Germany, and are forced to publish their works through firms established for this purpose. You know, of course, that an entire "Emigrantenpresse" has sprung up these last two years, which is not confined to daily or weekly papers but also comprises novels and poetry. This "Emigrantenpresse" is, quite justly, attacked by a part of the remaining press, and there are few things which, in my opinion, are so apt to create anti-semitism, even in those places where up to now it has been unknown, as this phenomenon. Some of these authors are, of course, very good writers, and even poets, but it seems to me that it would be very dangerous, to say the least, to presume that the whole German modern literature is represented by them. You will find this confirmed in the article by Hermann Hesse in the Neue Züricher [sic] Zeitung. Hermann Hesse is a very good writer himself and, as far as I know, neither given to anti-semitism, nor a friend of the Nazi regime in Germany. The same holds true with regard to the Neue Züricher [sic] Zeitung, the editors of which we know are personally fighting at least as good a battle against cultural Nazism as any of us. You will note that the publishing firms mentioned in the list are almost entirely the same mentioned in Hermann Hesse's article, and that one of the authors which he misses in the "Emigrantenpresse" appears on our list. Personally, I am of the same opinion, viz. that the list which is to appear in the Library Journal and which is to give a representative picture of modern German literature ought to comprise: Gerhard Hauptmann, Hans Carossa, Rudolf [sic] Alexander Schröder, Jakob Schaffner, Emil Strauss (all of them mentioned by Hesse), to whom might be added: Hermann Hesse himself, Annette Kolb, Hans Fallada, Hermann Stehr, and even Hanns Johst, though the latter has turned Nazi. On the other hand, it seems to be absolutely partial to mention three works by Lion Furchtwanger [sic!], three by Werfel and three by Zweig, considering that so many excellent writers have not been included. The same holds true with regard to the four works by Emil Ludwig and the four by Stefan Zweig mentioned under the heading "Biographies". Please do not misinterpret my meaning: I am fully aware of and sincerely appreciate your intentions in allowing the jewish [sic] authors their full share in German literature, but in a representative list, intended for a scientific journal, such a one-sided picture would give an absolutely wrong impression, and I am afraid that the ultimate result would be the contrary to what you, and I and all of us would wish.

I regret to say that I have not quite finished yet, and I am afraid that you will consider me a terrible bore if I continue, but, on the other hand, you know that I am only acting out of consideration for the present delicate situation.

My second objection refers to the list of works on history. It does not, as the two other lists, comprise a preponderance of jewish [sic] authors, but it does, on the other hand, leave out a considerable number of excellent books which have appeared in the last five years, the political conviction of the authors perhaps not being shared by the compiler. I am sending you a list of those which our Dr. Meier has suggested ought to be added. The same holds true with regard to this as with regard to the other list: If an unbiassed [sic] picture of the standing of the German historiography is to be given, it should contain the most representative works. In the list you sent me there are several works which may safely be left out, first of all the two works by Rudolph [sic] Olden. Olden was the former editor of the Berliner Tageblatt, and the works mentioned here are mere political pamphlets. It also seems strange that the book by Holborn has been mentioned, or the first item of Rosenberg's, which is his dissertation, or the Hutten by Graf Stollberg. If you should wish to insert works more or less connected with "Tagespolitik", I would suggest, for instance, the work by Marcks on Hindenburg, Friedrich Meinecke on "Staat und Persönlichkeit", or Gerhard Masur on Stahl.

Again, dear Miss Simpson, please let me say that I do not wish to create unnecessary difficulties, and I do not, of course, wish to do anything which might harm or offend either the authors mentioned in the list or the compilers. However, I do think, and so do my colleagues, that in the present situation it would be most dangerous to publish a list of German books which could not be looked upon as impartial.

Yours sincerely,[18]

A few days later, Simpson thanked Bing 'for all the trouble' she had taken with the list of books for the 'Library Association Record': 'We appreciate your co-operation very greatly.'[19] Two things stand out here: that members of The Warburg Institute were called upon to give their opinion on matters German and that by doing so they discharged their duties in a non-partisan way. Phrasing carefully, so as not to offend anybody, Bing grasped the nettle. She spoke up for German scholarship, regardless whether it was Jewish or Aryan, realizing that philo-semitism was another form of discrimination. True, it was not as damaging as anti-semitism, but people in her situation, with her experience of having been uprooted, had to be the ones who could openly say that any form of discrimination was to be avoided.

For Saxl, the problems of setting up a research institute in London were not unlike the problems encountered in the early 1920s in Hamburg, when he had taken over the running of the Warburg library, only now with the additional task of helping the great number of refugee scholars who had made the Institute their first port of call and place of work.[20] They hoped that people who had shared their experience of homelessness would be in a position to understand their predicament.

To help scholars from the Continent was never easy and requests for help were many and manifold. An institute which had come from abroad was a valuable ally for refugee scholars from abroad. From the very beginning of its work in London one of the big topics in the correspondence files of the institute were pleas for help to obtain lecture invitations, lectureships, teaching contracts, research contracts, publication contracts, loans for completing degree course studies,[21] requests to give references and views matching vacancies with experts.[22] There were also, as a matter of course, requests for information as to whether a particular man or woman was a bona fide job seeker from Germany and not a surreptitious Nazi who would infiltrate a household in England under false pretences.[23]

Many harrowing letters by Jewish and non-Jewish scholars, Socialists, Catholics, speaking of loss of employment, poverty, illness, loss of family, reached members of The Warburg Institute, if the applicant was known to Institute personnel or somehow in touch with them — relatives, friends and friends of friends. The largest correspondence file is that of the letters sent on to Walter Adams, the General Secretary of the Academic Assistance Council in London.

In the years 1934 to 1936 there were appeals — among others — from or on behalf of F. Antal, Arthur Beer, Edgar Breitenbach, Otto Brendel, Heinrich Walter Cassirer, Carl Einstein, Hermann Fränkel, Robert Freyhan, von Fritz, Adelheid Heimann, Paul Kraus, Helmuth Kuhn, Lotte Labowsky, Ulrich Middeldorf, Ernst Moering, Gunther Neufeld, Jacob Hans Polotsky, Otto Rosenthal, Richard Salomon, Manfred Sandmann, Wolfgang Stechow, Franz Urbach, Friedrich Waismann, Richard Walzer, Martin Weinberger, Paul Wescher, Theodor Wiesengrund-Adorno, Fritz Wohlwill.

In the years 1937-38 they also dealt with requests — amongst others — from and on behalf of Bruno Adler, Berthold Altmann, Alfons Barb, Hans Baron, Marion Bartmann, Arthur Beer, Klaus Berger, Eva Bradt,

Edgar Breitenbach, Hugo Buchthal, Ernst H. Buschbeck, Guido Calef, Hans Calmann, Otto Demus, David Diringer, Heinz and Iwan Döry, Albert Ehrenzweig, Mussia Eisenstadt, Dora Ettlinger, Martin Feddersen, Ludwig Feuchtwanger, Liselotte Frankel, Helmut Fuerst, Günther Goldschmidt, Werner Goldschmidt, Ernst H. Gombrich, Werner Gramberg, Gustav von Grünebaum, Gertrud Hallo, H. P. Heckscher, Adelheid Heimann, Ida Herz, Jacob Hess, Heinrich Heydenreich, Paul Hofmann, Felix Horb, Frau von Hornbostel, Elisabeth Jastrow, Ernst Kapp, Emil Kaufmann, Victor Klemperer, Sonja Klibansky, Fritz Kormis, Olga Koseleff, Ernst Kris, Paul Oskar Kristeller, Helmut Kuhn, Betty Kurth, Otto Kurz, Gerhard Ladner, Erich Langstadt, Helmar Lerski, Hans Liebeschütz, Aenne Liebreich, Ernst Moritz Manasse, S. Marck, Johanna Meyer-Udewald, Ludwig Münz, Mrs. Neumann-Tönniessen, Otto Pächt, Franz Rapp, Wilhelm Rechnitz, Franz Rosenthal, Hans Rothfeld, Richard Salomon, Gertrud Saxl, Marianne Schmidl, Guido Schönberger, Leo Schrade, Marianna Schubart, Maks Seidmann, K. E. Simon, Walter Solmitz, Clemens Sommer, Otto Stein, Ernst Sternfeld, Miss St. Goar, Ernst Strauss, Friedrich Stross, Erica and Hans Tietze, Hans Tritsch, Klaus Wachsmann, Martin Weinberger, Paul Wescher, Ilse Wittenberg, Theodor Zondek.[24] (Work at cataloguing the entire correspondence collection is in progress.[25])

One letter shows that the newly arrived scholars themselves wanted to do their bit for raising funds. Edgar Schiff had proposed a series of lectures 'by German scholars the proceeds from which would go partly to the Academic Assistance Council.' Adams turned it down, it would be too much effort organising the lectures, and more, he queried whether it would be counter-productive for 'German scholars to lecture as Germans': 'We feel that as far as possible the German scholars have got to be absorbed into the ordinary university and research world in this country and it is not desirable therefore to emphasise their distinctive position as foreigners.'[26] Although this initiative did not bear fruit, it must be said that a great number of those who were newly arrived in the country contributed to funds helping others to come. A list of fourteen pages with names of contributors to the 'Selbsthilfe deutscher Ausgewanderter' makes impressive reading.[27] Equally impressive is a short note to Esther Simpson in September 1938, the Secretary of the Society for the Protection of Science and Learning, listing 'those connected with our Institute who would like to give their services to the British Community in case of war': Fritz

Saxl, Hans Meier, Edgar Wind, Hugo Buchthal, Ernst Gombrich, Otto Kurz, Otto Pächt, Ludwig Münz, Leopold Ettlinger, Gertrud Bing, Elsbeth Jaffé, Adelheid Heimann, Erna Mandowsky — in fact, the entire staff.[28] Requests by foreigners for help were usually directed to Gertrud Bing, the Deputy Director of The Warburg Institute from 1933 to 1955 (and Director from 1955 to 1959) and not to Saxl, who was very good at finding people who were interested in the work of the institute, less so at finding the necessary resources. She handled the bulk of this correspondence, lending a sympathetic ear to everybody. She was a good listener, a tireless letter-writer, interested in people beyond her work in the Institute. 'Herself an immigrant, she cared uncomplainingly for others.' ('Selbst heimatlos geworden, sorgte sie klaglos nur für andere.')[29] The obituary in *The Times* wrote of her

> miraculous reserves of strength and human warmth. An ever-increasing stream of homeless and bewildered scholars and refugees sought her advice, and few can have left her little office in the makeshift rooms of the expatriate library without having received comfort and solid help.[30]

The Warburg Institute did not only correspond with the Academic Assistance Council, but with a variety of organisations which were involved in helping refugees to find employment, accommodation and so on: American Joint Distribution Committee — European Executive Offices — Paris, Anglo-German Academic Bureau/ Deutscher Akademischer Austauschdienst London, Aquinas Society, Au Pair & Interchange Association, Board of Deputies of British Jews, Central British Fund for German Jewry, The Classical Association, Commercial Advice for Germans — Robert Kauffmann, The English Association, Georgian Historical Society, International Federation of University Women, International Missionary Council, International Student Service, Inter-Aid Committee for Children from Germany, Jewish Historical Society, Jewish Refugee Committee, Library Association, Lingard Society, London Association of University Women, London Missionary Society, Maison de l'Institut de France, Fondation Edmond de Rothschild London, Medieval Group, miscellaneous publication bodies, parties, leagues, Modern Language Associations, 'Notgemeinschaft Deutscher Wissenschaftler im Ausland', Royal Commission of Historical Manuscripts, The Pilgrim Trust, Royal Historical Society, Royal Society, Royal Society of Medicine, Royal Society of Teachers, Society for the Promotion of Roman Studies, Society of Friends/ German Emergency Committee, Society of Jews and Christians, Workers Travel Association.

Two publications are important in this context, taking the form of 'tributes' and 'reminiscences', *Refugee Scholars*[31] by Esther Simpson, the Secretary of the Academic Assistance Council (later the Society for the Protection of Science and Learning), and *Retrospective Sympathetic Affection. A Tribute to the Academic Community*[32] by Ray Cooper. Both their accounts stress the generosity of the British people, '[T]hat generous impulse of British academics in Britain to come to the rescue of their colleagues who had fallen victim to the madness of racial and political intolerance', as Ernst Gombrich put it.[33] These books are valuable contributions to the literature on assistance to foreigners. With their help, gaps in biographical material and understanding of this particular time can be closed. Ray Cooper credited The Warburg Institute with having 'transformed studies of art and history of art'.[34]

An Institute, dépaysé, not exiled in its narrow sense, but transplanted from its soil to service a different academic tradition, faced, like so many immigrants, the options of alienation or assimilation and absorption. The process of taking root was made easier because the Institute as an organisation and its individual members actively sought contact with scholars and institutions in Britain and, in time, were able to carve out a niche which became uniquely its own, a development beyond the Hamburg confines, borne out of the experience of working in Britain. Thus, the period from 1933 to 1939 was a period for establishing the work of the Institute in Britain by a variety of means, including accepting invitations to garden parties, dinners and visits to English friends in their houses in the country. The kind of intellectual exchange that took place in Hamburg between scholars of different disciplines was pursued upon arrival in London. The lecture programme for 1936 and 1937 featured lectures by Jurgis Baltrusaitis, Niels Bohrs, Otto Brendel, Ernst Cassirer, W. G. Constable, Henri Focillon, Johan Huizinga, Raymond Klibanksy, Alexander Koyré, Ernst Kris, Konrad Lorenz, E. A. Lowes, Paul Schrecker, Edgar Wind, Francis Wormald. In 1939 there were lectures by Isaiah Berlin, Anthony Blunt, George Clutton, Roger Hinks, Otto Pächt, Beryl Smalley, Rudolf Wittkower, Frances Yates. The series of publications called *Studien der Bibliothek Warburg* became *Studies of the Warburg Institute*, with important contributions such as *Studies in Seventeenth-Century Imagery* by Mario Praz, *Catalogue Raisonnée* by Rudolf Wittkower of the drawings by

Poussin, edited by Walter Friedlaender and Anthony Blunt, and Jean
Seznec's *La survivance des dieux antiques*. In addition, a new series, *The
Journal of the Warburg Institute*, was started in 1937, which continued as
Journal of the Warburg and Courtauld Institutes. *Surveys* continued as
Surveys and Texts. The new series *Oxford-Warburg Studies*, *Warburg
Institute Colloquia* and *Kleine Schriften* followed in time.[35]

The Warburg Institute with its lecture and publication programme
clearly could not continue simply on the various short-lease arrangements
of its early years in Britain. It was a natural progression that the Institute,
with its reputation as a research resource for the intellectual and cultural
history of post-classical Europe, was taken into public ownership.

Negotiations started with the University authorities which led to the
decision by the Trustees to hand over The Warburg Institute to the
University of London on 28 November 1944. It took over financial
responsibility for the running of the Institute.[36] It was 'A Present from
Germany', as headlined in the *Observer* on 24 December 1944: 'The
nation's greatest Christmas present of the year comes from Hamburg. It is
the unique library of art and letters collected by the Warburg family [...].'
It was not 'Hitler's gift to Britain', as is so often wrongly quoted today with
a blatant disregard for historical facts.

One of the factors which led to this decisive turn of events, the
British taxpayer assuming responsibility for the continuance of the
Institute, was, to quote Gombrich,

> a comparison that had been made by way of spot checks between the Institute's
> library and that of the British Museum. It showed that some thirty percent of the
> titles of books and periodicals brought over from Hamburg were not to be found in
> that great treasure-house of books.[37]

An enlightened decision to accept new blood meant that the staff of six,
their research concerns and their books, had become an integral part of the
intellectual landscape of the UK. The Institute could employ more staff and
mesh with the academic home community. It had proved a successful
transplantation of an institute and centre of learning.

> Warburg's idea had taken root and the Institute was saved for the future. The Wbg
> family gave it as a donation to London University which agreed to provide for it
> permanently. Thus an Institute created by a German scholar was handed over by
> American citizens to become a British Institution, in the expectation that it will serve
> the students of this country and be a worthy member of the international family of
> learned Institutions

— this is how Saxl summarized the momentous move in his unfinished biography of Warburg, drafted in 1944-1945.[38]

Gertrud Bing, the trusted librarian from the Hamburg days, became deputy director and then director from 1955 to 1959, and saw the Institute into its new and permanent home in Woburn Square, next to the School of Oriental and African Studies in Central London.

Fifty years after incorporation into the University of London, the Institute's position has been even more firmly secured: from 1 August 1994 it became one of the founder-members of a new federation of research institutes, the School of Advanced Studies, within the University. The Institute's pluri-disciplinarity and tradition of cross-cultural research proved a method which has enriched British academic life.

Notes

[1] E. Gombrich, *Aby Warburg. An Intellectual Biography* (Oxford: Phaidon, 1970), pp. 65-66.

[2] G. Bing, 'Fritz Saxl (1890-1948): A memoir', in *Fritz Saxl 1890-1948. A Volume of Memorial Essays from his friends in England*, ed. by D.J. Gordon (London: Nelson, 1957), pp. 1-46 (p. 28.)

[3] Memorial address by Max M. Warburg on 5 December 1929, quoted in E. Gombrich, *Aby Warburg,* p. 22.

[4] The Warburg Institute Archives (WIA), General Correspondence (GC), A. Warburg to his mother Charlotte Warburg, 26.01.1887.

[5] *Sandro Botticellis 'Geburt der Venus' und 'Frühling'. Eine Untersuchung über die Vorstellungen von der Antike in der italienischen Frührenaissance* (Hamburg und Leipzig: Leopold Voss, 1893).

[6] WIA, GC, Warburg to A. Doren, n.d., 1910.

[7] F. Saxl, 'The History of Warburg's Library (1886-1944)', in E. Gombrich, *Aby Warburg*, pp. 325-338 (p. 327).

[8] Cf. 'Die Bibliotheken der Jahrhundertwende, die Berufsausbildung und die Schaffung eines neuen Frauenberufes', in Hans Michael Schäfer, *Die Kulturwissenschaftliche Bibliothek Warburg. Persönlichkeiten im Dienst der Bibliothek: Biographische Skizzen und Einblick in die bibliothekarischen Entwicklungen. Eine Untersuchung anhand von Publikationen und Korrespondenzen* (Hausarbeit, University of Hamburg, unpublished, 1997), pp. 7-8.

[9] Fritz Saxl, in E. Gombrich, *Aby Warburg,* p. 326.

[10] WIA, GC, Max M. Warburg to F. Saxl, 03.11.1919.

[11] 'Andere reiche Familien haben ihren Rennstall, ihr habt meine Bibliothek — und das ist mehr.' C. G. Heise, *Persönliche Erinnerungen an Aby Warburg* (New York: Copyright Eric M. Warburg, 1947), p. 23.

[12] Cf. the detailed account of developments from 1929 to 1933 by Bernhard Buschendorf, 'Auf dem Weg nach England. Edgar Wind und die Emigration der Bibliothek Warburg', in *Porträt aus Büchern. Bibliothek Warburg & Warburg Institute. Hamburg. 1933. London*, ed. by Michael Diers, Kleine Schriften des Warburg-Archivs im Kunstgeschichtlichen Seminar der Universität Hamburg, Heft 1 (Hamburg: Dölling & Galitz, 1993) pp. 85-128.

[13] WIA, GC, G. Bing to E. Warburg, 28.09.1933. Erich Warburg is the son of Max M. Warburg, the head of the bank M.M. Warburg & Co.

[14] G. Bing, 'Fritz Saxl (1890-1948): A memoir', p.17.

[15] E. Gombrich, 'Introduction', in *A Heritage of Images. A Selection of lectures by Fritz Saxl*, ed. by Hugh Honour and John Fleming (Harmondsworth: Penguin, 1970), p. 12. On the beginnings of the academic discipline History of Art in Great Britain cf. Dieter Wuttke, 'Die Emigration der Kulturwissenschaftlichen Bibliothek Warburg und die Anfänge des Universitätsfaches Kunstgeschichte in Großbritannien', in *Aby Warburg. Akten des internationalen Symposions. Hamburg 1990*, ed. by Horst Bredekamp, Michael Diers and Charlotte Schoell-Glass (Weinheim: VCH, Acta Humaniora, 1991), pp. 141-163.

[16] WIA, GC, Assistance 1, I.9.1., 1934-1936, E. Simpson to F. Saxl, 08/01/1926.

[17] WIA, GC, Assistance 1, I.9.1., enclosure with letter E. Simpson to G. Bing, 24/01/1936.

[18] WIA, GC, Assistance 1, I.9.1., G. Bing to E. Simpson, 27/01/1926

[19] WIA, GC, Assistance 1, I.9.1., E. Simpson to G. Bing, 03/02/1936.

[20] Cf. G. Bing, passim.

[21] As an example of a letter of recommendation cf. WIA, GC, G. Bing to The Secretary, Central Bureau Loan Fund, 54, Russell Sw, W.C.1, 28/09/1923:
'Dear Madam,
Mrs. Mitchell (formerly Miss Prudence Yalden-Thomson) has suggested that I might approach you for help in the following case. There is a very gifted and capable German-Jewish girl over here, Miss Bradt, who is training to become an architect. She has already passed her Intermediate examination, so that only two more years of training remain. She has already won a competition for a school building and seems altogether very promising. She receives £10 a month from Germany through a transfer from 'Hilfe und Aufbau', but another transfer, which up till now has covered her school fees, has now stopped. The whole fees amount to £150, that is, £75 per annum, and though the amount is high I think it would be well worth while for her to continue her training, since she is so far on her way and has done so well.
Miss Bradt, whose address is 49, Nassington Road, N.W.3, would be most grateful if she might come and see you. She could then furnish further particulars, and I feel confident that she would make a favourable impression and justify her application for a loan. If your Committee could see its way to helping in this case, I should be very grateful.
Yours truly
The Warburg Institute
Assistant Director.'

[22] A specimen in WIA, GC, G. Bing to W. Adams, 25/05/1926:
'Dear Mr. Adams,
You have asked me to give you my opinion on Dr. Edgar Breitenbach as a possible candidate for a Library Directorship. Dr. Breitenbach is one of the oldest pupils of this Institute. He was trained at Hamburg University under our supervision and we have always taken the liveliest interest in his career. He studied art history, and very soon specialised in the study of illuminated manuscripts and of illuminated printed books. It was at our suggestion that he entered the career of librarianship, because even as a student he acted as voluntary assistant in the library of this Institute and showed remarkably good gifts for the profession of librarian. His subsequent career as a librarian justified all our expectations. He did very well during his training at Göttingen University, which, I may add, has the reputation of being one of the best schools of librarianship in Germany; and he was promoted to the position of Senior Librarian (Bibliotheksrat) at a remarkably early age. This accounts for his wide experience, and for the great amount of organisation which he has already done. His testimonials show that he gave satisfaction in all the posts he has held, and I should like to add that he is a very keen worker of a sociable disposition able to get on well with his colleagues as well as with his subordinates, and though he has devoted all his energies to his library work he has still kept up his interest in and his ability for research work. His publications cover both these fields and his activities as a librarian have always profited by his research work and vice versa. He is now engaged on a bibliography of illustrated English books of the 18th century, which we hope will be published in English. We sincerely hope that Dr. Breitenbach will find a position suited to his abilities, and I feel sure that he will fulfil his duties very well.'

[23] WIA, GC, Alan Taylor, of Manchester University, to F. Saxl, 18.12.1936: 'I wonder if you can tell me anything about a Hamburg family of the name of Maass. I ask for this reason: we have been put in touch with a girl to act as nurse for our future family. She is English trained, but has returned to Hamburg. Her brother lives in England and has been over to see us: he mentioned that his parents knew you. All we want to know is that we are not introducing a Nazi into our house and we thought you might be able to tell us whether they are non-Aryans, or at any rate non-Nazi.' Bing, in Saxl's absence, replied on 23.12.1936: 'As it happens, she is a distant relation of one of our collaborators, Dr.Elsbeth Jaffé, who knew her as a child and who has since heard that she is said to have developed into a very capable young woman. She is Jewish and was sent here immediately after Hitler came into power. She has had a domestic training in Germany and was employed here in that capacity before she took up her training as a nurse.'

[24] WIA, GC, box 2.4.

[25] WIA, GC, Correspondence re. Assistance for 1939-1941 in box 3.6. and for 1942-46 in box 4.3.

[26] WIA, GC, W. Adams to E. Wind, 03/02/1926.

[27] WIA, GC, box 2.4.

[28] WIA, GC, box 2.4., G. Bing to E. Simpson, 28/09/1938.

[29] E. Gombrich, 'Gertrud Bing zum Gedenken', *Jahrbuch der Hamburger Kunst-sammlungen* (Hamburg: Hauswedell, 1965), vol.10, p. 9.

[30] 06-07-1964, reprinted in *Gertrud Bing 1892-1964* (London: The Warburg Institute, 1965), p. 4:

[31] E. Simpson, *Refugee Scholars* (Leeds: Moorland Books, 1992, without index).

32 R. Cooper, *Retrospective Sympathetic Affection. A Tribute to the Academic Community* (Leeds: Moorland Books, 1996, without index).

33 Ibid., p. 12.

34 Ibid., p. 95.

35 Cf. Nicholas Mann, '"Kulturwissenschaft" in London: Englisches Fortleben einer europäischen Tradition', in *Aby M. Warburg. "Ekstatische Nymphe ... trauernder Flußgott". Portrait eines Gelehrten*, ed. by R. Galitz and B. Reimers (Hamburg: Dölling und Galitz, 1995), p. 211. German translation of English lecture '"Kulturwissenschaft" in London: The English Avatars of a European Tradition'.

36 Cf. Eric M. Warburg, 'The Transfer of The Warburg Institute to England in 1933'. Appendix to *The University of London. The Warburg Institute Annual Report 1952-1953* (London: University of London, pp. 13-16).

37 E. Gombrich, *Aby Warburg*, p. 338.

38 WIA, Cabinet 8, top drawer, F. Saxl, 'Notes for Warburg Biography, (mainly 1945)', p.1.

Jennifer Taylor

The 'Endsieg' as Ever-Receding Goal. Literary Propaganda by Bruno Adler and Robert Lucas for BBC Radio

March 1999 marked the end of the BBC German Service, established at the time of the Munich Crisis. Now, different priorities have emerged. This paper is concerned with broadcasts during the Second World War, when speaking to Germans in their native language was very much on the political agenda. The paper examines the way in which the propaganda aims of the British government were cloaked in literary garments by exiled writers from Germany and Austria to produce programmes which, aided by state-of-the-art technology, were broadcast by the BBC Features Department. The conclusion is that the result was very different from that achieved by the exiles in the Soviet Union.

On New Year's Eve 1941 the BBC German Service sent season's greetings to Germany. Listeners who were brave enough to risk fines, imprisonment or death for the crime of tuning in to foreign broadcasts heard from Frau Wernicke, a Berlin housewife, Adolf Hirnschal, a private in Hitler's army, Kurt Krüger, a senior teacher, and Willy Schimanski, an official in the German Propaganda Ministry. These were not real people but successful series characters created by exiled writers working for the BBC.
'Kurt und Willi' and 'Frau Wernicke' by Bruno Adler,[1] and 'Adolf Hirnschal' by Robert Lucas were broadcast weekly from mid-1940 until the end of the war.[2] These short, satirical scenes constitute the most extensive examples available of literary propaganda by established authors — for a similar exercise by exiled German writers in the Soviet Union was confined to a shorter time scale. For example, the scenes written by Friedrich Wolf and broadcast to the beleaguered German troops at Stalingrad by loudspeaker van were drafted between November 1942 and November 1943,[3] while Erich Weinert's 'Frau Künecke will jarnischt gesagt haben' (one example of several similar series) could be heard on Radio Moscow from June 1942 to March 1943.[4] Nevertheless, a comparison of the British output, drafted to conform to Government propaganda aims,[5] with the scenes written in the Soviet Union can be a fruitful exercise. For as differences in tone, emphasis and working practice are revealed, the specific characteristics of BBC propaganda can be discerned. Similarly, recognition of the literary components of these broadcasts and

identification of their literary antecedents will enable this large body of work to take its place in the corpus of German exile literature.

These works were part of a campaign of psychological warfare, a campaign to win the hearts and minds of the German people. The aim, to impair morale both on the home front and the battle front and so sap the fighting spirit. The appeal, not to the lofty ideals of heroic resistance and revolution, but to the less noble motive of self-interest. The target, the average man or woman faced with the seemingly never-ending war. The weapons: references to food and clothing shortages, reminders of the high loss of life from enemy bombs at home and the high casualty rate on the battlefield, ridicule of Germany's political leaders and, finally, chilling parallels with the First World War, which had ended so ignominiously in Germany's defeat.

The style of the BBC series was influenced by the working practices of the Corporation. Familiarity with the language currently spoken and written in Hitler's Germany from which the writers had been separated by several years of exile was the first requirement for an author of such works. Moscow and London solved this problem in different ways. In the Soviet Union Wolf, Weinert and Johannes R. Becher were afforded privileged access to German prisoners-of-war, including censoring their letters. (It will be remembered that a German soldier's letter inspired Becher's five-act tragedy *Schlacht um Moskau* [1941-2], later renamed *Winterschlacht)*. Wolf's work benefitted from this contact with his younger compatriots, gaining freshness and immediacy. The writers working in England were not afforded such opportunities. Instead, the BBC placed an extensive library of the German national and regional press at their disposal. But sole reliance on the written is no substitute for human contact. At times, a certain bookishness pervades the pieces written in London so that the sheer weight of the written material the writer has had to absorb inhibits the immediacy and freshness of the drama. Such weakness is particularly evident in some of the 'Kurt und Willi' scenes.

A more felicitious influence was provided by the state-of-the-art technology of the BBC sound archive. At a time when voice recording was technically difficult, the BBC possessed a complete set of Hitler's speeches. Careful editing, aided by a comprehensive cross-reference system and the prodigious memory of the young Martin Esslin made it possible to compose a programme solely from Hitler's own words, showing him contradicting himself, reneging on his promises and unable to fulfil his grandiose claims.[6] Adler and Lucas incorporated this technique of antithetical juxtaposition into their work so that contrast was built into the structure of the pieces.

The three series we are concerned with were all successful productions of the Features Department, whose brief was to infuse documentary material with popular appeal. Dramatisation was an obvious tool to this end, and so the nature of these scenes as literary constructs is indicated by their place in the BBC's tripartite structure.[7] Furthermore, aspects of the dramatisation were dictated by contemporary conditions and the demands of psychological warfare. As propaganda broadcasts had to be short (between three and seven minutes) to minimise the danger of detection, an elaborate approach was not appropriate. Discrete plays, for instance, would be ineffectual, since there was insufficient time to establish the characters. One or two strongly delineated figures, easily identifiable in the first few seconds of the broadcast, were needed. In this way a rapport could be established and empathy result.

The most obvious dramatic format was a dialogue. This afforded authors the opportunity of creating an informed interlocutor who would refute the snippets of propaganda mindlessly repeated by a naive speaker. This scheme, widely used by Friedrich Wolf, was also employed by Bruno Adler in 'Kurt und Willi', which he wrote in collaboration with the British writer Norman Cameron.[8] In this series the unquestioning patriotism of Kurt Krüger, a senior teacher, is countered by the worldly cynicism of Willi Schimanski, an official from the Ministry of Propaganda, two friends who meet regularly in a café on the Potsdamer Platz to discuss the progress of the war.

The scenes are loosely constructed (usually Kurt and Willi discuss more than one topic), the dialogue often unpolished and laconic. Typical examples of Kurt's utterances are: 'Oder habt ihr Propagandafritzen da vielleicht wieder 'n Ding gedreht?' (23 July 1941), 'Aber Willi ... jeder wünscht den Bolschewiken eins auf den Kopp.' (25 June 1941)[9] This is the overheated world of spin doctors where, in the light of the appalling casualty figures, even Hitler himself is in danger of being used as a scapegoat. For Willi, the propagandists' propagandist (much admired, it was said, in the German Ministry itself),[10] is engaged in an internecine feud with the High Command of the Armed Forces (OKW). In this battle victory will be accorded to the the one who first succeeds in issuing massaged figures. For example, in the wake of severe Allied bombing raids

Willi avoids publishing the mass casualty lists which would depress civilian
morale simply by introducing regional editions of the *Völkischer
Beobachter.*

In creating this work in which paper prevails over flesh and blood
the authors' dependence on written sources is often evident. For instance,
to emphasise the casualty rates among German sub-mariners during the
Battle of the Atlantic Willi refers to actuarial tables issued by a Swiss life
assurance company (13 August 1941). A similar artlessness was reflected in
the original production arrangements. The scripts were read by whoever
happened to be the duty announcers on the day of the broadcasts. Nor were
the parts differentiated — on separate occasions Carl Brinitzer read both
Kurt and Willi. Eventually, though, it was realized that the best
performances were given by two announcers who were in fact trained
actors, and the parts were assigned on a permanent basis. Kurt was read by
Fritz Wendhausen and Willi by Peter Illing (formerly Peter Ihle of the
Volksbühne in Berlin).

The dialogues as conceived have two advantages. Firstly, they
provided the authors with an excellent vehicle for discrediting National
Socialist leaders. Secondly, including a character such as Willi who prides
himself on his inside knowledge made it possible to use information gained
from the clandestine sources to which Adler had access by virtue of his
employment at the Political Warfare Executive, which at that time was
running the BBC. But in spite of these strengths Adler (an art historian
who had not previously worked as a professional dramatist) encountered
difficulties of language and dramatic structure which were never fully
resolved.

In 'Kurt und Willi' Adler was aiming at a similar effect to that
successfully achieved by the master of satire, Karl Kraus, in those short,
transitional scenes in *Die letzten Tage der Menschheit* where the naive,
cliché-ridden militaristic utterances of 'der Optimist' are complemented by
the cynical comments of 'der Nörgler':

> Die Völker werden aus dem Kriege nur lernen/daß
> sie ihn künftig nicht unterlassen sollen.
> Wir sind mit den Deutschen verbunden auf Gedeih und
> /Verderb!
> Diese Photographie sagt Ihnen also / daß ein
> Renngigerl die Welt in den Tod geführt hat! [11]

In Kraus' work, since the Nörgler completes the Optimist's sentences to bathetic, anti-heroic effect, the antithesis is effectively embedded in the syntax. That Adler never quite attained this standard of witty repartee is illustrated by the following example from a 1944 broadcast in which Willi is the first to speak:

> Warum kann uns denn eigentlich nischt passieren?
>
> Weil unsere Befestigungen am Atlantikwall
>
> unüberwindlich sind.
>
> Unüberwindlich?
>
> Allerdings. Das sagt man doch alle Tage mehrere
>
> Male![12]

Furthermore, the concept itself was flawed, for the listeners had no character with which to identify. This point can perhaps best be made by seeing how Friedrich Wolf went about a similar task. 'Zwischenrufe aus dem Dritten Reich' feature friends who, like Kurt and Willi, are of equal social status. But Schramm counters Schroeder's naiveté with patient Socratic questioning, and manages to persuade him to his way of thinking without undermining his dignity. The dramatic climax is a synthesis of the argument, usually embodying an agitational aim, and often summarised in proverbial form: 'Ungerecht Gut gedeihet nicht',[13] 'Der Krug geht solange zum Grunde, bis er bricht!', 'Wer Wind sät, wird Sturm ernten!'[14] This simpler, more didactic pattern means that the person countering the Nazi propaganda becomes an object of admiration since he is in the right. Such in not the case with 'Kurt und Willi', for neither character is admirable. The listener must perforce despise Willi's cynicism, while at the same time denigrating Kurt's weakness, gullibility and tunnel vision.

However, where the central concept of the devious manipulator generates sufficient moral outrage for the listener to identify with Kurt, an effective dramatic climax can be reached, as in 'Kurt and Willi on Hitler's Responsibility' (6 August 1941). The listeners learn that the slaughter on the Russian front has unleashed an inter-departmental feud between the Propaganda Ministry who are intent on exonerating Hitler, and the OKW, who wish the Führer to shoulder the blame. This battle has been won by the Ministry at the expense of the career of a hapless military attaché. Kurt finds this news difficult to reconcile with his absolutist ideal, 'Der Führer ist die verkörperte Ehre', but eventually achieves a synthesis by concluding, 'Aber schließlich, jeder von uns muß bereit sein, für den Führer alles zu opfern.' In this exchange Kurt's utterances border on a dignified if misguided patriotism, and so he becomes an object of pity rather than ridicule. It was not long before the advantages of such an adjustment to the characterisation were realized. A fortnight later a script condemning war profiteering ('Kurt and Willi on Soldiers and Shares', 20 August 1941) had a typewritten note appended, which read, 'Kurt ist [...] diesmal etwas weniger heiter und naiv als sonst und soll in seinem Ausbruch am Ende des Gesprächs echt menschlich wirken.' Willi, drinking champagne, explains that he has made a killing on the stock exchange. However, his investment would be adversely affected by German victories on the eastern front. This attitude prompts the following indignant outburst from Kurt:

> Fast jeden Tag höre ich, daß einer meiner alten Schüler auf dem Felde der Ehre gefallen ist, für Führer und Vaterland [...] und jetzt, wenn ich hier sitze, und anhören muß, was du und deine ehrenwerten Freunde [...] treiben, und wie ihr hofft, daß unsere Truppen nicht zuviele Siege gewinnen, damit eure dreckige Spekulation nicht schiefgeht, dann... .

Indignantly refusing a second glass of champagne, Kurt storms out of the café.

Rarely was such a satisfying dramatic structure achieved. More usually, the need to inform overburdened the fragile structure. Such was the importance attached to the informative aspect that, despite the dramatic shortcomings, the series was maintained until the end of the war and served as a model for the 'Pacher and Pachulke' series written by Robert Lucas when the Austrian Service was established in 1943.[15] And in many ways Willi can be seen as a distant ancestor of Sir Humphrey Appleby, that devious civil servant who started life in the BBC radio comedy series 'Yes Minister' in the early 'eighties.

Although the dialogue was the most obvious vehicle to express the dialectical pattern of propaganda work, monologues, too, had their advantages. Firstly, there is the economy of scale, since only one actor is needed. Secondly, as this format demands pre-editing, the resulting authorial compression can ensure a higher literary quality. This is the case in the 'Frau Wernicke' series. Adler achieved a tighter format and so avoided some of the linguistic and dramatic difficulties encountered when writing the 'Kurt und Willi' dialogues.

'Kurt und Willi' represent the governing classes. 'Frau Wernicke' (written solely by Adler) is set firmly among the petit bourgeoisie, the small, independent tradesmen and their families, the ordinary people at

whom the British propaganda campaign was primarily targetted. Frau
Gertrud Wernicke, who lives in an unprepossessing Berlin suburb near the
Schlesischer Bahnhof, is married to such a tradesman, Gustav, a First-
World-War veteran. In the creation of this *persona* Adler was assisted by
the actress who portrayed Frau Wernicke throughout the series. Annemarie
Hase (whose voice can still be heard on the few remaining recordings
which survive)[16] had worked in cabaret in Berlin, an experience which
obviously stood her in good stead when delivering lines in the
uncompromising Berlin dialect in which the series was written. So
instrumental was the actress in the definition of this character that the
premature termination of the series (the last broadcast was on 29 January
1944) is most likely due to her indisposition — she had an eye operation at
that time.

'Frau Wernicke', like 'Kurt und Willi', is set in Berlin, although in
this case there is more variation in the locale. This vantage point on the
home front affords Frau Wernicke the opportunity (as befits her gender)
of commenting on shortages of food and clothing. But although the series
was originally assigned to a slot in the women's programme, Frau
Wernicke's probing intellect is not confined to domestic matters. Reference
is made to the high casualty rate among German troops (20 September
1941), conditions on the eastern front (21 November 1942), defection (6
March 1943), German territorial losses and allied advances (3 September
1943, 20 November 1943), while those at home are portrayed as
increasingly beleaguered, facing an incursion of refugees from the west of
Germany (3 September 1943) and bombing from all directions (2 October
1943), day and night (16 October 1943).[17] Running through the programme like a leitmotif are comparisons to 1918, when Germany was
defeated and demoralised, intensified by frequent reminders of the Nazi
glorification of war and death.

The earliest scenes are set in Frau Wernicke's parlour (her 'gute
Stube') where friends have gathered to knit or to renovate clothes that in
peacetime would have been thrown away. As the war progresses, the locale
becomes increasingly public. Subsequent scenes are set at the offices where
clothing coupons are obtained (29 November 1941) and where old clothes
are collected (19 January 1942). She is shown in the street collecting for
the 'Kriegswinterhilfe' (4 October 1941)[18] and looking for war work (30
May 1942). She eventually finds employment in a restaurant (20 June

1942), where she meets the Ukranian 'Zwangsarbeiter' working as a waiter who becomes her most frequent interlocutor.

The subversive nature of Frau Wernicke's comments are dictated by aspects of her character: her volubility and her robust common sense. The examples which follow offer evidence of more careful sentence construction, tighter drafting and more compression than 'Kurt und Willi'. 'Jeht ihm aber jut, wat? Uneinberufen jut?' Frau Wernicke enquires of her friend's husband (19 April 1941, p. 5), while she defends her Ukranian colleague in the following terms, 'det is doch keen Bolschewike, det is doch'n injedeutscher Aushilfsjermane aus de Ukraine, eijenhändig von mir jezähmt' (20 November 1943, p. 143). Frequently there is an antithetical structure to her statement: the second part of her sentence counters and thus discredits the pro-Nazi proposition which precedes it, a technique reminiscent of the edited versions of Hitler speeches broadcast by the BBC. Additionally, Adler uses a variety of devices to enhance the effect. There is the rhetorical question,'[ich habe gelesen] det ne deutsche Mutta nich bloß einen Sohn opfern muß, sondern alle ihre Söhne, soville se hat, und zwar "damit das Vaterland lebe". Wat wa mi n Vaterland anfange, wenn wir alle Söhne jeopfert haben?' (22 March 1941*), contradiction, 'Det deutsche Volk führt doch [...] nen Verteidijungskriech, den wo uns de Feinde uffjezwungen haben, nich wahr? Und in den Vateidijungskriech ham wa nun schon so viel erobat ...' (3 May 1941, p. 12) and contrast, 'Entweder wa verzichten uff de Führer, oder wa verzichten uff Frieden. Der Mensch kann ebent nich allet zujleich haben.' (16 October 1943, p. 139)

The emphasis on shortages of food and clothing, the high loss of life at home and on the battlefront, and the equation of National Socialism with militarism and death in these carefully constructed sentences constitute subversive statements which would effectively impair the working and fighting morale of the German people and persuade them to end the war. Nevertheless, after the series had been on the air for about nine months, Adler resorted to a plotting device to account for his character's motivation for making political statements. Frau Wernicke reports that she had spent a short period in a concentration camp but had been released on the understanding that she would disseminate pro-Nazi propaganda (22 March 1941*). One year later, on 4 April 1942, she reminds her listeners of this undertaking. Thus her status as an officially sanctioned — if not coerced — disseminator of the Party line adds another level to the irony, since she has agreed to embrace a role she is temperamentally incapable of fulfilling.

This gives the pieces a comic dimension so singularly lacking in 'Kurt und Willi', for in place of Willi's world-weary cynicism we have a forceful personality whose emphatic volubility and unremitting common sense traduce the message it carries. The resultant situation comedy invites comparison with Gerhart Hauptmann's *Der Biberpelz*, in which the washerwoman Frau Wolff (Frau Wernicke's most obvious literary antecedent) enjoys a reputation for probity and hard work while all the time she and her family are conspiring to defraud their neighbours.[19]

A similarly archetypal figure was chosen by Robert Lucas when devising 'Adolf Hirnschal', the third and final series to be considered here. Hirnschal, a First-World-War veteran, writes a weekly letter from the front to his wife at home. Before despatch, each letter is read aloud to Emil Jaschke, Hirnschal's comrade-in-arms. As these letters contain copious amount of direct speech, they are in effect dramatised monologues. Although Lucas denied that he had consciously used the good soldier Schwejk as a model,[20] Hirnschal exhibits a similar simplicity masking a shrewd common sense. And Lucas, like Hasek, uses the satirical device of *reductio ad absurdum*.

As the first of these radio series to be published,[21] 'Adolf Hirnschal' is the best known of the three,[22] and deservedly so, since it is qualitatively the most accomplished. Lucas, formerly Robert Ehrenzweig, a qualified chemist who later worked as a journalist, had extensive experience with political cabaret in Vienna, which stood him in good stead when writing this series.

Careful drafting is evident in the references to the minor characters, acquaintances from Zwieselsdorf, Hirnschal's home town, whose names and descriptions evince a euphonious resonance. There is Theodorich Zwanzig, 'Schaubudenbesitzer' and proprietor of a 'motorisierte Flohzirkus', Dagobert Streckfuß, member of the 'Freiwilliger Feuerbestattungsverein Vergissmeinnicht' and Eberhard Wundrisch, 'Blutordensanwärter und Bademeister im Städischen Schwimmbad'. Additionally, such references evoke a cosy, provincial atmosphere, in contrast to the unashamedly metropolitan tones of Kurt and Willi or the Berlin dialect of Frau Wernicke. Great care was exercised to ensure this distinction was maintained. It was felt at the BBC that Hirnschal should not be identified with any particular town or region and Fritz Schecker, the actor who interpreted Hirnschal, was carefully schooled in a non-specific dialect. The result of such attention to detail in both drafting and interpretation is that a

more polished effect is achieved in this series than in either of the other
two.

Setting the scenes at the front gives the author great flexibility, for
he is able to move his character around the theatre of war, and this in itself
serves as a comment on its course. So Hirnschal is first shown serving in
France, but is moved to the Eastern Front in the summer of 1941. In
September 1943 he is in hospital in Warsaw with a head wound, but in his
confused state thinks he is in Moscow. On his release from hospital he is
attacked by partisans before he can rejoin his regiment. Subsequently he
serves in Romania, and, in 1944, he is transferred to the Western Front,
from which vantage point he witnesses the final disintegration of the Third
Reich.

Whereas the antithetical structure of Frau Wernicke's sentences
ensures the balance is restored by the protagonist's robust common sense,
Lucas uses reductive devices to discredit Nazi propaganda. One such
technique is to establish an incongruous juxtaposition which, at times, veers
on the scatalogical. For example, while the soldiers are listening to Hitler's
speech on the 'Tag der nationalen Erhebung', they are pre-occupied with
delousing, worried about vermin and the spread of disease in their barracks
(1 February 1942), where the latrine is referred to as 'Das Braune Haus'
(14 November 1942). Another, more extensively used device is the
anecdote, which achieves bathetic effect by portraying matters of national
or strategic importance from the perspective of Zwieselsdorf. This device
is used to particularly good effect when commenting on strategic or tactical
problems. Asked by an SS officer to define 'Frontbegradigung', Hirnschal
is reminded of the occasion when the village idiot Eberhardt Knackfuß had
tried to cut his garden hedge. Unsatisfied with the results, 'sie [ist] voll
Löcher und Einbuchtungen', Knackfuß works on it for a week, 'und hat
hier etwas weggenommen und dort etwas abgeschnitten [...] bis zum Schluß
überhaupt nichts mehr übrig war von der Hecke.' (4 October 1943, p.
118)[23]

In keeping with the battlefront setting, the predominant emphasis of
the propaganda is on discrediting the leaders — especially the military
leaders. The breach of faith between the leaders and the people, illustrated
by the anecdote of the confidence trickster who duped Hirnschal's aunt
Pauline (29 November 1943), is reinforced by the sustained metaphor of
Fritz Ziegenbart's unfaithful wife who is having an affair with a Party
official while her husband is at the front (18 July 1942, 14 November

1942). Frequent mention is made of the identification of National Socialism with war, destruction and death, and the war news itself is used to refute Hitler's claim that the 'Endsieg' was in sight. As the German military offensive is repulsed, German victory is shown to be an ever-receding goal. On one such occasion, when asked to explain the Führer's recent statement that 'Der Ausfall Italiens hat sehr wenig zu bedeuten', Hirnschal's reply consists of a pastiche of inaccurate predictions from official German sources:

> Es gibt zwei Erklärungen für diesen Ausspruch des Führers [...] Die eine Erklärung, daß unser geliebter Führer dies in demselben Sinne gesagt hat, in dem er vor einem Jahr erkärt hat, daß wir Stalingrad nehmen werden. Die andere Erklärung ist, daß unser geliebter Führer diesen Ausspruch in demselben Sinne getan hat, in dem der Reichsmarschall vor vier Jahren versichert hat, der Feind werde keine einzige Bombe auf Deutschland werfen. (4 October 1943, p. 119)

So impressed are his superiors by his grasp of the rhetoric that Hirnschal is encouraged to apply for a transfer to the Ministry of Propaganda. In this capacity he travels to the besieged Cherkassy ('the second Stalingrad') to boost morale. However, he is unable to fulfill his mission since his exit from the aeroplane is blocked by the stampede of officers anxious to escape the stricken city.[24] This plot development, after the programme had been on the air for nearly three years, can be seen as an acknowledgement of the extent to which the author relied on the broadcasting media for his material. If Willi is the propagandists' propagandist, Hirnschal can be said to be the broadcasters' broadcaster. As such, he reflects the important role this medium was accorded by the German authorities as a means of maintaining the morale of their troops and influencing their opinions.[25] Frequently the soldiers are shown in barracks waiting to listen to a Hitler speech, an activity which was compulsory (22 November 1941, 1 February 1942), Hirnschal himself takes part in a live broadcast from the front (27 September 1941), Leutenant Krickwitz mistakenly tunes to Radio Moscow when conducting a propaganda campaign in the Ukraine (18 July 1942). Finally, when, on New Year's Eve, the radio breaks down before the soldiers can hear Hitler's address to the nation, Hirnschal drafts a speech for the officer to give. But once power is restored it becomes evident that this speech bears a close resemblance to that actually given by Hitler (3 January 1944).

It is noticeable that the atrocious conditions faced by the men fighting on the Eastern Front are rarely described directly, but mediated through literary conceits. For example, in the terrible cold of January 1942 the hypnotist Hans-Joachim Blitz persuades a soldier suffering from hypothermia he is warm, so that he dies with a smile on his face (18 January 1942). Contrast to this the immediacy of Wolf's detailed descriptions of privations faced by the ill-equipped troops, 'An der Ostfront hatten wir bloß unsere leichten Sommerlatscher', the resultant injuries, 'Der Fuß ist abgefroren, weil die Schuhe zerfetzt waren und nur bis zum Knöchel gingen,'[26] and the medical treatment, informed by the author's expert knowledge (Wolf was a qualified doctor), 'Erst nehmen sie ihm den Fuß ab, dann immer noch ein bißchen mehr, weil das alles erfroren und verfault war.'[27] Several of Wolf's scenes end with an explicit exhortation to desert, 'Wir sollten, anstatt uns hier mit den Kosaken herumzuschlagen, schleunigst nach Deutschland zurück',[28] 'Ich bin dafür, daß wir hier 'ne scharfe Kehrtwendung machen und uns unsre Frauen und Werkbänke und unser Deutschland zurückerobern!'[29] Lucas, however, handles the question of defection obliquely. When Hirnschal discovers that a prisoner taken by his unit is not a deaf and dumb Russian peasant, as had hitherto been supposed, but a neighbour from Zwieselsdorf who had been attempting to give himself up to the Russians, he keeps the secret, 'So sag' ich ihm, er soll weiter das Maul halten, denn sonst geht noch das halbe Regiment mit ihm.' (2 August 1941, p. 49)

Furthermore, attacks on the destructive nature of war are expressed in terms of the great imponderables of life, death and faith. A montage-like sequence where Hirnschal, in charge of the ciné projector, mistakenly runs the film backwards, is expressed in cadences of Biblical resonance:

> [...] und wie sie laufen, verschwinden die Löcher in ihren Uniformen, und die Wunden an ihren Gliedern heilen [...] und aus dem Schnee kommen die Erforenen und aus dem Staub die Verdursteten [...] und auf einmal ziehen sie wieder in Panzern und Lastern zurück nach Westen. (7 February 1945, p. 165)

A draft of the 1943 Christmas broadcast shows an even greater influence of a religious tradition. Hirnschal, lying wounded in a hospital in Russia, dreams he is in hell with the Nazi leaders. Subsequently he is shown sueing for entry into heaven, where he is granted a vision of the Christ child, worshiped by the Magi, who are then transformed into Roosevelt, Stalin and Churchill.[30] Such was the extravagance of this vision that, hardly surprisingly, the script was rejected by the BBC. Nevertheless, in the final stages of the war, when Germany's imminent defeat made the antithetical balance of any argument difficult to maintain, dream sequences re-appear;

a modest one is used on 21 February 1945, while the final broadcast, 1 May 1945, is conceived in terms of a grandiose Wagnerian 'Götterdämmerung'.

Behind the topicality of the satire, whose style was derived from the relatively recent literary institutions of the cabaret and the *Kleinkunstbühne*, there can be discerned the influence of an older dramatic tradition. It is that of those sweeping surveys of human life and death which constitute the mediaeval mystery plays, a genre revived in Salzburg under the aegis of Hugo von Hofmannsthal. For when, marooned on the Russian steppes, surrounded by the corpses of his dead comrades, Hirnschal remarks, 'Wir sind nur Tote auf Urlaub' (p. 86), he is exhibiting neither revolutionary fervour, nor the resolve to desert or defect, but rather an ironic resignation to the vagaries of the human condition.

It is evident, then, that Adler and Lucas, these two highly successful propaganda writers working in Britain, came from a different tradition to that of the committed communists exiled in the Soviet Union. For while Wolf adopts the direct approach developed during the Weimar Republic, when his writing pilloried social injustice, Adler and Lucas employ a more oblique and allusive style. This style reflected the Austrian tradition from which they came, but it was also influenced by contemporary factors, by the circumstances of production, by their distance from the theatre of war, and by their reliance on printed sources for information. In short, it was a style which accorded well with the donnish atmosphere prevalent in the BBC German Service at that time, an atmosphere generated by the high number of academics who had been recruited for the duration.

Acknowledgements

My thanks to BBC Written Archives Centre, Caversham, Reading, for affording me access to the original scripts of the three series described in this article, and to the Friedrich Wolf Archive, Lehnitz, for sending me copies of Wolf's unpublished scenes.

Additionally, in preparing this article I have relied heavily on the following published sources: Bernhard Wittek, *Der britische Ätherkrieg gegen das Dritte Reich*, C. J. Fahle: Münster, 1962; Carl Brinitzer, *Hier spricht London*, Hoffmann und Campe: Hamburg, 1969, in particular Chapter 9; and Uwe Naumann, *Zwischen Tränen und Gelächter,* Pahl-Rugenstein: Cologne, 1983, especially Chapter 3.

Notes

1 Broadcasting commenced early summer 1940; the earliest broadcasts are no longer extant.

2 Broadcasting commenced December 1940.

3 See the present author's 'Propaganda as an Art Form? Some reflections on Friedrich Wolf's Work in the Soviet Union in 1942', *GLL*, 2 (1985), 138-154.

4 See Simone Barck, 'Zur Tätigkeit deutscher Schriftsteller und Künstler am Moskauer Rundfunk (1935-1945)', in *Exil in der UdSSR*, ed. Klaus Jarmatz and others, (Leipzig: Reclam, 1979), pp. 348-356.

5 Cf. Tom Kuhn, 'Under the Crooked Cross: Brecht's *Furcht und Elend* at the BBC', in *England? Aber wo liegt es?*, ed. Charmian Brinson and others (Munich: Iudicium, 1996), p. 185.

6 See Brinitzer, pp. 188-7 for an example.

7 See Kevin Gough-Yates, 'The BBC as a Source of Employment for Film Workers and Composers during the War', in *Zwischenwelt 4: Exil in Großbritannien*, ed. Siglinde Bolbecher and others (Vienna: Verlag für Gesellschaftskritik, 1995), pp. 215-240 (p. 217).

8 The precise degree of collaboration has yet to be established; Gough-Yates (p. 219) states categorically that Adler translated the scenes which had been drafted by Cameron; Naumann, in his latest study, 'Kampf auf Ätherwellen. Die deutschsprachigen Satiren der BBC im Zweiten Weltkrieg' in *Keine Klage über England*, ed. Charmian Brinson and others (Munich: Iudicium, 1998), pp. 34-35 implies that Adler's participation was greater than this.

9 These scenes have never been published; scripts, from March 1941, available in BBC Written Archives; references are to the date of broadcast.

10 Gough-Yates, pp. 218-9.

11 Quotations from Karl Kraus, *Die letzten Tage der Menschheit*, I, 4, II, 2, III, 41 respectively, edn used Munich: DTV, 1978.

12 Broadcast 30 May 1944, quoted after Brinitzer, p. 239.

13 Friedrich Wolf, *Hörspiele, Laienspiele, Szenen* (Berlin and Weimar: Aufbau, 1965), p. 432.

14 Eponymous scenes not published, ms. in Wolf Archive.

15 See Susanne Gföller, 'Pacher und Pachulke — Doppelconférence im Österreichischen Dienst der BBC', *Mit der Ziehharmonika*, 1 (1996), 28-29.

16 Three recordings of 'Frau Wernicke', three of 'Kurt und Willi' and the sole remaining 'Hirnschal' recording from the BBC Sound Archive were issued as audio-cassettes to accompany the following publication, *Der Kampf um die Ätherwellen*, ed. Hans Sarkowicz and Michael Crone (Frankfurt/M.: Eichborn, 1990).

17 See Bruno Adler, *Frau Wernicke. Kommentare einer 'Volksjenossin'*, ed. Uwe Naumann (Mannheim: persona, 1990). Page references to this edition.

18 Not published; BBC Written Archives. Subsequent references to unpublished scenes denoted by an asterisk.

19 Frau Wernicke is erroneously referred to as a washerwoman by Brinitzer (p. 113); this error is compounded in Günter Scholdt, *Autoren über Hitler. Deutschsprachige Schriftsteller 1919-1945 und ihr Bild vom 'Führer'* (Bonn: Bouvier, 1993), p. 901.

20 Robert Lucas, 'Über den Gefreiten Hirnschal und seine Briefe', *Literatur und Kritik*, 128 (1978), 453.

21 A selection of 50 scripts published as Robert Lucas, *Teuere Amalia. Vielgeliebtes Weib! Die Briefe des Gefreiten Adolf Hirnschal an seine Frau in Zwieselsdorf* (Zurich: Europa Verlag, 1946). Page references to this edition.

22 Subsequent editions expanded by five scripts: under the same title, ed. Uwe Naumann (Frankfurt/M.: Fischer, 1984); *Die Briefe des Gefreien Hirnschal. BBC-Radio-Satiren 1940-1945*, ed. Uwe Naumann (Vienna: Verlag für Gesellschaftskritik, 1994).

23 Further examples in Naumann, *Tränen und Gelächter*, pp. 143-4.

24 Broadcast on 21 February 1944, omitted from the original edition, included in subsequent editions.

25 See Klaus Scheel, *Krieg über Ätherwellen* (Berlin: Verlag der Wissenschaften, 1970). The photograph opposite p. 145 shows a group of soldiers listening to the radio.

26 Friedrich Wolf, 'Die Verwesungskompanie', ms. in Wolf Archive.

27 Friedrich Wolf, 'Zwischenrufe', ms. in Wolf Archive.

28 Friedrich Wolf, 'Der Kilometerkrieg', ms. in Wolf Archive.

29 Friedrich Wolf, 'Neu Babylon', ms. in Wolf Archive.

30 Robert Lucas, 'Der Weihnachtsbrief des Gefreiten Adolf Hirnschal an seine Frau Amalia', *Mit der Ziehharmonika*, 4 (1994), 19-24.

J. M. Ritchie

The *Thomas Mann Newsletter* in London 1940-1942

As a Czech citizen in exile in Switzerland Thomas Mann regularly visited Czechoslovakia where a Thomas Mann Society had been formed to aid refugee writers. When forced to move to London, this society continued its activities with the help of the Czech Refugee Trust Fund. From 1940 till 1945 the Thomas Mann Society issued a *Thomas Mann Newsletter* containing concise information on writers and artists and their fate in exile. Of particular interest is the light this *Newsletter* sheds on the exile scene in Great Britain in these years, especially the effects of internment and deportation on literary and artistic circles.

When after some hesitation Thomas Mann decided to go into exile and thereby lose his German citizenship he had difficult choices to make. As a world-famous author he would have been welcomed in many countries. In fact he chose to become a Czech citizen. There were various reasons for this choice. Czechoslovakia was near the German border and hence a country favoured by many refugees from National Socialism. It also had a German-language reading public among whom he had a following. In addition he had visited the country many times, had excellent contacts there and his works were widely commented on in that country. But there was also a more compelling reason why he chose Czechoslovakia. He had a family example to follow. His brother Heinrich, a prominent anti-Nazi, had been one of the first to have to leave Germany and he had accepted Czech citizenship, having been sponsored by a little town called Prosec. Despite the hostility of the pro-Nazi sections of the Czech press which this act of sponsoring an anti-Nazi had provoked the same little town seemed willing to sponsor Thomas Mann too. So he submitted an application and to his delight the council of Prosec voted in favour of granting him and his family the requested Czech citizenship. Needless to say this was widely reported in the Czech press, evoking a wave of positive and negative reactions. In fact Thomas Mann was by then living in Switzerland and it was in that country that, on 23 November, he swore the oath of allegiance before the Czech consul. In January of the following year he was able to come to Czechoslovakia as a Czech citizen in order to thank the people of Prosec personally. As one newspaper reported at the time: 'Eine kleine Stadt bekommt einen großen Sohn'.[1] Thomas Mann was to remain a Czech citizen for the next eight years. While continuing to live in Switzerland, he returned frequently to Czechoslovakia. He also wrote for Czech journals and exile newspapers published in that country, was the guest of Czech PEN, and was received by the President of the Republic. Every move he made in Czechoslovakia was widely reported.

After 1933 various anti-Nazi clubs were formed in Czechoslovakia of which the most prominent were the Bert Brecht Club and the Oskar Kokoschka Club. As early as 1935, Friedrich Burschell, who had emigrated to Czechoslovakia from Nazi Germany, had also established a "Notgemeinschaft deutscher emigrierter Schriftsteller", the first organisation in Prague to attempt to do something practical to help exiled writers. Heinrich Mann was the president and Arnold Zweig and Lion Feuchtwanger were committee members. Burschell then looked around for a prominent patron and in January 1935 managed to interest Thomas Mann who was in Prague. It took another two years of badgering by Burschell before Thomas Mann came back to Prague to attend the meeting to constitute a 'Thomas-Mann-Fonds'. This Thomas Mann Fund was then transformed into a Thomas Mann Society of which the first full meeting took place on 9 November 1937 under the chairmanship of Professor Jan Blahoslav Kozák, a prominent politician and anti-Nazi. This new society was to prove one of the most effective of all the many organisations set up to alleviate the lot of refugee writers.

As far as exile in Great Britain is concerned the history of the Thomas Mann Society is important because the exodus from Czecho-slovakia meant that the Thomas Mann Society was forced to move from Prague to London. Burschell, the first secretary of the society, moved to London with it in December 1938 and remained in England till 1954, eventually becoming a British citizen. In London the Thomas Mann Society worked in parallel with the Czech Refugee Trust Fund, which had funds set aside by the British government. The Thomas Mann Society accordingly not only had an immensely influential figure as its titular head, it also had access to significant resources which it could administer for the benefit of the many refugees, *Reichsdeutsche*, Austrians and Czechs, who had managed to find refuge in England by way of Czechoslovakia. This in itself was worthy enough. In addition, however, though Burschell's original plan that the society should have its own *Thomas-Mann-Jahrbuch* was never realised, the society did keep in touch with its members by issuing a

*Thomas Mann Newsletter.*2 Walter A. Berendsohn, in his pioneering introduction to exile literature, reported on this briefly as follows:

> Für die Thomas-Mann-Gruppe in London, ursprünglich eine internationale Organisation, die von Prag ausging, gab W. Sternfeld hektographierte Nachrichtenblätter in 200 Exemplaren heraus, die sich auf ganz knappe Informationen über Schriftsteller, Künstler und Forscher und ihre Leistungen beschränkten und gratis an die Mitglieder und interessierten Kreise verteilt wurden.3

On 20 October 1940 the first number of the *Thomas Mann Newsletter* was sent out with Bernhard Menne and Wilhelm Sternfeld named as editor and co-editor respectively acting on behalf of the Thomas Mann Group of the Czech Refugee Trust Fund, the address for which was given as 81 Montague Street, London W. C. 1. In appearance the *Thomas Mann Newsletter* was not very impressive — it consisted of an almost illegible, duplicated typescript. Nevertheless the newsletter did have certain advantages, for the persons named as editing the newsletter *were* impressive. Bernhard Menne was an experienced German journalist, who, after emigration to Prague, had been editor-in-chief of the *Prager Mittag*. His co-editor, Willy Sternfeld, was also an experienced journalist who had made his way from France to Prague, where he had succeeded Friedrich Burschell as secretary to the Thomas Mann Society. In other words, the amateurish appearance of this exile publication was deceptive. Both of its editors had an extensive background in editorial and journalistic work. Berendsohn's description of the notes in the 'Nachrichtenblätter' also turns out to be an accurate one. There are no editorials or attempts at opinion forming. At first at least the 'news' imparted generally takes the form of lists of names and facts. So, for example, the newsletter starts off on the very first page of the first number with the names of two colleagues who have arrived in Canada, namely Fritz Wallensteiner (= Fritz Walter Nielsen) and Peter Margital. Although he did significant anti-Nazi work in Prague at the time (he was a founder of the Studio 34 Group) Wallensteiner-Nielsen is today a forgotten figure. Peter Margital is even less well known. More interesting is the longer list which follows of those deported to Australia: Albin Stübs, Justin Steinfeld, Walter D. Schultz, Hans Riepl, Josef Diamant-Almas, Joachim Werner Cohn, Bernhard Koch, Max Zimmering, Alexander Vogel, Otto Wolfgang, Jacques Bacharach, Alfred Joachim Fischer and finally Werner Tuerk, who is described as the co-founder of the Thomas Mann Society. Such lists are a reflection of the

British government policy of the time, namely to deport as many refugees as possible. (Later newsletters record the names of those returning from deportation, as government policy changes). Not surprisingly, there are literary figures among those listed as deportees. The Berliner, Albin Stübs, had been active in exile literary circles in Prague, had been a member of the Bert Brecht Club there and had also given the speech at a writers' gathering in honour of Thomas Mann in 1935. His anti-Nazi play *Der Rattenfänger bei den Schildbürgern* had been performed with some success in Prague in 1938 and on his return from Australia his volume of poetry, *Spanischer Tod*, was to be one of the few exile books published in German in Britain in wartime. Hans Riepl was a publisher and Bernhard Koch was also a publisher; Alfred Joachim Fischer was a very successful journalist and Walter D. Schultz was also a journalist, but he is remembered today rather as the friend and colleague of one of the most brilliant figures of the Weimar Republic, Kurt Hiller. Like so many others he later returned to London from deportation with the help of PEN and the News Chronicle Fund. Max Zimmering, a prominent literary figure in the German Democratic Republic after the war, had made an adventurous escape from the Nazis before reaching Britain from Prague by way of Poland, only to be deported to Australia: Werner Tuerk (or Thürk) was yet another Berliner and radical German writer who had been very active in exile circles in Prague. He too had made a speech in Prague in June 1935 on the occasion of Thomas Mann's sixtieth birthday and had been critical of the great man's silence vis-à-vis Nazi Germany. His novel, *Kleiner Mann in Uniform*, had been published in Prague in 1934. Depicting as it did the evolution of a petit-bourgeois civil servant into an SA man it had made quite a stir. Justin Steinfeld (who used the pseudonym Jonathan Swift) was a North German journalist, a member of the Bert Brecht Club, and hence clearly also of a left-wing persuasion. After his return from Australia he was to spend the rest of his life in England. He died in Baldock on 15 May 1970. The Australian government, like that in Canada, had been led to believe that they were going to be giving custody to dangerous Nazis; instead, as this list shows, they were about to receive writers and intellectuals, publishers and journalists with years of anti-Nazi activities behind them. Little wonder that protests soon mounted from all quarters.

Almost immediately too, on the first page of *Thomas Mann Newsletter No.1*, the editors have to report an aspect of refugee existence in Great Britain almost as troubling as deportation, namely internment.

Fortunately, however, the news was in some respects good, because by then British government policy was already under revision, and the newsletter was able to report the names of those who were being released — although so far only on health grounds. Among the names listed the most famous is that of Helmut Herzfelde, better known as John Heartfield, yet another Berliner who had come to England by way of Czechoslovakia. Once released from internment he was to be active and successful for several years in England until 1950, when he opted for the German Democratic Republic. After internment matters a third section of the newsletter is devoted to arrivals from elsewhere. In this instance the report focuses on Erika Mann who had come from America for some weeks to prepare programmes for the BBC. Thomas Mann, the titular head of the Thomas Mann Society, also made programmes for the BBC for transmission to Nazi Germany, but they were recorded in America where he had settled by then. Erika Mann came to Britain personally and on one occasion also shared the experience of the Blitz with real Londoners since she lost all her possessions after her hotel was hit by a bomb. This time she promised to raise funds to help refugees still in internment. Further help according to the newsletter was also promised from the newly established Advisory Committee for Refugees from Europe, which had Thomas Mann and Albert Einstein on its advisory board. Closer to home it was reported that those in internment would also be helped by the exile PEN Club of which Friedrich Burschell, the first secretary of the Thomas Mann Group, was the secretary of the German section, while British PEN had been given the task of forming the advisory board which would assist the tribunals dealing with release from internment, when questions of literary standing were involved.

The first page of *Newsletter No.1* then concludes with some bad news, namely the announcement of the death of four persons very close to the Thomas Mann Group: Rudolf and Ika Olden and Dr Lenyi, the husband of Thomas Mann's daughter Monika, had died when the "City of Benares" taking them to Canada was sunk by enemy action, while Frank Warschauer, the German journalist, author of *Prag heute* (1937), and one of the original founders of the Prague Thomas Mann Society, had taken his own life in Holland. Suicide is a recurring feature of exile life and the numbers of the newsletter which follow have more than once to report such a fate. Meanwhile the first number finally closes with a list of names of those who, as a result of the actions of Thomas Mann and the German Labour

Delegation in America, had managed to escape from France to find refuge in North America, namely Heinrich Mann, Lion Feuchtwanger, Fritz von Unruh, Leopold Schwarzschild, Herta Pauli, Alfred Döblin, Leo Lania, Adrienne Thomas, Alfred Polgar, Friedrich Torberg and many others. As one indication of how unreliable sources of information at that time could be, the name of Willy Münzenberg is included among those who have managed to escape. In fact, as was later revealed, he died under mysterious circumstances in France. The same uncertainty also emerges from the later list appended for the benefit of those still in internment. In it Anna Seghers is listed as missing in France, while Irmgard Keun is reported as having committed suicide like Walter Hasenclever and Carl Einstein. In the case of the latter two this regrettably proved to be the case, whereas Irmgard Keun in fact survived by smuggling herself back into Nazi Germany and going underground. Finally the Berlin poet and doctor Karl Theodor Bluth is reported as having taken up a post at Stanford University. In fact he was in London, where he remained until his death in 1964. Yet despite such uncertainties, so characteristic of the rumour-laden atmosphere of the time, the newsletter, with its three closely typed pages, does contain a fascinating amount of first-hand information on figures from the world of science, literature, theatre, music, film and the arts.

Newsletter No.2, which came out on 25 November 1940, followed the same pattern as the first, starting with a list of prominent refugees like Leonhard Frank, who have arrived in the U.S.A., before once again noting deaths and suicides. So it is noted that in France Erich Kaiser, the former editor of the *Berliner Zeitung* and editor of the exile newspaper *Pariser Zeitung,* had committed suicide, as too had Walter Benjamin. As far as literature is concerned books published by refugees are noted, such as, for example, one by Franz Höllering, the Austrian writer and founder of the exile newspaper *Prager Mittag*. His book, *The Defenders*, dealing with the suppression of the Austrian workers in January 1934, was published by Routledge in London in 1940; Gustav Regler's *The Great Crusade*, dealing with the Spanish Civil War, had been published by Longman's, while *Suicide of a Democracy*, a book covering the collapse of France by the Berliner Heinz Pol, also found a publisher and came out in 1940. Clearly there was interest in Britain in what was going on in Europe, and British publishers were prepared to publish the first-hand material made available by survivors. The coverage of music, theatre and cinema is also extremely good, particularly for America, but the focus is not exclusively on

Hollywood or Broadway. There are also items for those interested in the exile scene in England. The careers of stars like Conrad Veidt and Paul Henried are obviously of great interest and the fact that Elisabeth Bergner had abandoned her successful career on stage and screen in England and had left for Hollywood is noted without further comment. Erich Pommer is singled out as another film great who had ceased film-making in Britain and departed for the greater possibilities Hollywood had to offer. Briefly noted too is the dramatic turn in the career of E. W. Pabst who had stopped being a 'freiwilliger Emigrant' in Paris and had returned to make films in Nazi Germany.

After a rapid survey of the political situation in various occupied countries of Europe *Newsletter No.2* focuses on France and the anti-Jewish laws introduced by the Vichy regime. Clearly the situation of refugees in French internment camps was far worse than that of refugees in British internment and cause for considerable concern. The issue raised is not that of eventual release but of the need for immediate rescue, especially of former members of the International Brigade who, it is suggested, should be transferred from France to Mexico. Also reported are the repercussions following the murder of von Rat, a German Embassy official, in Paris. Special funds have had to be raised and further rescue operations set in motion to alleviate the desperate situation this has caused in refugee circles. By now it is obvious that a newsletter of this kind cannot restrict itself to bare lists of facts but has to respond to extreme events as they happen. So *Newsletter No.2* closes with a supplementary list of names of individuals as information about them comes in. Regretted at the end is the fact that Stefan Zweig, a long-term resident in England, has left for Brazil.

Newsletter No.3 was sent out on 7 January 1941 with an apology for lateness, caused by the non-arrival of those overseas newspapers which were the compilers' main sources of information. Erika Mann is once again thanked for her efforts in America on behalf of refugees in England. Reading between the lines, however, another general exile problem emerges, namely that of visas. Thousands of refugees in various countries, including England, were obviously encountering enormous difficulties in their attempts to enter the United States of America, because that country operated strict quotas by country. Erika Mann's reports to Britain indicate that the American President had been forced to appoint a coordinating 'Super-Committee' to unscramble conflicts between various government bodies causing unseemly delays. Still, some visas were being granted and among the many names of those who had succeeded in reaching the United States is that of Franz Pfemfert, the famous editor of the expressionist journal *Die Aktion*. (In fact a remarkable number of Expressionists would end up in exile in Great Britain). Meanwhile in England the burning issue, apart from visas, was still internment and the newsletter is able to report that the process of release is continuing. The poet Jesse Thoor had been released as too had Eugen Brehm, while the release of the Nuremberger Kurt Doberer was expected. All three were to play a significant part in exile literary life in England where they became as active as they had been in Prague up to 1938. Doberer remained in England until 1949. Both Jesse Thoor and Eugen Brehm died in England. Regrettably another suicide, this time that in Paris of the novelist Ernst Weiss, has to be noted. On a happier note the newsletter marks the successes in exile of Alfred Döblin, Heinrich Mann, Franz Werfel, Alfred Polgar, and Friedrich Wolf, while the reports indicate how much the worlds of art, music, theatre and film in America had gained from the arrival of such figures as Erwin Piscator, Wilhelm Dieterle and Marlene Dietrich.

Newsletter No.4, dated 25 January 1941, starts immediately with news of the release from internment of Friedrich Burschell and Julius Vogel, both of whom had been founder members of the original Thomas Mann Group in Czechoslovakia. Equally important is the news that refugees deported to Canada were now returning to Britain. Important information is also contained about the working of President Roosevelt's Advisory Committee, the question of the resettlement of refugees already in America and the mechanism for the granting of emergency visas through Lisbon for refugees from European countries. Deaths are noted and escapees to America from France welcomed, especially prominent figures like Ludwig Marcuse, who were thought to have been rounded up. On the literary scene the new organisation founded in New York called 'European Writers' is welcomed, as too is the opening of a new branch of the Fischer Verlag, especially as it is expected to start its operation with the launch of an edition of Thomas Mann's *Lotte in Weimar* in German. Once again the coverage of the various spheres of literature, academic life, art, music and theatre for the whole of North America is extensive. Regrettably however, there is correspondingly less news about refugee life in England. Nevertheless this number of the newsletter does close with the doubtless important information that the trustees of the Czech Refugee Trust Fund

have agreed to grant every member of the fund in internment the sum of
£2 for clothes. Unfortunately this good news has immediately to be
corrected in the following newsletter. The clothing allowance would be
based on two shillings per week of internment.

Where the previous newsletter had been lacking in news of refugees
in Great Britain, this is made up for in *Newsletter No.4*, dated 18 February
1941. More releases from internment are noted, including that of one of
the most famous journalists of the Weimar Republic, Kurt Hiller, who after
appalling treatment at the hands of the Gestapo had managed to escape to
Czechoslovakia and from there to England. A new volume of poetry by the
Czech writer Rudolf Fuchs (presumably *Gedichte aus Reigate*) is acclaimed
and it is reported that Dosio Koffler, the Austrian dramatist who had
published the anti-Hitler comedy *Die Liebesinsel* in Prague in 1938, would
shortly be publishing in London his *Deutsche Walpurgisnacht* in English
and in German. This proved to be an accurate report as both books duly
appeared. Further publications were also expected in the near future from
the German journalist Wilhelm Necker, from a Dr Rosenzweig
(presumably Wilhelm Rosenzweig, the Austrian Social Democrat), and
from Egon Larsen, who, once released from internment, would have a
major part to play in the satirical revues of the 'Kleine Bühne' of the Free
German League of Culture. *Newsletter No.5*, which followed on 18
February 1941, also returned to events in Britain. The German writer,
member of the BPRS and of the Bert Brecht Club in Prague, Werner
Ilberg, it is noted, had been released from internment. He would remain in
England until 1949; Kurt Doberer was also free at last, as too was Hans
Jaeger, the Berlin journalist and politician, remembered now for his essay
'A New Face of Democracy' in the volume *After Nazism Democracy*,
edited by Kurt Hiller and published by Lindsay Drummond in London in
1945. (Earlier in Prague, however, he had published *Das wahre Gesicht
Hitlers und der NSDAP* in 1933). Thereafter the newsletter follows its
established format, listing prominent arrivals in the USA, noting deaths and
then, under the rubric 'Literature', drawing particular attention to Thomas
Mann's broadcasts for the BBC and to Klaus Mann's new journal *Decision*.
Interestingly, the film news is not taken up exclusively with tidbits from
Hollywood, for there are also reminders that Britain had a lively film
industry in wartime and that German and Austrian exiles were active in it.
So, for example, the Viennese dramatist, Richard Duschinsky, responsible
for the satirical features *Pacher und Pachulke* and *Frau Schiernagel* for the

BBC, is reported as working on three films in London based on plays by J. B. Priestley. This newsletter closes with a letter from Kurt Pine, a former journalist with the *Vossische Zeitung*, who draws attention to Mexico as a possibility for onward emigration. While this is a useful reminder (Mexico was indeed to prove a safe haven for many including Anna Seghers), the next newsletter also contains information about another possible escape route from the Nazi noose, for it starts with a note to the effect that the Czech journalist Kurt Raphael, an early member of the Thomas Mann Group, had managed to make his way to Shanghai. In this he was to be by no means unusual, for Shanghai became home to thousands of refugees, despite the Japanese presence. Under the heading 'In USA trafen ein' it is noted that Hans Gál, 'früher an der Oper in Wien und in Mannheim' was expected. In fact Hans Gál was to spend the rest of his life in Great Britain. As already noted, uncertainties of this kind are understandable and some idea of the manner in which news and gossip was gathered can be gained from the first paragraph of *Newsletter No.7*. This goes on to mention Herta Pauli, Hans Natonek, Raoul Arnheimer, Berthold Viertel and Harry Klapeter (by then also in Shanghai). The film-maker and theatre director Berthold Viertel spent long periods in London, which he seemed to prefer to Hollywood. Piscator is recorded as working on a *Chalk Circle* in English in New York, while Ernst Deutsch and Peter Lorre, having left behind their brief careers in London, are busy on stage and screen in America, and Bruno Frank, another great favourite in London, had apparently written a play about Tibet, which was going to be filmed by Korda. Leaving the film world and turning to politics, close readers of the newsletter would have picked up an item of burning interest regarding the Nazi agent Hans Wesemann, who had not only been responsible for arranging the seizure of Berthold Jacob by the Gestapo but had also managed to infiltrate refugee circles in London. Widespread fear of just such infiltration had been a feature of refugee life in all cities like prewar London.

Perhaps because the Thomas Mann Group was having to move location *Newsletter No.8*, dated 15 April 1941, is a comparatively short one. Other changes were obviously also afoot, because British government policy had changed in wartime. Not only were 'enemy aliens' being released from internment, they were now being allowed to work and members of the group therefore no longer needed to rely on financial support from the Czech Refugee Trust Fund. The next step would be that refugees would not only be allowed to work, they would be encouraged to join the armed forces. With regret the newsletter has to announce the death of the poet Max Herrmann-Neiße in a London he never grew to love, though he did manage to publish his poetry there. *Newsletter No.9* appeared on 30 May 1941, still edited by Bernhard Menne and Wilhelm Sternfeld, but now at a new address, 128 Westbourne Terrace, London W. 22. It is back to its normal size and full of information, starting with releases from internment including those of Walter D. Schultz and Joachim Werner Cohn. Reports on literary life in exile in North America are fuller than ever. Leopold Schwarzschild, the former editor of the *Neues Tage-Buch*, was said to be bringing out an important survey with Oxford University Press, and Johannes Urzidil was publishing *Wenzel Hollar, a Czech Emigré in England*. Of even wider interest is the news that: 'Das neue Stück von Carl Zuckmayer und Friedrich Kortner *Somewhere in France* erzielte bei der Uraufführung in Washington und der Erstaufführung in New York einen starken Erfolg'. Both Kortner and Zuckmayer had started their exile lives in London. Yet though the newsletter seemed to be getting back into a regular routine this was almost immediately interrupted again and *Newsletter No.9* did not reach its two hundred subscribers till some time in October. This number contains more information about returnees from Australia, paying particular attention to such returning members of the Thomas Mann Group as Max Zimmering and Werner Thürk. The latter two, though interned on their return on the Isle of Man, were expected to be released soon. Other group members such as Albin Stübs and Josef Diamant-Almas were still in Australia, but their early release was also expected. Once again the unsatisfactory nature of some sources of information for the newsletter is indicated by the fact that Georg Kaiser was expected to leave Switzerland and make for England. He never did. Similarly, under the rubric 'those who have died', Walter A. Berendsohn is said to have taken his own life in Denmark whereas, as is now known, he had managed to make his way to safety in Sweden where he became the founder of Exile Studies there. The very last item returns to the mysterious fate of Willy Münzenberg.

    Newsletter No.12 is dated simply 'Mitte November 1941'. After the customary report on exile activities in the United States the editors turn once again to matters affecting exile life in Great Britain. It is noted that the Czech government in exile had awarded the Prize for Literature for the year 1941 to Maurice Hindus for his books *To sing with the Angel* and *We*

Shall Live Again. Ferdinand Bruckner had apparently published an article in the American exile journal *Aufbau* against the London PEN conference, against Erika Mann and against Alfred Kerr, the president of London PEN. Interestingly, in this number Bert Brecht is mentioned for the first time: he had apparently arrived in Hollywood and made a statement about Carola Neher being condemned to six years in a Soviet forced-labour camp. Also noted are productions of his *Mutter Courage und ihre Kinder* in Zürich and *The Good Woman of Sezuan* in New York.

Following this issue members had to wait till the beginning of March 1942 before they received *Newletters No.13* and *No.14* as one issue. This was a bumper issue packed full of information and gossip. Regrettably the death of Rudolf Fuchs had to be reported (he was killed by a bus in the London blackout), followed by the news that Jesse Thoor, better known as a poet, had completed a bust of Winston Churchill. The list of those who had died in the last months is long, as too is that of exile literary activity. This includes a note on Anna Reiner's 'emigration novel' *The Coward Heart* and of Leo Lania's *The Darkest Hour*. Both of these women writers had found refuge in England, Leo Lania for a short period, Anna Reiner/Gmeyner for the rest of her life. The next double number, *Newsletter No.15/16*, came out about the end of May and once more was packed with information. Particularly interesting from the point of view of exile in Great Britain is the brief paragraph on Thomas Mann Group members:

> Justin Steinfeld hat ein Stück *Offero* verfaßt, das in Baldock von der Christopher-Gruppe aufgeführt wurde. Seine Gattin Käthe Behrens wirkte dabei zum ersten Male als Schauspielerin in englischer Sprache — Egon Lehrburger ist einer der Autoren des im Freien Deutschen Kulturbund aufgeführten Stückes *In Hampstead ist Holzauktion*. Im Juli soll ein neues Stück von ihm und Fritz Gottfurcht *Mr Gulliver goes to School* aufgeführt werden. Julius Gellner führt zur Zeit Regie des *Othello* im Old Vic Theatre. An der gleichen Bühne spielt Friedrich Richter mit großem Erfolg den Shylock. Paul Demel spielt augenblicklich englisch in *The Doctor's Dilemma*. Die Freunde Paul Lewitt, Paul Hardtmuth und Dr Rudolf Spitz spielten in *Volpone* im Laterndl, Arnold Marlé, Lilli Molnar und Lili Strich-Rohne waren bei Arthur Hellmers 'österreichische Bühne' in *Unentschuldigte Stunde* verpflichtet.- Julius Gutmann singt die Bass-Partie in *The Tales of Hoffmann* Strand Theatre.

This gives some idea of theatre life in the London of the time in which exile members were involved. Some time later in the packed pages of the newsletter mention is made of Anna Maria Jokl who 'wurde von der Arbeitsgemeinschaft sudetendeutscher Schriftsteller (Vorsitzender Peter Pont, Stellvertreter Dr Ernst Sommer) zur Schriftführerin bestellt'. This is a brief reminder that Sudeten German writers too had set up an exile organisation in London to look after their affairs.

By the time *Newsletter No.17/18* came out in September 1942 the format had had to change again, because the entry of the United States into the war had more or less brought immigration into that country to a standstill. Gone now is the section devoted to new arrivals in America, but the list of those who have recently died is still a long one. Equally long is the list of literary activities in the United States, some of them now, in wartime, directed to explicitly overt propaganda purposes. British exile activities receive only an occasional mention, particularly the newly constituted German PEN in London, at whose first meeting Alfred Kerr had given a talk on Robert Musil, Monty Jacobs had spoken on Erich Kästner, while Bernhard Menne had spoken on 'Emigrantenschicksale'. Erika Mann was expected in London for yet another visit. More information of a local nature is contained about the middle of November 1942 in the first section of *Newsletter No.19/20*. This was to become the last number. Particular attention is paid to the death in Epsom of Stefan Pollatschek, who briefly gained an international reputation with his biographical novels on Vincent Van Gogh and on John Law, the latter an exiled Scotsman who rose to the dizziest heights in seventeenth-century France, when he introduced paper money instead of currencies based on gold. Information is also given on the 'Deutsche PEN in England' under Alfred Kerr, Friedrich Burschell, Richard Friedenthal and Leon Zeitlin, one of the founders of the PEN-Zentrum deutschsprachiger Autoren im Ausland. He died in London in 1967. Mention is also made of GUDA, the breakaway Group of Independent German Authors in Exile in London formed by Kurt Hiller. Altogether exile cultural life is made to sound lively and exciting with a dramatic work and a poetry cycle announced by Albin Stübs, a book on Karl Kraus promised by Heinrich Fischer, a play called *A Message from Moscow* in production in Glasgow and reports of theatrical successes both on the limited stages of refugee clubs of the FDKB, the Austrian Centre in London and on the stages of West End theatres.

In this, the final number, as in all previous numbers, several pages are devoted to the literary activities of exiles in the USA. However there are also occasional references to exile activities in Great Britain. British publishers obviously continued to take an interest in exile work. Hutchinson had brought out *The Fight for Freedom*, a pamphlet by Bernhard Menne; James Clark had brought out Elisabeth Castonier's *Eternal Front*, a book about the contribution of the churches in resistance to National Socialism and Frederick Muller had bought the rights to Hermynia Zur Mühlen's novel *Ewiges Schattenspiel*, which eventually came out under the title *We Poor Shadows*. Hermynia Zur Mühlen would go on to a successful career as a writer in Britain, once she had changed language from German to English as so many others did .

After eight closely typed, single-spaced, A-4 pages of documentation on refugee fates around the world the *Thomas Mann Newsletter* closes for the last time with a little appendix on Emil Ludwig's latest book,which has been published by Whittlesey House in New York under the title *The Mediterranean*, while the German edition is to be published by Oprecht in Zurich under the title *Das Mittelmeer*; Hans Natonek, it is reported, has sold *To Whom It May Concern*, the first book he had written in the United States, to Putnams, while Georg Kaiser it is reported is still living in the Swiss mountains, where he had completed a play called *Das Floß der Medusa*. As far as Great Britain is concerned the important news is that Alfred Kerr is celebrating his seventy-fifth birthday in exile in London on 25 December 1942. No reason is given as to why the newsletter then ceased to appear. Perhaps it was simply that by then there were many other sources of information with which a newsletter of this kind could not compete. The British government sponsored newspaper *Die Zeitung* was by then in existence, as too was the Austrian *Zeitspiegel* and the Sudeten-German journal *Die Einheit. PEMS Private Bulletin* also contained an almost unbroken stream of information on the exile worlds of literature, cinema, theatre and the arts. Yet the experience of information-gathering gained in the issuing of a newsletter of this kind was to prove invaluable, for it was Wilhelm Sternfeld, one of the editors of the *Thomas Mann Newsletter*, who became the main source for the first exile bibliography after the war, *Deutsche Exil-Literatur 1933-1945: Eine Bio-Bibliographie*, mit einem Vorwort von Hanns Eppelsheimer (Heidelberg and Darmstadt: Lambert Schneider, 1962), a reference work which was to prove an absolutely essential tool for all future researchers in this field.

Notes

1 In an article entitled 'Zur Begrüßung' in the *Volks-Illustrierte*, 27 January 1937, p. 32.

2 The grateful thanks of the author go to Dr Brita Eckert, Leiterin of the Deutsches Exilarchiv in the Deutsche Bibliothek, Adickesallee 1, 60322 Frankfurt/M., Germany, who made copies of the *Thomas Mann Newsletter* available for this survey. A full set of the *Newsletter* is held in the Exilarchiv, except for one number, No. 10 1941. — For many of the exiles mentioned in the 'Nachrichtenblätter' bio- and bibliographical information is available in *International Biographical Dictionary of Central European Emigrés 1933-1945*, vols. 1-4 (Munich and London: Saur, 1980-83), so for Peter Margital, Hans Riepl the publisher, Josef Diamant-Almas, Joachim Werner Cohn, Bernhard Koch another publisher and book-seller, Alexander Vogel, Otto Wolfgang, Jacques Bacharach, Alfred Joachim Fischer the journalist, and others. For the association of the Mann family with Czechoslovakia and their citizenship of that country the best source is *Exil und Asyl. Antifaschistische deutsche Literatur in der Tschechoslowakei 1933-1938*. Von einem Autorenkollektiv unter der Leitung von Miroslav Beck und Jîrí Vesely (Berlin: Volk und Wissen, 1981). This volume also has bio- and bibliographical details on many of the Austrians, Germans and Czechs mentioned in the *Thomas Mann Newsletter*, e.g. on Bernhard Menne, Wilhelm Sternfeld, Friedrich Burschell, Fritz Wallensteiner, Fritz Bruegel, Paul Deml, Kurt Doberer, Paul Dornberger, Heinrich Fischer, Rudolf Fuchs, John Heartfield, Franz Höllering, Werner Ilberg, Hans Jaeger, Anna Maria Jokl, Dosio Koffler, Oskar Kosta, Charlotte Küter, Paul Lewitt, Wilhelm Necker, Heinz Pol, Justin Sternfeld, Albin Stübs, Werner Thürk, Franz Warschauer, Max Zimmering.

3 Walter A. Berendsohn, *Die humanistische Front*, vol. 1: *Von 1933 bis zum Kriegsausbruch 1939* (Zurich: Europa, 1946, reprint Worms: Heintz, 1978); vol. 2: *Vom Kriegsausbruch 1939 bis Ende 1946* (Worms: Heintz, 1978). Here vol. 2, p. 68.

Jörg Thunecke

'Characterology', not 'Ideology': Sebastian Haffner's Refutation of Daniel Goldhagen in *Germany: Jekyll and Hyde* (1940)

Sebastian Haffner's *Germany - Jekyll and Hyde*, written and published in exile in England in 1939/40, is a study of two types of Germans living side-by-side in Nazi Germany, anticipating in an uncanny way charges levelled by Daniel Goldhagen in his 1996 bestseller *Hitler's Willing Executioners*, in which it is claimed that pre-1945 Germany was permeated by a particular radical and vicious brand of *eliminatory* anti-Semitism. Haffner's putative conclusion suffices to refute Goldhagen's claims, more that half a century prior to their being made, and amounts to the discovery of a vital difference between the first and second generation of Nazi followers, thus nullifying the American's contention that ordinary Germans were responsible for the killing fields in the East.

Raimund Pretzel (1907-1999) — in exile he adopted the pen name Sebastian Haffner[1] — was the son of a liberal Prussian school inspector, who grew up in Berlin where he studied law and had plans to become a judge. Yet the completion of his studies in 1933 ('Referendarexamen') coincided with Hitler's accession to power; and since Haffner felt little inclination to be a cog on the wheel of the Nazi administration (especially after the passing of the 'Nuremberg Laws'), he quit the civil service in 1936 (having got his doctorate in 1935),[2] and switched to journalism, writing light-hearted, non-political contributions for various Berlin magazines and newspapers, like the *Berliner Illustrirte*, the *Neue Modenwelt*, and the *Vossische Zeitung*.[3] In connection with such journalistic work, Haffner succeeded in mid-1938 in obtaining permission to work as a reporter in England,[4] arriving in London on 29 August 1938,[5] where he was reunited with his Jewish girl friend, Erika Hirsch, whom he had known since 1934 and who had emigrated at an earlier stage. Initially the couple lived in Cambridge, except for extensive working visits to London, married and had two children; but in February 1940, barely a year and a half after his arrival in England, Haffner, by then classed a Category 'A' alien, was interned at Warner's Camp in Seaton (Devonshire).[6] Meanwhile though his first English-language publication, *Germany: Jekyll and Hyde*, had been published in London,[7] in which, among many other things, he had mounted a spirited attack on French internment policies during the first

half of 1940.[8] The book's positive reception, as well as Secker &
Warburg's intervention with the British authorities on behalf of their
author, secured Haffner's release in April of that year. However, just over
a month later he was re-interned, following the military defeat of the Low
Countries in May 1940, his permanent release, in August 1940, being the
result of a Parliamentary inquiry in July 1940.[9]

The contact with Secker & Warburg, leading to the publication of his
first book, had been established by Hans Lothar (1900-1944), formerly
managing director of the *Frankfurter Zeitung*, who had left Germany in
1936, subsequently to become an employee of the London publishers.[10]
During their joint internment in 1940, Haffner put the idea of a German
exile paper to Lothar, who in turn, in late 1940, managed to draw the
attention of Duff Cooper, in charge of the UK Ministery of Information
(MOI), to these plans.[11] The paper, simply called *Die Zeitung*, was first
published on 12 March 1941 (until 1 June 1945): Lothar became its first
editor-in-chief, Haffner one of the staff reporters. However, as a result of
ongoing opposition by left-wing exile organisations to Lothar's and
Haffner's political views, advocating the break-up of Germany and her
replacement by a confederation of smaller states,[12] Haffner eventually left
Die Zeitung and joined the editorial staff of the *Observer* newspaper in
July 1942.[13] Apart from a spell as press officer for the Allied Forces in
post-war Germany (having been granted British nationality in 1948),
Haffner worked for the *Observer* until 1961, becoming the paper's chief
German correspondent in 1954, based in Berlin. However, the paper's
stance in the wake of the erection of the Berlin Wall in August 1961 (at this
stage Haffner was still considered a 'cold-war warrior') led to the parting
of the ways, and Haffner worked for a short spell for the Springer papers
Die Welt and *Christ und Welt*. The *Spiegel*-affair in October/November
1962 though led to yet another change in alliances,[14] and from then on,
until his retirement from journalism, Haffner became a weekly columnist
for the magazine *Stern*,[15] got his own TV programme ('Berliner Fenster',
from 1965) with the Sender Freies Berlin, became a regular member of
Werner Höfer's 'Internationaler Frühschoppen', wrote, from 1964 to 1972,
for the radical student paper *konkret* (edited by Klaus Rainer Röhl and
Ulrike Meinhoff),[16] and in 1967/68 even lent his support to the German
student revolution.[17] Following the death of his first wife Erika in
December 1969, Haffner re-married (Christa Rotzoll [1982]),[18] but in
1975 withdrew from day-to-day journalism to concentrate on writing

books, the most famous being *Anmerkungen zu Hitler* (1978), and *Von
Hitler zu Bismarck. Ein Rückblick* (1987).[19] Growing more and more
frail, Haffner gradually withdrew from public life (especially following the
death of his second wife in 1995), and died, at the beginning of this year,
after prolonged illness.

*

'Zweifellos war das Exil *die* Zäsur im Leben des Sebastian Haffner [my
emphasis]',[20] as the columnist of the German weekly *Die Zeit* claimed in a
recent obituary; and of all events during the émigré's years in England
none shaped his future more decisively than the publication of *Jekyll and
Hyde* in early 1940. In fact, this book had a dual impact:

> The first was that Haffner came to the attention of the British Foreign Office. [...]
> At least some members of the British Government were still keen to drive [...] a
> wedge between the Nazis and the German people. [...] One result was the creation
> by the Foreign Office of a German language newspaper, called simply *Die Zeitung*,
> whose aim was the marshalling of the Nazis' German enemies. Haffner was seen
> as an ideal candidate for the editorship. Through this book he also came to the
> attention of the remarkable David Astor [...] already being groomed by his father
> (who owned *The Observer*) as a future editor. [...] In 1941 Haffner began to write
> for *The Observer* (resigning from *Die Zeitung* in 1943, by which time Whitehall's
> support for anti-Nazi Germans had evaporated entirely). He soon became its chief
> leader writer and established for it an enviable reputation as a paper which took
> foreign policy analysis as seriously as domestic comment.[21]

As it happened, by joining the editorial staff of such a reputable Sunday
paper, Haffner also became a member of 'that constellation of Central
European geniuses assembled in the Forties by David Astor to write *The
Observer* [sic].'[22] Nicknamed the 'Professorate', contributors like Isaac
Deutscher, Jon Kimche, Arthur Koestler, George Orwell, and, of course,
Sebastian Haffner 'made it the most influential weekly paper in the
world.'[23] As pointed out in an obituary in *Die Welt* by Arnulf Baring, who
probably knew Haffner better than most contemporaries, it was indeed 'ein
bewegendes Zeugnis britischer Liberalität' that some of the most important
journalists, writing for the *Observer* during World War II, were non-
British, and Baring was not far off the mark either in his claim that it was
'Haffners größte Lebensleistung: während des Krieges in einem der
wichtigsten britischen Blätter Einfluß zu gewinnen.'[24]

    Yet it was his study *Germany: Jekyll and Hyde*, published with
Secker & Warburg in 1940, which 'was acclaimed in Britain as one of the

first books to attack Hitler and Nazism from a conservative perspective, so
giving the lie to the widespread notion that the only opposition worth
recognition came from the Left';[25] for in this book – a 'Parabel von der
gespaltenen Persönlichkeit'[26] – Haffner set out to explain to his British
hosts the complexities of the German national character: 'Nicht als
amüsante ethnologische Fingerübung, sondern als Studie zur Optimierung
des Propagandakrieges.'[27] That is to say, Haffner 'wollte den Briten über
Nazideutschland die Augen öffnen, damit sie ihre Propaganda noch
wirkungsvoller einsetzen konnten',[28] wanted to impress on them that even
in 1939/40 a substantial minority of the German population was leading 'a
double life like Dr. Jekyll and Mr. Hyde' (H117), that side by side with 'the
excessively familiar, crudely placarded Germany of swastika flags,
uniforms and marching-columns, there is yet another, very different,
secret Germany, a shadow Germany, intangible but omnipresent.' (H153)
And that he indeed succeeded in doing just that is supported by the fact that
a German library copy, originally belonging to the Intelligence Unit of the
Rhine Army's 21st Corps, had apparently been used for denazification
purposes in the British Occupation Zone immediately after the war.[29]
Though, according to Haffner's own testimony, the book did not sell well,
it '"erregte aber Aufsehen".'[30] It also 'made him instantly famous for what
Thomas Mann called "superb analysis",'[31] and certainly helped to secure
his early release from internment. Above all though, '[d]er
unverwechselbare Haffner-Ton war in seinem Erstling bereits ausgebildet:
eine zupackende, klare Sprache, die pointenreich ihren Gegenstand
umkreist und vor Übertreibungen nicht zurückschreckt'.[32] Here, and even
more so in his two bestsellers *Anmerkungen zu Hitler* and *Von Bismarck
zu Hitler. Ein Rückblick,* Haffner proved himself to be a master of the art
'einfache Fragen zu stellen, die überraschend neue Perspektiven auf
vermeintlich längst bekannte Zusammenhänge oder historische Tatbestände
eröffneten.'[33]

It is in this context – as pointed out only recently by the doyen of
German historians of the Third Reich[34] – that Haffner's early publication
may serve as a useful corrective to sweeping claims by Harvard political
scientist Daniel J. Goldhagen in his recent bestseller *Hitler's Willing
Executioners. Ordinary Germans and the Holocaust,*[35] which received
overwhelming approval by the general public and most journalists on both
sides of the Atlantic in 1996, but was roundly condemned by the bulk of
professional historians worldwide, resulting in an international contro-

versy.[36] Some sixty years prior to publication of Goldhagen's work Haffner had anticipated and, I suggest, refuted some of the main claims he had put forward.

One of Goldhagen's chief detractors, the Canadian historian Ruth Birn, has summarized his arguments as follows:

> Germany was permeated by a particularly radical and vicious brand of anti-Semitism whose aim was the elimination of Jews. The author defines this 'eliminationist anti-Semitism'. The viral strain of anti-Semitism, he states, 'resided ultimately in the heart of German political culture, in German society itself' (p.428). Medieval anti-Semitism, based as it was on the teachings of the Christian religion, was so 'integral to German culture' (p. 55) that with the emergence of the modern era it did not disappear but rather took on new forms of expression, in particular, racial aspects. By the end of the nineteenth century 'eliminationist anti-Semitism' dominated the German political scene. In the Weimar Republic, it grew more virulent even before Hitler came to power. The Nazi machine merely turned this ideology into reality. The course of its actualization was not deterred by anything save bare necessity: 'the road to Auschwitz was not twisted' (p. 425). When the 'genocidal program' was implemented along with the German attack on the Soviet Union, it was supported by the general German population, by the 'ordinary Germans' – the key phrase of the book – who became 'willing executioners'. They had no need of special orders, coercion or pressure because their 'cognitive model' showed them that Jews were 'ultimately fit only to suffer and to die' (p. 316).[37]

Had Goldhagen been familiar with two of Sebastian Haffner's key studies,[38] *Anmerkungen zu Hitler (The Meaning of Hitler)* and *Von Bismarck zu Hitler. Ein Rückblick (The Ailing Empire. Germany from Bismarck to Hitler)*,[39] he might well have avoided some of the more obvious pitfalls in his contentious survey of the role of 'ordinary' Germans in the Holocaust;[40] for Haffner, like Victor Klemperer in his recently published diaries,[41] was not merely a reliable eye-witness of the political scenario as it unfolded in Germany during the quarter of a century after the end of the First World War.[42] He also approached the objects of his observation 'mit einfachen Fragen und kam zuverlässig zu anderen Urteilen als die akademische Forschung',[43] his trademark being '[e]ine hartnäckige Unbefangenheit im Aufspüren ideologischer Tretminen'. While other critics gave such explosive issues a wide berth, 'ließ [er] sie hochgehen',[44] which, no doubt, is exactly what he would have done with Goldhagen's concept of 'eliminationist anti-Semitism' as genocidal motivation, summarized in the opening statement of the Chapter 16 of the American's book:

> That the perpetrators approved of the mass slaughter, that they willingly gave assent
> to their own participation in the slaughter, is certain. That their approval derived in
> the main from their own conception of Jews is all but certain, for no other source of
> motivation can plausibly account for their actions. This means that had they not
> been antisemites, and antisemites of a particular kind, then they would not have
> taken part in the extermination, and Hitler's campaign against the Jews would have
> unfolded substantially differently from how it did. The perpetrators' antisemitism,
> and hence their motivation to kill, was, furthermore, not derived from some other
> non-identical source. It is not an intervening variable, but an independent one. It is
> not reducible to any other factor. (G416)

Condensed in the sentence: 'non-ideological factors were mainly irrelevant to the perpetration of the Holocaust' (G417), this was indeed a highly charged historical issue reflected in the ensuing debate in Germany in the autumn of 1996, except that — unknown to the person triggering the controversy and to most of the expert participants — it had already been adequately defused two decades earlier by Haffner who — in *The Meaning of Hitler* — identified Hitler's specific kind of anti-Semitism as being of East European extraction:

> In Western Europe and also in Germany anti-semitism was on the wane about the
> turn of the century; assimilation and integration of the Jews was desired and was in
> full swing. But in Eastern and South Eastern Europe, where the numerous Jews
> were living, voluntarily or involuntarily, as a separate nation within the nation, anti-
> semitism was (and is?) endemic and murderous, directed not towards assimilation
> or integration but towards liquidation and extermination. And this murderous East
> European anti-semitism, which allowed the Jews no escape, reached as far as
> Vienna in whose third district according to Metternich's famous dictum, the Balkan
> begins. There the youthful Hitler picked it up.[45]

And Haffner further reinforced this line of argument by maintaining that

> Hitler's variety of anti-semitism, demanding extermination, existed nowhere except
> in eastern Europe, from where he himself had got it; and even there, it must be said
> to the credit of the Ukrainians, Poles and Lithuanians, it was based not on Hitler's
> fantasies of a world-wide Jewish conspiracy to enslave or exterminate 'Aryan'
> humanity, but upon the plain fact that the Jews in those countries were settled as a
> compact alien people. This was not the case anywhere else, and accordingly anti-
> semitism elsewhere never aimed at the extermination or the 'removal' of the
> Jews.[46]

Twenty years later Haffner's assertion was vindicated retrospectively when — at the height of the Goldhagen controversy — the Israeli historian Robert Wistrich referred to the fact that 'in any ranking of anti-Semitism in the pre-1914 era, Germany must be put some distance behind not only Austria but several other European countries',[47] and that one can 'make a plausible case that Austria, *not* Germany, was the crucible of Nazi-style anti-Semitism [my emphasis]';[48] for 'anti-Semitism in the pre-Hitler era was undoubtedly much more intense in Austria than in Germany':[49]

[P]roportionally twice as many Austrians joined the Nazi party as Germans, and Austrians, though a mere 8 percent of the population of greater Germany after the 1938 *Anschluss*, made up 14 percent of the SS, 40 percent of the staff of the death camps, and 70 percent of Adolf Eichmann's staff. A significant number of prime movers in the 'Final Solution' were themselves Austrians, including Hitler, Eichmann, Ernst Kaltenbrunner (head of the Reich Main Security Office), and Odilo Globocnik (in charge of the death camps in Poland), and others.[50]

Not only did Haffner therefore manage to refute in *The Meaning of Hitler,* two decades *prior* to its conception in *Hitler's Willing Executioners,* Goldhagen's main thesis that eliminationist anti-Semitism was the root cause for the murderous activities of ordinary Germans in Eastern Europe,[51] but he was also able to lay to rest — in *The Ailing Empire* — Goldhagen's other main assertion that anti-Semitism was rampant in Germany throughout the 19th and 20th centuries. After all: neither the German Reich of the Hohenzollerns nor the Prussia of Hardenberg and Bismarck, thus Haffner's counter-claim, had been anti-Semitic states. On the contrary: 'The anti-Semitism of the German people was at most "conventional"; in the provinces Jews were not always liked and often socially isolated. There was some resentment against their attraction to certain professions [...], but it was a social, nonviolent anti-Semitism. And it was not shared by the majority of the people.'[52] In any case, anti-Semitism, as emphasized by Omer Bartov in a review-article of Goldhagen's book, is '*not* sufficient as a single factor in explaining the conduct of individual German soldiers, policemen, SS or SD men, or anyone involved in murder during that period. It is much more convincing to argue that such actions were the result of a cluster of conditions, some ideological and some existential, some reality and others rooted in a distorted perception of it. *No* single element can explain this terrible phenomenon [my emphasis].'[53]

*

Another issue, closely related to the monocausal concept of eliminationist anti-Semitism — '[b]rutality, mass killings, torture, sadism, and everything that Goldhagen is at pains to describe in gory detail'[54] — was also brought to the fore by the American political scientist's study, despite the fact that it is common knowledge that such atrocities are 'as old as humanity itself' and 'not particularly unique to the Holocaust';[55] while what *was* unprecedented about the Holocaust — 'the industrial killing of millions of human beings in factories of death, ordered by a modern state, organized by a conscientious bureaucracy, and supported by a law-abiding, patriotic, "civilized" society'[56] — was carefully omitted by Goldhagen from his investigation.

In fact, his contention that the 'culture of cruelty' (G255) — exemplified by the murderous brutality of many supposedly ordinary Germans, attached to police battalions and 'Einsatzgruppen' behind the advancing German armies in Eastern Europe and the Soviet Union after mid-1941,[57] and assigned the job of exterminating the Jewish population in these areas — was the result of eliminationist anti-Semitism is as erroneous as the assumption that anti-Semitic sentiments had enjoyed widespread acceptance among the German people since medieval times, misconceptions that could have been quite easily avoided had Goldhagen been familiar with *Germany: Jekyll and Hyde*, Sebastian Haffner's first major book, written in exile, on the Third Reich — and especially his chapter on the Nazis.[58]

According to Haffner, it was 'not easy to pierce political realities in Germany' (H69) at the time he was compiling this survey in 1939/40. However, based on first-hand experience, dating back a mere twelve months since his own 'emigration', he came to the conclusion that there existed a solid kernel of real Nazis flourishing under the regime, 'highly organized, determined, armed, unscrupulous, and morally inaccessible.' (H73) In an attempt to establish who these *real* Nazis were and how they could be identified, Haffner in turn concluded that — despite the fact that it was not easy to recognize them from external signs and badges — 'there [were] some shibboleths, some touchstones' (H76), the most important and most simple being their attitude towards the Jews: for a Nazi — this being Haffner's 'provozierende These',[59] indirectly linking it to Goldhagen's case studies in Part III of his book[60] — 'is one who assents unreservedly to [a] general and permanent sadistic orgy, and takes part in it.' (H77)

*

One of the chief aims of anti-Semitism in the Third Reich — on this point at least Goldhagen and Haffner would have concurred — was a conscience-killing course in the education of the first generation of Germans involved in building the Third Reich,[61] i.e. basically of all those men born between 1900 and 1910 (H85), tallying, as it happened, with the age profile of the majority of men attached to Police Battalion 101, on whom Goldhagen's first case study is based:

> Their mean age, when their genocidal killing began, was 36.5 years old. Only 42 of them were younger than thirty, a measly 8.1 percent. One hundred fifty-three of them, a shade under 30 percent, were older than forty. Nine of them were over fifty. Fully 382 of them, or almost three quarters (73.6 percent) came from the birth cohorts of 1900-1909, the cohorts of men who were generally deemed to be too old to be desirable for military service and from which most reservists who served in the police battalions were raised. That they were older is significant. They were mature men who had life experience, who had families and children. The overwhelming majority of them had reached adulthood before the Nazis ascended to power. They had known other political dispensations, had lived in other ideological climates. They were not wide-eyed youngsters ready to believe whatever they were told. (G206)

Of the 550 men assigned to Police Battalion 101, 179 were members of the Nazi Party, composing 32.5 percent of the unit. However, for Goldhagen '[t]he major issue here [...] is not the percentage of these men who were Nazified according to institutional affiliation in comparison to the national average, and therefore how *representative* a sample these men form in this respect'; instead, for him those with Nazi or SS affiliation 'were analytically the most significant people, because they (and thousands like them in other police battalions [sic]) provide[d] insight into the likely conduct of other ordinary Germans, had they too been asked to become genocidal killer.' (G208) How one can possibly deduce from these figures, as Goldhagen did — bearing in mind that by the early 1940s seven million Germans were members of the NSDAP, i.e. approximately 20 percent of the adult male German population (G206), a figure confirmed by Haffner (H75) — that '[a]s a group, the men of Police Battalion 101 were *not* an unusually Nazified lot for German people [my emphasis]' (G208), while at the same time admitting that 'their Nazi Party and SS membership was somewhat higher than the national average' (G210), is hard to comprehend; and neither is it easy to follow Goldhagen's additional argument that 'the most remarkable and significant fact is that 96 percent of these men were not in the SS, the association of the true believers.' (G208)[62]

Goldhagen is of the opinion that '[n]o other country's antisemitism was at once so widespread as to have been a cultural axiom, was so firmly wedded to racism, had as its foundation such a pernicious image of Jews that deemed them to be a mortal threat to the *Volk*, and was so deadly in content, producing, even in the nineteenth century, such frequent and explicit calls for the extermination of the Jews, calls which expressed the logic of the racist eliminationist antisemitism that prevailed in Germany.' (G419) He also believes that 'the long-incubating, pervasive, virulent, racist, eliminationist antisemitism of German culture' (G419) was supposedly mobilized by a criminal regime to turn its 'ordinary' citizens into 'ideological warriors' ('Weltanschauungskrieger' [G190]). By contrast, Haffner — from his contemporary vantage point, and in opposition to Goldhagen — maintained that anti-Semitism was nothing more than an 'iron chain of common crime' (H77), joining all those Germans together who, without pretext, were able to torture, beat, hunt and murder: 'To the Nazis', Haffner insisted, 'this, and this alone, is the significance, all-important and fundamental, of anti-Semitism, and not the "purity of the German race," the "suppression of all un-German influences," the "defensive war against the Jewish world conspiracy" or any such nonsense.' (H77-78) In other words, Haffner did *not*, like Goldhagen, consider Jews to be the 'metaphysical enemies' of the German people to be eliminated by 'ideological warriors' (G241), but thought that anti-Semitism served the Nazis as 'a means of selection and trial', 'a test not of courage but of lack of scruple' (78). Or, to put it in a nutshell, as Haffner so often did with his inimitable 'stilistische Brillanz' and his 'magistrale Knappheit':[63] '*Nazism is no ideology but a magic formula which attracts a definite type of men. It is a form of "characterology," not ideology. To be a Nazi means to be a definite type of human being.*' (H79-80) Consequently, to look for any further explanations for anti-Semitism was, in Haffner's opinion, pointless.

Returning, however, to the topic of Nazi brutality, one must, as Haffner did, emphasize that Hitler's repeated claim that heroism and self-sacrifice were the essential traits of his followers was in fact a lie; for it was not to heroism that he appealed, 'but rather to sadism, to the pleasure [...] in "brutal," "fanatical," "merciless" oppression and persecution of those who ha[d] already been overpowered and rendered defenceless [...].' (H82-83) This being the case, Haffner felt obliged to return once again to his original query:

What kind of man was it who felt himself instinctively lured by Hitler, by his
promises, his threats, his furious rage against all and sundry [...]? What kind of
man was it who responded without fail to this extremely complex mixture of
rigidity, roughness, discipline, self-effacement, and Spartanism, combined with
heroic phrase-making, sensationalism, never-ending adventure, luxury, and
collective debauchery; to this strange alloy of bulldog faithfulness and corruptness,
of old-fashioned German simplicity and hypermodern organization, of 'back to the
soil,' and stream-lined cars and super-aeroplanes, of the 'master-race' and standing
to attention, of camp fires and rewards for denunciation? (H83)

In other words: 'Where lies the Archimedean point in the mass-soul of the
Nazis [...]? What united the Nazis since it cannot be the fraudulent
collection of contradictions that constitutes their "world-conception"?'
(H83-84). These — according to Haffner — were the vital questions,
without an answer to which there could be no pretence of knowing the
enemy — which, of course, was the purpose of *Jekyll and Hyde*, a book
whose intention it was — among other things — to open 'seinen neuen
Landsleuten die Augen über die deutsche Gewaltherrschaft und ihre
historischen Potenzen.'[64]

As mentioned earlier, both Haffner and Goldhagen, in their
respective studies, are essentially dealing with the first generation of
genuine Nazis, born between 1900 and 1910,[65] men in whom all the
resentments and all the negations of Nazidom had accumulated,[66] and who
apparently gained great satisfaction to be able at last quite openly to 'set
their foot on the neck of the strange, uncomprehended, and despised world
of the spirit, of civilization, of the "bourgeoisie".' (H88)

> To say nothing of the Jews, who seemed to be created to be beaten, just because
> they were utterly unable to beat back. Shabby curs they were, with their spirituality,
> sentimentality, family life, prickly individualism, fine feelings, showily displayed
> culture, love of Art and — curse them! — of money. (H89)

By contrast, the second Nazi generation, that is roughly speaking all men
born after 1918, had for the most part never come into contact with the
values, problems and ideas which had troubled their elders. Of such things
these young people only had a vague idea, because '[t]o all from childhood
Nazism had been offered as their sole spiritual food.' (H104) This
generation of Nazis knew no sentimentality, their style was almost dry, '[t]o
them murder, torture, and destruction are no more voluptuous disorder but
"the New Order",' and '[t]he apostle of this generation [...] [was] Himmler,
the man of pedantic methodical extermination.' (H105) That is to say, we
are here dealing with men who had 'lost all connection with mankind and

live[d] by plan', men 'from whom conscience, mind, and soul ha[d] been extracted as by an operation' (H106), the essential difference between the two successive generations being that the former had this 'operation' done with some sort of ideological pretext remaining, whereas in the latter's case this pretext had ceased to exist,[67] giving rise to the question 'whether these beings [were] still to be called men.' (H106) For Haffner at least, had a selection been required, the choice would have been an obvious one: 'those hystericals, in spite of everything [were] not quite so utterly repulsive as these prize scholars of inhumanity.' (H105). However, the distinction between first and second generation Nazis — which apparently came quite naturally to Haffner — *never* seems to have occurred to Goldhagen, though it should in fact have caused him a major headache. After all, the break- down of the age profile of men attached to Police Battalion 101, the core material of his first case study, makes it quite clear that of the 550 men known to have served in this battalion merely 42 were younger than thirty, i.e. born after 1918, a measly 8.1 percent, as the author himself has to admit (G206). And it is therefore a statistical impossibility that these forty- odd men could have made up the core of 'ideological warriors', that such a small sample could have carried the torch of 'eliminationist anti-Semitism'. For, by and large, the destruction of European Jewry in the East — prior to the establishment of extermination camps as part of the so-called 'Endlösung' — were the deeds of the first, and *not* the second generation of Nazis, whose 'characterology' (Haffner), *not* their 'ideology' (Goldhagen), made them commit these atrocities (cf. H80).

As Haffner never tired of reiterating, the qualities essential for being a *genuine* Nazi 'were an urge for activity, craving for sensation, and lust for adventure on the one hand, combined with mental laziness, lack of imagination, and a want of talent for life on the other' (H91), meaning that the practical danger and strength of the Nazis went hand in glove with their spiritual baseness: because they were men psychically deficient, of which their cruelty was just one striking example, proven for years in the daily abominations inside and outside concentration camps.

Yet, it is this very deficiency which oddly enough offers a plausible answer to Goldhagen's statistical problem. If one studies the subjective side of many Nazi cases a surprise awaits the investigator, comparable to the unexpected result of Hannah Arendt's findings in her report on the Eichmann trial in the early 1960s; for it emerges that '[t]he doer does not fit the deeds', that '[t]he enormity is committed by extraordinarily banal, weak, and insignificant men' (H92):

> They are merely men of unusually gross, dull, and stupid insensitivity. They increase the agonies of their victims and daily think out fresh torture in order to drag out of themselves a little sadistic satisfaction, as an impotent man seeks to stimulate himself with every perversion. (H92)

And just as Hannah Arendt — to the howls of the victims of Nazi atrocities worldwide — pointedly added a telling subtitle to her famous book,[68] Haffner noticed little difference between the perpetrators at the forefront of the 'action' and their bureaucratic colleagues, the so-called 'Schreibtischtäter', concluding that '[e]verywhere this sadism is pedantic and crude, and the agonies of the victims [...] thereby intensified to an unbearable pitch.' (H93) In fact, the resurrection of sadism was, in Haffner's opinion, 'the solitary contribution of the Nazis to the History of Culture, with which they [left] their mark on history!' (H93), a view shared by Chaim Kaplan in his 'Warsaw Diary':

> The beast within the Nazi is whole, completely healthy — it attacks and preys upon others; but the man within him is pathologically ill. Nature has struck him down with the illness of sadism, and this disease has penetrated into the very fiber of his being. There is no Nazi whose soul is not diseased, who is not tyrannical, sadistic [...].[69]

All the same, even this form of brutality — as mentioned above — must be considered the result of insufficiency rather than of excess; for the Nazis had 'the whole orchestra of sadism playing, but they [could] not rise above the note of brutality.' (H93) At the bottom of their feverish dynamic lay the fear of nothingness, prompting Haffner to reduce Nazism to its shortest formula: 'nihilism in action, world-domination out of boredom.' (H93)

Overall then, Haffner's provocative and farsighted conclusion in *Jekyll and Hyde*,[70] which can be used to refute Goldhagen's *Willing Executioners*, amounted to the discovery of a vital difference between the first and second generation of *real* Nazis: for only members of the latter — scarcely represented in police battalions like those studied by Goldhagen — can conceivably be considered 'ideological warriors' along the lines of eliminationist anti-Semitism, nullifying the American political scientist's conclusion that 'ordinary' Germans were responsible for the killing fields in the East. This result may come as a surprise, yet it is quintessentially Haffner, and surely also one of the reasons why his slim volumes on the history of the Third Reich will still be read and discussed, 'wenn die meisten dickleibigen Geschichtsbücher längst vergessen sind.'[71]

Notes

[1] The pseudonym — reflecting his admiration for the composers Bach and Mozart — was to ensure the safety of his relatives back home in Germany (cf. Volker Ullrich, 'Der helle Klang. Ein Nachruf auf Sebastian Haffner, den großen Stilisten und begnadeten Geschichtserzähler', *Die Zeit*, 7 January 1999, no. 2, p. 2); yet this particular pen name was also chosen because it was easily pronounceable by English speakers and readily identified him as a non-Jewish German (cf. the recent TV documentary *Mit scharfer Zunge. Sebastian Haffner wird neunzig*; directed by Christian Walther and edited by Gert Monheim [broadcast in the WDR-series *Menschen Hautnah* on 5 January 1998]).

[2] Cf. Arnulf Baring, 'Anmerkungen zu Haffner', *Die Welt*, 4 January 1999, p. 3.

[3] His last article in the *Vossische Zeitung* in 1934 was entitled 'Das Leben der Fußgänger' (cf. 'Sebastian Haffner 1907 bis 1999 — Nachruf', *Der Spiegel*, 11 January 1999, no. 2, p. 173).

[4] To write a report on Britain for the Deutscher Verlag, previously known as Ullstein Verlag.

[5] According to a postcard (date-stamped 26 August 1938), cited by Haffner's daughter Sarah in the TV documentary mentioned above, her father left Berlin on 28 August 1938, arriving a day later in London via Cologne, Hook van Holland and Harwich.

[6] Cf. Michael Seyfert, *Im Niemandsland. Deutsche Exilliteratur in britischer Internierung. Ein unbekanntes Kapitel der Kulturgeschichte des Zweiten Weltkrieges* (Berlin: Das Arsenal, 1984), p. 25; cf. also Seyfert's earlier contribution on this topic, entitled '"His Majesty's Most Loyal Internees": Die Internierung und Deportation deutscher und österreichischer Flüchtlinge als "enemy aliens"' (in: *Exil in Großbritannien. Zur Emigration aus dem nationalsozialistischen Deutschland*, ed. by Gerhard Hirschfeld [Stuttgart: Klett-Cotta, 1983], pp. 155-82).

[7] The UK edition was published by Secker & Warburg in London in 1940, the US edition in New York by E. P. Dutton & Co. in 1941 (H plus page references in the text refer to the UK edition); the translation was rendered by Wilfrid David, but the orginal manuscript was lost; a German edition, initiated by Uwe Soukup (cf. his 'Nachwort', pp. 282-84) and translated by Kurt Baudisch (*Germany: Jekyll and Hyde. 1939 — Deutschland von innen betrachtet*), was not published until 1996 (Berlin: Verlag 1900); in 1941 Secker & Warburg also published another book of Haffner's entitled *Offensive against Germany*.

[8] Cf. Ch. VII: 'The Émigrés', pp. 249-50: 'Whilst in England there has been no change in policy, France has declared war on the German emigrants no less than on Hitler. Immediately after the outbreak of war, all adult male German emigrants, with a few exceptions, were arrested. The fact was deliberately ignored that they were exiles and they were treated like the Nazi agents, with whom they were imprisoned. An army of valuable allies has been destroyed in order to get, at small cost, a number of prisoners of war. Something much worse than an injustice has been perpetrated; a grave, a catastrophic defeat on the psychological battle-field.'

[9] Cf. *Hansard* (vol. 363, col. 623 of 23 July 1940) regarding a Commons question tabled by an MP named Parker (addressed to Home Secretary John Anderson) concerning Haffner's internee-status (cited by Seyfert, *Im Niemandsland*, p. 201, fnt. 41).

[10] Cf. *Biographisches Handbuch der deutschsprachigen Emigration nach 1933*, vol. 1: *Politik, Wirtschaft, Öffentliches Leben*, ed. by Werner Röder and Herbert A. Strauss (München: Saur, 1980), p. 461.

[11] Ibid., p. 262; cf. also Werner Röder, *Die deutschen sozialistischen Exilgruppen in Großbritannien 1940-1945* (Bonn-Bad Godesberg: Verlag Neue Gesellschaft, 1968), p. 132 and Ch. 17 (= 'Minister of Morale') in John Charmley, *Duff Cooper. The Authorised Biography* (London: Phoenix, 1997; 1986), pp. 141-53, although there is no specific mention of either Lothar, Haffner or *Die Zeitung*; see furthermore Ch. 5 '"The Same Old Hun": Anti-German Propaganda', in Ian McLaine, *Ministry of Morale. Home Front and the Ministry of Information in World War II* (London: Allen & Unwin, 1979), pp. 137-70 and Anthony Glees, *Exile Politics during the Second World War. The German Social Democrats in Britain* (Oxford: Clarendon Press, 1982), p. 81.

[12] Cf. Röder/Strauss, p. 262.

[13] *Die Zeitung* was published at the London premises of *The Observer* (Ludgate House, 107 Fleet Street).

[14] Cf. his famous 'Panorama' broadcast on 2 November 1962 in which he maintained: 'Wenn die deutsche Öffentlichkeit sich das gefallen läßt, wenn sie nicht nachhaltig auf Aufklärung dringt, dann adieu Pressefreiheit, adieu Rechtsstaat, adieu Demokratie!'

[15] Maligned by the Springer press as 'Paradepferd des Ulbricht-Regimes'.

[16] His regular column in *konkret* was called 'Sebastian Haffners Monatslektüre'.

[17] Cf. his support for the student movement in a broadcast on 2 June 1967 under the heading 'Die Nacht der langen Knüppel', calling for the expropriation of the Springer press, and as result being labelled 'Staranwalt der APO'.

[18] Cf. Munzinger Archiv/Internationales Biographisches Archiv — Personen Aktuell.

[19] Among the most important titles are: *Winston Churchill* (1967); *Der Teufelspakt. 50 Jahre deutsch-russische Beziehungen* (1968); *Die verratene Revolution. Deutschland 1918/19* (1970); *Der Selbstmord des Deutschen Reiches* (1970); *Anmerkungen zu Hitler* (1978); *Preußen ohne Legende* (1979); *Preußische Profile* (1980); *Überlegungen eines Wechselwählers* (1980); *Von Bismarck zu Hitler. Ein Rückblick* (1987); *Germany: Jekyll & Hyde. 1939. Deutschland von innen betrachtet* (1996).

[20] Ullrich (1999).

[21] 'Sebastian Haffner — Obituary', *The Times*, 5 January 1999, p. 19.

[22] Neal Ascherson, 'In the name of Haffner, give us back our talking heads', *The Observer*, 10 January 1999, p. 27.

23 Ibid.; Haffner's lead articles were published anonymously under the pseudonym 'A Student of Europe' (cf. Röder/Strauss, p. 262); a cursory survey of the *Observer* for the year 1943 at the British Newspaper Library (Colindale) unearthed the following contributions on Germany and Austria under this pseudonym: 'Hitler's Double Gamble' (7 February 1943), 'Diminishing German Manpower' (6 June 1943), 'The Battle of the Ruhr' (27 July 1943), 'All Routes Lead to Berlin' (5 September 1943), 'What Hitler has at Stake' (12 September 1943), 'When Will Germany Crack?' (31 October 1943), 'The Restoration of Austria' (26 December 1943); only once, on 27 September 1942, did Haffner publish a review ('Hitler as Orator of the Day') under his 'real' name.

24 Baring (cf. note 2).

25 *The Times* (cf. note 21).

26 *Spiegel* (cf. note 3).

27 Christian Walther, 'Deutschland und die Deutschen erklären', *die tageszeitung*, 4 January 1999, p. 15.

28 Ullrich (cf. note 1).

29 Mönchengladbach Public Library, date-stamped July 1945.

30 Cited by Marlis Menge, 'Wilhelm II. war immerhin Kaiser — Unterwegs mit Sebastian Haffner', *Die Zeit*, 26 September 1997, no. 40, p. 22.

31 In a diary entry on 15 May 1940 Thomas Mann first mentioned Haffner's *Jekyll and Hyde*, calling it 'ausgezeichnet'; and in a further note on 22 May 1940 he praised the book as a 'vorzügliche Analyse' (cf. *Thomas Mann: Tagebücher 1940-1943*, ed. by Peter de Mendelssohn [Frankfurt a.M.: S. Fischer, 1982], p. 76 & p. 80).

32 Volker Ullrich, 'Ein gelassener Unruhestifter', *Die Zeit*, 26 December 1997, no. 1, p. 6.

33 Johannes Willms, 'Skeptiker und Provokateur. Zum Tod des Publizisten Sebastian Haffner', *Süddeutsche Zeitung*, 4 January 1999, no. 2, p. 15.

34 'In der Tat sind, wie kürzlich wieder Hans Mommsen bemerkte, Haffners Studien zu Hitler von keiner historischen Spezialforschung überholt worden [...].' (Ulrich Raulff, 'Ein Meister der vorletzten Dinge', *Frankfurter Allgemeine Zeitung*, 4 January 1999, no. 2, p. 45).

35 New York: Knopf, 1996; London: Little Brown & Co, 1996 (G plus page references in the text refer to the UK edition).

36 Cf. *Ein Volk von Mördern? Die Dokumentation zur Goldhagen-Kontroverse und die Rolle der Deutschen im Holocaust*, ed. by Julius H. Schoeps (Hamburg: Hoffmann & Campe, 1996); *Die Deutschen — ein Volk von Tätern? Zur historischen Debatte um das Buch von Daniel Jonah Goldhagen 'Hitlers Willige Vollstrecker. Ganz gewöhnliche Deutsche und der Holocaust'*, ed. by Dieter Dowe (Bonn: Friedrich Ebert Stiftung, 1996); Wolfgang Wippermann, *Wessen Schuld? Vom Historikerstreit zur Goldhagen-Kontroverse* (Berlin: Elefanten Press, 1997); Harald Schmid, 'Vom "Henker" zum "Wunderheiler".

Gerechtigkeit für Goldhagen?', *Menora. Jahrbuch für deutsch-jüdische Geschichte*, 8 (1997), 16-50; Dieter Pohl, 'Die Holocaust-Forschung und Goldhagens Thesen', *Vierteljahrshefte für Zeitgeschichte*, 45 (1997), 1, 1-48; *Geschichtswissenschaft und Öffentlichkeit. Der Streit um Daniel J. Goldhagen*, ed. by Johannes Heil and Rainer Erb (Frankfurt a.M.: S. Fischer, 1998); *A Nation on Trial. The Goldhagen Thesis and Historical Truth*, ed. by Norman G. Finkelstein and Ruth Bettina Birn (New York: Metropolitan Books 1998); *Eine Nation auf dem Prüfstand. Die Goldhagen-These und die historische Wahrheit. Mit einer Einleitung von Hans Mommsen*, ed. by Norman G. Finkelstein and Ruth Bettina Birn (Hildesheim: Claassen, 1998).

[37] Ruth Bettina Birn, 'Revising the Holocaust', *The Historical Journal* 40 (1997), 1, 195 (page references refer to the UK edition of Goldhagen's book).

[38] Goldhagen's use of the relevant specialized literature ('Fachliteratur') is highly selective, and according to Clive James '[f]or a work as important as Goldhagen's, the absence of a bibliography is a bizarre publishing development.' ('Blaming the Germans', *The New Yorker*, 22 April 1996, pp. 45-46).

[39] *The Meaning of Hitler* (Cambridge, MA: Harvard UP, 1979); *The Ailing Empire. Germany from Bismarck to Hitler* (New York: Fromm, 1989).

[40] Cf. Christopher R Browning, *Ordinary Men. Reserve Police Battalion 101 and the Final Solution in Poland* (New York: HarperCollins, 1992) and Raul Hilberg, *Perpetrators Victims Bystanders. The Jewish Catastrophe 1933-1945* (New York: HarperCollins, 1992).

[41] *Leben sammeln und nicht fragen wozu und warum. Tagebücher 1918-1932*, 2 vols (Berlin: Aufbau, 1996) and *Ich will Zeugnis ablegen bis zum letzten. Tagebücher 1933-1946*, 2 vols (Berlin: Aufbau, 1995).

[42] Haffner's assessment was confirmed in a recent study (Dirk Walter, *Antisemitische Kriminalität und Gewalt. Judenfeindschaft in der Weimarer Republik* [Bonn: J.H.W. Dietz 1999]), which shows *no* evidence of 'eliminatory' anti-Semitism, and expressly refutes Goldhagen's claims as far as the Weimar era is concerned (p. 17).

[43] *Spiegel* (see note 3).

[44] Markus Schwering, 'Provokateur und trauriger Patriot. Sebastian Haffner — wider den Zeitgeist. Nachruf', *Kölner Stadtanzeiger*, 4 January 1999, no. 2, p. 2.

[45] Sebastian Haffner, *The Meaning of Hitler* , p. 9 (*Anmerkungen zu Hitler*, p. 16); cf. also Brigitte Hamann, *Hitlers Wien. Lehrjahre eines Diktators* (München: Piper, 1996).

[46] Haffner, *The Meaning of Hitler*, p. 91 (*Anmerkungen zu Hitler*, p. 117).

[47] Robert S. Wistrich, 'Helping Hitler', *Commentary*, July 1996, p. 29.

[48] Ibid., p. 28.

[49] Ibid.

[50] Ibid., p. 29.

[51] In the TV documentary mentioned above (cf. fnt. 1), Haffner frankly admitted: 'ich sah den Holocaust nicht voraus.'

[52] *The Ailing Empire*, p. 206 (*Von Bismarck zu Hitler. Ein Rückblick*, p. 264).

[53] Omer Bartov, 'Ordinary Monsters', *The New Republic*, 29 April 1996, p. 36.

[54] Ibid., p. 38

[55] Wistrich, p. 31.

[56] Bartov, p. 38.

[57] Not 'ordinary men' of various nationalities, as Browning's study suggests (cf. note 40).

[58] Cf. Ch. 3 (= 'The Nazis'), pp. 68-108.

[59] Willms (see note 33).

[60] Cf. especially Chs. 6-9, pp. 181-280.

[61] Haffner equated the generation of Germans born before the turn of the century with the first generation of Nazis, but at a later stage calls the generation born between 1900 and 1910 the first generation of *real* Nazis (i.e. the second generation), and all those men born after 1918 the second generation of *real* Nazis (i.e. the third generation [H103]); in order not to complicate the issue I have *not* adopted his division, calling all those men born *before* 1910 first, and all those born *after* 1918 second generation Nazis.

[62] Cf. Dieter Pohl's comments ('Die Holocaust-Forschung und Goldhagens Thesen', *Vierteljahrsheft für Zeitgeschichte*, 45 [1997], 1, 25) on this issue: 'Die Polizeieinheiten [...] fügen sich nicht völlig bruchlos in das Konzept von den 'gewöhnlichen Deutschen' ein. Zwar bestanden die Reservepolizeibataillone tatsächlich aus einem einigermaßen repräsentativen Querschnitt deutscher Männer zwischen 18 und 40 Jahren. Diese handelten jedoch in quasi-militärischen Verbänden, und die Institution Ordnungspolizei gehörte per se zu Himmlers 'Endlösungs'-Apparat. Neuere Untersuchungen zeigen auch, daß die preußische Schutzpolizei bereits vor 1933 autoritär ausgerichtet war. Die Laufbahn-Polizisten, die hier des öfteren neben den einfachen Reservepolizisten beispielhaft genannt werden, kann man kaum noch als 'gewöhnliche Deutsche' bezeichnen. Sie waren zum Teil langjährige SS-Mitglieder, und gerade sie stellten als Rückgrat der Bataillone die personelle Verbindung zwischen Weltanschauungsapparat und durchschnittlichen Polizisten dar.'

[63] Raulff (see note 34); Haffner's 'nüchterne[], schnörkellose[] Sprache' (Ulrich Schlie, 'Kein Blatt vor dem Mund. Zum Tod von Sebastian Haffner', *Neue Zürcher Zeitung*, 4 January 1999, no. 1, p. 32) contrasts sharply with Goldhagen's 'clumsy and jargon-filled English' (Jerry Adler, 'Why Did They Do It?' *Newsweek*, 29 April 1996, p. 42).

[64] Raulff (see note 34).

[65] Cf. note 61.

[66] Consequently it is fitting that, at one stage, Haffner should define Nazidom as a 'social solvent' (H158).

[67] This 'ideological pretext' refers to the cultural and political conditions of the Weimar Republic in general, and *not* to anti-Semitism (cf. also H77-78).

[68] *Eichmann in Jerusalem. A Report on the Banality of Evil* (New York: Viking, 1963).

[69] *Scroll of Agony. The Warsaw Diary of A. Kaplan*, ed. by Abraham I. Katsh (New York: Macmillan, 1965), p. 87; for Goldhagen, in a footnote (p. 583, fnt. 53) to claim that 'Kaplan's use of "Nazis" should be read as "Germans"' is an absurdity.

[70] 'Dabei war der liberale Konservative journalistischen Kollegen und auch der Zunft der Historiker mit seinen provozierenden wie hellsichtigen Analysen oft weit voraus [...].' ('Tod eines großen Historikers — Nachruf', *Stern*, 7 January 1999, no. 2, p. 17).

[71] Ullrich (see note 1); cf. also Horst Köpke's comment: 'Noch bedeutender als der Tagesschriftsteller war der Buchautor Haffner. Er [...] erarbeitete neuartige Thesen, auch dabei stets bedacht, allgemeinverständlich zu bleiben und seine Leser nicht mittels dicker Wälzer zu überfordern.' ('Abseits der politischen Ströme. Zum Tode des Publizisten und Historikers Sebastian Haffner', *Frankfurter Rundschau*, 4 January 1999, no. 2, S. 5).

Jonathan Ross

'Grenzüberschreitungen'
The Life and Works of Werner Ilberg (1896-1978)[1]

This article is an exploratory study of the German-Jewish author Werner Ilberg. Although focusing on his exile in Britain, it also portrays his colourful personal, ideological and artistic background. Ilberg had been associated with various political and literary movements, including Zionism, Expressionism, and the 'Bund proletarisch-revolutionärer Schriftsteller', and contributed to some of the key debates among anti-Nazi émigrés. He came to England as a staunch Communist, and the article documents his attempts to influence the Manchester branch of the Free German League of Culture in line with the philosophy of the German Communist Party (KPD). In addition, Ilberg's writing in Britain is examined, and his shift from the production of fiction to literary criticism is discussed with reference to his important essay on 'Schriftstellernöte'. Archive material is used throughout, particularly to reconstruct the more practical aspects of Ilberg's exile, such as his internment and employment.

In the epilogue of his unpublished autobiography, *Grenzüberschreitungen*,[2] the German-Jewish author Werner Martin Ilberg, who was in exile in Britain, reflects on the fate of his short-story 'Der Wirrweg der Maria Böttcher'. Written in Prague in the mid-1930s, it was due to be published in Moscow, but the war prevented this. Dejectedly, and not entirely logically, the author comments, 'Die literaturpolitische Folge war und ist, daß ich mit meinem Werk, meinen poetischen, essayistischen und kritischen Bemühungen nicht in die Periodisierung unserer Literaturhistoriker hineinpasse...'[3]

Ilberg was certainly justified in claiming that his efforts had been overlooked by literary-historians in the German Democratic Republic. This is where he settled in 1956, having spent the early post-war period in his hometown of Wolfenbüttel, Lower Saxony. Although there is an entry for him in the lexicon *Schriftsteller der DDR*,[4] he is absent from other reference works which cover equally unsung East German writers. The impetus for his claim could have been his exclusion from the authorised tome *Geschichte der Literatur der Deutschen Demokratischen Republik* which came out at the time Ilberg was preparing his autobiography.[5]

Were he alive today, Ilberg would also have grounds for complaining that his life and work in England between 1938 and 1947 had

largely been neglected by scholars in the field of exile studies. He is
omitted from the foremost early works on exile literature, such as Walter
Berendsohn's *Die humanistische Front* and Wilhelm Sternfeld's *Deutsche
Exil-Literatur 1933-1945*, even though Sternfeld and Ilberg knew each
other in Britain.[6] Given that Ilberg settled in the GDR, it is not surprising
that the most extensive coverage of his exile is in the East German series
Kunst und Literatur im antifaschistischen Exil 1933-1945.[7] Nevertheless,
here, as in Hans-Albert Walter's *Deutsche Exilliteratur 1933-1950*,[8] the
majority of references relate to his activities in Czechoslovakia between
1933 and 1938, rather than to his stay in the UK.

One can easily see why Ilberg has not attracted the attention of
scholars of exile and GDR literature. On first appearances, he was not a
prolific writer of fiction, with a single novel to his name, *Die Fahne der
Witwe Grasbach*. Although this won him second prize in a competition
organised by the Swiss Gutenberg Book Guild in 1935, it was not published
until 1948. The publisher, East Berlin's Neues Leben, also brought out a
collection of short-stories by Ilberg entitled *Rastlose Jahre*. This included
'Der Wirrweg der Maria Böttcher' and two short-stories Ilberg had written
in the UK. Apart from these, all that remains of Ilberg's work from exile
are brief essays, poems, and *Erzählungen* which appeared in anti-fascist
periodicals and anthologies.

Although recent years have seen a profusion of research into
German and Austrian exiles in Britain, Ilberg has not benefited from it. As
far as I have been able to ascertain, his name appears only twice in the mass
of scholarly literature that has emerged. And on both occasions, he is of
little importance in his own right, but is named as the recipient of a letter
from a better-known exile, Rudolf Olden.[9]

In the post-war years, Ilberg barely produced any imaginative
literature. He concentrated instead on literary biography (Heine, Bernhard
Kellermann, Hans Marchwitza, and the French author Romain Rolland),
criticism,[10] and editing the works of earlier authors, namely Georg
Lichtenberg, Ferdinand Freiligrath and Ludwig Turek.

The works of fiction by Ilberg that still exist are actually a fraction
of what he wrote. Amongst the freight which he despatched from Prague,
but which never arrived in London, for example, were numerous
manuscripts.[11] These included 'eine Auseinandersetzung mit dem
Zionismus' in novel-form, which Ilberg had started writing in 1933.[12]
Another novel, *Das Teufelsrad*, submitted for a literary competition

organised by the American Guild for German Cultural Freedom in 1938, also appears to have vanished. In short, Ilberg was not as unproductive as his publication record would suggest.

Nevertheless, one could hardly describe him as an outstanding writer. In terms of both form and content, his works are indistinguishable from those by other second-rate Communist authors who have likewise been more or less forgotten. His poetry, for example, typifies the blatant, and often formally clumsy, propagandistic verse which was churned out for the anti-fascist struggle. In *Grenzüberschreitungen*, Ilberg actually acknowledges the embarrassing mediocrity of one of his early efforts. Describing the first of the two times he was arrested and imprisoned by the SA, he mentions that he was repeatedly asked by his fellow-inmates to recite a poem he had composed shortly after the *Reichstag* fire. He admits

> [...] obwohl ich es in jenem Bunker oft genug aufsagen mußte, ist mir nur der Anfang im Gedächtnis geblieben: 'Aus des Reichstags grau Gemäuer — Feuer, Feuer.' Darauf hat sich dann in den folgenden Strophen alles Mögliche gereimt: Teuer, geheuer oder ungeheuer, neuer und was weiß ich. Das letzte Wort war dann Euer, jedenfalls war es schaurig schön, und es ist nicht schade, daß ich nichts mehr davon weiß.[13]

Apart from his meagre and mediocre literary output, a specific reason springs to mind why Ilberg has not attracted the attention of researchers into the UK-exile: he seemingly made little impression on his fellow émigrés, which would suggest that he was not noticeably involved in the public life of the exile community. Whereas other Communist writers who were in Britain, such as Kurt Barthel (Kuba), Jan Petersen and Max Zimmering, are referred to in the reminiscences of fellow UK-émigrés such as Emmy Koenen,[14] Jan Koplowitz[15] and Jürgen Kuczynski,[16] as well as in biographies by lesser-known refugees,[17] Ilberg's name does not occur in any of these works.

Nevertheless, Ilberg was not dormant as a writer and political activist whilst in England. And although his autobiographical works only furnish limited information about his stay in Britain, they show that he endeavoured to be an engaged member of the émigré community.[18] Unpublished sources, such as documents from the 'Deutsches Exilarchiv' in Frankfurt and observations from acquaintances, give additional insight into Ilberg's public activities, and help fill some of the gaps in the autobiographical writings. They tell us about the more mundane aspects of Ilberg's exile in the UK — his addresses, his employment and financial circumstances. Whilst adding to our knowledge of the living conditions of exiles in the UK, such information also offers clues as to why Ilberg was not as prominent in émigré affairs as some of his contemporaries.

The focus in this article is obviously on Ilberg's life and work in the UK. However, since these were inevitably linked to what he had experienced and done before, it is worthwhile first summarising his personal, political and artistic development prior to his arrival in England. Another reason for doing this is that Ilberg is an unknown entity with a quite fascinating biography. The latter owes much to the fact that he really did cross a considerable number of borders, as the title of his autobiography implies. As will become clear, these were not just geographical borders, but also political, linguistic, cultural and artistic ones.

In *Grenzüberschreitungen*, Ilberg portrays the hybrid Jewish milieu in which he was raised. The family of his father were archetypal assimilationists. Many had converted to Christianity to facilitate their social mobility; one had managed to become the Kaiser's personal doctor. Ilberg's mother's family were less eager to abandon their heritage, and she observed orthodox customs quite fastidiously. Ilberg epitomises the difference between his parents in his description of their respective diets.[19] Whereas his father would sometimes eat ham or bacon, the mother and children stuck to traditional Jewish dishes such as *lokshen*.

Ilberg received his secondary education at the local Jewish boarding-school. As a writer, he would frequently draw on the knowledge of ancient Jewish literature he acquired there, and deploy models from the Bible and post-Biblical writings to clarify the topical phenomena he was describing. The foreword to *Rastlose Jahre*, for instance, opens, 'Deutschland ist Sodom. Es ist das Reich des Bösen.'[20] Having likened the condition of contemporary Germany to the city in Genesis, Ilberg emphasises that the fate of the former will be determined very differently to that of the latter. It is no longer decisive — as it was in Abraham's day — whether ten or a million righteous people exist, who can convince God to be merciful. What matters now is that these people bring about the vanquishing of the ill. Writing as a Communist, and presumably also as an atheist, Ilberg evidently believed that it was humans alone who made history. But he was prepared to invoke paradigms from the Jewish tradition with which he was familiar in order to convey the momentousness of current events.

After finishing school, Ilberg trained as a textile-merchant, and later ran the family textile-retailing business in Wolfenbüttel. This, however, went bankrupt in 1930, and Ilberg was soon to join the millions of unemployed Germans. At this time, he started to write. He was heavily encouraged by Ruzena Lechner (known as Rosi), a Jewish woman of Galician origin, who was later to become Ilberg's second wife — he had married his cousin Klara in 1923. The couple moved to Berlin, in the hope of furthering Ilberg's literary career. There, he attempted (unsuccessfully) to have his efforts published in various Left-wing newspapers, whilst earning a living running a book-cart.

The First World War, in which Ilberg served three years on the front, helped determine his political development. But whereas it led others to align themselves with the revolutionary Left, it made Ilberg question his fervent patriotism, and set him on the path towards becoming a Zionist. One factor was his enormous disappointment at the count of Jews in clerical positions in the army which the Prussian War Ministry implemented in 1916. A Zionist fellow-private was also influential, particularly since he seized on the 'Judenzählung' to support his argument that the Germans would always be prejudiced against the Jews.

In the early 1920s, Ilberg became involved in the Left-wing Zionist youth group 'Ha'poel Ha'tsair', and later in the Zionist organisation in Braunschweig. He supplemented his Jewish education, reading the works of the major Zionist theoreticians and the classics of Yiddish literature, and attending lectures by, and discussing with, German-Jewish intellectuals such as Arnold Zweig and Ernst Toller. At one point, he belonged to the 'Landesvorstand' of the German Zionist organisation.[21]

The next two decades, however, saw further 'Grenzüber-schreitungen' in Ilberg's political evolution. In 1925, he broke his rule of not engaging in German politics when he joined the SPD. Four years later, he left the Zionist organisation in protest at the suppression of the Arab uprising in Palestine, although retaining his belief in the need for a Jewish state. Gradually, he became disenchanted with what he saw as the irresolution of the Social Democrats, and gravitated towards the KPD. By 1935, he had presumably overcome his earlier reservations about this party, which largely concerned the Communists' theoretical position on the 'Jewish question' and the suppression of Zionism in the USSR. For in that year, he and Rosi successfully applied to become members of the KPD.

Three years earlier, Ilberg had met the poet Walter Stolle in Berlin, and it was Stolle who recommended him to become a bookseller. He also suggested that Ilberg should attend a meeting of the Berlin branch of the 'Bund proletarisch-revolutionärer Schriftsteller'. He did so, and after the Nazis took power, continued to participate in rendezvous of the now banned organisation. When, for conspiratorial reasons, the branch was broken up into five-person cells, Ilberg joined one of these. His work included assessing new authors, and producing flyers and stickers bearing agitational verse.[22]

Despite the precautions taken by Ilberg and the other members of the cell, he was arrested twice. An incident during his first imprisonment testifies to his extraordinary courage and selflessness.[23] In the 'Prügelkolonne' in which he was being held, Ilberg found himself next to a seriously ill prisoner. When that man's name was called, which meant that he was next in line for a beating, Ilberg took his place to spare him. After his second spell behind bars, Ilberg was advised by Jan Petersen, on behalf of the KPD, to leave Germany. In November 1933, he managed to escape to Prague.[24]

Ilberg was actively involved in the affairs of the German political and literary emigration in Prague. He took part in the weekly gatherings of the KPD-group in the emigrant-home where he was living, and in the regular Monday-night discussions of the 'Bert-Brecht-Klub'. He thus became acquainted with leading figures on the German Left, such as Ernst Bloch, Bruno Frei, and Wieland Herzfelde. On one occasion, Ilberg attended a meeting of the Prague 'B'nei B'rith' lodge which was addressed by Max Brod, and ended up at loggerheads with the speaker on the subject of Soviet culture.[25] Ilberg himself lectured at one of the meetings of the 'Kulturausschuß der Liga für Menschenrechte',[26] and wrote reviews of novels for the Liga's periodical *Abend*.[27]

Whilst in Czechoslovakia, he was certainly quite productive as an author. As well as writing *Die Fahne der Witwe Grasbach*, 'Der Wirrweg der Maria Böttcher', and *Das Teufelsrad*, Ilberg contributed numerous short texts to a range of exile newspapers and periodicals.[28] Many of these appeared under the pseudonym 'Martin Grebly'.

His articles which were published in the Moscow-based periodical *Das Wort* can be seen as indicative of his political outlook and standpoint on artistic questions prior to his departure to Britain. With 'Der Förster und der Wilderer',[29] Ilberg showed himself to be a naive accessory to

Stalinist injustice, for this parable was a transparent legitimisation of the show-trials.[30] In his two articles on literary topics, Ilberg displayed more independent thinking. The first of these was a contribution to the Expressionism debate which Alfred Kurella had initiated in September 1937 with a polemic against Gottfried Benn.[31] Whereas Kurella had claimed that there was a similarity between the spirit from which Expressionism derived and the spirit behind the ideology of fascism, Ilberg denied any such link. For him, Expressionism was 'der Punkt, an dem der Weg sich gabelt.'[32] Some Expressionists went on to ally themselves with 'the class bearing the future' (a euphemism for becoming socialist), whilst the likes of Benn chose the path 'backwards'. Benn's fall, then, could not have been a consequence of his Expressionism alone.

In Ilberg's opinion, although the Expressionists lacked the necessary 'knowledge', particularly of the 'social-political' kind, they had commendable objectives: to depict as starkly as possible the cold world of insecure and isolated people, and to conjure up from their imaginations a new, warming alternative to this. And despite the fact that Expressionism did not go beyond subversion, it still had progressive aspects. By exposing the foulness of the old world, it helped pave the way for a better one, which was why the fascists hated it. What is more, it undoubtedly had a distinct style. This, Ilberg admits, is more than one could say for the literature of the German Leftist emigration: 'Es fehlt der zwingende, der mitreißende Ausdruck für unser Wollen. Ihn aber haben die Expressionisten damals gehabt.'[33]

Ilberg arrived in Britain on the 19th November 1938.[34] Like most KPD members in Czechoslovakia, he and Rosi had opted for England when, following the Munich Conference of 30th September, the Party told them that they should leave the country as soon as possible. Wilhelm Koenen, leader of the German Communist émigrés in Czechoslovakia, also warned them that the prudish English would not approve of them, an unmarried couple, cohabiting.[35] This explains why they got married within days of Rosi arriving from Prague, approximately six months after Werner.[36]

They were permitted to enter Britain as members of the 'Schmidt-Gruppe'. This comprised around three hundred and fifty German Communist refugees from Czechoslovakia, for whom Heinz H. Schmidt, a member of the Central Committee of the KPD, procured visas. Schmidt represented 'his' refugees within the British Committee for Refugees from

Czechoslovakia and its successor, the Czech Refugee Trust Fund. Since the latter was subsidised by the British government, it could be quite generous with its payments to refugees. Ilberg's living-costs from the time of his arrival in Britain until July 1941, for example, were paid for by the Fund.[37] In addition, he received small grants from the Thomas Mann group and the English PEN-Centre.[38]

Ilberg was evidently eager to maintain the relationships he had developed with other refugee authors, and to forge links with English colleagues. In early December, he informed Rudolf Olden that his new home in Chiswick[39] had become a meeting point for various acquaintances from Prague and other authors they had met on the journey from Czechoslovakia.[40] He also divulged to Olden that he and his friends were disconcerted about their relationship to the English PEN-Centre. Whilst they appreciated the generous financial support they received from that organisation, they regretted that they had not yet met any of the writers actually involved in it.

Following Rosi's arrival and their subsequent marriage, the couple were advised by the Fund to go to Clacton on Sea in order to recuperate from their recent turbulent experiences. After spending a seemingly fruitful quarter of a year there,[41] they were sent to Manchester — presumably by the Party — to help set up a branch of the Free German League of Culture. Unfortunately, it has not been possible to examine internal documents of the League or the KPD in the UK which could reveal more about Ilberg's 'mission'.[42] Nonetheless, the fact that he was entrusted with such a task would suggest that the Party leadership in Britain, which was so influential in the League's founding and development, viewed him as a reliable guardian of its interests, and that he had considerable status within the League itself. We know that he belonged to the board of the League in October 1944,[43] and he is likely to have been more than an ordinary member five years earlier.

Ilberg had little time to develop the branch, however, for within nine months of arriving in Manchester, he and most other male Central European refugees were interned. As he had been placed in category C,[44] the first wave of internment following the outbreak of the war left him untouched. But he was affected by the declaration of general internment on the 11th June 1940, and spent the period between 28th June and 22nd February 1941 in Huyton Camp near Liverpool.[45] This was unusual, since

Huyton was a transit camp, from which internees were normally deported to the Isle of Man or abroad.

Another noteworthy aspect to Ilberg's stay in Huyton is that, unlike almost all of his fellow-writers, he does not seem to have contributed to the vibrant cultural life that developed there, as in all of the internment camps.[46] One can only surmise the reasons for this. According to Heinz Kamnitzer and Jan Koplowitz, Ilberg was a withdrawn man, and this may have inhibited him from participating in plays, recitals, lectures, exhibitions and the like. Having said this, he was hardly a hermit when he was not interned, so his personality was probably not the only reason for his inactivity. Another possibility is that he was ill, as he appears to have been for much of his stay in Britain.

Following his release from internment, Ilberg's time seems to have been taken up with three main activities: paid employment, assorted literary projects, and organisational and political work for the League and other groupings. He was first employed in July 1941. From December of that year until April 1944, he worked as a capstan operator for the Empire Engineering Company.[47] This firm was involved in armaments production and Ilberg was obviously pleased to be not just earning a living but also contributing to the war effort. In 1943, when he was clearly exasperated with the Germans for their failure to demonstrate any opposition to their regime, Ilberg wrote of his hope that the weapons he was manufacturing would be used by the Allies to blast holes in the thick heads of his countrymen, so that the light of reason could get through to them.[48]

Ilberg's life as a worker was not without its problems. On one occasion he was threatened with dismissal, but a show of solidarity from his English colleagues supposedly persuaded his manager to retract this.[49] In addition, he was plagued by illness, and this caused him to accumulate debts to the Czech Refugee Trust Fund which supported him when he was unable to work. In October 1942, Ilberg wrote to Wilhelm Sternfeld, who was responsible for allocating the loans of the Fund, apologising for being in arrears and explaining that the sole reason for this was that he had been laid low by a thrombosis of the leg.[50] He also mentioned that he still had outstanding debts to the Fund for financial assistance at the time of his first illness during his 'working period'. Since Ilberg only started working in July 1941, this means that he was dehabilitated twice in the space of little more than a year. And Ilberg's condition does not appear to have improved; in April 1944 he was laid off due to ill health.[51] Whilst this was, of course, financially inopportune, it meant that he could concentrate on his writing.

Throughout its existence, Ilberg belonged to the Writers' Section of the Free German League of Culture. However, judging from the bulletins of the London branch of the League and of the Free German Youth, in all this time he was prominently involved in just one event. This was on the 16th April 1944 when, alongside Grete Fischer, Erich Fried and Rita Hausdorff, Ilberg read from his new works in the third literary matinee of the Section.[52] According to Jan Koplowitz, a regular at events at the clubhouse in Hampstead, Ilberg did not simply shun the limelight at gatherings of the 'Schriftstellersektion'; he rarely attended them.

No doubt this was mainly because he lived in Manchester. When he was not working, Ilberg seems to have been convalescing, and even if he had the time to travel to London, this would have entailed considerable trouble and expense. Significantly, the one occasion that he actually made it to London was shortly after he had stopped working. Ilberg appears to have made the most of his new-found freedom. The May/ June issue of *Freie Deutsche Kultur* contains two items by him: a satirical poem, and a review of the Soviet playwright Rakhmanov's *Professor Polezhayev*, which had been performed in London by the Austrian Centre's theatre-group *Laterndl*.[53]

Whilst Ilberg was a very inactive member of the Writers' Section, he did not stop writing in the UK. As well as composing the two 'Erzählungen' which later appeared in *Rastlose Jahre*, he had four brief texts published in anthologies brought out by the League and the Free German Youth: triumphal hymns to the Soviet Union and Maxim Gorky,[54] a revised excerpt from *Die Fahne der Witwe Grasbach*[55] and a short-story 'Die Entbindung'.[56]

Admittedly, this was a meagre output for an author over a period of almost nine years. But it was not all Ilberg produced; during his stay in Britain he gravitated towards writing about the works of others. In the letter-essay 'Schriftstellernöte' of 1943, Ilberg outlined his reasons for almost abandoning fiction.[57] In so doing, he raises a number of fundamental problems confronting German émigré writers, and for this reason it is worth dwelling on this text.

Ilberg starts by answering the unnamed addressee of his letter, who has suggested that the main cause of his writing crisis is that he has been working between ten and twelve hours a day in a factory. Ilberg's response is that there are more profound reasons for this crisis. The first is the fact that, as an exiled writer, he is no longer surrounded by the language in which he feels at home and in which he is used to writing. In Germany, he could overhear people in the street and, from the way they spoke, surmise something about their social and individual characteristics. Frequently, such people provided the models for his literary figures. In England, however, this is not possible, since he is not sensitive to the nuances of everyday speech.

The second reason Ilberg gives for his inability to write fiction is that he finds it impossible to depict the Third Reich, because he simply cannot imagine the conditions there. The daily life of the Germans now seems more alien to him than that of the inhabitants of the darkest corners of the earth. It is, moreover, extremely difficult for exiles to grasp how much the minds of their compatriots have been contaminated by Nazi propaganda. Sometimes it seems that they no longer even speak the same language; what is called the 'Herrenvolk' inside Germany, for example, is 'versklavt wie nie zuvor' (p. 53). Ilberg wonders how many Germans can still decipher 'Nazideutsch' and find a way to the truth.

Finally, he suggests that émigré authors should revise the way they portray the German populace. So far, they have focused on the few courageous resisters, leaving the masses in the background. If they want to be realistic, writers ought to show how the vast majority of Germans have been so corrupted by the regime that they are now rotten to the core. Ilberg maintains that he could write a lengthy treatise on this problem. To represent it in works of fiction, though, involving 'Menschen von Fleisch und Blut' (p. 53), is another matter. He realises how necessary such prose is, but admits that he has been incapable of producing it. Were he in the Soviet Union and had the opportunity to speak with German prisoners of war, he might learn from them 'wie die Realität der Lüge zuhause aussieht.' Then he could resume writing. Without this opportunity — Ilberg concludes resignedly — writing fiction is impossible, and he must wait for his return to Germany.

'Schriftstellernöte' undoubtedly helps explains why Ilberg wrote so little fiction during the war. Yet it could not be said that he practised exactly what he preached in it. He continued to produce the kind of 'heroic' narratives which, according to 'Schriftstellernöte', did not tell the whole truth about Nazi Germany. 'Die Entbindung', for example, which is set in the maternity ward of a prison-hospital, focuses above all on the determination of the wife of an executed anti-fascist. Gertrud Schwiebau's sole concern is to give birth to their child, in the hope that it will perpetuate the ideas for which she and her husband have struggled.

Other than 'Die Nacht der Entscheidung', 'Die Entbindung' was the only imaginative text of any length Ilberg wrote in the UK. But it would be wrong to interpret his 'migration' to critical literature as a retreat from political engagement. Ilberg invariably examined the ideological content of works and the philosophies of their creators, to establish what use they could be in the struggle against fascism. His survey of 'German Literature in Exile', which appeared in a special English-language number of *Freie Deutsche Kultur* in 1942, opens tellingly with a quotation from the Russian critic Vengerov: 'The novel and the reality mutually influence each other.'[58] Ilberg's essay on Ernst Wiechert from the same year revolves around the question of whether this 'inner emigrant' would find the courage to try and 'influence the reality' by inciting active resistance through his writing, or whether he would evade his responsibility and produce escapist literature, as he seemed to have done with *Das einfache Leben*.[59]

Ilberg also looked back at earlier periods of literature, but always highlighted the pertinence of works to the contemporary situation. In October 1944, Dr. Karl Wolff gave a lecture on Schiller's idea of freedom,[60] and Ilberg was one of thirteen members of the League and the breakaway Club 1943 whose responses to this were published.[61] Taking up Wolff's observations on *Wilhelm Tell*, Ilberg argues that in this play, Schiller identifies what is necessary for a freedom-struggle to be successful. Among the factors listed by Ilberg are unity across social divisions, the openness of the movement to people who previously followed the wrong path, but who have learnt the error of their ways, and the importance of participants in the struggle dedicating themselves entirely to the common cause. Ilberg does not make the point explicitly, but there is an unmistakable analogy between these principles and the 'Volksfront' ideology promulgated by the KPD. Émigré authors frequently tried to enlist posthumously the great figures in German literature as allies in the fight against Nazism. But rarely did an author suggest such a concrete parallel between the content of the work of one of these figures and the strategy of the anti-fascists.

A good deal of Ilberg's time in the UK was devoted to preparing a biography of the French intellectual Romain Rolland.[62] Rolland had long been a popular figure among German and Austrian writers, and exiles in the UK honoured him with numerous events and publications.[63] Presumably, at least part of Ilberg's research was carried out in the British Library; in a letter of July 1944 he mentioned his intention to travel to London 'um *wieder* im Britischen Museum zu arbeiten' (my italics).[64] Although the first fruit of this work was an article in the London-based *Modern Quarterly*, which appeared in 1947, Ilberg's more extensive treatments of Rolland were published in the GDR.[65]

Unfortunately, there are few sources available which can provide details of Ilberg's work within the Manchester branch of the Free German League of Culture.[66] However, an account by Ludwig Meyer, who joined the branch in Autumn 1941, gives some insight into his function and the objective underlying his efforts. Ilberg was responsible for chairing meetings, and, in Meyer's opinion, he consistently used his position to steer the branch in line with the philosophy of the KPD. This was exemplified by a meeting which included a lecture on Nietzsche who was, of course, a bogeyman for Communist émigrés everywhere. Luckily for Ilberg, the speaker had nothing positive to say about Nietzsche. Nevertheless,

> After the lecture, Ilberg as the chairman thanked the speaker and congratulated him 'for tearing the whole Nietzsche to shreds for all of us', meaning that all those present would abominate henceforth Nietzsche and all his writings.

Grenzüberschreitungen records another occasion when Ilberg offered ideological guidance to members of the branch.[67] Around 1941, E. M. Butler, Professor of German at Manchester University, purportedly declared, 'The Germans are predestined slaves.' To Ilberg, this resembled the view of contemporary Germany being propagated by the British 'Reaktion', above all by the influential civil servant Vansittart, who maintained that the Germans were currently behaving the way they were because of their congenital national characteristics. Like many Leftist émigrés, and in line with the KPD position at that time, Ilberg took it upon himself to refute 'Vansittartism'. He composed a fable, 'Die Zwei Pferde', which was displayed in the reception of the branch, and recited at meetings. It was later printed alongside Butler's comment in *Rastlose Jahre* .[68]

In 'Die Zwei Pferde', an old farm horse tells an impetuous young dapple-grey that he cannot understand how he bears the brutality which his owner inflicts on him. To his senior, the dapple-grey appears to be 'der geborene Sklave.' The latter replies that he would be treated as mildly as the older horse is treated by his master, if he were equally harmless. 'Mein Herr wäre kein Tyrann,' he concludes, 'wäre ich kein Rebell.'

A reader familiar with Butler's labelling of the Germans as 'predestined slaves' might have understood the older horse's designation of the younger as 'der geborene Sklave' as an allusion to this. (S)he may have regarded the dapple-grey as a *Schlüsselfigur* for the German people. Yet if this were so, the reader would have arrived at the conclusion that the Germans only appeared subservient because they were oppressed, but that this happened because they were so rebellious.

Today, this seems an extremely illusory view of early 1940s Germany. But it is precisely what Communists loyal to the Party line were then contending. Until approximately 1944, they clung to the belief that an opposition to fascism existed inside Germany, and that this was getting broader and stronger every day.[69]

There are, however, grounds for arguing that Ilberg would not have wanted his fable to be understood thus. Personally, he may not have been so convinced as to the existence of anti-fascist opposition within Germany. Two years after writing 'Die Zwei Pferde', before the Party changed its assessment of the opposition, he asserted that authors had been wrong to focus on resistance, because this was so negligible within Nazi Germany.[70] He might well have harboured similar thoughts previously.

Another argument is that Ilberg signalled through the form of 'Die Zwei Pferde' that it should not be read as a *Schlüsseltext*. It is a beast fable in the tradition of Aesop, and the events and figures in such texts rarely stood for actual historical events and figures. Authors normally used beast fables to illustrate, and comment on, more general issues and problems. The fundamental point of 'Die Zwei Pferde' seems to be that individuals or peoples are not born servile or rebellious, tyrannical or permissive. They become like this through their relations with others. The dapple-grey is not subordinate by nature, but has been subordinated by his owner. And he, in turn, is autocratic because he is faced with such a rebellious horse.

Ilberg intended to publish 'Die Zwei Pferde', yet once more circumstances conspired against him. In *Grenzüberschreitungen*, he outlines the new position regarding 'the Germans' which emerged in the Soviet Union after the invasion of June 1941.[71] Following the writer Ilya Ehrenburg, Soviet ideologues began to argue that the misdeeds of the Reichswehr troops manifested malicious traits in the German national character. These arguments were not dissimilar to those of the

Vansittartists which the Communists had hitherto refuted and, as such, they were hardly reconcilable with the moral of 'Die Zwei Pferde'. From around the beginning of 1944, the KPD in the UK under the leadership of Wilhelm Koenen effectively adopted the so-called 'Ehrenburg-Linie'. Although this position did not go unchallenged, most Communists went along with it obediently, as they had done with the many volte-faces in recent times. Ilberg's response to the new line is not documented. What is clear, however, is that the sentiment of 'Die Zwei Pferde' was outmoded, and that no publisher linked to the Party would have been interested in publishing Ilberg's fable.

A final example of Ilberg's involvement in central debates within the émigré community is a letter he had printed in the January 1944 edition of *Freie Tribüne*.[72] This was his contribution to an ongoing discussion about the position of Jewish refugees towards the recently founded Free German Movement. At issue was whether, in the light of the continuing atrocities against their co-religionists in Germany and elsewhere in Europe, Jews from Germany should renounce all ties with their homeland, or if they could still consider themselves German Jews, and fight for a 'better Germany' as part of the Movement.

To Ilberg, this debate was little more than the age-old battle between assimilationists and 'Nationaljuden', and was an anachronism. Invoking as examples Heinrich Heine and Arnold Zweig, Ilberg asserted that 'the German Jew' belonged to both the German and Jewish traditions. Repressing either of these components of his essence would only restrict him. Rejecting both total assimilation and the Jewish separatism he had earlier advocated, Ilberg contends: 'Das Deutsche, das wir lieben, muss wieder erkämpft werden ohne dass wir das Jüdische, das wir lieben, opfern.' (p. 13).

Ilberg's letter is noteworthy in two respects. First, he diverges from Communist orthodoxy in implying that Jews should preserve something of their 'difference'. In his standard 'historical materialist' treatment of the 'Jewish question' published in 1931, Otto Heller had contended that the disappearance of the Jewish people through assimilation was an inevitable and desirable process.[73] Those who tried to prevent this, such as Zionists, were acting against the movement of history. Yet Ilberg was arguing unequivocally that 'das Jüdische' should be retained!

What is more, he was doing so as a Communist who openly referred to himself as a Jew. It was much more usual for German Communists of

Jewish descent either to define themselves as such, or to deny that they were Jewish at all. The justification for the latter being that Jewishness was purely a matter of religious confession and, as 'the opiate of the masses', religion should be anathema to any decent Communist. In his letter, Ilberg was clearly exhibiting a personal standpoint, which took him beyond Marxist-Leninist orthodoxy.

The memoirs of Bruno Retzlaff-Kresse, another German Communist exile in Manchester, indicate that Ilberg was not only active in the League. He was among the Communist exiles in Manchester who used every opportunity to address (in English) local Leftist groups, such as trade-unions, Labour Party branches, and the Left Book Club.[74] In late 1946, after most of the émigré groups had been dissolved, Ilberg still attended meetings of an organisation with the name 'Deutsche Antifaschisten, Manchester'. On 19th October, he read from, and elucidated, parts of Heinrich Heine's *Deutschland, ein Wintermärchen*.[75]

With the possible exception of 'Deutsche Juden', it could be said that, whilst in the UK, Ilberg remained within the borders set by the KPD. He was an obedient servant of the Party, and used every opportunity to propagate its position on fascism, and its general philosophy. The major shifts in his world-view had occurred prior to 1939, such as his commitment to, and then abandonment of, Zionism. For this reason, his years in England may seem rather colourless in comparison with those that preceded them.

This, however, is only an exploratory study of Ilberg. Other sources, such as the archive of the Czech Refugee Trust Fund held at the Public Record Office, Kew, and documents relating to the KPD and Free German League of Culture at SAPMO in Berlin might augment, or even explode, the impression I have given of him. In the meantime, I hope to have provided a taste of the background and exile experience of a hitherto disregarded émigré; outlining the practical and personal hindrances Ilberg faced in the UK, at the same time as drawing attention to his contributions to exile-culture, some of which — such as 'Schriftstellernöte' — deserve wider recognition.

Notes
[1] I am grateful to many people for assisting me with this article: to Professor Ian Wallace, for inviting me to contribute to the *Yearbook*; to Frau Hahn at the Deutsche Bibliothek, Deutsches Exilarchiv 1933-1945, Frankfurt/M. (the holdings of which are indicated by EB), and to Frau Möller and Frau Wolf, archivists of the Werner-Ilberg-Archiv (WIA) and

Heinz-Worner-Archiv of the Stiftung Archiv der Akademie der Künste in Berlin; to Dr. Ulrich Schwarz at the Niedersächsisches Staatsarchiv in Wolfenbüttel, and to the town archivist in Wolfenbüttel; to William Abbey, Dr. Charmian Brinson, Ludwig Meyer, Professor J. M. Ritchie, and Harold Ross in the UK; to Professors Ursula Adam and Heinz Kamnitzer, Jan Koplowitz, Heinz Worner and Frau Wolf, Basri and Gülay Kuran in Berlin; and to the Department of German, King's College London, for the provision of a research grant which enabled me to travel to Berlin. I was unsuccessful in my attempt to contact the executors of Wener Ilberg's literary estate, Ursula and Dieter Gomolka.

2 The WIA contains several drafts of *Grenzüberschreitungen*. All quotations in this article, however, refer to the manuscript with the shelf-mark WIA 142/2, which Ilberg submitted to the Mitteldeutscher Verlag, Halle in 1978. The archive also includes correspondence between Ilberg and Mitteldeutscher Verlag (WIA 142/9) concerning the proposed publication of *Grenzüberschreitungen*. This informs us that, although he agreed on the 12th June 1974 to complete three hundred pages within approximately one year, he did not finish his manuscript until the Summer of 1978. In a letter dated 6th September 1978, Ilberg was told that the publishers were not satisfied with the draft and believed that he would need outside assistance to produce a publishable version. There proved, however, to be no time for a collective rewriting of *Grenzüberschreitungen*, as Ilberg died on the 30th December 1978.

3 *Grenzüberschreitungen*, p. 305.

4 (Leipzig: VEB Bibliographisches Institut, 1974), pp. 235-6.

5 Horst Haase and others, *Geschichte der Literatur der Deutschen Demokratischen Republik*, Geschichte der Deutschen Literatur von den Anfängen bis zur Gegenwart, 11 (Berlin: Volk und Wissen, 1976).

6 Walter A. Berendsohn, *Die humanistische Front. Einführung in die deutsche Emigrantenliteratur*, vol. 1: *Von 1933 bis zum Kriegsausbruch 1939* (Zurich: Europa, 1946, reprint Worms: Heintz, 1978); vol. 2: *Vom Kriegsausbruch 1939 bis Ende 1946* (Worms: Heintz, 1978); Wilhelm Sternfeld, *Deutsche Exil-Literatur 1933-1945. Eine Bio-Bibliographie* (Heidelberg: Lambert Schneider, 2. verb. u. stark erw. Aufl., 1970).

7 *Exil in der Tschechoslowakei, in Großbritannien, Skandinavien und Palästina*, ed. by Ludwig Hoffmann and others, Kunst und Literatur im antifaschistischen Exil 1933-1945 in sieben Bänden, 5, 2nd edn (Leipzig: Reclam, 1987).

8 Hans-Albert Walter, *Deutsche Exilliteratur 1933-1950*, 3 vols (Stuttgart: Metzler, 1978-1988).

9 Charmian Brinson and Marian Malet, 'Rudolf Olden in England', in *Literatur und Kultur des Exils in Großbritannien*, Zwischenwelt, 4, ed. by Siglinde Bolbecher and others (Vienna: Theodor Kramer Gesellschaft, 1995), pp. 193-214 (p. 208); William Abbey, '"Die Illusion genannt Deutscher Pen-Club". The Pen-German Group and the English Centre, 1933-45', in *Between Two Languages. German-speaking Exiles in Great Britain 1933-45*, ed. by William Abbey and others, Stuttgarter Arbeiten zur Germanistik (Stuttgart: Verlag Hans-Dieter Heinz und Akademischer Verlag, 1995), pp. 135-53 (p. 143).

10 Numerous articles by Ilberg are listed in *Bibliographische Kalenderblätter der Berliner Stadtbibliothek* (East Berlin: July-September 1966), Part III, pp. 25-9.

11 *Grenzüberschreitungen*, p. 297.

[12] Ibid., p. 207.

[13] Ibid., p. 190.

[14] 'Erinnerungen', *Beiträge zur Geschichte der Arbeiterbewegung*, 20 (1978), 540-63.

[15] *Geschichten aus dem Ölpapier* (Halle: Mitteldeutcher Verlag, 1972).

[16] *Memoiren. Die Erziehung des J. K. zum Kommunisten und Wissenschaftler*, 2nd edn (Berlin and Weimar: Aufbau, 1975).

[17] *Das war unser Leben. Erinnerungen und Dokumente zur Geschichte der Freien Deutschen Jugend in Großbritannien 1939-1946*, ed. by Alfred Fleischhacker and Holger Stoeker (Berlin: Neues Leben, 1996); Alice and Gerhard Zadek, *Mit dem letzten Zug nach England* (Berlin: Dietz, 1992).

[18] The main part of *Grenzüberschreitungen* ends with Ilberg's arrival in Britain. On a few occasions, however, he refers ahead to experiences in the UK. In the epilogue (pp. 305-8), he dwells on several incidents during his stay in Britain obviously considered to be especially significant. Ilberg also looked back on his exile years in the two short texts he contributed to the anthology *Hammer und Feder. Deutsche Schriftsteller aus ihrem Leben und Schaffen* , ed. by Karl Grünberg and others (Berlin: Tribüne, 1955): pp. 182-8 ('Wie meine Umerziehung begann'); pp. 189-205 ('Ernstes — heiter gesagt').

[19] *Grenzüberschreitungen*, p. 11.

[20] Werner Ilberg, *Rastlose Jahre* (Berlin: Neues Leben, 1948), p. 7.

[21] 'Biographien / Bibliographien', *Das Wort*, 4-5 (1937), 174.

[22] Wolfgang Brekle, *Schriftsteller im antifaschistischen Widerstand 1933-1945 in Deutschland* (Berlin and Weimar: Aufbau, 1985), p. 40.

[23] I was made aware of this incident by Jan Koplowitz during an interview in Berlin.

[24] 'Fragebogen der Deutschen Akademie für Sprache und Dichtung (Darmstadt)' (EB 75/177 - A. IV. 9).

[25] *Grenzüberschreitungen*, pp. 271f.

[26] *Exil in der Tschechoslowakei, in Großbritannien*, p. 85.

[27] *Exil und Asyl. Antifaschistische deutsche Literatur in der Tschechoslowakei 1933-1938*, ed. by Miroslav Beck and Jiří Vesely (Berlin: Volk und Wissen, 1981), p. 341.

[28] These are listed in Lieselotte Maas, *Handbuch der deutschen Exilpresse 1933-1945*, 4 vols (Munich: Hanser, 1976-1990).

[29] *Das Wort*, 12 (1937), 15-6.

[30] In an essay 'Jüdische Politik und Sowjetunion' which appeared in the Czech-based Jewish-nationalist *Jüdische Revue* (11 (1937), 671-2), Ilberg even justified the persecution of alleged Zionists in the Soviet Union. He criticises delegates at the recent twentieth

Zionist congress for being preoccupied with the situation of the Soviet Zionists, whilst remaining silent on anti-Semitism in Central Europe and Poland; this was misplaced, since Jews were otherwise thriving as individuals and as a people in the Soviet Union. In any case — Ilberg contends — 'credible reports' show that no-one is condemned in the Soviet Union because of their convictions, 'sondern nur um staatsfeindlicher Taten willen.' (p. 672). Implicit in this, of course, is the belief that the charges against the accused had a factual basis.

31 'Die Beiden Seiten des Expressionismus', *Das Wort*, 6 (1938), 94-8. The later article was one of two reviews of Remarque's *Die Kameraden* which appeared in the July 1938 issue of *Das Wort* under the title 'Zwei Stimmen zu einem Buch' (129-34). The other critic, F. C. Weiskopf, castigated Remarque for depicting the decadence of bourgeois society without pointing a way out of it. Ilberg's review was a good deal more sympathetic. In *Grenzüberschreitungen* (p. 256), he speculates that the editors of *Das Wort* decided to print it alongside Weiskopf's review, because it exemplified the kind of fraternity towards bourgeois colleagues like Remarque which was called for in the era of the *Volksfront.*

32 'Die Beiden Seiten des Expressionismus', p. 95.

33 Ibid., p. 98.

34 'Fragebogen der Menne Gruppe', undated (EB 75/177 — D. II. 2).

35 *Grenzüberschreitungen*, p. 295.

36 A marriage certificate in the restitution files of the local government in Braunschweig (4 Nds Zg. 41/1992 Nr. 1080) is dated 10th May 1939.

37 'Fragebogen der Thomas Mann-Gruppe', dated 1/4/1942 (EB 75/177 — D. II. 2).

38 It is possible that Ilberg owed his rescue not only to Schmidt and his co-workers, but also to the Exil-PEN club and its English supporters. He had been seventh in a list of seventeen German and Austrian writers who were still in Prague on the 3rd November 1938, and whose escape Exil-PEN was eager to facilitate. (Item 457 in *Der deutsche PEN-Club im Exil 1933-1948. Eine Ausstellung der Deutschen Bibliothek Frankfurt am Main* (Frankfurt/M.: Buchhändler-Vereinigung, 1980), p. 313).

39 In *Grenzüberschreitungen* (p. 296), Ilberg notes that his first lodging in Britain was in a garage provided by a 'Schriftstellerin Mitchell'. Since he only gives her surname, and because there is no evidence of a female writer named Mitchell assisting refugees, one can only speculate as to her identity. But it is most likely that she was the crime-writer Gladys Mitchell who was teaching at a girls' school in Hanwell, London at the time Ilberg arrived in the UK.

40 Ilberg to Exil-PEN (Rudolf Olden), around 6th December 1938 (EB 75/175 — 846).

41 *Hammer und Feder*, pp. 184-8.

42 These might be available in the relevant sections of the Stiftung Archiv der Parteien und Massenorganisationen der DDR im Bundesarchiv in Berlin (SAPMO).

43 'Become a member of the FREE GERMAN LEAGUE OF CULTURE', *Freie Deutsche Kultur*, October 1944, 14.

44 'Fragebogen der Menne Gruppe'.

45 'Fragebogen der Thomas Mann-Gruppe'.

46 Ilberg is not mentioned in any general treatments of internment, nor in Michael Seyfert's detailed examinations of literary activity in the camps: *Im Niemandsland. Deutsche Exilliteratur in britischer Internierung. Ein unbekanntes Kapitel der Kulturgeschichte des Zweiten Weltkrieges* (Berlin: Arsenal, 1984); '"His Majesty's Most Loyal Internees". The Internment and Deportation of German and Austrian Refugees as "enemy aliens". Historical, cultural and literary aspects', in *Exile in Great Britain. Refugees from Hitler's Germany*, ed. by Gerhard Hirschfeld (Leamington Spa: Berg, 1984), pp. 163-93 (pp. 180-7).

47 'Fragebogen der Thomas Mann-Gruppe'.

48 'Schriftstellernöte', in *Zehn Jahre Kulturbarbarei im Dritten Reich, zehn Jahre freie deutsche Kultur im Exil* (London: Free German League of Culture in Great Britain, 1943), pp. 52-4 (p. 54).

49 *Hammer und Feder*, p. 183.

50 Ilberg to Sternfeld, 12th October 1942 (EB 75/177 — A. I. 2).

51 Ilberg to Sternfeld, 3rd July 1944 (EB 75/177 — A. I. 2).

52 *Freier Deutscher Kulturbund-Nachrichten* (London), April 1944, p. 8.

53 J. M. Ritchie, 'Theatre and Exile in Great Britain', in J. M. Ritchie, *German Exiles. British Perspectives* (New York: Peter Lang, 1997), pp. 96-128 (p. 123).

54 'Tod und Leben: der Sowjetunion zum 25. Jahrestag' and 'Gorki', in *Und sie bewegt sich doch! Freie deutsche Dichtung* (London: Verlag Freie Deutsche Jugend, 1943), pp. 13-5.

55 'Die Umstellung', in *Weg durch die Nacht. Erzählungen*, ed. by Jan Petersen (London: Free German League of Culture in Great Britain, 1944), pp. 3-8.

56 In *Kleine Sammlung 1946* (London: Free German League of Culture in Great Britain, 1946), pp. 4-8.

57 *Zehn Jahre Kulturbarbarei im Dritten Reich*, pp. 52-4.

58 'German Literature in Exile', *Freie Deutsche Kultur*, March 1942, 8.

59 'Die Stimme in der Wüste', in *Verbannte und Verbrannte* (London: Free German League of Culture in Great Britain, 1942), pp. 17-19.

60 'Schiller und die Idee der Freiheit', in *Freier Deutscher Kulturbund-Nachrichten*, November 1944, 6.

61 '"Der Güter höchstens dürfen wir verteid'gen"', in Karl Wolff, *Schiller und die Idee der Freiheit* (London: Free German League of Culture in Great Britain, 1945), pp. 8-10.

62 *Grenzüberschreitungen*, p. 276.

63 *Freie Tribüne* (2 [1944], 10), for example, mentions a 'Feier für Romain Rolland' as having taken place in the League clubhouse. The first issue of the same periodical in 1945 included an essay on Rolland by Wilhelm Unger.

64 Ilberg to Sternfeld, 3rd July 1944 (EB 75/177 — A. I. 2). Rather strangely, according to Christopher Date, archivist at the British Museum, there are no records of Ilberg ever having used the British Library.

65 *Traum und Tat. Romain Rolland in seinem Verhältnis zu Deutschland und zur Sowjet-Union* (Halle: Mitteldeutscher Verlag, 1950), republished in 1951 by Rütten und Loening as *Romain Rolland*; *Der schwere Weg*; *Leben und Werk Romain Rollands* (Schwerin: Petermänken, 1955).

66 *Freie Deutsche Kultur*, *Freie Tribüne* and their antecedents generally only contain notices for, and reviews of, events held in London. One exception is a letter from Manchester which was printed in *Freie Deutsche Kultur* in February 1942 (p. 4). However, since Ilberg is not mentioned by name, this is of little relevance to the present context. Alice and Gerhard Zadek write about the League in Manchester in their autobiographical *Mit dem letzten Zug nach England*. But although they mention the vice-chairman of the branch, a Dr. Hans Nathan, Ilberg's name does not crop up.

67 *Grenzüberschreitungen*, pp. 306-7.

68 *Rastlose Jahre*, p. 7.

69 Werner Röder, *Die deutschen sozialistischen Exilgruppen in Großbritannien 1940-1945. Ein Beitrag zur Geschichte des Widerstandes gegen den Nationalsozialismus*, Schriftenreihe des Forschungsinstitutes der Friedrich-Ebert-Stiftung, 58 (Bonn and Bad Godesberg: Neue Gesellschaft, 1973), pp. 208-10.

70 'Schriftstellernöte', p. 53.

71 *Grenzüberschreitungen*, p. 307.

72 'Deutsche Juden', *Freie Tribüne*, January 1944, 12f.

73 Otto Heller, *Der Untergang des Judentums. Die Judenfrage. Ihre Kritik. Ihre Lösung durch den Sozialismus* (Vienna and Berlin: Verlag für Literatur und Politik, 1931).

74 Bruno Retzlaff-Kresse, *Illegalität — Kerker — Exil: Erinnerungen aus dem antifaschistischen Kampf* (Berlin: Dietz, 1980), p. 231.

75 Retzlaff-Kresse, p. 317.

Charmian Brinson / N. A. Furness†

'Im politischen Niemandsland der Heimatlosen, Staatenlosen, Konfessionslosen, Portemonnaielosen...'[1] : Otto Lehmann-Russbueldt in British Exile

This article considers the life and work of the exiled pacifist and writer, Otto Lehmann-Russbueldt, during the 18 years he spent in British exile, from 1933 to 1951. It examines his efforts on behalf of world peace, in pre-war, wartime and post-war conditions, as well as the ways in which both he and his work were marked by the circumstances of a life in exile.

> This essay is dedicated to the memory of N. A. Furness (†31 December 1995) to whose researches it is greatly indebted.

Among the thousands of men and women to be arrested by the National Socialist regime in the hours following the Reichstag fire of 27 January 1933 was the sixty-year-old pacifist, writer and journalist Otto Lehmann-Russbueldt.[2] Remarkably, he was released after only ten days, a fate in marked contrast to that suffered by fellow prisoners Carl von Ossietzky and Erich Mühsam and one attributed by his elder daughter Ingeborg Wolske (née Lehmann) to official confusion about his name.[3] Nevertheless, it was clear that, given his past political record, Lehmann-Russbueldt would henceforth be in danger in Germany and that his emigration was imperative.

His escape from Germany on 30 March 1933 took place under hazardous circumstances: disguising himself as one of a group of psychiatric patients out on a walk, he was escorted across the Dutch border by two Catholic priests, members of the 'Friedensbund deutscher Katholiken'. 'Mein Vater erzählte mir später lachend', Ingeborg Wolske would recall, 'daß er immer mit dem Kopf gewackelt und vor sich hingelallt hat.'[4] In Holland, where in August 1933 he learned of his inclusion on the first 'Ausbürgerungsliste',[5] he took refuge with friends from the peace movement; but later that year, on 30 October, he made a further move to England, 'um meine Aufklärungsarbeit über den preußischen Militarismus fortzusetzen'.[6]

Such work was, in fact, the stuff of Lehmann-Russbueldt's entire life. Prior to his exile, he had played a leading role in the German peace and civil rights movements, being a co-founder in November 1914 of the 'Bund Neues Vaterland'. Standing for international reconciliation, the 'Bund' had attracted such diverse members as Albert Einstein, the former German ambassador to London Fürst Lichnowsky, Karl Liebknecht and the post-war mayor of West Berlin, Ernst Reuter. Soon after the First World War it had changed its name to 'Deutsche Liga für Menschenrechte' and for some years Lehmann-Russbueldt served as its Secretary, devoting himself particularly to such causes as Franco-German and German-Polish understanding and, one exceptionally close to his heart, to the ideal of a United States of Europe.[7] During the 1920s, he also began to concern himself increasingly with questions of the international arms trade, peace and disarmament, propagating his ideas in articles, lectures and books such as *Die blutige Internationale der Rüstungsindustrie* (1929) which found a worldwide readership.[8]

Because of the international nature of his work, Lehmann-Russbueldt was not short of ready-made contacts in Britain. He had originally visited Britain in 1920 when his host had been the future Lord Noel-Buxton, an important associate of his in later British exile, and his acquaintance with the Quaker Corder Catchpool also dated from this time. Lord Cecil, the President of the League of Nations Union, was another very significant contact of his; it was Cecil who supported Lehmann-Russbueldt's entry to Britain in 1933 and took an enduring interest in him and his work thereafter. Most vital of all to Lehmann-Russbueldt, however, was undoubtedly his acquaintance and later friendship with the former editor of *The Times*, Wickham Steed, 'mein Beschützer und Meister in diesem widerspruchsvollen Volk'.[9] Steed, whom he had met in Geneva in September 1926 on the eve of Germany's entry into the League of Nations, not only actively encouraged his work in exile but also helped to organise financial support for him. Moreover, in the spring of 1939, he and his wife Violet took Lehmann-Russbueldt's younger daughter Yvonne into their own family.

Lehmann-Russbueldt who, in his *Wann ist der Krieg aus?*, observed that he found himself 'im derzeitig größten aller Vaterländer [...] wo man gar nicht Vaterland sagt, sondern bloß "this country"',[10] had considerable respect for his host country and indeed an appreciation of many of its characteristics: Yvonne Wells (née Lehmann) recently recalled both her father's admiration for British democracy and his liking for British politeness.[11] Yet the fact that he did not feel in any way at home in Britain is clear from a letter from 1934 where he lamented that, were it not for occasional pleasures like music, 'würde ich hier in diesem Lande vollendeter Correktheit und Nüchternheit umkommen'.[12] And undoubtedly the life and work in England of this elderly exile was further burdened by communication problems; for although he came to read English with considerable ease, 'his spoken English was non-existent'.[13]

Though Lehmann-Russbueldt came to Britain with the aim of alerting the British to the threat to world peace posed by the Nazi regime, the task was no easy one for him or like-minded exiles. Disclosures of the German secret rearmament programme, for instance, that appeared in the *Sunday Referee*[14] and were raised in the House of Commons in February 1934 (based on material provided by Lehmann-Russbueldt and his fellow campaigner Dora Fabian), were dismissed as exaggerated by the majority of British MPs. 'Nur Winston Churchill signalisierte am 8. März 1934 die drohende Gefahr im House of Commons,' Lehmann-Russbueldt would record. 'Sein Warnruf verwehte gänzlich.'[15] In 1936, in an article for an exile journal, he considered where the causes of this British shortsightedness might lie:

> Es kommen verschiedene Umstände zusammen, daß man in England die Tücken der Nazis nicht durchschaut. Man kann sich nicht denken, daß Deutschland noch einmal so wahnsinnig sein sollte, mit dem British Empire anzubinden. Hinzu kommt, daß die Labour Leute dem inneren politischen Gegner nicht Recht geben wollen. Winston Churchill hat einmal gesagt, daß alle speziellen englischen Schmerzen verschwinden würden, wenn man das Inselland von Europa fortlegen könnte. Das trifft den Nagel auf den Kopf. Jede politische Überlegung — ob von rechts oder von links — ist im geheimen von der Vorstellung beherrscht: 'Mögen sich doch die verrückten Kontinentalen gegenseitig totschlagen; was geht uns das an?'[16]

Despite such fundamental difficulties, however, Lehmann-Russbueldt worked unremittingly to communicate his message, even while he was afraid of the possible consequences for his wife and younger daughter, still in Berlin. 'Die kleinste Unvorsichtigkeit kann sich furchtbar an meiner Frau rächen,' he would tell his friend J. B. Hugenholtz in July 1933.[17] He wrote numerous articles, more than 50 for the German exile press alone — in particular for the *Pariser Tageblatt* (later *Pariser Tageszeitung*) and for *Sozialistische Warte* — on the plight of political prisoners in Germany, on the armaments industry, on German militarism and on the future shape of Europe. And, despite the language problems, he managed to place articles in British journals, too, in the *Contemporary Review*,[18] for instance, whose editor, G. P. Gooch, was encouraging to refugee writers. One of the publishing successes in which Lehmann-Russbueldt took the greatest satisfaction was the appearance in mid-1934 of two articles, under Wickham Steed's name, in Steed's journal *The Nineteenth Century and After*, on secret German experiments into bacteriological and gas warfare carried out in the Paris and London underground systems; these articles were based on material copied from the records of the Junkers concern at Dessau that Lehmann-Russbueldt obtained through a German contact.[19]

In fact, despite his desire for caution, Lehmann-Russbueldt had been identified by the German agent Hans Wesemann[20] as being connected with these disclosures and indeed had been described in one of Wesemann's reports as 'die intellektuelle Seele des Londoner Hetzkreises gegen Deutschland [...], der trotz seines Alters und seiner Zerfahrenheit eine gewisse Leitung der übrigen in den Händen hat'.[21] Political exiles in London, as elsewhere, were well aware of the National Socialist espionage network operating in the countries of emigration. Thus, by 1935, when his highly controversial book *Germany's Air Force* was due to appear,[22] Lehmann-Russbueldt deemed it essential to bring his wife and younger daughter to safety in England. (They finally arrived on 1 July 1935.) Certainly Lehmann-Russbueldt took pains to delay the publication of *Germany's Air Force* until after his family had left Germany. However:

> Irgendwie hatte der deutsche Nachrichtendienst, anscheinend durch eine verfrühte buchhändlerische Anzeige, Wind von dem Erscheinen des Buches bekommen, sodaß man nur am Ostertag 21. April 1935 einen als englischen Kriminalbeamten mit falschem Ausweis versehenen Nazispion in die Londoner Wohnung schickte, der in meiner Abwesenheit meine Papiere beschlagnahmen wollte. Ein benachbarter Freund vereitelte das Manöver, das nicht das erste und nicht das letzte seiner Art in England war.[23]

If this was one kind of difficulty, admittedly a dramatic one, associated with the books Lehmann-Russbueldt wrote in Britain, it was by no means the only kind. Above all, the conditions for writing were very far from ideal, as he recounted to the Hugenholtz family:

> An 2 Büchern arbeite ich [...] Es geht alles nur mit den größten Schwierigkeiten. Vor allem, weil die Geldmittel fehlen, um in Ruhe zu arbeiten, da gleichzeitig den Freunden in Deutschland geholfen werden muß.[24]

The history of two further pre-war works, *Neues Deutschtum* and *Der strategische Imperativ*, both of them prophesying the total destruction of

Europe by the 'furor teutonicus', illustrates some of the problems of producing political literature in turbulent times.[25] *Neues Deutschtum*, on which he was working in 1937, took so long to find a publisher that the *Anschluss* intervened, necessitating a significant revision of the manuscript. The work, supported by a grant from Prince Hubertus zu Löwenstein's American Guild for German Cultural Freedom, was subsequently accepted by a Paris publishing house, but:

> Die Fertigstellung des Buches hat sich so verzögert, daß es gerade in die Grenze des Überganges vom sogenannten Frieden zum Krieg fiel. Dadurch, daß es in Paris gedruckt wurde, trat eine weitere Verzögerung in der Ankunft des Buches hier ein. Ich habe mir überlegt, ob ich in einem beigefügten Blatt die veränderte Situation berücksichtigen soll. Vorläufig ist das nicht nötig [...][26]

As for *Der strategische Imperativ*, Lehmann-Russbueldt was afraid that the same fate would befall it, writing to Löwenstein in July 1938 of his desire to complete the work before it, too, could be rendered obsolete by events.[27] By March 1939, in fact, he was hopeful that it might appear in the Penguin *6d* series,[28] where it would have achieved a wide readership, but these hopes were not fulfilled. In the end Lehmann-Russbueldt had to content himself with the publication merely of extracts from the work in *Sozialistische Warte*.[29]

* * * * *

By the time Lucia and Yvonne Lehmann arrived in London in July 1935, Otto Lehmann-Russbueldt was already a resident at his third London address. Initially he had found accommodation in a house in Gloucester Place, London W1, where, as it happened, a room had also been taken by the young exiled socialist Dora Fabian who began to assist him on a number of antifascist projects.[30] On 9 December 1933, Lehmann-Russbueldt was conveying to Hugenholtz something of the urgency that he felt and of the sort of conditions under which he was living:

> Ich arbeite aber viel mehr, muß es tun, denn die Zeit drängt immer mehr. Hier ist kein Garten, ich komme nicht einmal jeden Tag in den Park. Dafür habe ich jeden Tag ein Bad, sonst wäre es nicht zum Aushalten. Aber ich muß hier bleiben, weil man hier ganz andere Verbindungen aufnehmen kann.[31]

From Gloucester Place, he moved at the beginning of 1934 to become a subtenant of the refugee writer Fritz Gross,[32] in a house at 3 Regent Square in Bloomsbury,[33] and here too, in Gross himself and in other residents and visitors, he found kindred spirits. In regular correspondence with a friend, Gross would often comment upon the cordial relations between himself and his tenant, 'den beiden intellektuellen Schwerarbeitern'[34] in the house, reporting in June 1934, for instance: 'Mit L.R. stehe ich gut und freundschaftlich, er war bei der Vorlesung mit [of Gross's unpublished novel 'Wien'] [...] Im übrigen gebe ich ihm Anregungen für Arbeiten und er macht auch was in der Richtung.'[35]

Lehmann-Russbueldt's next move was merely to a house across the square where he rented two rooms and, as Yvonne Wells remembers, lived in near penury:

> The first morning after our arrival, O. L.-R. bought me an exercise book which cost a penny. I knew he had but one pound in all the wide world, and that there were 240 pennies to a pound. My exercise book seemed a great extravagance.[36]

But his financial difficulties in exile were as nothing compared to the fact that his (second) wife Lucia, to whom he was devoted, had been diagnosed as suffering from Hodgkin's Disease. She died in France, after much suffering, in July 1937, aged only 30. Yvonne, meanwhile, was cared for in a London children's home until being invited to live with the Steeds.

During these first exile years, moreover, even the prolongation of Lehmann-Russbueldt's permit to reside in Britain seems to have been far from certain. He had had his German passport impounded even before his flight from Germany, and travelled initially on Czech papers, secured through his old acquaintance with the Czech President Masaryk. Early correspondence between Lehmann-Russbueldt and the British Home Office records a series of difficulties caused by the fact that the dates on his Czech papers, on the one hand, and his Home Office permit, on the other, frequently failed to coincide.[37]

Then, early in April 1935, his young comrade in exile, Dora Fabian, and her flatmate Mathilde Wurm, were found dead in their Bloomsbury flat in circumstances that have never been fully explained, causing a flurry of anxiety within the émigré community in Britain and an increase in British official attention towards the refugees;[38] and it is probably no coincidence that Home Office and Security Service interest in Lehmann-Russbueldt seem also to have intensified at around this time. In the Home Office, in response to one of Lehmann-Russbueldt's regular requests for an extension, a handwritten report, dated 6 April 1935, was drawn up on his financial situation: a fund (of £45, with a further £20 outstanding) had been raised by the Peace Council to support his work, it was recorded. The jacket of Lehmann-Russbueldt's Home Office file bears a minute from the same date, commenting: 'It is satisfactory that his support is assured but I think we should know a little more about his plans.' These plans — to the effect that he wished to remain in Britain for the present and to undertake a revision of his manuscript *Germany's Air Force* as well as a study of the armaments industry — were elicited from him later that month and the desired extension granted. Yet it is perhaps not uninteresting in this connection that on 4 June 1935 MI5 expressed a wish to review Lehmann-Russbueldt's papers (no details of their observations are available).

On the other hand, it should be recalled that Lehmann-Russbueldt's position in Britain was undoubtedly strengthened by the existence of powerful British sponsors. Thus, in October 1934, when one of his extension applications had been rejected, Lord Cecil had written to the Home Office in his support, while Lehmann-Russbueldt himself could claim: 'As a writer I am working for the aims of the League of Nations in collaboration with Lord Robert Cecil, Mr Wickham Steed, Philip Noel Baker [...] Professor Gooch, Editor of the Contemporary Review and the National Peace Council.'[39]

Lucia's death in mid-1937 must have represented the nadir of Lehmann-Russbueldt's years of exile. A letter to Willi Eichler from the end of that year testifies to his feeling of 'Ohnmacht gegenüber dem sogenannten Schicksal' and, uncharacteristically, expresses deep discouragement.[40] On his return to England, after having been with Lucia in France at the time of her death, Lehmann-Russbueldt moved into a flat in Oppidans Road (near Primrose Hill) where he shared rather more spacious accommodation — three rooms, bathroom and kitchen — than he had previously enjoyed. Money remained a problem, of course: Yvonne Wells recalls how her father would postpone his shopping until Saturday evening in order to take advantage of the fact that food was then sold off cheaply.[41]

An unusually detailed account of Lehmann-Russbueldt's circumstances at that time, as well as of his work in the first years of exile, is contained in a statement of means he submitted to the Home Office in October 1938 in support of an application for permanent residence in Britain. Since 1933, so he reported, he had earned a total of £72 from his books, that is for *Germany's Air Force*, 1935; *Landesverteidigung ohne Profit*, 1936; *Wer rettet Europa? Die wehrpolitische Lage der kleinen Staaten*, 1936; and for a Danish translation of one of his earlier works.[42] Articles in journals had earned him a bare £18.10.0 over the same period.

His major sources of income, however, were scholarships 'granted by English and American friends', amounting to £12 per month (around £350 in today's figures), for research into the League of Nations and Collective Security, as well as a further scholarship of £150 awarded him in late 1936 by the Nobel Prize Committee in Oslo for work on 'Why the disarmament conference failed'. As for his outgoings, so Lehmann-Russbueldt informed the Home Office, 'my standard of living is accordingly [sic]'.[43]

In the event, Lehmann-Russbueldt did not obtain the status of permanent resident at that time since his financial position was considered 'risky'.[44] It would not be long, however, before a Home Office minute would note resignedly: 'The Czechs will not renew his doc[umen]t [...] The new Czechoslovakia must presumably disown him and we are stuck with him.'[45]

From Lehmann-Russbueldt's extensive correspondence, it is clear that it was above all his work that sustained him through this critical period in his life. A Circular to the National Peace Congress of 1935, drawn up by Lehmann-Russbueldt in the name of 'several German refugees', listed some of his main concerns in the pre-war exile years, namely political, religious and racial persecution in Germany, abuses of criminal justice and harsh prison conditions there, German rearmament and German agents abroad.[46] Lehmann-Russbueldt's efforts through the Society of Friends, for instance, and in conjunction with Lord Cecil, on behalf of political prisoners in Germany — such as Hans Litten, Fritz Küster and other pacifists, socialists and radicals — have been documented in an earlier article,[47] as has the active part he played in the campaign on behalf of the imprisoned *Weltbühne* editor, Carl von Ossietzky.[48] Ossietzky's fate — he died of tuberculosis in 1938 after much suffering at the hands of the National Socialists — continued to haunt Lehmann-Russbueldt for years after the event, as is evident from post-war articles on the subject (in the *Contemporary Review* for example, in 1946[49] and the Berlin *Tagesspiegel* in 1949[50]) and from a passage in a letter to Wilhelm Sternfeld of 25 June 1956 in which he contended: 'Es ist ein Skandal für West-D[eu]tschl[an]d, daß es nicht gelang, für ihn dauernd an seinem Todestag ein Gedenken auf ihn zu richten. Ich habe das damals von London aus versucht.'[51]

Lehmann-Russbueldt demonstrated a similarly enduring concern in the misfortunes of the fiercely anti-Nazi journalist Berthold Jacob, kidnapped by National Socialist agents — Hans Wesemann among them — in Switzerland in 1935; held in and then released from a Berlin prison later

that same year following international protests; and finally abducted by
German agents for a second time in 1941 (he died in Berlin in 1944). In
the wake of the first kidnapping incident, Lehmann-Russbueldt contacted
the Society of Friends, among others, to alert them to the case,[52] while a
letter to Lord Noel-Buxton, published in the *Pariser Tageblatt*, urged him
to intervene with the German government on Jacob's behalf.[53] As he
explained to Hugenholtz, Jacob's kidnapping represented one of a whole
series of blows he had to endure at that time:

> Ich erlebe — wie alle, es ist nichts Besonderes — immer ernste oder tragische
> Dinge. Im Sommer wird Erich Mühsam, ein liebster Freund und ganz ganz reiner
> Charakter, zu Tode gefoltert, jetzt läßt sich Berthold Jacob, ein treuester und
> klügster Kamerad, gefangen nehmen, bald darauf gehen Mathilde Wurm und Dora
> Fabian freiwillig in den Tod.[54]

Berthold Jacob was, by general consensus, an 'überhaupt nicht leicht zu
behandelnder Mann', as Lehmann-Russbueldt would maintain to Karl
Retzlaw,[55] with a tendency to create enemies; moreover his unexpected
release from prison in September 1935 had rendered him politically
suspect in some sections of the overwrought German exile community.
When, therefore, in 1941, desperate letters began arriving from 'Marcel
Rollin' (Jacob's pseudonym) from France, Spain and finally Portugal,
pleading financial distress and appealing for help in obtaining an overseas
visa, it proved difficult for Lehmann-Russbueldt and Retzlaw to mobilise
any support for him. In particular, exiled SPD politicians in Britain
evinced a total unwillingness to vouch for Jacob in the matter of a visa,
indeed as Retzlaw reported to Jacob on 30 August 1941, 'der
Parteivorstand der SP verbreitet Verleumdungen über Dich'.[56] Lehmann-
Russbueldt's efforts to prevail upon Victor Schiff and Hans Vogel led
merely to an angry dispute between them.[57] Nor did it prove any easier to
raise money on Jacob's behalf, as Retzlaw explained:

> Lehmann und ich liefen tagelang herum danach. Lehmann setzt sich sehr für Dich
> ein, aber nicht einen Penny kriegen wir. Es geht uns allen nicht besonders gut. Wir
> sind froh, das Brot zu bekommen, und das ist noch bitter genug.[58]

Jacob's repeat kidnapping by Nazi agents occurred in Lisbon in
September 1941. A letter from Lehmann-Russbueldt to W. F. Stein, from
1947, suggests that a British visa may finally have been obtained for Jacob
but that it came too late.[59] By 1942, in any case, Lehmann-Russbueldt
seems to have felt it incumbent upon him to mount a defence of Jacob,
initially in the form of a 'Rundschreiben':

Diese Skizze über B.J. Tätigkeit als Schriftsteller und politische[n] Kämpfer gegen den deutschen Militarismus hat den Zweck, über seine Person aufzuklären, nachdem allerlei Mißverständnisse über ihn entstanden sind. Wenn die gefährliche Wirkung dieser Mißverständnisse anhält, werde ich ein Untersuchungs- und Schiedsverfahren innerhalb der deutschen Emigration beantragen.[60]

It is interesting to note that, as with Ossietzky, Lehmann-Russbueldt continued to be preoccupied with Jacob for years after, recalling the treatment of 'unseren Freund Besa' (as Jacob was known) at the hands of the SPD in a letter to Retzlaw of January 1945,[61] and managing soon after the end of the war to trace a contact of Jacob's from his time in Lisbon.[62] In later years, there are references in Lehmann-Russbueldt's letters to assistance to Jacob's widow and, in 1954, to an article to mark the tenth anniversary of Jacob's death in the newly revived journal of the 'Deutsche Liga für Menschenrechte'.[63]

As this suggests, Lehmann-Russbueldt was uncommonly loyal to his friends; Yvonne Wells has recorded that he was also generous to a fault where fellow refugees were concerned (even if this led to hardship for himself and his family, as it frequently did).[64] In 1944, when his old friend Fritz Gross had become a virtual invalid, Lehmann-Russbueldt organised an 'Aktion' in the form of a collection of money under the discreet heading 'Sammlung für einen Emigrantenfreund'.[65] Such behaviour fits neatly, as it happens, with a memory of Yvonne Wells from her student days: 'Once at Oxford (and of course it would coincide with one of my own financial crises) I got an SOS from O. L.-R. "Send 2/6d. Fritz Gross [...] has angina. He needs milk."'[66] It was a gesture characteristic of the man which combined extreme kind-heartedness with a high degree of impracticality.

* * * * *

On 3 September 1939, the day Britain declared war on Germany, Lehmann-Russbueldt was listening to Chamberlain's radio broadcast to the nation with his friend and fellow tenant Bernhard Reichenbach. Turning to Reichenbach, he predicted: 'Dieser Krieg bedeutet die Auflösung des British Empire.'[67] More immediately for the refugees, the war exacerbated the difficulties of life in Britain: they were summoned before tribunals whose task it was to categorise them according to the degree of security risk they were perceived to represent. For tribunal purposes, Lehmann-Russbueldt received a statement of support from Lord Cecil who attested that he had 'always appeared to me to be a genuine worker for peace and, as such, politically hostile to the present Government of Germany; and I believe you to be an able as well as a very honest man'.[68] Appearing before Tribunal No. 6 on 5 December 1939, Lehmann-Russbueldt was placed in the unobjectionable 'C' category. Yet although at that stage in the war category 'C' refugees were still exempt from internment, by the following summer the situation had changed radically: the fall of France and the fear of an invasion of Britain led to the indiscriminate internment of aliens, including that of the 67-year old Otto Lehmann-Russbueldt. Thus, on 2 July 1940, he was arrested by a plain-clothes police officer — 'er war höflich und machte keinerlei Haussuchung' — and was initially held for two days at Kempton Park before being transported to Huyton by Grenadier Guards armed with bayonets.[69]

Huyton, where Lehmann-Russbueldt spent the best part of two months, was in fact a transit camp, set up on an unfinished council estate, where fellow internees included the writers Robert Neumann and Hans José Rehfisch, the politicians Hans Gottfurcht and Hans Ebeling, and other well-known figures in the refugee community such as Kuba (Kurt Barthel) and Kurt Joos. Enlightened public opinion in Britain was not slow in protesting against the internment of proven antifascists; and a letter, appearing in the *Manchester Guardian* on the subject on 25 July 1940, cited the case of Otto Lehmann-Russbueldt, together with those of Rudolf Olden, Wilhelm Necker and Friedrich Burschell among others, as examples of British misguidedness:

> Does not the internment of these men mean a very serious diminution of our ability
> at the right time to make effective appeal to the German people to throw off the yoke
> of their Nazi tyrants?[70]

In a report designed for Lord Lytton, the Chairman of the Advisory Council on Aliens, Lehmann-Russbueldt criticised the rough and ready conditions in Huyton, though acknowledging that definite improvements had followed the visits to the camp made by prominent British champions of the refugees like Eleanor Rathbone MP and the Bishop of Chichester. Not that this rendered the British policy of mass alien internment any more acceptable, he argued:

> Alle wesentlichen Milderungen der ursprünglichen Form des Internment konnten
> uns aber nicht darüber hinwegtäuschen, daß wir als Feinde des englischen Volkes
> behandelt wurden und in einer Lebensgemeinschaft mit Nazisympathisierenden
> eingesperrt waren. Alle Beschwichtigungen, unsere Einsperrung geschähe zu
> unserem Schutz, sie sei nichts unehrenhaftes, sie sollte nur dazu dienen, etwaige
> Hitleragenten zu erfassen, erschienen uns hohl und nichtig.[71]

On the other hand, some years later, Lehmann-Russbueldt would express his appreciation of the support the refugees had received, recalling how he had come to learn of it and been encouraged by it even under camp conditions:

> Die Psychose der Engländer aus Angst und Ärger über uns Deutsche führte zunächst dazu, daß man uns keine Zeitungen im Camp zu lesen gab. Es entstand ein Schleichhandel damit, wodurch wir erfuhren, in welcher Weise einige englische Männer und Frauen für uns kämpften [...] In Deutschland hätte ein solches Eintreten für 'Landesfeinde' dazu geführt, daß man die edlen Beschützer dazu sperrte.[72]

Lehmann-Russbueldt was released from Huyton for medical reasons on 22 August 1940; he had been diagnosed by the camp's Medical Officer as suffering, inter alia, from angina.[73] In fact, he had already appealed for release the month before on the grounds of his age and state of health and of his antifascist record, through the distinguished refugee lawyer, E. J. Cohn. Cohn had maintained of his client that there were few men in the world at the time 'who can claim to have been more farsighted with regard to the danger of German militarism'[74] while further weight had been added to the appeal by a letter from the Chargé d'Affaires at the Czech Legation and another from Wickham Steed. Steed's had concluded: 'To treat this man as though he were in any way suspect or likely to render any service, direct or indirect, to Hitler's Germany, strikes me as so serious an error of judgement as to be incomprehensible.'[75]

On 20 August 1940, the day on which Lehmann-Russbueldt's release was eventually agreed, there was an illuminating exchange of Home Office minutes on the subject. The first contended that 'the fewer of these political agitators at large during the War the better. (See S1051.) Refuse appeal.' An answering minute enquired: 'Even if they agitate against the Nazis?' The third minute, in the original hand, read simply 'Yes'.[76] File S1051, it should be noted, to which reference is made here (but which is no longer extant), was that of the beleaguered Berthold Jacob Salomon, better known as Berthold Jacob.[77]

It is interesting to compare the British nervousness apparent from this 1940 exchange with the more tempered views manifested in Home Office documents of the following year when, in November 1941, Lehmann-Russbueldt applied for official recognition as a 'Refugee from Nazi Oppression'. Although not automatically qualifying for such a status — being neither 'non-Aryan' nor registered with one of the recognised refugee organisations — his request was granted nonetheless 'on his whole record as known to us'.[78]

Shortly after his release from internment, Lehmann-Russbueldt married his third wife, Jeanette Saphir, a Jewish refugee from Vienna. Writing of the occasion to Wilhelm Sternfeld some eleven years later, Lehmann-Russbueldt recalled that, in spite of the customary exhortation to kiss the bride, 'bei uns unterließ man das, weil es Bomben hagelte, damals September 1940'.[79] His *Wann ist der Krieg aus?*, as it happens, includes a memorable first-hand description of Londoners fleeing from the bombing into the underground stations

> wenn zur Nacht sich die Anwohner zum Beziehen der Schlafstätten rüsten. Nicht alle finden Drahtgestelle. Alte Mütterchen und zitternde Greise breiten spärliche Decken und Packpapier auf dem kalten Steinboden. Dazwischen hocken junge Mütter mit Babies im Arm. Anfangs jauchzen die Kleinen fröhlich, wenn die Züge vorbeirasen. Aber dann weinen sie, wenn das Licht ihre Augen stundenlang blendet. Erst wenn der Verkehr ruht, können sie einige Stunden schlummern [...] Auch in ruhigen Wochen eilen sie in diese Schutzräume, weil sie sonst den Anspruch auf den Platz verlieren.[80]

Although, according to his daughter, Lehmann-Russbueldt himself was not unduly anxious about the Blitz, Jeanette was of a 'nervous disposition', such that the couple soon decided to move from London to Leicester.[81] Here Lehmann-Russbueldt spent a large part of the war though he continued to make frequent visits to London in connection with his work. The war depressed him, of course — in his memoirs he refers to a brief fit of melancholy he experienced after the Fall of Tobruk. But yet, so he adds: 'Ich gedachte all der bitteren Dinge, von denen sich eines an das andere gereiht hatte. Keines hatte mich mehr gebeugt, als ich aushalten konnte.'[82]

However, it would be untrue to say that the experiences of exile and war failed to take their toll on Lehmann-Russbueldt. Eugen Brehm recalls visiting him in 1943 or 1944 and finding

> this tall and virile man considerably aged. He was still very active and full of ideas, but some of them seemed to me rather unco-ordinated, even ill-digested; he showed signs of a permanent restlessness which I had not noticed before.[83]

Throughout the war, Lehmann-Russbueldt continued to write compulsively and to undertake speaking engagements when the opportunity arose, even volunteering to speak in English, for the first time, at the Leicester Rotary Club in June 1944.[84] He sent off letters and articles to English-language newspapers and journals, too, in an attempt to reach the British public, including a noteworthy piece that was published in the *Contemporary Review*, under his pseudonym 'Argus', entitled 'Friendly Enemy Aliens'; this was written as if by a British critic of the policy of interning 'loyal friends of this country and bitter foes of Hitler'.[85] Later letters — one appearing in the *Central European Observer* in September 1942 entitled 'Occupation of Germany'[86] and one, 'Germany Decentralised',[87] written jointly with Carl Herz, in the *Times* in March 1944 — looked ahead to the end of the war and beyond.

However, his most sustained publishing activity in wartime and the immediate post-war period was the series of 25 news sheets, his *Circular Letters of the Refugee/Rundbriefe des Flüchtlings*, produced between July 1941 and February/March 1948. In these, as in his letters to the press, he focused on serious current problems: the state of the German internal opposition, the treatment to be meted out to Hitler's supporters, Lord Vansittart's views on Germany, the identification of war aims, the formation of the National Committee of Free Germany in Moscow, the desirability of collective security, the Deprussianisation of Germany, the re-education of the Germans after the war and similar. These news sheets started life in a small way, with the first two issues addressing themselves merely 'an einige Freunde' in response to a single article of Bernhard Reichenbach's, 'Die Stunde der Opposition', which had appeared in *Die Zeitung* on 7 July 1941. A note to Retzlaw, however, of 24 July 1941, which accompanied the second *Rundbrief*, referred to a plan to turn the news sheet into 'eine kleine Corr.[Correspondence] für ca. 30-50 Leute'[88] while, in a letter to Herz later that year, Lehmann-Russbueldt considered the financial implications: 'Sie wird sich nicht "rentieren". Aber die Selbstkosten brächte ich schon rein.'[89] (Indeed, a typical addendum to later *Rundbriefe* would run: 'Für die Selbstkosten der Rundbriefe und deren Verbreitung erbitte ich Beiträge nach Selbsteinschätzung.')[90] By the fifth *Rundbrief*, dated 11 October 1941, Lehmann-Russbueldt had introduced a system of distribution along the following lines: 'Ich setze den Versuch der Zirkulare fort, indem ich diesmal numerierte Exemplare an deutsche Freunde sende, ferner an englische Persönlichkeiten, die deutsch lesen können.'[91] To increase his readership further, later issues were published in English and even in French.

While it has not proved possible to ascertain precise circulation figures, Eugen Brehm, writing in 1991, estimated a total of between 100 and 200, adding further: 'They were sent to a gradually expanding number of individuals, British as well as Allied and German — including some in the USA and probably Latin America.'[92] As to their message, the *Rundbriefe* were essentially an expression of Lehmann-Russbueldt's own views[93] even if, in Brehm's view, 'occasionally he allowed himself to be influenced by others. I think I influenced him a little at times and so did Hans Jaeger and "Ali" [Alois Ernst]'.[94] It is, in any case, clear from contemporary correspondence that Lehmann-Russbueldt sought and received advice from a wide circle of people before finalising his texts: thus on 21 November and 8 December 1941, he addresses himself to such friends as Fritz Demuth, Willi Eichler, Carl Herz, and Walter Loeb to elicit comments on his draft of *Rundbrief* No 6[95] while others called upon at various times for the purpose included Wickham Steed and Karl Retzlaw.

Whether or not the *Rundbriefe* can be said to have exerted any real influence is hard to determine, though Brehm does recall that they were 'often the subject within refugee circles of positive or adverse comment'.[96] They were appreciated by the readership, that much is clear, with Carl Herz, for one, reporting on a proposal that a copy of *Rundbrief* No 3 — on Vansittart — be supplied to Ivonne Kirkpatrick at the Ministry of Information.[97] Of *Rundbriefe* Nos 11 and 13, dealing with one of Lehmann-Russbueldt's recurrent preoccupations, the Deprussianisation of Germany, Alois Ernst would comment in May 1944: 'Ich halte es für außerordentlich wertvoll, daß endlich einmal an die vordringlichste deutsche Nachkriegsaufgabe mit praktischen Vorschlägen herangegangen ist.'[98] And finally it should be recognised that the production of the news sheets represented a most time-consuming and exacting task for the seventy year old exile who — to take one example from many — recorded ruefully on 3 August 1944: 'Ich arbeite seit Wochen an einem neuen Rundbrief, den ich immer wieder feile und umschreibe.'[99]

To Herz, in December 1941, Lehmann-Russbueldt would write of himself: 'Ich *dachte* stets *ohne* Partei und ohne Konfession.'[100] His daughter Yvonne has surmised, in fact, that his life would have been rather easier had he not declined to join a political party.[101] One benefit from this, however, was undoubtedly the fact that in exile Lehmann-Russbueldt was able to maintain friendly relations with an unusual number of refugee organisations, particularly though by no means exclusively with those of the non-Communist radical Left. Thus he was on good terms with members of the exiled 'Sozialistische Arbeiterpartei' (SAP)[102] and enjoyed friendly relations with the 'Internationaler Sozialistischer Kampfbund' (ISK), keeping in regular touch with ISK leader Willi Eichler.[103] And despite earlier disagreements with the SPD leadership over Berthold Jacob, communication was not broken off with the Social Democrats either: Lehmann-Russbueldt became a regular attender at meetings of the 'Union deutscher sozialistischer Organisationen in Großbritannien' (of which the SPD was the leading member).[104]

Lehmann-Russbueldt was also in touch with Kurt Hiller's 'Freiheitsbund deutscher Sozialisten', though he found Hiller difficult, while he enjoyed positively close relations with the 'Deutsche Volkssozialistische Bewegung', particularly since a number of its leading members, such as Hans Jaeger, Alois Ernst and Eugen Brehm, were counted among his personal and political friends. In September 1942, Jaeger founded the 'Klub Konstruktivisten' to bring together a circle of sympathisers to discuss current problems, in particular the reconstruction of post-war Germany, on a non-party basis; and Lehmann-Russbueldt became a signatory to its 'Plattform', its founding statement. Here the 'Konstruktivisten' pledged themselves 'gegen das heutige, deutsche Regime, gegen Diktatur, Nationalsozialismus, Militarismus, für eine politische, wirtschaftliche, kulturelle Neugestaltung Deutschlands'. The future defeat of Germany, which they were prepared 'mit herbeiführen zu helfen', was already assumed.[105]

The 'Konstruktivisten' were opposed by the Social Democrats and others as being pro-Vansittartist. So, too, of course, was the Fight For Freedom Group, whose leading German members included Walter Loeb, Curt Geyer and Bernhard Menne, for maintaining, as Vansittart did, that Hitler had been brought to power by a great mass movement of the German people and that the war was supported by the German majority. Lehmann-Russbueldt was in regular contact with Vansittart and agreed with some, though not all, of what Vansittart professed[106] — he himself would in fact define his position as: 'Ich bin jenseits von Vansittartismus und Anti-Vansittartismus.'[107] Despite certain disagreements with Loeb, Lehmann-Russbueldt maintained generally cordial relations with the Fight For Freedom Group and indeed his 1942 book, *Aggression: The Origin of Germany's War Machine*, appeared in the Fight For Freedom publication series.[108]

At the same time, Lehmann-Russbueldt was a participant, initially at least, in the activities of the Communist-inspired 'Freier Deutscher

Kulturbund' (FDKB) — later in Berlin, in very different political circumstances, he would be dubbed a 'Mitläufer des Kulturbunds' for his pains.[109] In 1942 he spoke on the subject of 'Neues Deutschtum' at the FDKB, while on 23 January 1943 the 'Kulturbund' even organised an event, 'Ein Friedenskämpfer und seine Zeit', to mark the occasion of Lehmann-Russbueldt's seventieth birthday. However, with the increasing Communist domination of the FDKB, Lehmann-Russbueldt soon found himself quietly eased out, as he subsequently reported to Sternfeld: 'Als ich mich später an den näheren Arbeiten beteiligen wollte — wie ich's wollte — hat man mich schweigend hinauskomplimentiert.'[110]

Thus, when in 1943 a group of members seceded from the FDKB to form the 'unpolitical' Club 1943, it would not be long before Lehmann-Russbueldt would join them. He addressed Club 1943, too, on a number of occasions, speaking on 'Letzte Begegnungen mit Carl von Ossietzky' in February 1944 and on 'Der Kampf der Liga für Menschenrechte' in December 1945. Jennifer Taylor, in a study of Club 1943, has pointed out that, while neither of these lectures appears to have been deemed controversial, in general Lehmann-Russbueldt 'seemed to have particular difficulty in getting his proposals past the committee'.[111] A suggestion for April 1946, 'Vatikan, Kreml und Wall Street' was rejected as 'zu heikel';[112] and when, in June 1946, he was set to speak on 'Das Verhältnis der kleinen Nationen zu den Großmächten', this, too, aroused such apprehension that Hermann Friedmann, as prospective Chairman, had to assure the Committee that 'er werde dafür sorgen, daß nichts passiere'.[113] In the event the lecture itself passed off without incident and the succeeding discussion started calmly enough — but 'dann sei ein Pandaemonium erfolgt'. A terrible argument ensued on the relative evils of the Soviet Union and the National Socialist regime in which a Czech guest to the Club reportedly enquired whether the Club's President, H. J. Rehfisch, was in the pay of the Soviet Union. To make matters worse, Rehfisch was shouted down by two women from the audience, a Fräulein Löwenschuss and none other than Lehmann-Russbueldt's wife Jeanette, with no intervention forthcoming from the Chair.[114] That same day, Rehfisch drafted his letter of resignation (though remaining in office, in fact, for a further three months). It just remains to be said that, despite the rumpus his lecture seems to have occasioned, Lehmann-Russbueldt was invited back to address the Club again and was still a regular recipient of Club 1943 literature in Berlin during the 1950s!

Similarly, even after his return to Germany, he retained his membership of the German PEN Club in Exile, a group he supported actively for years. Writing on the occasion of Lehmann-Russbueldt's eightieth birthday, Wilhelm Sternfeld, as PEN Secretary, would pay him a warm tribute in this regard:

> Sie, lieber Herr Lehmann-Russbueldt, sind nicht nur dem Lebensalter nach unser ältestes Mitglied (an zweiter Stelle steht unser Ehrenpräsident Thomas Mann), auch nach den Jahren der Zugehörigkeit sind Sie heute unsere Nummer 1. Während dieser achtzehn Jahre sind Sie eines unserer treuesten Mitglieder gewesen, das sein Interesse nicht nur durch Teilnahme an fast allen Veranstaltungen bekundete, sondern durch wertvolle Anregungen unsere Arbeit oft wesentlich gefördert hat [...]
>
> Keiner unter unseren Freunden — ja wohl auch unter den Mitgliedern aller anderen Zentren — hat in solchem Masse wie Sie den hohen Zielen der PEN-Charta nachgelebt und nachgestrebt, niemand den Kampf für Frieden und Freiheit in stärkerem Masse wie Sie zur eigenen Lebensaufgabe gemacht.[115]

The closest to his heart of all these allegiances, however, was doubtless his longstanding membership of the 'Deutsche Liga für Menschenrechte' (DLM), represented in Britain during the 1930s, though without any organisational framework, by Rudolf Olden, Ernst Toller and Lehmann-Russbueldt himself and then, after Olden's and Toller's untimely deaths, by Lehmann-Russbueldt alone. The exiled DLM had been active in 1934 and 1935 in the Nobel prize campaign for Carl von Ossietzky and, in 1935, in the Volksfront experiment in Paris, in which Lehmann-Russbueldt had been a participant. Thereafter, however, it had proved virtually impossible for the DLM to play any real part in the life of the political emigration. When, late in 1944, there were plans to revive the DLM, Lehmann-Russbueldt appears to have considered it necessary to issue an explanation of the organisation's recent inactivity:

> Seitdem ich Herbst 1933 in England eintraf, wurde mehrfach angeregt, die Tätigkeit der L.F.M. [Liga für Menschenrechte] als Liga im Exil wieder aufzunehmen. Bisher lehnte ich für meine Person ab, weil ich vom Anfang an der Auffassung war, daß nach der Niederlage der Linken in Deutschland die Gründung von Parteien, Bünden im Exil nur legitimiert werden kann durch die inneren Kräfte der Opposition in Deutschland, also weder durch Emigrantenorganisationen noch durch unsere Gastländer. Daraus folgt, daß bis zur Befreiung der deutschen Länder alle 'Ämter' erloschen sind.[116]

Despite this, however, it should be noted that during the wartime years Lehmann-Russbueldt had been drawn into certain refugee organisations specifically as a representative of the 'Deutsche Liga für Menschenrechte'. One of these was Heinrich Fraenkel's '7. November Ausschuss' of 1942, a group of Communists, Democrats and Pacifists wishing to celebrate the Soviet Union's 25 years of existence;[117] another, prior to that, had been Karl Höltermann's short-lived 'Gruppe der Parlamentarier' which had had plans to establish a representative body for the German emigration.[118] And in spite of Lehmann-Russbueldt's personal reservations — 'Sie können durch noch so viel "Lebenskraft" keinen Leichnam zum Auferstehen bringen', he would write to Karl Retzlaw in September 1944, 'Sie können nur einen neuen Menschen machen'[119] — steps were taken to re-establish the DLM in British exile, if initially on a provisional basis, in October 1944, with a committee consisting of Max Bergenthal, Retzlaw and Lehmann-Russbueldt.[120] One of the early concerns of the renascent DLM was the plight of the 'drangsalirten Anti Nazi in den Gefangenen Lagern [sic]', with Lehmann-Russbueldt himself first attempting, vainly, to interest Vansittart, and then calling on Ernst, Jaeger and Retzlaw to enlist the help of potential British sympathisers.[121] In fact, Lehmann-Russbueldt's association with the DLM would remain his abiding interest back in Germany, too, at least until 1954 when an internal disagreement would cause him to tender his resignation.

* * * * * * *

Looking back over the first four years of the war, Lehmann-Russbueldt observes in his *Interviews im Jenseits*: 'Ich dachte selten daran, daß Berlin meine Geburtsstadt war. So sehr war mir das Weltall zur Heimat geworden, da jede Heimat auf Erden trostlos war.'[122] At the end of 1945, indeed, he had written to Hugenholtz and other Dutch friends: 'Vorläufig gehe ich nicht zurück nach Deutschland.'[123] However, a letter from fellow pacifist Fritz Küster, to Lehmann-Russbueldt's elder daughter Ingeborg, from March 1946, perhaps indicates that a return was already under consideration:

> Ob Sie Ihren Vater zur Rückkehr anregen sollen, ist natürlich schwer zu sagen, weil man nicht weiß, wie er sich in England eingelebt hat. An sich wäre es natürlich wünschenswert, daß er zurückkommt. Nur weiß ich nicht, ob die Emigranten sich nicht manchmal vor unseren jetzigen Verhältnissen eine ganz falsche Vorstellung machen.[124]

It may be that, in postponing his return until 1951, Lehmann-Russbueldt was influenced by his wife Jeanette who, as a Jew, seems to have been understandably less keen on the idea of life in Germany — indeed she applied for British citizenship in 1949 (which was granted in 1950). In the Special Branch report relating to her application, there is the following comment on her husband's position:

> Both Home Office and Police papers show that Otto Lehmann has previously indicated his intention of seeking naturalisation — but, according to the applicant, her husband (who appears not to speak English at all well) is not really interested in the question of nationality, considers himself a 'European' and seeks the attainment of a United Europe.[125]

In the meantime, Lehmann-Russbueldt's life in post-war Britain was continuing along familiar lines. He still worked indefatigably, excusing his failure to reply to a letter, in November 1945, on the grounds that 'ich keine Sekunde Ruhe hatte, weniger als im "Kriege". Ich bin immer noch auf dem Kriegspfad gegen den Krieg.'[126] Eighteen months later, he would complain to Carl Herz of his 'dauernder Überarbeit' as well as of the fact that 'die "Einnahmen" stehen in umgekehrtem Verhältnis'.[127] Certainly Special Branch would describe the income he derived from his freelance writing as 'spasmodic and not very extensive'.[128] It is true that other work came his way at the end of the war: he was invited to lecture to German prisoners of war, his audience on one occasion consisting of no fewer than 80 generals (of whom between 30 and 40 would ostentatiously leave the lecture hall),[129] and he was twice given the opportunity to broadcast on the BBC German Service.[130] However, as he observed to Herz in October 1947: 'Ein eigentliches Emigrations-Leben besteht eigentlich nur noch bei der hiesigen SPD.'[131]

In August 1951, therefore, Otto Lehmann-Russbueldt decided to return to Berlin, initially as a temporary measure, in order to investigate the possibilities open to him there. He was received warmly and, on the basis of a pension arranged for him by Ernst Reuter, he and Jeanette soon moved back permanently (though keeping on their London flat as a precautionary measure). On 20 January 1953 Lehmann-Russbueldt was accorded the 'Großes Bundesverdienstkreuz'. Reuter, on making the award, 'gab [...] seiner Freude Ausdruck, daß Lehmann-Russbueldt nach den Jahren der Naziherrschaft wieder an seinen alten Wirkungskreis Berlin zurückgekehrt sei'. In reply, Lehmann-Russbueldt pledged himself in dem Geiste weiterzuarbeiten, den er seit 1915 zu erfüllen sich bemüht habe, nämlich einzutreten für ein neues Deutschland und ein neues Europa, mit dem Ziele der Wohlfahrt und des Friedens für alle Menschen und alle Völker.[132] He continued to write, work and campaign for peace, becoming increasingly concerned at the prospect of a further world war, for the rest of his life. He died in October 1964 in Berlin, aged 91. During the 1940s and '50s, Otto Lehmann-Russbueldt was nominated on several occasions and twice shortlisted for the Nobel Peace Prize, an honour of which he was justifiably proud.

His last visit to England, and to his daughter Yvonne and her children, had been in late 1961 and early 1962. Though Lehmann-Russbueldt was by no means well-off in his final Berlin years, his life there would prove considerably easier[133] than in the insecure period of British exile. As Yvonne Wells has recorded: 'Years later I asked O.L.-R. how on earth he (and everybody else) had managed, and he could only shrug his shoulders and shake his head.'[134] In all, Otto Lehmann-Russbueldt spent eighteen years in Britain; the presence here of that 'prodigious and unquenchable spirit'[135] is recalled today by a seat inscribed in his memory and situated in the grounds of Kenwood House, Hampstead,[136] a part of London of which he was particularly fond.

Notes

Acknowledgements
Grateful thanks are due to the following for access to archive material as well as for information and advice: the Auswärtiges Amt, Bonn; the Bibliothek van het Vredespaleis, The Hague; the British Library, London; the Deutsches Exilarchiv 1933-1945, Deutsche Bibliothek, Frankfurt/M. (and in particular Marie-Luise Hahn); the Friedrich-Ebert-Stiftung, Bonn; the Fritz-Küster-Archiv, Oldenburg; the Home Office, London (and in particular J. M. Lloyd); the Internationaal Instituut voor Sociale Geschiedenis, Amsterdam; the John Rylands University Library of Manchester; the Library of the Religious Society of Friends, London; the Public Record Office, London. Thanks are due also to the late Eugen Brehm, to Peter Gross for permission to quote from the letters of Fritz Gross, and above all to Yvonne Wells, née Lehmann, for much help and encouragement.

1 Otto Lehmann-Russbueldt [O.L.-R.], *Interviews im Jenseits: Plaudereien, Satiren und Visionen eines Weltbürgers* (Hamburg: Hamburger Kulturverlag, 1948), p. 80.

2 He was born Otto Lehmann but assumed the further name Rußbüldt by way of thanks to a family of that name who took an interest in him during his otherwise deprived youth. In British exile, 'Rußbüldt' was then rendered as 'Russbueldt'.

3 Ingeborg Wolske to Gerhard Kraiker, 1 September 1990, Fritz-Küster-Archiv, Oldenburg. But see also O.L.-R.'s own explanation: 'Ich war der erste Entlassene, aber gleichzeitig wurden auch einige Kommunisten und Pazifisten entlassen. Der Inspektor

kannte meine Bücher [...] Das erklärte mir das Rätsel' (in O.L.-R., 'Lebenserinnerungen bis zur Jahreswende 1932-1933', unpubl. ms. in private possession of Yvonne Wells, p. 115).

4 Ingeborg Wolske to Gerhard Kraiker, 1 September 1990, Fritz-Küster-Archiv.

5 Among members of the political emigration, it was considered an honour to appear on one of these lists. See, for example, in O.L.-R. to Wilhelm Sternfeld, 1 August 1944, 'das unendliche Vergnügen "ausgebürgert" zu sein' (Deutsches Exilarchiv [DE], Deutsche Bibliothek, Frankfurt/M., NL Sternfeld, EB 75/177).

6 O.L.-R. to 'Vereinigung Deutscher Juristen in Großbritannien', n.d. [early 1946], Fritz-Küster-Archiv, NL Fritz Küster.

7 See N. A. Furness, 'Otto Lehmann-Russbueldt: Forgotten Prophet of a Federal Europe', in: *'England? Aber wo liegt es?' Deutsche und Österreichische Emigranten in Großbritannien 1933-1945*, ed. by Charmian Brinson, Richard Dove, Marian Malet and Jennifer Taylor (Munich: Iudicium, 1996), pp. 87-97.

8 *Die blutige Internationale der Rüstungsindustrie*, Hamburg-Bergedorf: Fackelreiter-Verlag, 1929.

9 O.L.-R., 'Mein Leben' (handwritten continuation of 'Lebenserinnerungen'), unpubl. ms., Archiv der sozialen Demokratie der Friedrich-Ebert-Stiftung [AdsD], Bonn, Personalia-Sammlung L, p. 133.

10 O.L.-R, *Wann ist der Krieg aus? Interviews im Jenseits mit Aristophanes, dem Lustspieldichter aus Athen, Thomas Paine, dem heimatlosen Propheten der Menschenrechte aus England und Graf Yorck, dem Generalstabler aus Preußen* (Leicester, 1942) (self-published first series of *Interviews im Jenseits* (see footnote 1, above), p. 1.

11 Author's interview with Yvonne Wells, 5 February 1997.

12 O.L.-R. to Jacob Ter Meulen, 6 June 1934, Vredespaleis [VP], The Hague, LO8.

13 Yvonne Wells, 'Otto Lehmann-Russbueldt, 1873-1964', unpubl. ms. in private possession of the author, p. 8.

14 'Troops, Tanks and 'Planes', *Sunday Referee*, 4 February 1934, p. 1.

15 O.L.-R., 'Lebenserinnerungen', p. 121.

16 O.L-R., 'Aufrüstung?', *Sozialistische Warte*, X, 7 (1 May 1936), p. 172.

17 O.L.-R. to J.B. and E.M. Hugenholtz, 29 July 1933, VP, LO8.

18 See, for example, O.L.-R., 'The Military and Political Strength of the Smaller Nations', *Contemporary Review*, CLI, February 1937, pp. 200-09.

19 'Aerial Warfare: Secret German Plans' and 'The Future of Warfare' appeared in *The Nineteenth Century and After*, DCLXXIX (July 1934), pp. 1-15, and DCXC (August 1934), pp. 129-140. For the background to this, see Steed to W.P. Crozier, 18 May 1934, *Manchester Guardian* Archive (John Rylands University Library, Manchester),

B/5327/3a-3f. See also, Martin Hugh-Jones, 'Wickham Steed and German Biological Warfare Research', *Intelligence and National Security*, 7, 4 (October 1992), pp. 379-402.

[20] For Wesemann, see Charmian Brinson, 'The Gestapo and the Political Exiles in Britain during the 1930's: the Case of Hans Wesemann — and Others', *German Life and Letters*, LI, 1 (January 1998), pp. 43-64.

[21] 'Aufzeichnung' (Rüter), 28 April 1934, Politisches Archiv des Auswärtigen Amts, Bonn, Inland II A/B, R99578.

[22] *Germany's Air Force* (London: Allen & Unwin, 1935)

[23] O.L.-R., 'Lebenserinnerungen', p. 124.

[24] O.L.-R. to J.B. and E.M. Hugenholtz, 21 April 1935, VP, LO8.

[25] *Neues Deutschtum* (Paris: Editions Nouvelles Internationales, 1939).

[26] O.L.-R. to Prince Hubertus zu Löwenstein, 24 September 1939, DE, American Guild, EB 70/117.

[27] Ibid., 13 July 1938.

[28] Ibid., 18 March 1939.

[29] In XIV, 10 (10 March 1939), pp. 244-248, and XIV, 11 (18 March 1939), pp. 263-68.

[30] See Charmian Brinson, *The Strange Case of Dora Fabian and Mathilde Wurm: a Study of German Political Exiles in London during the 1930's* (Berne: Lang, 1997), pp. 129f.

[31] O.L.-R. to J.B. Hugenholtz, 9 December 1933, VP, LO8.

[32] See Charmian Brinson and Marian Malet, 'Fritz Gross: An Exile in Britain', *German Life and Letters*, XLIX, 3 (July 1996), pp. 339-57.

[33] See Charmian Brinson and Marian Malet, 'The House at 3 Regent Square', in: *'England? Aber wo liegt es?'*, pp. 99-113.

[34] Fritz Gross to Magda Hoppstock-Huth, 7 March 1934, letter in private possession of Peter Gross, Australia.

[35] Ibid., 1 June 1934.

[36] Yvonne Wells, 'Recollections 1930-1946', unpubl. ms. in private possession of the author, p. 17.

[37] See Otto Lehmann file in Home Office [HO], Aliens Department, L43569.

[38] See Brinson, *The Strange Case of Dora Fabian and Mathilde Wurm*, passim.

[39] O.L.-R. to Home Office, 30 October 1934, HO, Aliens Department, L43569.

[40] O.L.-R. to Willi Eichler, 7 December 1937, AdsD, Bestand II ISK, Box 33.

41 Yvonne Wells, 'Recollections 1930-1946', p. 36.

42 *Landesverteidigung ohne Profit* (London: Internationale Verlags-Anstalt, 1936); *Wer rettet Europa? Die wehrpolitische Lage der kleinen Staaten* (Zürich: Zentralstelle für Friedensarbeit, [1936]); the Danish translation was of *Die blutige Internationale der Rüstungsindustrie* (see note 8, above).

43 O.L.-R. to Home Office, 13 October 1938, HO, Aliens Department, L43569.

44 Minute on jacket of Lehmann-Russbueldt file, 31 October 1938, HO, Aliens Department, L43569.

45 Ibid., 3 February 1939.

46 Circular 'to the Honorary National Committee of the National Peace Congress being held in London from 28 June to 2 July 1935, and to the Organisations represented on the General Committee of the Congress', VP, LO8.

47 See N. A. Furness, 'The Moral Imperative of Exile: Otto Lehmann-Russbueldt's Mediation for Victims of Nazi Persecution', in: *Between Two Languages: German-speaking Exiles in Great Britain 1933-45*, ed. by William Abbey, Charmian Brinson, Richard Dove, Marian Malet and Jennifer Taylor, Stuttgarter Arbeiten zur Germanistik 308/ Publications of the Institute of Germanic Studies 59 (Stuttgart: Akademischer Verlag, 1995), pp. 59-75.

48 Ibid. See also *Rettet Ossietzky! Dokumente aus dem Nachlaß von Rudolf Olden*, ed. by Charmian Brinson and Marian Malet (Oldenburg: Universität Oldenburg, 1990).

49 O.L.-R, 'Carl von Ossietzky: In Memoriam', *Contemporary Review*, CLXX, December 1946, pp. 340-43.

50 O.L.-R., 'Carl von Ossietzky als Symbol', *Tagesspiegel*, 27 November 1949, [p. 3].

51 DE, NL Sternfeld, EB 75/175.

52 O.L.-R. to Elizabeth Fox-Howard, 22 May 1935, Library of the Religious Society of Friends, FCRA 19/1.

53 O.L.-R., 'Offener Brief an Lord Noel-Buxton', *Pariser Tageblatt*, 20 May 1935, p. 1.

54 O.L.-R. to J.B. Hugenholtz, 21 April 1935, VP, LO8.

55 O.L.-R. to Karl Retzlaw, 3 July 1941, DE, NL Retzlaw, EB 80/169.

56 S. [Karl] Retzlaw to Marcel Rollin [i.e. Berthold Jacob], 30 August 1941, DE, NL Retzlaw, EB 80/169.

57 See, for example, O.L.-R. to Karl Retzlaw, 24 September 1941, DE, NL Retzlaw, EB 80/169: 'Mit Schiff hatte ich Krach. Ich sandte Briefe an Vogel. Schiff sandte seine 5 Seiten auch an Vogel.'

58 S. [Karl] Retzlaw to Marcel Rollin, 30 August 1941, DE, NL Retzlaw, EB 80/169.

59 Letter dated 4 February 1947, quoted in: Jost Nikolaus Willi, *Der Fall Jacob-Wesemann (1935/1936): Ein Beitrag zur Geschichte der Schweiz in der Zwischenkriegszeit* (Berne/Frankfurt/M.: Lang, 1972), p. 48: 'Da war es aber zu spät: Die Engländer zögerten [...] nachdem die Amerikaner abgelehnt hatten.'

60 O.L.-R., 'Rundschreiben zum Fall Berthold Jacob', June 1942, DE, NL Sternfeld, EB 75/177, p. 4.

61 O.L.-R. to Karl Retzlaw, 18 January 1945, DE, NL Retzlaw, EB 80/169.

62 Ibid., 7 September 1945.

63 O.L.-R., 'Zu Berthold Jacobs zehnjährigem Todestag am 26 Februar 1944', *Die Menschenrechte*, 20 (N.F.3), 2 (Februar/März 1954), p. 5. The article was also intended for, but failed to appear in, the *Frankfurter Rundschau*.

64 Yvonne Wells interview.

65 See O.L.-R. to Karl Retzlaw, 17 November 1944, DE, NL Retzlaw, EB 80/169.

66 Yvonne Wells, 'Otto Lehmann-Russbueldt, 1873-1964', p. 3. She adds: 'Did they really give milk to people with angina pectoris in those days?'

67 O.L.-R., 'Mein Leben', p. 146.

68 Lord Cecil to O.L.-R., 1 November 1939, British Library, Cecil Papers, Add MS, 51145, f.76.

69 O.L.-R., 'Alien Internment Camp Huyton-Liverpool: Erlebnisse und Beobachtungen zweier Monate', 3 September 1940, DE, NL Sternfeld, EB 75/177, p. 1.

70 Ivor C. Lewis, Hon. Sec. Progressive League, 'Interned Enemies of Hitler: A few Examples', *Manchester Guardian*, 25 July 1940, p. 10.

71 O.L.-R., 'Alien Internment Camp Huyton-Liverpool', p. 9.

72 *Wann ist der Krieg aus?*, p. 15.

73 Medical report dated 16 August 1940, HO, Aliens Department, L43569.

74 E. J. Cohn to Home Office, 19 July 1940, ibid.

75 Wickham Steed to E.J. Cohn, 15 July 1940, ibid.

76 On jacket of Lehmann-Russbueldt file, ibid.

77 This was not the first time that O.L.-R. and Berthold Jacob had been associated in Home Office documents. See also an earlier undated minute [1934], ibid.: 'There is a somewhat unfavourable reference to this man [O.L.-R.] by MI5 on S1051.'

78 Minute on jacket of Lehmann-Russbueldt file, 17 November 1941, ibid.

79 15 December 1951, DE, NL Sternfeld, EB 75/177.

[80] O.L.-R., *Wann ist der Krieg aus?*, p. 37.

[81] Yvonne Wells interview.

[82] O.L.-R., 'Mein Leben', pp. 152-53.

[83] Eugen Brehm to N. A. Furness, 18 February 1991.

[84] See O.L.-R. to Carl Herz, 19 May 1944, Internationaal Instituut voor sociale Geschiedenis [IISG], Amsterdam, Herz Archive, 46/39. The Leicester Rotary Club is not able to verify whether the proposed lecture actually took place, however.

[85] *Contemporary Review*, CLIX, January 1941, pp. 53-60.

[86] *Central European Observer*, 19, 19 (18 September 1942), pp. 305-06.

[87] *The Times*, 31 March 1944, p. 5.

[88] DE, NL Retzlaw, EB 80/169.

[89] 27 November 1941, IISG, Herz Archive, 46/3-5.

[90] *Rundbriefe des Flüchtlings*, 21, June 1945, p. 4.

[91] The copy held in the Deutsche Bibliothek is marked 'Ex. No. 50'. (This system appears to have ceased after a few issues, however.)

[92] Eugen Brehm to N. A. Furness, 3 June 1991.

[93] When, late in 1944, the 'Deutsche Liga für Menschenrechte' was reconstituted in Britain, Lehmann-Russbueldt, who was the Honorary Secretary, specifically stated that he regarded the *Rundbriefe* as independent of it (see *Rundbriefe des Flüchtlings*, 18, November 1944, p. 9). Nevertheless, it should be noted that the *Rundbriefe* do appear to have been sent out by him in his DLM capacity from No 22, August 1945 on.

[94] Eugen Brehm to N. A. Furness, 3 June 1991.

[95] IISG, Herz Archive, 336/3 and 336/4.

[96] Eugen Brehm to N. A. Furness, 3 June 1991.

[97] Carl Herz to O.L.-R., 23 October 1941, IISG, Herz Archive, 328/2.

[98] Alois Ernst to O.L.-R., 15 May 1944, IISG, Herz Archive, 333/1.

[99] O.L.-R. to Wilhelm Sternfeld, 3 August 1944, DE, NL Sternfeld, EB 75/177.

[100] 12 December 1941, IISG, Herz Archive, 46/6.

[101] Yvonne Wells interview.

[102] As indicated, for instance, by correspondence of the London group of the exiled SAP, held at the Arbeiderbewegelsens Arkiv og Bibliotek, Oslo.

103 See, for example, O.L.-R.'s correspondence with Eichler, held at AdsD (ISK Archive).

104 As documented in Ludwig Eiber, *Die Sozialdemokratie in der Emigration: Die 'Union deutscher sozialistischer Organisationen in Großbritannien' 1941-1946 und ihre Mitglieder* (Bonn: Dietz, 1998), pp. 388, 427, 433 and 445.

105 A copy of the 'Plattform' is held at the Public Record Office, FO 371/30911, together with a curious report on the 'Konstruktivisten' from W. F. Henson, Ministry of Information, to Geoffrey Harrison, Foreign Office, 19 November 1942: 'Apropos of this club — at a recent meeting at which a number of British officers were present, a statement was made on the following lines: — a time would come, it was argued, coincident with the establishment of a second front, during which all Germans resident in this country would be in danger of internment with the exception of the members of the 'Konstruktivisten' group which "the British Government looked upon as definitely anti-Nazi and pro-Allied". The bogey of internment was raised in order to enrol members. I think the 'Konstruktivisten' would be worth watching.'

106 For O.L.-R.'s views on Vansittart, see, inter alia, *Rundbriefe* Nos 3, 4 and 6.

107 O.L.-R. to Wilhelm Sternfeld, 6 September 1944, DE, NL Sternfeld, EB 75/177.

108 *Aggression: The Origin of Germany's War Machine* (London: Hutchinson, 1942)

109 O.L.-R. to Wilhelm Sternfeld, 20 December 1952, DE, NL Sternfeld, EB 75/177.

110 Ibid.

111 Jennifer Taylor, 'Dachshund or St Bernard? The contribution of Club 1943 to the history of German-speaking exiles in Great Britain, 1943-1949', in: *Zwischenwelt 4: Literatur und Kultur des Exils in Großbritannien*, ed. by Siglinde Bolbecher, Konstantin Kaiser, Donal McLaughlin, J. M. Ritchie (Vienna: Verlag für Gesellschaftskritik, 1995), p. 62.

112 Protokoll der außerordentlichen Vorstandssitzung, 16 March 1946, DE, Club 43 Archive, EB 95/208.

113 Vorstandssitzung, 20 June 1946, ibid.

114 Ibid.

115 PEN Vorstand to O.L.-R., 20 December 1953, DE, Exil PEN, EB 75/175.

116 O.L.-R., 'An ehemalige Mitglieder und Freunde der deutschen Liga für Menschenrechte im Exil', n.d. [c. 26 October 1944], DE, NL Retzlaw, EB 80/169.

117 Other refugees involved in the venture included Wolfgang von Einsiedel, Hans Flesch, Wilhelm Necker, Richard Löwenthal, Wilhelm Sternfeld, and Oskar Kokoschka.

118 On this, see Werner Röder, *Die deutschen sozialistischen Exilgruppen in Großbritannien 1940-1945: Ein Beitrag zur Geschichte des Widerstandes gegen den Nationalsozialismus* (Bonn-Bad Godesberg: Verlag Neue Gesellschaft, 1968), pp. 31f.

119 8 September 1944, DE, NL Retzlaw, EB 80/169.

120 See O.L.-R., 'An ehemalige Mitglieder und Freunde der deutschen Liga für Menschenrechte im Exil'.

121 O.L.-R. to Alois Ernst, Hans Jaeger and S. [Karl] Retzlaw, 22 February 1945, DE, NL Retzlaw, EB 80/169.

122 On p. 79.

123 O.L.-R. to J. B. Hugenholtz et al., 30 November 1945, VP, LO8.

124 Ingeborg Lehmann to Fritz Küster, 18 March 1946, Fritz-Küster-Archiv, NL Fritz Küster.

125 Metropolitan Police Special Branch Report, 5 January 1950, HO, Aliens Department, L43569.

126 O.L.-R. to Carl Herz, 27 March 1947, IISG, Herz Archive, 46/53.

127 O.L.-R. to J. B. Hugenholtz, n.d., (on reverse of O.L.-R. to Hugenholtz et al., 28 November 1945), IISG, LO8.

128 Metropolitan Police Special Branch Report, 5 January 1950, HO, Aliens Department, L43569.

129 See O.L.-R., *Landesverteidigung: Vortrag vor deutschen Kriegsgefangenen in England* (Hamburg: Hamburger Kulturverlag, 1947), p. 71.

130 On 26 November 1946 on 'In Memoriam: Carl von Ossietzky' and on 3 January 1948 as a contributor to a magazine programme, 'The Roving Microphone'.

131 O.L.-R. to Carl Herz, 7 October 1947, IISG, Herz Archive, 46/69.

132 'Die Ehrung Otto Lehmann-Russbueldts', 20 January 1953, Senat von Berlin, Presseamt.

133 See, for example, O.L.-R. to Wilhelm Sternfeld, 25 June 1956, DE, NL Sternfeld, EB 75/177, in which he reports on his current economic circumstances.

134 In 'Recollections 1930-1946', p. 18.

135 Yvonne Wells, 'Otto Lehmann-Russbueldt 1873-1964', p. 2.

136 We are indebted to Simon Jones of English Heritage for his kind assistance in locating it.

Steven W. Lawrie

Erich Fried — Language and *Heimat*

Although all writers share a special relationship to language as the material with which they work, for the writer in exile language assumes a heightened significance. This is true of the Austrian-born poet Erich Fried. During his long years in exile in Britain he consciously resisted the threat posed by the foreign language environment to his mother tongue. Fried's translation work made him a cultural go-between, but his attention was always focused on the German-speaking countries. The German language remained the major link with his lost childhood home and ultimately assumed the role of 'Heimat'.

When driven from Austria in 1938, Erich Fried was deprived of a substantial part of his identity: his nationality and his home. Instead, the status was forced upon him of a Jewish refugee of Austrian origins. In retrospect Fried provided a very negative evaluation of exile, equating it with 'abgebrochenes Studium, verlorene Jahre, Entwurzelung'.[1] Yet despite this very black picture, Fried's status as cultural go-between and his own literary innovations would be unthinkable without contact with the foreign environment, as a result of which his native language was 'zugleich bedroht und fruchtbar in Frage gestellt'.[2] The following examination will consider Fried's attitude to his native tongue and his native country in the light of his experience of exile.

I

Fried's cross-cultural activity was almost exclusively a one-way street, from English to German, and his impact on the Anglo-Saxon countries was modest, both in respect of his own work and in his function as translator.

Fried's contact with English writers and publishers was limited. During the War Fried may have encountered English writers at the 'Literarische Tees' (Literary Teas) organised by the London Free German League of Culture for that very purpose.[3] In the post-war period Fried was indeed involved in British culture and attended publishers' parties, perhaps when still hoping for an English version of his novel. But he spent increasing periods in Germany and also in Austria and was, from 1972 onwards, permanently 'auf Achse'[4] in continental Europe. His impact on Britain was restricted to a handful of English anthologies of his work. Georg Rapp brought out a translation of some of Fried's poems in 1968, but *Last Honours* appeared in a limited edition of only 150 copies. In 1969 the volume *On Pain of Seeing*, which included poems from *Anfechtungen*, *...und Vietnam und...*, *Warngedichte* and *Zeitfragen* appeared, again in Rapp's translation. The volume *100 Poems without a Country* was translated by Stuart Hood in 1977, but the second edition did not follow until 1990. More recently, *Love Poems* (1991) appeared on the British market as well as a collection of prose from various volumes, translated by Martin Chalmers, *Children and Fools* (1992).

The lack of impact can be accounted for by Fried's ambitions to become a German (i.e. German-language) writer, despite his position far from the language community in which he wished to publish. Fried was concerned with cultural and political aspects of the German-speaking countries and of the Federal Republic in particular, and consequently his interest lay with the German language.

There is no indication of a will to switch language. Had Fried ever considered this step, the year 1945 might have been the time to change, as the German and Austrian exile organisations in London were wound up and German-language publications discontinued.

In contrast to other exile writers such as Hilde Spiel or Robert Neumann, who wrote in a convincing English idiom, Fried decided against the exhausting process which Hilde Spiel perceived as the essential prerequisite to writing in the English language. Spiel, who made a conscious and conscientious attempt to attain the level of fluency required of a writer, commented on the difficulties associated with this step with the following observation:

> Wie ich nach London kam, hab ich gemerkt, daß ich nicht versteh, wie der Grünzeughändler redet oder die Greißler, oder sogar die Nachrichtensprecher hab ich nicht verstanden, weil das alles viel zu rasch und viel zu sehr in einem lokalen Idiom vor sich gegangen ist. Also das hat Monate und dann später Jahre gedauert, bis ich mich getraut habe, Englisch auch zu schreiben. Das war ein sehr mühsamer Vorgang.[5]

Fried categorically rejected the notion of language-switching and suggested: 'So gut wie niemand kann wirklich in einer anderen als der eigenen Muttersprache schreiben. Journalisten vielleicht noch, Schriftsteller kaum je. Sie sind mehr mit ihrer Muttersprache untrennbar verknüpft.'[6] And despite his success, Robert Neumann appears to concur with Fried when he describes the reaction to his own work in English. Neumann describes his novel *Scene in Passing* as 'in einer Sprache geschrieben, die

Nichtengländer für englisch halten, Engländer für "irgendwoher von den Äußeren Hebriden vielleicht" oder amerikanisch, Amerikaner ebenfalls für amerikanisch, "aber nicht dorther, wo ich zu Hause bin — Amerika ist ein großes Land!"'.[7] However well the exile writer may have mastered the new language, he will never be completely at home in it as the reactions of native speakers referred to by Neumann suggest. Another language-switcher, Ernst Bornemann, clearly anticipated a comparable reaction to his prose and chose for that reason to disguise his own German origins behind the American Glaswegian identity of his narrator in *The Face on the Cutting-Room Floor*.[8] Bornemann did indeed achieve his aim, although it has been shown that he nevertheless made some errors in idiom and grammar.[9]

In his rejection of language-switching Fried makes an important distinction between the writer and the journalist, and in so doing he echoes the pronouncement of another exile writer, Lion Feuchtwanger. On the same issue Feuchtwanger asserts: 'Gewiß man kann lernen, sich in einer fremden Sprache auszudrücken: *die letzten Gefühlswerte* des fremden Tonfalls lernen kann man nicht. In einer fremden Sprache dichten, in einer fremden Sprache gestalten, kann man nicht.'[10] Whether it is, or is not possible to function satisfactorily as a writer in a language other than one's own mother tongue, is a difficult question to answer, particularly as it has as a prerequisite a definition of the term 'dichten', but it is a question which is perhaps answered by the very existence of linguistic border-crossers such as Neumann, Spiel and Bornemann as well as others such as Klaus Mann, Jakov Lind, Hans Flesch-Brunningen and Peter de Mendelssohn.[11]

In any case, Feuchtwanger was in a privileged position, was a well-established figure of international repute belonging to the literary elite amongst exile writers and could consequently reach an audience via the translator. Fried, however, would, like Brecht, learn that: 'Das Handwerk des Exilierten ist das Hoffen.'[12] Writing in the German language was a luxury which was to demand many years of perseverance before Fried reached an audience of any considerable size.

Fried's theoretical pronouncement on language-switching was based on his own experience, for it is improbable that he would ever have been able to do justice to his literary intentions in the medium of the English language. Admittedly Fried, who was to become a recognised and much praised translator of the works of, among others, William Shakespeare, had remarkable *passive* language skills. His active linguistic skills were less remarkable. Fried's first — and last — independent publication in English, the pamphlet *They Fight in the Dark* (1944),[13] which describes Austrian anti-Nazi resistance activities, is so full of errors in basic vocabulary and syntax that it fails in its propagandistic intention and gives an indication of its author's linguistic limitations. Apart from this work written in the war period Fried never wrote in English save for some love poems, not intended for publication.[14] His spoken and written English after the war would not have permitted him to switch languages. Stuart Hood commented that Fried had 'no sense of the idea of simplicity and clarity in English' and that Fried needed his help to correct letters to English newspapers.[15] Hood is here referring to the mid-1950s, so that it may be concluded that in 1945 Fried's English was even poorer. Fried's resistance to the English language was also reflected in his spoken English, which, even after fifty years in London, was clearly marked by language interference from German and by an unmistakable, thick Austrian accent.[16]

In addition, Fried's linguistic ability was restricted by the psychological factor which occasioned a conscious resistance to complete linguistic integration into the British environment. When the young refugee arrived in London in 1938 he was accompanied by the firm intention of becoming a German writer,[17] an intention consequent on the persecution experienced in Austria and maintained as an act of defiance against National Socialism.[18] Characteristic of this stubborn attitude was the later statement in which Fried insisted: 'I am an Austrian. That was my formative country and that's my mother tongue. And I won't permit Hitler to get me away from that.'[19] Hence, in one respect his tenacity stemmed from a resistance to the lasting effects of National Socialism in the form of his extended exile. Fried viewed his existence in London after 1945 as an extended exile. His comments on the issue of exile indicate that from his point of view exile lasted long after the end of the war:

> Zwei Aussprüche fallen mir ein. Der eine auf einer Exilliteratur-Tagung in England vor einigen Jahren, von einem angeblichen Experten für Exilliteratur aus Frankfurt am Main, der das dort unterrichtete: 'Exilliteratur hört natürlich 1945 auf, denn dann konnte man wieder im deutschen Sprachgebiet veröffentlichen.' Der Lyriker Michael Hamburger und ich fanden, das verdiene einen Dummheitspreis.
>
> Den anderen Ausspruch hat Oskar Maria Graf in Amerika nach Kriegsende getan: 'Jetzt fängt das Exil eigentlich erst an.'[20]

In another respect the importance of the German language derived from the threat posed by the foreign surroundings. He was 'determined not to give priority to the foreign language',[21] and consciously tried to avert the process described in Feuchtwanger's essay 'Arbeitsprobleme des Schriftstellers im Exil'. Feuchtwanger writes:

> Da ist zunächst die bittere Erfahrung, abgespalten zu sein vom lebendigen Strom der Muttersprache. [...] Immer und für alles haben wir den Klang der fremden Sprache im Ohr, ihre Zeichen dringen täglich, stündlich auf uns ein, sie knabbern an unserem Ausdrucksvermögen.[22]

In order to counter the threat from English, Fried maintained contact with German-speakers. During the war years Fried was greatly involved in the cultural and political activities of the major exile organisations, the Austrian Centre and the Free German League of Culture. He was in touch with the Club 43 which had a distinctly continental bias and where 'readings from poetry or fiction were held in German only'.[23] One commentator states that Fried occasionally helped organise evenings at the Club 43, and in 1955 Fried and Flesch-Brunningen gave a talk on Dylan Thomas, while Fried gave a reading from his own work in April 1957.[24] Keen to associate with literary colleagues, he established in 1949 a group of German-speaking exile writers in London, which included H. G. Adler and Franz Baermann Steiner,[25] while his work with the BBC Austrian and later German Services also allowed him to practise his mother tongue. Stuart Hood, who shared a flat with Fried from 1954 to 1956, recalled regular visits from Germans with whom Fried would retire for discussions after Saturday lunch.[26] Later, too, Fried's home was the port of call for German visitors to London such as Rudi Dutschke and Fritz Teufel.[27] Fried's last wife, Catherine Fried-Boswell, talked of a 'constant flow of visitors, mostly students and political figures',[28] while a literary colleague, Anne Duden, confirmed that it was always 'full house' in Fried's home. In his final years, in order to be able to speak German Fried had long telephone conversations both with Duden in London and with other friends in Germany.[29]

However, Fried's attitude to his native tongue was also encouraged by another factor, for he shared with his war-time fellow-exiles the conviction that they represented the better Germany (or Austria). Both the Germans and the Austrians in exile were convinced of their mission, and numerous examples of this attitude could be cited. One example from the exile periodical *Inside Nazi Germany* is typical of the prevailing mood. In

an article entitled 'The German Language versus Hitler' Fritz Gottfurcht
writes: 'A great responsibility lies with the writers, artists, musicians who
have left Nazi Germany. It is given into their hands to keep German
culture, the very language of their country, alive.'[30] Fried, in constant
contact with thoughts such as these during the war years, therefore also
resisted the influence of the English language in the belief — along with
other writers — that German culture and the German language were being
nurtured and preserved by themselves for a future Germany and Austria.

Fried, like so many other exiles, worked as a translator after the
war. On one hand the *German* language and his own literary output in that
language were of paramount importance to him, on the other hand Fried's
return home, if not physically then at least in his function as a writer, was
directly attributable to his translation work as a cultural go-between.

In his efforts to secure post-war publications in Germany Fried
attempted to capitalise on his position in prolonged exile and, in the context
of his correspondence with the Claassen Verlag, emphasised his particular
suitability as a translator in view of his exile experience.[31] The same
sentiment was shared by the other members of the aforementioned group
of London exile poets. Citing the supposed mass of poor quality
translations from English into German, Fried attempted to persuade Eugen
Claassen of the group's merits and wrote on behalf of the group:

> Wir haben eine Sonderentwicklung durchgemacht, sind von einigen deutschen
> Krankheiten verschont geblieben [...] und können durch unser ganzes Wesen
> nicht anders, als zwischen deutscher und englischer Kultur vermitteln, ohne
> dabei die eine oder andere mit Nachdruck zur Schau zu stellen.[32]

Despite the ultimate failure of the group's intention of functioning as
cultural ambassadors between the languages, Fried himself fulfilled the
function of go-between as of 1948 in his work for the BBC Austrian and
German Services, whereby Fried made a virtue of a necessity in that his
familiarity with British culture and English language and literature, a
result of his enforced encounter with the foreign language environment,
could be exploited in order to gain access to a German audience and
ultimately gain a foothold in German literary life.

His work at the BBC consisted of features on English poetry as well
as poetry translations, and it was targeted at an audience which had largely
been cut-off from foreign writers and culture during the Nazi period.
Alongside entire broadcasts on the theme of English poetry[33] Fried carried
out translations of English literature by T. S. Eliot, John Donne, John

Milton, Thomas Hardy, Dylan Thomas and many more. In addition to translations, Fried also introduced his German listeners to broader aspects of British culture, producing original German verse for the monthly series 'In England'. German listeners learnt, for example, about the 'Festival of Britain' or about Christmas and Easter in Britain. A translation of Dylan Thomas's radio play *Under Milk Wood*, arguably the deciding factor in Fried's literary return, was also commissioned by the BBC so that Fried's function as go-between was directly linked to his own literary 'return'.

II

Fried termed Germany his 'sprachliche Heimat'.[34] Austria was essentially associated with his memories of childhood and adolescence, whereas modern-day Austria had changed so much that it had ceased to resemble Fried's impressions from childhood. He comments:

> Was die Heimat mir bedeutet? Österreich viel zumindest die Teile Österreichs, die ich als Kind gesehen habe und die sich gar nicht so wesentlich verändert haben — das ist meine Heimat. Ich habe viele Freunde dort. Aber das Milieu, aus dem ich komme, gibt's nicht mehr. In dieser Hinsicht fühle ich mich wie mein eigenes Gespenst, wenn ich dort bin.[35]

In spite of the repeated statements made by Fried regarding his Austrian nationality, he did not return to live there and seems never to have seriously considered remigration to his native country. This may be accounted for by the memories of persecution which the country held for him. Nor was Fried's Jewish identity strong enough to entice him to emigrate to Israel, particularly as he became increasingly critical of the Israeli state.[36] There is evidence that he was considering, albeit with some hesitation, a move to Palestine in June 1940,[37] but Fried had grown up in an assimilated Jewish family and his interest in Jewish culture did not extend as far as Zionism.

In war-time London Fried's attitude to Austria wavered between the official Free Austrian Movement (FAM) line and his own misgivings. The FAM viewed Austria as the first victim of National Socialist aggression, and Fried projected just such an image in his earlier war-time work, invoking and articulating the concept of home. This is evident in poems such as 'Das Herz rückt ein'[38] which urges the reader towards increased production in an armaments factory as part of the antifascist war effort, or 'Wir stürmen das Land'[39] which contains an optimistic rallying-call to the

exiles, urging them to help defeat the Nazis. The ultimate goal in each case
is the liberation of and return to one's native country. The view in other
poems is directed towards a happier future after the end of exile, such as in
'Alte Mutter in Wien'[40] which describes a reunion with a loved one in
Vienna, or 'Vor der Ankunft'[41] which provides a poetic and moving
description of a return journey to Austria by train. At times Fried falls
prey to romantic recollections of home and resorts to the use of clichés,
intended to transport the reader back home to 'Der Stallgeruch, der an den
Hang gebaute Ort,/ der Wildbach und das Mundartwort.'[42] Austria is
frequently reduced to romantic pictures which provide an escape, even if
only imagined, from the drudgery of the exile existence.[43]

In a number of prose pieces Fried also complied with FAM policy by
emphasising the existence of resistance within Austria. One example of this,
'Die Fabriksmauer' [sic],[44] clearly distinguishes between Austrians and
'preussische Nazi' [sic].[45] The pamphlet *They Fight in the Dark*, mentioned
above, likewise seeks to portray Austria in as positive a light as possible, by
contrasting 'brave young Austrian patriots' with 'German hangmen'.[46]

However, amidst his prose and poetry pieces which corresponded to
the official FAM line, can be found a less optimistic portrayal of his
country. In one instance the memories of Austria engendered in Fried
relate to his own final days before leaving[47] and he reminds the reader that
Austria had been moving in the direction of fascism for some time even
before the *Anschluß*. There is little sentimentalising of the term 'Heimat' in
this case. In a poem bearing just this title,[48] written in 1941, the poet
criticises an apparent tendency to lose sight of the real Austria as a result of
a preoccupation with nostalgic associations such as the 'Bergluft' and
'Seen'[49] and warns against the danger of the term 'Austria' becoming so
filled with the images projected upon it by those in exile that it ceases to
bear any similarity to political reality, for the Austrian exiles are described
as: 'Knüpfer sind wir und Fäden, / Selber dich webend!'[50]

In these examples he is out of step with the patriotic slant in the
Austrian exile camp, a standpoint he would maintain later in the collection
of poems *Österreich* (1946). Fried already harboured doubts about his
native country during the war years and the question of a return home to
Austria gradually became less important. In his novel *Ein Soldat und ein
Mädchen*, begun in 1947 and published in 1960, there is no explicit
mention made of remigration. In one section of the novel the subject of
return is adapted. In 'Heimkehr' home has ceased to signify a specific place

in a specific country. In returning home the narrator goes back to his
childhood, the memories of which have supplanted a geographical location
as the concept of home, as is the case in the works of some other exile
writers. In Hilde Spiel's novel *Lisas Zimmer* the character of Lisa makes
the same connection between home and childhood, as does the character of
Martin in Klaus Mann's exile novel *Der Vulkan* whose drug addiction is
directly linked to his childhood memories of home. Echoing some further
sentiments expressed in *Der Vulkan*, exile is presented by Fried not as a
spatial concept but rather as an existential one. Life is seen as a period of
exile ended only by death, here by a bullet in the head.

   In the last example Fried's homelessness engenders a very negative
comparison, but by the late 1950s his concept of home and emotional
attachment to any particular geographical area had undergone a change.
Warngedichte (1964) contains one poem in particular which is striking in
its treatment of the theme of the lost home. In 'Untergang'[51] the lyrical
persona is unexpectedly deprived of the security of home when his house is
occupied by the sea. This is one of the few humorous poems in the
collection and it is significant that Fried chooses to present the theme in this
way and with self-irony. The lyrical I of the poem initially refuses to
recognise the fact that his home has been taken over by the sea — even
despite the movement of the tides and the presence of a shipwreck.
Empirical reality is ignored in an attempt to continue with everyday life.
As if in suspended animation, life goes on, although this is clearly
impossible. He drowns only at the point where he becomes intellectually
convinced that he has indeed lost his home to the sea: "Haben Sie doch ein
Einsehen!'/ Gut. Ich ertrank.'[52] The light-hearted note suggests that the
poet had become less emotionally dependent on the concept of 'home', a
development echoed in the title of Fried's prize-winning collection *100
Gedichte ohne Vaterland*, whereby homelessness takes on positive
connotations.

   From the mid-1960s poems dealing specifically with Austria
illustrate the reason for a detachment from his former country. On his
visits to Austria, Fried felt an unease, as is indicated in his comment on
this: 'You find a few people from the olden days like their own ghosts.
Even if there is a school fellow who has survived [...] there is this
strangeness: Why did *he* survive?'[53] In returning to his childhood home
Fried was reminded of the traumatic experiences which followed the
annexation. Although he returned to Austria in the 1960s[54] and continued

to attend conferences there, the ghosts from the past were still present. In a poem entitled 'Sommer der Verjährung', whose title is a reference to the debate at that time in Germany on the lapsing of Nazi crimes, Fried indicates the haunting presence of the past. In the first of three stanzas Fried writes:

> Es hat geregnet
> es ist wieder heiß
> das staubige Pflaster
> *sind schuld*
> der Liechtensteinstraße
> trocknet
> *sind unser Unglück*
> und riecht noch
> wie nach der Schule
> *müssen vernichtet werden*[55]

In 1980 Fried's Austrian citizenship was restored[56] but this formal reinstatement did not alter his reservations about Austria. He was quite clear about Austria's complicity in the rise of National Socialism, for it was 'ein Land, daß [*sic*] an der Nazitradition Anteil hatte'.[57]

'Sommer der Verjährung' and other poems referring to the National Socialist past were included by Fried in the anthology *Im Brennpunkt: Ein Österreich*[58] which appeared in the year in which Austria celebrated its 1,000 year existence. His choice of poems for an anthology on the subject of Austria is significant and quite clearly illustrates the unpleasant memories associated with that country. Although he was offered various places to live in Austria, he never returned.[59] Fried's main sphere of activity remained the Federal Republic, where his most important publishers were located. Austrian themes and issues are occasional excursions. There is, for example, no Austrian equivalent of *So kam ich unter die Deutschen* (1977), and an examination of Fried's many poetry volumes reveals a clear preoccupation with the Federal Republic.

III

As discussed above, the theme of Austria is generally linked to the past and to the poet's childhood. One critic has noted: 'Fried ist der Herkunft nach Österreicher, England wurde seine zweite Heimat. Die alte konnte er sich nur in der Sprache bewahren; sie, die Sprache, half ihm die Trennung von

Raum und Zeit seiner Jugend überwinden.'[60] The German language was indeed Fried's primary link with his lost home, but ultimately that language came to replace his lost home. Indeed language came to replace any home in the conventional sense and it is no coincidence that Fried chose the title *100 Gedichte ohne Vaterland* for his prize-winning entry to the 'Prix International des Editeurs' in 1977. The title of the volume indicates not only the anti-fascist slant to many of the poems, since they reject the chauvinistic concept of 'Vaterland', but more importantly it reveals Fried's own conception of his work and of himself as a writer who was not bound by national ties to any one country in particular.

Peter de Mendelssohn has provided a suitable description of the situation of writers in exile. He writes:

> Der Flüchtlings-Schriftsteller schreibt nicht nur, sondern lebt in seiner eigenen Sprache. Die Welt seiner Vorstellungen ist unlösbar verknüpft mit der Sprache seiner Träume — die natürlich seine Muttersprache ist. Er lebt nur in der Erinnerung.[61]

In the poetry volume *Reich der Steine* (1963) Fried does exactly this. In 'Rückschritt'[62] he writes: 'Wer in der Welt nicht/ daheim ist/ geht insgeheim heim',[63] and subsequently returns to the world of his childhood in order to portray a child's perception and interpretation of words and their meanings. Although the cycle is at times puzzling, it nevertheless demonstrates Fried's very close examination of language, of the meaning and associations of individual words, leading to the frequent use of the pun.

Fried's activity was previously described as a one-way street, with Fried producing German versions of works of English literature. He made little contribution to movement in the other direction. However, besides his activity as translator, his own work itself was influenced by the encounter with British culture and the English language, for example in the late 'forties in his experiments with half-rhyme, which were inspired by Wilfred Owen among others.[64] Fried's use of the pun is well-documented. Initially this personal innovation proved puzzling to readers, such as in his volume *Reich der Steine*, as indeed Fried himself anticipated at the time of publication, describing them as 'Gedichtzyklen [...], die für Unverständlichkeit im landläufigen Gebrauchslyriksinn von selbst sorgen.'[65] The use of punning was not refined until later, when a synthesis was arrived at between form and content, whereby Fried used the pun to startling effect to reveal unexpected insights, frequently of a political nature.

Besides this obvious aspect, immersion in the English language had
the more subtle effect of heightening the poet's awareness of and sensitivity
to his native language. On the subject of the writer and the foreign
linguistic environment Feuchtwanger notes:

> Der im fremden Sprachkreis lebende Autor kontrolliert beinahe automatisch das
> eigene Wort ständig am fremden. Häufig sieht er, daß die fremde Sprache ein
> treffenderes Wort hat für das, was er ausdrücken will. Er gibt sich dann nicht
> zufrieden mit dem, was ihm die eigene Sprache darbietet, sondern er schärft, feilt
> und poliert an dem Vorhandenen so lange, bis es ein Neues geworden ist, bis er
> der eigenen Sprache das neue, schärfere Wort abgerungen hat.[66]

It is an interesting coincidence that Fried should choose to use the same
term to describe the process of writing in the final poem of his collection
Österreich. The last stanza of 'Abgesang', which reads as follows, suggests
Fried was indeed engaged in a process of refinement inspired by the
influence of the language of his host country:

> Aber es glückt mir vielleicht,
> wenn ich träume und feile,
> daß dann und wann eine Zeile
> bis zu dir reicht.[67]

The gradual refinement ('feilen'), induced, it may be concluded, by the
process described by Feuchtwanger, acts as an aid to establishing a link, if
only in the poet's mind, to his native country.

Fried was influenced by constant exposure to the English language in
as far as it caused him to reflect closely upon the *use* of the German
language. In another respect he was made very sensitive to the *misuse* of
German. Language is reported to have been very important to Fried and
was 'almost like a person'.[68] It is consequently not surprising if Fried
objected to the maltreatment of this 'person'. The following poem, entitled
'Deutsche Sprachübung', demonstrates the poet's keen sensitivity to the use
of language and to what language can reveal.

> Lies
> einen Satz
> der beginnt
> 'Wir verfolgen
> aufmerksam
> und bereit...'
> mit den Augen
> der aufmerksam

und bereit

Verfolgten[69]

The sensitivity towards the official misuse of language is also in evidence elsewhere. Fried took exception, for example, to the expression created to define the fatal use of fire-arms by the West German police. This was termed euphemistically 'gezielter polizeilicher Todesschuß' and then 'finaler Rettungsschuß'.[70] Fried concluded that: 'die Sprache wird verbogen und verlogen'.[71] In the same way, Fried attempted to counter the misleading expression 'Radikalenerlaß' by explaining the actual implications of this.[72] His best-known confrontation with the West German authorities revolved around the discrepancy between official use of language and Fried's own. In a reader's letter to *Der Spiegel* Fried described the killing by the Berlin police of Georg von Rauch as 'Vorbeugemord'.[73] Fried was found not guilty of the charge of slander brought by the Berlin Chief of Police, but the Klaus Wagenbach Verlag eventually lost a similar case which revolved around the use of the word 'Mord' in connection with the deaths of von Rauch and Thomas Weißbecker.[74] In his reaction to the Wagenbach judgement Fried described the implications of the outlawing of the word 'Mord' as 'eine furchtbare Verzerrung der deutschen Sprache'.[75] Heinrich Böll, who as an expert witness helped in Fried's defence at the slander trial in January 1974, later that year thematised the use and misuse of language by the police and the right-wing press in his story *Die verlorene Ehre der Katharina Blum* (1974). Both writers had experienced the Nazi era and were keenly aware of the link between language and behaviour, identified as early as 1946 by Victor Klemperer. In *LTI* Klemperer argues, 'zu verschwinden hat nicht nur das nazistische Tun, sondern auch die nazistische Gesinnung, die nazistische Denkgewöhnung und ihr Nährboden: die Sprache des Nazismus.'[76] Fried, having been persecuted as a Jew, readily made the connection between what he perceived to be the use of language in the present to that of the National Socialist past, as he did for example in documenting the case of the doctor Peter Augst who had described soldiers as potential murderers. In the poem 'Ein bundesdeutsches Urteil' Fried writes:

Angeklagt wegen Beleidigung

und wegen Volksverhetzung

(ein zur Hitlerzeit gängiger Ausdruck)

wurde der Arzt verurteilt

zu 10 500 Mark[77]

One feature of a totalitarian state is the manipulation of language as a means of oppression and it is not surprising that Fried, given his preoccupation with the spoken and written word, was quick to attack the misuse of language. Although all writers have in common a special relationship to language, it may be argued that Fried had a particularly finely-tuned sensitivity to language and that this was the result of his enforced exile as well as his long years in an English-speaking environment.

Although Fried made contradictory statements on the subject of home at different stages in his life, it is tempting to attach more weight to later comments, in which he has the benefit of hindsight. When asked shortly before the poet's death where he felt at home Fried named, next to antifascism and Marxism, 'in der deutschen Sprache, im Schreiben'.[78] This may be accounted for by the loss of his childhood home and by the fact that the German language remained a major link with Fried's past and with that home.

In his political and literary work Erich Fried confirmed Reich-Ranicki's assertion: 'Wer einmal exiliert war, hört niemals auf, ein Exilierter zu sein',[79] but Fried was never 'exiled' from the German language. The process of 'feilen' already discussed, of working in and with the German language replaced the original aim of the activity, of intellectually reaching the writer's lost home. Other exile writers may have felt at home in both English and German. In the case of Erich Fried, however, there could be no question of language-switching, not merely because German was a link with home, but because, for the exiled writer, that language had assumed the rôle of 'Heimat'.

Notes

[1] Erich Fried, 'Der Flüchtling und die Furcht vor der Heimkehr', in *Gedanken in und an Deutschland*, ed. Michael Lewin (Vienna: Europa-Verlag, 1988), pp. 150–160 (p. 160).

[2] Erich Fried, *Befreiung von der Flucht: Gedichte und Gegengedichte* (Frankfurt/M.: Fischer, 1984), p. 139.

[3] See for example the call in *Freie Deutsche Kultur*, May 1940, 4.

[4] Unpublished interview with Anne Duden, London, 18.12.90.

[5] Hilde Spiel, after: *Österreicher im Exil: Großbritannien 1938–1945. Eine Dokumentation*, ed. by Wolfgang Muchitsch (Vienna: Österreichischer Bundesverlag, 1992), pp. 406f.

6 Erich Fried, 'Der Flüchtling und die Furcht vor der Heimkehr', in *Gedanken*, p. 150.

7 Robert Neumann, *Ein leichtes Leben: Bericht über mich selbst und Zeitgenossen* (Vienna/ Munich/ Basle: Desch, 1963), pp. 156f.

8 Cameron McCabe (i.e. Ernst Bornemann), *The Face on the Cutting-Room Floor* (London: Gollancz; Harmondsworth: Penguin, 1986).

9 See James M. Ritchie, 'Ernst Bornemann and *The Face on the Cutting Room Floor*', in *Brücken schlagen... 'Weit draußen auf eigenen Füßen': Festschrift für Fernand Hoffmann*, ed. by Joseph Kohnen, Hans-Joachim Solms and Klaus-Peter Wegera (Frankfurt/M.: Peter Lang, 1994), pp. 213–230.

10 Lion Feuchtwanger, 'Arbeitsprobleme des Schriftstellers im Exil', *Freies Deutschland*, 3, no.4 (March 1944), 27–28 (p. 27).

11 See Waltraud Strickhausen, 'Schreiben in der Sprache des *Anderen*: Eine Vorstudie zu den Publikationsmöglichkeiten und der Wirkung englischsprachiger Exilwerke in Großbritannien', in *Die Resonanz des Exils: gelungene und mißlungene Rezeption deutschsprachiger Exilautoren*, ed. by Dieter Sevin (Amsterdam: Rodopi, 1992), pp. 369–382 and 'Anhang', ibid., pp. 383–396; and Richard Dove, 'The Gift of Tongues: German-speaking Novelists Writing in English', in *Between Two Languages: German-speaking Exiles in Great Britain, 1933–45*, ed. by William Abbey, Charmian Brinson, Richard Dove, Marian Malet and Jennifer Taylor, Stuttgarter Arbeiten zur Germanistik 308/ Publications of the Institute of Germanic Studies 59 (Stuttgart: Akademischer Verlag, 1995), pp. 95–115.

12 Bertolt Brecht, 'Die Courage lernt nichts: Stellungnahmen Brechts zu Aufführungen 1953 bis 1956', in *Brechts 'Mutter Courage und ihre Kinder'*, ed. by Klaus-Detlef Müller (Frankfurt/M.: Suhrkamp, 1982), pp. 246–249 (p. 246).

13 Erich Fried, *They Fight in the Dark: The Story of Austria's Youth* (London: Young Austria in Great Britain, 1944).

14 *'Habe Angst vor dem, der keine Zweifel kennt': Gespräche mit Erich Fried*, ed. by Joern Schlund (Basel: Z-Verlag, 1988), p. 141.

15 Unpublished interview with Stuart Hood, London, 20.12.90.

16 See *Exiles: Erich Fried, Austrian Poet*, BBC2, 2.6.1988.

17 Ibid.

18 Erich Fried, *Höre Israel!* (Hamburg: Association, 1974; enlarged edn, Frankfurt/M.: Athenäum, 1983), p. 11.

19 *Exiles: Erich Fried. Austrian Poet.*

20 'Zur Tagung: Emigration und Exil heute', in *Nicht verdrängen — Nicht gewöhnen: Texte zum Thema Österreich*, ed. by Michael Lewin (Vienna: Europa-Verlag, 1987), pp. 59–62 (p. 59).

21 Previously cited interview with Stuart Hood.

[22] Lion Feuchtwanger, 'Arbeitsprobleme des Schriftstellers im Exil', 27.

[23] Marion Berghahn, *Continental Britons: German-Jewish Refugees from Nazi-Germany* (London: Macmillan; Oxford, New York and Hamburg: Berg, 1988) p. 154.

[24] Volker Kaukoreit, *Vom Exil bis zum Protest gegen den Krieg in Vietnam: Frühe Stationen des Lyrikers Erich Fried. Werk und Biographie, 1938–1966* (Darmstadt: Häusser, 1991) pp. 172f.

[25] Letter of 16.3.1949 from Erich Fried to Eugen Claassen, in Claassen-Archiv, Deutsches Literaturarchiv, Marbach am Neckar.

[26] Previously cited interview with Stuart Hood.

[27] Ibid.

[28] Unpublished interview with Catherine Fried-Boswell, London, 20.12.90.

[29] Previously cited interview with Anne Duden.

[30] Fritz Gottfurcht, 'The German Language versus Hitler', *Inside Nazi Germany* 2, no. 2 (February 1940), 12.

[31] Letter (undated; after 27.8.1948) from Erich Fried to Elisabeth Langgässer, in (A: Langgässer) Erich Fried, Langgässer, Elisabeth, 1948 (70.3395/2), Deutsches Literaturarchiv, Marbach am Neckar.

[32] Letter of 16.3.1949 from Erich Fried to Eugen Claassen, in Claassen-Archiv, Kasten 27, Mappe 1, 1948–1957, Deutsches Literaturarchiv, Marbach am Neckar.

[33] 'English Poetry II', see Talks Booking Requisition of 10.3.1947 from German Features, in Erich Fried, Talks, File 1: 1944–62, BBC Written Archives Centre, Reading; and 'English Poetry No. 3', see memo of 15.4.1947 from German Features to Programme Copyright Department, in Fried, Copyright, File 1: 1947–1962, BBC Written Archives Centre, Reading.

[34] Erich Fried after Herlinde Koelbl, *Jüdische Portraits: Photographien und Interviews* (Frankfurt/M.: Fischer, 1989) p. 69.

[35] 'Fried im Gespräch', *Neue Deutsche Literatur*, 36, no. 9 (September 1987), 9–14 (p. 13).

[36] See Fried, *Höre Israel!*

[37] See Christiane Jessen, 'Erich Fried und das Judentum: Thematische und sprachliche Untersuchungen anhand seiner Lyrik' (unpublished Magisterarbeit, Freie Universität Berlin, 1997), p. 44.

[38] *Der Zeitspiegel*, 1 August 1942, p. 6.

[39] *Jugend voran*, October 1942, pp. 14f.

[40] *Mut: Gedichte junger Österreicher* (London: Verlag Jugend voran, 1943), p. 19.

41 Ibid., p. 21.

42 Erich Fried, *Frühe Gedichte* (Düsseldorf: Claassen; Frankfurt/M.: Fischer, 1989), p. 67.

43 See for example 'Drei Gebete aus London', in *Frühe Gedichte*, p. 63.

44 Erich Fried, 'Die Fabriksmauer', *Jugend voran*, 3, October 1942, 9–10.

45 This line was maintained by Fried in pieces such as 'Das Gewehr mit den zwei Seelen' (*Der Zeitspiegel*, 6 December 1941, p. 8) which describes the desertion of Austrians from the German Army. In the prose piece 'Frau Neumayer weint nicht mehr' (*Junges Österreich*, 23 October 1943, p. 2) Fried cites the example of an Austrian half-Jew who has been pressed into the army, and in 'Angst' (*Die Zeitung*, 10 December 1943, p. 6), which is a personal account of his attempt to help his imprisoned parents, Fried detects signs of '*deutscher* Gewissenhaftigkeit'(my emphasis) in the changed appearance of Vienna.

46 Fried, *They Fight in the Dark*, p. 1.

47 Erich Fried, 'Bücher verbrennen', *Junges Österreich*, 3, no. 8 (mid-April 1941), 4f.

48 Erich Fried, 'Heimat', *Der Zeitspiegel*, 19 October 1941, p. 6.

49 Ibid.

50 Ibid.

51 Erich Fried, *Warngedichte* (Munich: Hanser; Frankfurt/M.: Fischer, 1980), p. 19.

52 Fried, *Warngedichte*, p. 19.

53 *Exiles: Erich Fried. Austrian Poet.*

54 In June 1962 Fried was a guest of the Österreichische Gesellschaft für Literatur and again in September 1963. See letter of 27.6.1962 from Hilde Claassen to Erich Fried, Claassen-Archiv, Briefe 1961–1966, Deutsches Literaturarchiv, Marbach am Neckar; and letter of 26.9.1963 from Hilde Claassen to Erich Fried, ibid.

55 *Literatur und Kritik*, 3, no. 11 (1967), 31f.

56 Lydia Trueb, 'Leben — das ist Wärme', in *Rote Revue/ Profil*, no. 9 (1983), 14–20 (p. 19).

57 Stefan Koldenhoff and Michael Magner, 'Hol's der Teufel', *TAZ*, 29 November 1988, pp. 11–12 (p. 11).

58 *Im Brennpunkt: Ein Österreich. 14 Beiträge auf der Suche nach einer Konstante*, ed. by Manfred Wagner (Vienna: Europa-Verlag, 1976), pp. 19–30.

59 Previously cited interview with Stuart Hood.

60 Wieland Schmied, 'Buchbesprechungen (Erich Fried, *Gedichte*)', *Wort in der Zeit*, 5, no. 5 (1959), 54–55 (p. 55).

[61] Peter de Mendelssohn, 'Schriftsteller ohne Sprache', *Die Zeitung*, 9 October 1941, p. 3.

[62] Erich Fried, *Reich der Steine: Zyklische Gedichte* (Hamburg: Claassen; Frankfurt/M.: Fischer, 1986) pp. 45–50.

[63] Ibid., p. 45.

[64] See 'Dreier Toren Tod', in: *Blick in die Welt*, 2, no. 1 (1947), p. 17.

[65] Letter of March 1962 from Erich Fried to Hilde Claassen, Claassen-Verlag Briefe, Mappe 3, 1961–1966, Deutsches Literaturarchiv, Marbach am Neckar.

[66] Lion Feuchtwanger, 'Arbeitsprobleme des Schriftstellers im Exil', pp. 27f.

[67] Fried, *Frühe Gedichte*, p. 114.

[68] Unpublished interview with Gerhard Wilke, London, 20.12.90.

[69] Erich Fried, *Die bunten Getüme: Siebzig Gedichte* (Berlin: Wagenbach, 1977), p. 56.

[70] See Erich Fried, 'Finaler Rettungsschuß', in *Deutsche Stichworte*, ed. by Horst Kurnitzky and Marion Schmid (Frankfurt/M.: Neue Kritik, 1984), pp. 110–112 (p. 110).

[71] 'Brief an Bettina von Arnim', in *Abschiedsbriefe an Deutschland*, ed. by Hans-Jürgen Heinrichs (Frankfurt/M. and Paris: Qumran-Verlag, 1984), pp. 145–154 (p. 148).

[72] See *Kürbiskern*, no. 2 (1975), 7.

[73] *Der Spiegel*, 26, no. 7 (1972), 8.

[74] See *Die Erschießung des Georg von Rauch*, ed. by Heinrich Böll et al. (Berlin: Wagenbach, 1976).

[75] 'Über den Begriff "Mord"', in *Die Erschießung des Georg von Rauch*, pp. 67–71 (p. 67).

[76] Viktor Klemperer, *LTI: Notzbuch eines Philologen*, 3rd edn (Halle: Niemeyer; Leipzig: Reclam, 1975), p. 10.

[77] Erich Fried and Michael Helm, *Gegen das Vergessen: Texte und Radierungen* (Cologne: Bund, 1987), p. 106.

[78] 'Fried im Gespräch', *Neue Deutsche Literatur*, 36, no. 9 (September 1987), 9–14 (p. 13).

[79] Marcel Reich-Ranicki, 'Die Anläufe eines Heimatlosen', *Die Zeit*, 17 December 1965, p. 25.

Axel Goodbody

'Eine Synthese deutscher und englischer Dichtungstraditionen': Erich Fried and Michael Hamburger as translators and poets

Erich Fried's role as a literary mediator between Britain and the German-speaking world is compared and contrasted with that of his fellow émigré Michael Hamburger. Since Fried's breakthrough to a wider German audience as a poet in the 1960s, his earlier work as a translator from English into German has been largely forgotten. Hamburger has on the other hand had a distinguished career as a translator in the opposite direction, from German into English, while his own poetry, written in the English language, has suffered relative neglect. Both poets have sought in their writing to integrate elements from the two cultures. This account of their biographies, their translations and their poetry addresses questions concerning the linguistic impact of exile, and the relationship between cultural production and reproduction.

Erich Fried and Michael Hamburger were separated by only three years of age, but these three years, and the difference of five years in the date of their arrival in Britain, had lasting consequences for the linguistic and cultural impact of emigration on them. For while Fried, who was seventeen years old when he arrived in London in 1938, became a German writer in exile, Hamburger wrote his first poems *in English* in the same year, having been in the country since the age of nine. Besides writing poetry and prose, Fried was to translate Shakespeare and English contemporaries such as Dylan Thomas and Sylvia Plath into German, while Hamburger's poetry has been accompanied by translations of Hölderlin, Goethe, Büchner, Hofmannsthal, and a whole series of contemporary German poets into English, as well as critical studies of German literature. They differ, then, in the direction of their literary mediation. In both cases, however, creative writing has been closely linked with translation and the presentation of literature in one language to readers of the other through introduction and commentary. Indeed, the literary breakthrough to a wider public came in both instances first as a translator, and only subsequently as a writer.

Fried's and Hamburger's literary development prompts questions about the impact on writers of living in a foreign language context, the difficulties it confronts them with, and what stimulus for literary creativity can be derived from linguistic and cultural dislocation. It examines the relationship between creative writing and translation, the problems

associated with the transmission of the cultural trends and poetic techniques
prevailing in one country into the language of another, and last but not
least about the opportunity for a creative synthesis of the two literary
traditions.

Emigration and bilingualism
German and Austrian émigrés have been among the most important
cultural mediators between Britain and the German-speaking countries
since the Second World War. They were predestined by their personal
experience of life in Britain to contribute to exchanges between German
culture and that of the host country, and by their immersion in the foreign
language to act as translators.[1] Yet the linguistic situation of the émigré
was, for both Fried and Hamburger, more complex and fraught with more
difficulties than this suggests.

Fried arrived in London in August 1938 as a penniless refugee, but
determined to become a 'deutscher Dichter'. Literary ambition was
inseparable from personal and political aims: he wished to avenge his
father's death by exposing the origins of fascism and war, and combating
racism and social injustice in every form.[2] He would appear to have
learned quite quickly to speak, read and write English competently, and his
many translations are ample evidence of the remarkable passive linguistic
skills he acquired over the years. However, he retained a strong accent
throughout his life and traces of German syntax in his written and spoken
English. As this suggests, his integration in London social and literary life
was only partial. This was not merely due to what he has described as the
'non-assimilative' nature of British culture,[3] but also to a reluctance on his
own part to assimilate.[4] His social and literary contacts during the war
years were almost exclusively in émigré circles, and he remained
orientated towards a German-speaking audience in Europe up to his death
in 1987. In his first decade in London, most of his contact with Englishmen
and women was restricted to the working class in the factories where he
earned a living as an unskilled labourer. Everyday life thus involved code-
switching between English in the working environment, and German at
home and in the social circle provided by the Austrian Centre and the Free
League of German Culture.

German became Fried's literary language. He shared with other
émigrés a sense of mission to act as guardian of the language and culture of
the 'other' Germany in exile. But he was also motivated by a more personal
need to preserve his own identity, to foster the linguistic link with his

Viennese childhood and youth. Ironically, his first book publication was the
English-language brochure *They Fight in the Dark*.[5] This fictional account
of the Austrian resistance, based on factual information, was written for a
British audience, its function determining the choice of language. Fried was
never again to publish in English.[6] During the war, Fried gained a
reputation as a versatile journalist and translator, poet and dramatist from
readings, performances and publications in German-language exile journals
and anthologies, and published two significant poetry volumes, *Deutschland*
and *Österreich*.[7] Though he had expected to return to Austria at the end of
the war, he did not do so for reasons both political and personal.[8] He
continued to contemplate moving back to Austria or Germany at various
junctures, and travelled increasingly frequently from the 'fifties onwards,
coming by the 'eighties to spend four to five months a year abroad. But he
never gave up his home in London.[9]

In a speech at the London PEN Congress of September 1941 which
was much discussed at the time, 'Writers without Language', Peter de
Mendelssohn distinguished between two kinds of writers in exile, the
émigré and the *refugee*. For the former, the J. B. Priestleys of German
literature, the (political) message was paramount and language essentially a
tool, while the main preoccupation of the latter, the German Virginia
Woolfs, was 'their language, their style, their melody'. The first group
would go over to using English as the medium of their writing, while the
second would continue to write in German for the day when their work
could be read in Germany again. In the world after the war, both would be
'equally necessary and indispensable'.[10] Since Sylvia Patsch published her
book on Austrian writers in Britain in 1985 with chapters on the English-
language novels of Hans Flesch-Brunningen, Robert Neumann and
Hermynia Zur Mühlen, the hitherto neglected phenomenon of exile
novelists crossing the language barrier has attracted increasing attention.[11]
Peter de Mendelssohn's *The Hours and the Centuries*, Arthur Koestler's
Scum of the Earth and *Arrival and Departure* (though not his masterpiece
Darkness at Noon, which was translated from German), and Robert
Neumann's *The Inquest* are among the more significant works to have been
rediscovered or reassessed.[12] Historians and biographers found the
transition easier than novelists. However, writers like de Mendelssohn, who
had the benefit of a solid grounding in English from school, and his wife
Hilde Spiel, who embarked on an impressive programme of reading
English fiction and poetry, essays and literary journalism, were able to

acquire a more than adequate command of English in the space of a few years. Richard Dove makes a useful distinction between writers using the *denotative* and the *connotative* meanings of words: whereas changing languages was relatively unproblematic for those whose writing relied primarily on the former, it was inevitably more difficult for those concerned with verbal associations and connotations. Poets rarely adopted the foreign language.[13]

Fried once commented, looking back in the late 'seventies, that to write in English had always been out of the question for him. It would have meant losing all the unconscious elements so important in creative writing. Hardly anyone, he insisted, can really write in a foreign language:

> So gut wie niemand kann wirklich in einer anderen als der eigenen Muttersprache schreiben. Journalisten vielleicht noch, Schriftsteller kaum je. Sie sind mit ihrer Muttersprache untrennbar verknüpft. Das Mischungsverhältnis von bewußten und unbewußten Faktoren beim Schreiben geht auf frühkindheitliche Erfahrungen, auch Erfahrungen beim Sprechenlernen, zurück. [...] Während [Robert] Neumann in deutscher Sprache nicht nur ein guter Erzähler, sondern auch ein bemerkenswerter Stilist war, blieb sein Englisch wenig mehr als ein korrektes Kommunikationsmittel. Gelegentlich machte er sogar Fehler, die verrieten, daß er *deutsch dachte*. [...] Von den *Lyrikern* im englischen Exil hat meines Wissens keiner englische Gedichte zu schreiben versucht, außer in besonderen Notfällen, z.B. wenn sich einer in ein Mädchen verliebte, das nur englisch sprach.[14]

Fried described himself and other exile writers as caught between the atrophy of their own language and an imperfect command of the new. He spoke of the dangers of linguistic impoverishment, the writer being cut off from sources of enrichment and change, 'weil der Nachschub aus Dialekt und Umgangssprache, aus einem Dutzend Fachjargons und aus der Sprache der Halbwüchsigen einfach fehlt'.[15] The fresh vocabulary and idioms associated with new experiences can only be derived from the foreign language. As Lion Feuchtwanger expressed it wryly in 1943: 'Da ist zunächst die bittere Erfahrung, abgespalten zu sein vom lebendigen Strom der Muttersprache. [...] Immer und für alles haben wir den Klang der fremden Sprache im Ohr, ihre Zeichen dringen täglich, stündlich auf uns ein, *sie knabbern an unserem eigenen Ausdrucksvermögen*.'[16] (My emphasis — A.G.) German all too easily became stiff and dry in the attempt to prevent English language expressions encroaching: by the end of the war, according to Fried, many émigrés were writing 'ein manchmal fast peinlich halbwilhelminisches Deutsch'.[17]

One alternative was of course the deliberate integration of English words into German texts. Adrienne Ash defends Theodor Kramer's use of English (including terms without German equivalents such as 'roll-call' and 'black-out') in his exile poems as an intensification of 'the presentation of an alien environment and thus of the split personality of the poet adrift'.[18] But such code mixing, sometimes referred to as 'Emigranto', had the disadvantage of being only understood by the small émigré circle, and becoming dated when the political situation altered. Though some writers undoubtedly handled the interspersing of foreign language elements in German skilfully, it was usually to humorous effect, and in serious contexts has been felt by readers to be an intrinsically unsatisfactory 'contamination'.

Fried was nonetheless wrong to dismiss the option of switching languages and writing in English so emphatically. As Dieter Lamping has pointed out in an article challenging previous assumptions, there are plenty of successful examples of literary code switching.[19] These include not only writers who grew up with one language and subsequently learned a second, which became their literary medium (Joseph Conrad, Elias Canetti and Samuel Beckett), and representatives of 'small literatures' like Danish (Karen Blixen) and colonial literatures (Leopold Senghor, Salman Rushdie), but also exile writers whose linguistic situation was the result of political upheavals, such as Adelbert von Chamisso and Ludwig Börne in the nineteenth century, and Vladimir Nabokov, Peter Weiss and Klaus Mann in the twentieth. In any case, Richard Dove's recent article on Robert Neumann, 'Almost an English Author', suggests Fried's judgement of Neumann was unjust — *The Inquest* and other novels Neumann wrote in English after 1940 reveal a 'remarkable command of idiomatic English' and great sensitivity to formal and colloquial registers.[20] Dove and Waltraud Strickhausen both indicate German novelists were on the whole less hampered by their command of the English language than by their style, subject matter and cultural resonance, which did not always meet readers' (or reviewers') expectations.[21]

The reasons why Neumann and others switched to writing in English have recently been clarified by Dirk Wiemann. There was in fact no German publishing house in Britain which could have brought out longer prose works during the war. Wiemann distinguishes between two phases in the production and publication of exile novels in Britain. From 1933 up to 1938 relatively few émigrés found their way to Britain, and these did not establish significant cultural organisations. Émigrés writing in Britain typically sought publication by one of the continental exile publishers, for example Allert de Lange or Querido in Amsterdam, Oprecht in Zurich, or Bermann Fischer in Stockholm, and subsequently approached a British publisher to bring out an English translation. From 1939 on this was no longer possible. So at the very moment the German-speaking readership in Britain grew to a size which might have supported the publication of novels in German in this country, writers were forced to have their work appear in translation, if it was to be published at all. The move to circumvent the translator by writing in English from the start was a natural one, though it meant authors had to reorientate themselves towards the British reading public. Ironically, they lost many of their German readers in doing so. German exile literature was thus integrated into mainstream publishing to a much greater extent than in France.[22] This did not, however, hold true in equal measure for the publication of shorter prose and poetry, for which the German-language journals in London provided a ready outlet.

Wulf Köpke suggests in his article 'Die Wirkung des Exils auf Sprache und Stil' that language switching probably results in a greater intellectual awareness of language at the cost of associative richness and the unconscious element of poetic creativity, leading to a 'fundamentale Unsicherheit'.[23] There is doubtless truth in this, as in the observation that ambiguities, complex idioms, play on literary quotations and colloquialisms, images derived directly from the language, sarcasm, satire and caricature cannot easily be transferred from one language into another,[24] but there is no intrinsic reason why imaginative writing in two languages is either impossible or invalid.

Poets, too, have been known to write in more than one language – Lamping gives Swinburne and George, Rilke and Goll, Ungaretti and Marinetti, Pessoa and Eliot as examples. Nonetheless, Michael Hamburger, whose literary career would seem to contradict Fried's views outright, has described the impact of language switching in the autobiographical 'variations' which make up the first part of his book *Zwischen den Sprachen* in terms comparable to Köpke's. He interprets bilingualism as a curse rather than a blessing, and associates it with a destabilisation of personal identity. In *Zwischen den Sprachen* (and again in his autobiography *String of Beginnings*),[25] Hamburger recounts how, his family having left Berlin for Edinburgh when he was only nine, his secondary and higher education took place in English. In his first year, while his father, a paediatrician at the Charité with a flourishing private practice, was studying to take the British medical exams in Edinburgh, he learned English rapidly, winning a school prize for exceptional progress in the language. When the family moved to London, he attended Westminster public school (his merchant banking grandfather, who had also moved to England, probably paid the fees), won an exhibition to study at Christ Church, Oxford, in 1941, when not quite seventeen, and completed the process of British socialisation by joining the Army in 1943.

Like many young émigrés keen to integrate, Hamburger largely abandoned German for English: 'Jahrelang sprach ich kaum Deutsch, höchstens mit meiner Mutter, mit den Geschwistern kaum mehr, auch als die Familie noch nicht durch die Kriegsumstände zersprengt war; schrieb nur englisch, dachte und träumte englisch' (*ZdS* p. 29). Though his German vocabulary advanced far beyond that of a child as a result of his experiences in the army in Austria in 1945-7, and through reading German literature, he describes his German as 'schlechte[s], steife[s] und lückenhafte[s] Buchdeutsch' (*ZdS* p. 32). Contact with literary émigrés (Heinz Priebatsch, Franz Baermann Steiner and Jesse Thoor) in the late 1940s and early 1950s only made him more aware of his Englishness (*ZdS* p. 31).[26]

One of Hamburger's principal concerns in *Zwischen den Sprachen* is to dispel any illusions about bilingualism coming easily or being a simple phenomenon. It was not the 'Erschütterungen' of his move to England (*ZdS* p. 28) and first confrontation with the foreign language, but a second 'bilingualism', the experience of regional and social variation in language, learning the differences between Edinburgh and London English, and between the received pronunciation spoken in Westminster and the everyday language of the ranks in the army, which he describes as plunging him into a crisis 'in der Diktion meiner Lyrik und in meinem Verhältnis zur Sprache überhaupt'. (*ZdS* p. 30) For the time being, however, Hamburger learned to live with the situation, and it was only when he began writing in German fifteen years later that the crisis was to come to a head. After four years as a freelance writer, he became a lecturer in German at University College, London in 1952:

> Bald schrieb ich ab und zu kritische Beiträge für deutsche Zeitschriften, zuerst nur in englisch, dann mit Mühe und Not in deutsch. Erst elf Jahre später — und dreißig Jahre nach der Auswanderung — geschah es, daß ich ein nichtkritisches Prosastück

deutsch schrieb, und zwar nicht zufällig über die Wiederbegegnung mit Berlin.
(*ZdS* p. 33)

'Rediscovering' his German childhood and the German language on visits
to Berlin in 1956 and 1962, he was persuaded to write a first piece of non-
academic prose at the end of the 'fifties. Temporarily adopting the German
language as a literary medium, he found himself in a profoundly unsettling
situation:

> Mit genau vierzig Jahren [schrieb ich] mein erstes deutsches Gedicht [...]
> Erschreckend war das, weil ich die Zweisprachigkeit weder vorausgesehen noch
> erwünscht hatte, weil ich nun — auch in meinen englischen Gedichten — noch
> einmal emigrieren mußte, diesmal aber in ein Niemandsland. [...] Mein
> Niemandsland zwischen den Sprachen konnte eigentlich nur ein Land des
> Schweigens und der Nacktheit sein, denn nicht nur Kleider, sondern auch Wörter
> und Satzformen machen Leute. [...] Im Niemandsland wurde jedes Schreiben
> schwerer als je zuvor. Wer es einmal betreten hatte, gewöhnte sich an die tägliche
> Gefahr, an das tägliche Risiko des Verstummens zwischen den Sprachen. (*ZdS* p.
> 33)

The gain of German as a medium of expression is here presented as
outweighed by an unexpected, traumatic loss of instinctive command of
English. 'Wenn es Schichten gab, die mir nur durch deutsche Wörter
zugänglich waren, schien es fast gewiß, daß diese Schichten meinem
Englisch fehlten und immer fehlen würden. Das Wissen von dieser
Möglichkeit bedeutete aber, daß sie nun zum täglichen Risiko gehörte.'
(*ZdS* p. 34) The void opened up between the 'safe' territories of each
language threatened his creative writing and very sense of identity.

Painful though the 'silence' and 'nakedness' of this no man's land
between the languages was, it nevertheless provided a unique opportunity
to get behind the treacherous half-certainties of linguistic convention.
Echoing Hofmannsthal's language scepticism in the 'Brief des Lord
Chandos', Hamburger writes:

> Im reineren, nicht verschönenden Licht des Niemandslandes lächelte man über die
> Trachten und die beruflich maskierten Gesichter. Dort ging nämlich das absurde
> Gerücht, daß die Leute unter den Trachten nackt seien; auch daß unter den Worten
> eine Stille läge, an der nicht nur alle Menschen, sondern auch noch die Tiere,
> Pflanzen und Steine teilhaben. (*ZdS* p. 34)

The idea of a poetic language tapping into the universal 'Natursprache'
touched on here, possibly influenced by friendship with Johannes
Bobrowski, was to assume a key role in Hamburger's poetics. In the short
term the autobiographical prose and the handful of poems he wrote in

German[27] were 'der Beginn einer Zerrüttung, die sich ohne weiteren
Anlaß fortsetzte', reopening old wounds, and making him for the first time
fully aware of the rift between his German-language childhood and life in
England:

> Darum ist die Zweisprachigkeit für einen Schreibenden ein Unglück. Was ich auf
> deutsch erlebte, verlangt auf deutsch wiedergegeben zu werden. Aber das wenige
> Deutsch, welches mir aus der Kindheit erhalten blieb, reicht zum Schreiben nicht
> aus; und das später Erlernte bleibt, wie alles nur Erlernte, abstrakt, fügt sich nicht
> den Gedanken und dem Gefühl. Die Zerrissenheit des Erlebten ist arg genug; die
> Zweisprachigkeit zerreißt es noch einmal. (*ZdS* p. 26)

In the longer term, nonetheless, Hamburger's position in the no man's land
between the languages fostered a critical awareness of the shaping and
distorting of thought in each language, and encouraged exploration of the
possibility of a poetic language in which words are linked to the things they
describe by more than mere convention.

Fried and Hamburger have indicated the difficulties arising from the
language situations they found themselves in in no uncertain terms.
However, the émigré situation and the linguistic context were for both, I
hope to demonstrate, a productive irritation from which they ultimately
succeeded in deriving creative stimulus. Detachment from everyday use of
German was, for instance, acknowledged by Fried as having a positive
aspect: 'Ich hatte das Glück, in eine Zivilisation verschlagen zu werden, die
den Fremden kaum heimisch werden läßt', he wrote with irony in 1958.
'So blieb mir meine Sprache erhalten, bereichert und *zugleich bedroht und
fruchtbar in Frage gestellt* durch die Möglichkeit des Abstandes vom
Gebrauch und Mißbrauch des Alltags'.[28] (My emphasis — A.G.) For his
part, Hamburger was able to master the crisis when he ceased to attempt to
paper over the cracks, faced up to the rift in his identity, and took courage,
'nach der Rückkehr, entspannt [...], Fetzen zu verwerten, die Zerrissenheit
selber darzustellen'. He came to recognise that the gap left by the
disruption of the automatic link between thing and word which resulted
from writing in a language not his first could be accepted, left open and
explored, that if his identity had been called in question, this was in time to
facilitate 'den freieren Gebrauch des Ichs in Gedichten oder Prosa' (*ZdS*
pp. 27 and 35; *SoB* p. 93). Before examining their poetry and prose, it
will be useful to gain an impression of Fried's and Hamburger's
achievements in mediating between English and German literature as
translators.

Fried and Hamburger as translators

Fried's and Hamburger's translations in over four decades after the war are
too numerous for a comprehensive account here.[29] Volker Kaukoreit's
monograph of Fried's early writing,[30] the standard work on the poet,
provides much relevant information, including listings of his publications,
radio broadcasts and translations up to 1966. Steven Lawrie affords
additional insights through the focus of his book on 'the effect which
extended exile in an English-speaking environment had on his career'.[31]
Though the last ten years have seen the publication of a useful collection of
articles in the volume *Michael Hamburger: Dichter und Übersetzer*, and of
two German studies of Hamburger's poetry, there is as yet no account of
Michael Hamburger's writing comparable in scope or detail to those on
Fried, to which one can turn as a source regarding his translation. The
author's autobiography *String of Beginnings* provides helpful, though
scattered, information on Hamburger's activities as a translator, but only
covers the period up to 1954. For the years since I have consulted Ralf
Jeutter's bibliography, included information of Hamburger's work for the
BBC gathered from the Michael Hamburger files held at the BBC Written
Archives Centre, Caversham, and referred to Uta Kreuter's study of the
reception of German literature in Britain between 1960 and 1980.[32] The
following account of Hamburger's translations should nonetheless be
regarded as provisional.

In a radio interview in 1975 Fried described how he began
translating English poems he liked in order to make them his own by
putting them into his own tongue.[33] His first published translations were in
fact popular Russian political poems which he translated from English
versions for *Young Austria* in 1941/42. These were followed by other
short pieces for *Die Zeitung*. Fried's main social and literary contacts in
the war years were in émigré circles. Through the Austrian Centre and the
Free German League of Culture he appears to have met Stephen Spender,
the Australian novelist Jack Lindsay and the Hungarian-German émigré
poet David Martin.[34] Martin, together with Fried's friend and mentor
Joseph Kalmer, financed the publication of his first poetry volume
Deutschland. In gratitude, Fried reviewed Martin's poetry volume
Battlefields and Girls (1942) in *Der Zeitspiegel*, and even translated it into
German, but the translation was not published.[35] Towards the end of the
war, Fried began to take an increasing interest in English literature. He
became a member of the Club 1943, which served (and continues to serve

today) as a meeting place for émigrés with interested English circles. In the late 'forties, when the exile community was dispersing, he convened the 'London Group' of poets (Fried, Franz Baermann Steiner, Hans Eichner, H. G. Adler, Hans Werner Cohn and Georg Rapp). These poets read and discussed each other's work, but also contemporary English poetry, seeking to derive from T. S. Eliot in particular new impulses for their own writing. Fried also participated for a time in a British Marxist writers' group including Jack Lindsay, the Australian John Manifold and the anarchist writer Alex Comfort, where he gave a talk on the aesthetics of Christopher Caudwell, and he met other English writers through his work for the BBC.

Fried's contacts with English writers, however modest they were, are, like Michael Hamburger's with German and Austrian literary émigrés, which will be discussed later, of interest because of the generally accepted view that there was very little exchange between British writers and German émigrés in London.[36] The role of the English PEN Centre, and of its president and secretary Margaret Storm Jameson and Hermon Ould in particular, in working to integrate German and other émigrés in English literary life has recently been discussed,[37] and Ernst Toller and Arthur Koestler have been acknowledged as 'exceptions' who made a major impact on the English literary scene. Statements by émigrés (including Fried) on their isolation from the literary life of the host country may have been taken too readily at face value.

In the late 'forties Fried was effectively trained as a journalist and translator, and set exercises in poetic techniques, by his friend and mentor Joseph Kalmer. Kalmer was an excellent linguist, as well as a poet and journalist. As the owner of a literary agency, he was in a position to place over a hundred pieces of original writing and translation by Fried in German, Swiss and Austrian papers and magazines under a variety of pseudonyms. These were mostly of a trivial nature, but there was occasional scope for a more serious concern with contemporary poetry. In a hitherto unpublished letter to Franz Theodor Csokor written on the 12 May 1946 Fried mentions translating contemporary English poetry together with Kalmer among other literary projects in hand. After mentioning his poems, the more recent of which are less political than his wartime verse and experiment with surrealism and psychoanalysis as 'integrierende Bestandteile einer großzügigen Realismuskonzeption', as well as plans for short stories, he goes on:

Ansonsten befasse ich mich [...] zusammen mit Kalmer mit der Übersetzung englischer Lyrik aller Richtungen und Schulen aus den letzten Jahren (die so erscheinen soll, daß auf einer Seite der englische, auf der anderen der deutsche Text gedruckt wird).[38]

Elisabeth Langgässer, to whom Kalmer had given Fried an introduction, wrote to the publisher Eugen Claassen in 1948 recommending him as a poet and translator. Claassen visited Fried in London a few months later, and they discussed the possible publication of translations as well as Fried's own prose and poetry over a period of years. Unfortunately, the political and economic circumstances were not favourable. Fried was by this time writing and translating for the re-education journals *Neue Auslese* and *Blick in die Welt* published in 1945-50 by the Foreign Office. Within their broad brief of democratic re-education by familiarising German readers with the literature from around the world they had been cut off from since 1933, Fried was able to publish eighteen translations in *Neue Auslese*, including poetry and prose by Graham Greene, Sidney Keyes, John Masefield and Liam O'Flaherty. For *Blick in die Welt* he translated stories by Alex Comfort and Somerset Maugham. Among his translations for the *Englische Rundschau* in the early 'fifties was an essay by Stephen Spender on Rilke's influence in England.

It was radio, however, which was to play the crucial role in Fried's career as a translator. There is evidence he was already doing talks and translations for the BBC German Service by the end of the war, and worked there on an occasional basis up to 1949. From 1950 on he broadcast fairly regularly, especially after 1952, when he was employed by the German Soviet Zone Programme. He soon gained a reputation as a reliable and conscientious translator. The works he translated ranged from the medieval York miracle plays to hymns (for Christmas and Easter programmes), from the poetry of Donne and Milton to Eliot, Dylan Thomas and Sidney Keyes. Radio plays by H. G. Wells and John Masefield were broadcast in his German versions in the early 'fifties.

Fried's real breakthrough as a translator came with his version of Dylan Thomas's radio play *Under Milk Wood* in 1954. This was translated under extraordinary time pressure — Lawrie recounts how the German Soviet Zone Programme for which he was working as Political Commentator at the time released him for a mere week. Fried dictated to two typists, correcting the typescripts in the evenings.[39] He had known Thomas between 1950 and his death in 1953 and translated excerpts from his writing as early as 1943. However, his ability to translate such complex material in so short a time remains remarkable. *Unter dem Milchwald* was produced again by the German radio stations NWDR and SWF in September 1954, published, and adapted successfully for the stage. Fried's translation was widely acknowledged to be 'kongenial', doing justice to the alliteration and assonance of the original, its modulations of tempo, and the different levels of language, ranging from everyday speech with humorous, grotesque and vulgar elements, to the lyrical descriptive passages of the two narrators. It marked a turning point in his career, attracting the attention of both the German public and publishers. Commissions for further translation broadcasts and publications followed, and, as Lawrie has shown, there was a direct link with the publication of Fried's first post-war volume of poetry in 1958, and Fried's three radio plays broadcast in the first half of the 'sixties.[40]

In the late 1950s and early 1960s Fried completed translations of an astonishing range of contemporary English poetry and drama. This included Eliot and Thomas, Graham Greene, John Arden, Edith Sitwell and John Millington Synge, and the political playwrights Arnold Wesker and John Whiting. A reference to his translating ability by Rudolf Walter Leonhardt, who knew Fried from his days at the BBC, after Leonhardt had become literary editor of *Die Zeit*, led to Kurt Hübner commissioning him to translate Shakespeare's *Midsummer Night's Dream* for a production by Peter Zadek in Bremen in 1963. This was to be the first of no fewer than twenty-seven Shakespeare plays he translated, three more than Schlegel/ Tieck, as he took pleasure in pointing out. Fried's Shakespeare translations have been described by Klaus Reichert as 'ein verfeinerter und verbesserter, zuweilen bloß modernisierter Schlegel/ Tieck', but were widely praised for their accuracy, liveliness and suitedness to the stage, and are still in use today. They were a useful source of income at a time when, despite his growing fame as a poet and public figure, he had become persona non grata with radio stations and publishers following the publication of *und Vietnam und* and his controversial involvement in German politics.

Another important twentieth-century writer Fried introduced to the German public in the 1970s was Sylvia Plath. He turned down an offer to translate her novel *The Bell Jar*, because he could not afford the time, but lobbied Suhrkamp for ten years[41] to bring out a translation of her *Ariel* poems. His versions of the poems,[42] which came out in 1974, are, according to Heimann, remarkable for their faithfulness to Plath's

suggestive patterns of sound repetition, though they lack the rhythmic
intensity and verbal radicalism of the original. Ironically, they were
criticised precisely for Fried's efforts to find equivalents to Plath's
innovatory language.

Poetry was for Hamburger, as for Fried, an obsession. 'Mit sechzehn
Jahren schrieb und übersetzte ich schon so intensiv, daß über meinen Beruf
kein Zweifel mehr bestand.' (ZdS p. 28) But his approach was necessarily
oblique, via the translation and critical study of German literature:

> Wäre ich im November 1933 einige Jahre älter oder jünger gewesen, hätte ich
> vermutlich entweder deutsch zu schreiben angefangen, wäre also trotz der
> Emigration ein deutscher Schriftsteller geworden, oder hätte englisch geschrieben,
> ohne nötigerweise zum Übersetzer und Germanisten zu werden. Als ich aber mit
> vierzehn oder fünfzehn Jahren ernstlich zu schreiben begann, empfand ich zugleich
> das Bedürfnis, die im Deutschen verwurzelte Vergangenheit in das neue Leben und
> den neuen Sprachbereich hinüberzutragen. (ZdS p. 57)

Hamburger's preoccupation with German literature was on the one hand
necessary to 'preserve some continuity with my own childhood' (SoB pp.
44f.), on the other it was an effort to present to English readers of poetry
the 'other', humanist Germany.[43] His first translation in December 1939
was a sentimental poem of Theodor Körner's celebrating loyal friendship
in the face of separation. Not long afterwards he began translating
Hölderlin, and his first book was a volume of translations of Hölderlin
poems published to coincide with the centenary of the poet's death in
1943.[44] (The first volume of his own poems only followed in 1950.) The
Hölderlin vogue in Britain, which came in the 'forties in the wake of the
discovery of interest in Rilke, Kafka and Hofmannsthal, coincided with a
shift away from the socio-political commitment of the previous decade to a
more metaphysical, 'neoromantic' literature. Hardly had the book come out
than Hamburger set to work translating new Hölderlin poems and revising
those he had already translated. Translating Hölderlin and writing critical
introductions to the various editions which he has published since have been
the preoccupation of a lifetime. At first prompted by emotional
identification with Hölderlin and his fate, he soon came to focus on his art,
making close observance of the metre of the original his hallmark.

Studying Modern Languages at Oxford, Hamburger's interests
broadened into a more general appropriation of the tradition of European
modernism, in which the French Symbolists took a central place. He
contributed towards a volume of Kafka stories edited by the artist Vera

Leslie, which was published in 1945, and corresponded with Hermann Hesse concerning a possible translation of *Steppenwolf*. After only four terms he interrupted his university course to join the army, but had to wait until the end of the war before he was posted outside Britain, because, as he only later recognised, his German background was distrusted and the army 'didn't know what to do with him' (*SoB* p. 136). Between 1943 and 1945 he was stationed in a series of camps between the south coast and the Shetlands. During this period of 'unreality, almost escapism' (*SoB* p. 148) he had sufficient leisure to translate the sixteenth-century French poet Maurice Scève and Walter von der Vogelweide, and prepare translations of Novalis's aphorisms and Baudelaire's prose poems for publication. Friendly contact with the émigré Heinz Priebatsch led him to start translating a novel of Priebatsch's. This was to occupy him sporadically over the next ten years, though it was never published in either German or English.

After postings in Italy and Austria (as interpreter, and later as headmaster of a boarding school for the children of British soldiers) which permitted little leisure for literary activity, he was de-mobbed in the summer of 1947 and returned to Oxford. German now became his main subject, reflecting a concentration of interest in areas linked with his poetry and the 'peculiarities of German literature and their bearing on the breakdown of European civilisation' (*SoB* p. 195). He soon found that he was more interested in writing than philology or the history of literature, and became increasingly involved in translations and reviews. From the start critical study was for Hamburger an adjunct to translation: he writes of an early resistance to the 'pursuit of knowledge as an end in itself' (*SoB* p. 302). *Reason and Energy*, which consisted of studies of Hölderlin, Novalis, Kleist, Heine and Büchner, arguing for a synthesis of reason (empiricism, rationalism) with energy (imagination, vision), was in part a response to tensions within the author's poetic writing.[45] *The Truth of Poetry*, which examines American, French, English and German poetry and poetic theory, an important contribution to the debate on modern realism in contemporary poetry in the UK, pleading for a poetry combining subjectivity with objectivity, was similarly motivated by personal interests.[46] Hamburger, who reviewed hundreds of books for the *New Statesman*, *Spectator* and little magazines in Britain, America and Germany, and whose reviews of contemporary German poetry in the *TLS* in the 'sixties and 'seventies were to be a key factor in its reception in

Britain, has described his ideal of literary criticism as 'Einfühlungskunst'. 'Das kritische Werk zeichnet sich wie andere literarische Werke dadurch aus, daß es Inneres mit Äußerem, Eigenes mit Fremdem verschmilzt.' (*ZdS* p. 140)

In the late 'forties Hamburger made contact with a number of important German émigré writers in London. 'There was a time, in my late teens and early twenties', he writes in *String of Beginnings*,

> when I may have 'over-compensated' for my foreign origin, as naturalised subjects
> – not excluding my idol of that period, T.S. Eliot – are apt to do [...] Yet some
> instinct always warned me off the more extreme forms of mimesis [...] and, from
> the same early period, I had also felt the need to be in touch with refugees less
> assimilated than myself. (*SoB* p. 291)

Alfred Marnau, Jesse Thoor and Heinz Priebatsch had been among his earliest acquaintances who wrote in German. These were now joined by the Austrian poet Felix Braun, and by Erich Fried and Hans Werner Cohn, H. G. Adler and Franz Baermann Steiner. He was deeply impressed by Steiner, whose poem on the death of his relatives in the extermination camps he admired and translated as 'Prayer in the Garden'. Meetings with Jesse Thoor (Peter Höfler) laid the foundation for a later edition of Thoor's work published in Germany. Felix Braun introduced him to Celan's poetry at a time when the 'Todesfuge' had not yet appeared in a book publication, and a year of two later he met Celan at a reading in Fried's home.

After graduating in 1949, Hamburger became a freelance writer, but had to lecture for the Workers' Educational Association and teach private pupils alongside reviewing and writing programmes for the BBC to make ends meet. He took up work on new versions of Hölderlin again for a second edition, which duly came out in 1952, and translated Büchner's *Leonce und Lena*.[47] (He had already published a translation of *Lenz*.)[48] Translations of short prose by Kleist, and poems by Rilke and Trakl followed, and Hamburger embarked on a project funded by the Bollingen Foundation translating Hofmannsthal. After initially helping Stephen Spender, he later took over the edition and coordination of two volumes, the *Poems and Verse Plays*, and the *Plays and Libretti*, for both of which he also wrote critical introductions.[49] In the same year he was commissioned by Thames and Hudson to translate Beethoven's *Letters, Journals and Conversations*.[50]

The first of Hamburger's many literary talks for the BBC Third Programme was a broadcast on Rilke in December 1949 which involved the translation of selected passages from the poet's letters and journals, with linking narrative. This was followed by programmes on Edwin Muir, the poet and translator of Hölderlin and Kafka, Thomas Mann and Broch, on Hölderlin, and from 1957 on, on a series of contemporary German poets. These included Enzensberger and Grass (in 1966), Celan (1971), Huchel (1974), and Heißenbüttel (1977). His last significant work for radio consisted of three programmes on Goethe's poetry in 1982. Translations by Hamburger of plays by Albrecht Goes, Hofmannsthal, and Peter Weiss, of three of Günter Eich's radio plays, and of poetry and prose by Kunert, Bichsel and Kunze were also broadcast.

From the late 1950s on, Hamburger published translations of German poetry, including Trakl and Rilke, Benn and Brecht, Lehmann and Eich, Sachs and Bachmann in British and American magazines. The early 'sixties were a time when German novels, and even more so German poetry, were avidly read in Britain, and looked to for 'alternatives in literary expression' for English writing.[51] The 'epoch-making' anthology *Modern German Poetry 1910-1960*,[52] edited by Christopher Middleton and Michael Hamburger in 1962, presented in the original and what were acknowledged to be often inspired English translations a tradition of German poetry with its beginnings in Rilke and the pre-war Expressionists, including the nature poets and the émigrés, and culminating in Brecht and Huchel, Celan and Heißenbüttel, Fried and Bachmann, Enzensberger and Christoph Meckel. Hamburger's subsequent anthologies *East German Poetry* and *German Poetry 1910-1975*, which introduced many important younger poets, were also hailed as landmark publications.[53] By the late 'seventies there was scarcely a significant contemporary German poet who did not have Michael Hamburger to thank for his or her reception in English. Many became personal friends, and several translated poems of Hamburger's into German. Hamburger's many awards and honours for his translations include the prize of the Darmstadt Akademie für Sprache und Dichtung (1964), the Schlegel/Tieck prize (1978 and 1981), the Goethe medal (1986), the Friedrich Hölderlin prize (1991), the international Petrarca prize (1992), an OBE (1992), and honorary doctorates from British and German universities.[54]

Appropriation of aspects of the foreign poetic tradition

The questions of the linguistic impact of exile on Erich Fried, and of English influences on his writing, are addressed at various points in both Volker Kaukoreit's and Steven Lawrie's books. Kaukoreit's detailed study of the 'mittlere Werkphase' between 1946 (the end of exile poetry in the narrow sense of the word) and 1962/3 (when Fried wrote the *Warngedichte*),[55] which includes thoughtful interpretations of selected poems, offers significant insights not only into Fried's poetic aims and achievements, but also into the elements that may be attributed to his reading of English poetry. In keeping with his aim to discuss 'the effects of the poet's residence in Great Britain' and to investigate 'the influence of the English language and of British culture' (pp. 2-5), Lawrie similarly discusses English influences on Fried's poetic technique, and seeks out motifs derived from English works he translated.[56]

Fried's wartime poetry was not merely Socialist Realism. The influence of the 'social nature poet' Theodor Kramer, the Expressionists (Trakl) and Rilke, Rimbaud and Hofmannsthal is discernible in poetic 'dialogues' with these, in imagery and diction. In the post-war decade Fried was searching for a new way of writing, to get beyond the conventional forms and simplistic political commitment of exile poetry. His translations, articles and radio commentaries on contemporary English poetry undoubtedly played a role in his development from the *Tendenzdichtung* of the wartime volumes to the more complex themes and formal and linguistic experimentation of *Von Bis nach Seit, Reich der Steine*, and *Gedichte*.[57] In a letter to Eugen Claassen dated 16 March 1949, Fried claims for the London Group of poets, of which he was the principal organiser, 'aus dem englischen kulturellen Klima, aus der englischen Dichtung, aus der ganzen Art, wie die Engländer mit ihrer Sprache umgehen, viel gelernt zu haben'. He describes their natural role as that of cultural mediators: 'Wir [...] können durch unser ganzes Wesen nicht anders, als zwischen deutscher und englischer Kultur zu vermitteln'.[58]

Five principal aspects of English influence may be observed in Fried's writing: the pun, manipulation of words, half-rhyme and associated poetic structures, imagery, and themes. Fried explores links between seemingly unrelated spheres of reference by means of puns and similar-sounding words. Semantic shifts based on homonyms provide the impetus for often surprising progressions in poems from this period.[59] The serious pun, or 'ernsthaftes Wortspiel', as Fried describes it in *Ein Soldat und ein*

Mädchen,[60] derives from more than one source. Exile in itself led to a heightened awareness of the sound of the individual German word, of homonyms and homophones. Fried himself traced his use of the pun as a literary technique back to the poem 'Ton', which originated in his acquaintance with a girl who suffered from schizophrenia and formed a strange association between the words 'Ton' (clay) and 'Töne' (sounds).[61] Kaukoreit identifies the speculative etymologist Kurt Himer's pamphlet *Gewordenes Wort* as a further source (pp. 200-202). But Fried was also influenced by the puns he found in English literature. Looking back in 1978, he said in an interview:

> Dazu kam für mich in der englischen Literatur das ernste Sprachspiel, das – angefangen von Shakespeare und den sogennanten metaphysical poets bis zu seiner Spätblüte bei *Alice in Wonderland*, bei Lear im 19. Jahrhundert – im Englischen sehr stark ist und etwa von James Joyce in einer ganz anderen Form wieder aufgenommen wird.[62]

A second aspect of the attention devoted by Fried to the individual German word is word play or manipulation. He has been much criticised for his 'word acrobatics' (Lawrie), though his phonetic and morphological experimentation can usually be shown to reveal hidden meanings and semantically significant associations, rather than being practised for its own sake. Lawrie suggests the German language, Fried's link with his childhood, became a surrogate home, and 'almost like a person' to him.[63] Ceasing to perform their basic function of communication, words became detached from the objects and concepts they described, leading to hermeticism (Lawrie pp. 199f.). Lawrie's negative evaluation of Fried's word play (see pp. 201, 211, 274-276) ignores the dimensions of meaning revealed in Kaukoreit's close readings of poems such as 'Spruch', 'Der Sieger', 'Ton', and 'Männerlied'. In any case, poems like 'Ins Wort' and 'Logos' which thematise language directly suggest that everyday contact with English language and culture deautomatised Fried's linguistic processes, opening his eyes to the distortion of consciousness inherent in his native linguistic convention. In the *Warngedichte*, arguably Fried's best poetry, word play continues to feature prominently. Indeed, Fried's sensitivity to the use and misuse of language in a broader sense was to re-emerge in the mid-'sixties in his exposure of the ideological dimensions of sayings and idioms, euphemisms, and the language of the media.

A third complex is the use of partial rhyme (consonantal half-rhyme), internal rhyme, assonance and alliteration. These are striking

features of Fried's poetry after 1945, when he was trying to get away from
'das Reimgeklingel, das Heruntergekommensein des deutschen Reims, [...]
ohne deswegen eine strenge Form aufzugeben'. Here again Fried has
acknowledged his indebtedness to English literature:

> Versexperimente unserer Zeit von Gerard Manley Hopkins, Wilfred Owen u.a. –
> dies war also literarisch ungeheuer wichtig und war nicht nur bei mir so. Bei Hans
> Werner Cohn z.B., einem wenig bekannten Emigrationsdichter, haben dieselben
> Einflüsse unabhängig von mir fast dieselben Sprachexperimente hervorgebracht.
> Bei dem Anthropologen und Schriftsteller Franz Baermann Steiner sieht man
> ähnliche Entwicklungen.[64]

Fried has repeatedly spoken of the influence of Hopkins, Owen and Dylan
Thomas in this respect. However, his subtle and complex rhyme forms also
originated in Rilke and the Baroque writers he was introduced to by the
literary scholar Werner Milch.[65] An exercise book entitled 'Allerlei
Reimarten, 1947' held in the Erich Fried archive in Vienna confirms this
and indicates the lengths to which Fried went in his study of rhyme forms
at the time. 'ABLAUTREIM, als Endreime bei Wilfred Owen/ als
Binnenreim bei Rilke, (Orpheus-Son.)', he notes on page one.[66] In a letter
written to the Austrian anthologist Hans Weigel in 1952 Fried made the
English origins of the 'association technique' employed in his poem 'Zur
Zeit der Kriege' clear, and defended himself against accusations of playing
about with words:

> Ich weiß, daß viele mir vorwerfen werden, Wortspielerei zu betreiben. [...] Ob ich
> dieser Gefahr immer entgangen bin, das darf ich selbst nicht zu beurteilen
> versuchen. [...] Zu dieser Form kam ich vielleicht auch durch die Berührung mit
> der modernen englischen Literatur, wo Joyce namentlich in seinem *Finnegans
> Wake* ähnliches tut und wo es Lyriker gibt, wie Gerard Manley Hopkins und Dylan
> Thomas, deren Arbeiten ich in kleinen Bruchstücken übersetzt habe. Zuerst der
> 'Ablautreim' (Hand – Hund, Rand – rennt – rinnt – rund), der mich dann auf die
> Wortassoziation als Bindemittel brachte, weil ja Konsonantengefüge in
> indogermanischen Sprachen dauerhafte Stämme und Wurzeln bilden, während die
> Vokale sich ändern. Zwar macht kein englischer Dichter heute ähnliches wie die
> Assoziationsgedichte, aber doch ist es in mancher Hinsicht 'Englische Dichtung in
> deutscher Sprache'. Daß allerdings Ablaute und Assoziationsdichtung auch der
> deutschen Sprache entsprechen, zeigt die althochdeutsche Dichtung, vor allem aber
> die Barockdichtung, zum Beispiel Murner und Abraham a Sancta Clara. Wie weit
> man um der Assoziation willen dichtet? Nun, nicht weiter und nicht weniger weit
> als sonst um des Reimes willen.[67]

The question of Dylan Thomas's influence on Fried is complex, since several different aspects of Thomas's poetic style are involved. Responding to the reception of his poems in public readings in Germany in the previous year, Fried felt he had to defend himself against the accusation of simply copying Dylan Thomas, in the 'Nachwort' to the volume *Gedichte*. He is careful to stress his debt not only to 'der modernen englischen Lyrik und einzelnen älteren englischen Dichtern', but also to the 'Art und Weise, wie man in England — in jedem Land anders — mit Gedanken und Gefühlen umgeht, wie man sie gestaltet oder verschweigt, gegen sie oder mit ihnen lebt' (p. 108). 'In Wirklichkeit', he concludes, 'haben mich schon vorhandene Ähnlichkeiten der Auffassung, gemeinsame Einflüsse und Interessen (z.B. Bewunderung für Hopkins, Joyce, Owen, Cummings) zu ihm [i.e. Dylan Thomas] hingezogen.' (p. 109). The most likely influence lies in Thomas's associative imagery and use of assonance, alliteration and refrain. Despite Fried's interest in the poets of the 'New Apocalypse'[68] and Thomas's 'urwaldhafte[s] Durcheinander und Ineinander von Eindrücken, Symbolen, Bildern und barocker Wortmagie',[69] his own poetry does not share Thomas's exuberant rhetoric, and focuses on individual words and their sounds rather than emulating the Welsh poet's density of images. Significantly, his translations give rhyme and assonance priority over structural equivalence, rhythmic dynamism, complexity of imagery, and taughtness of form. His greatest strength lies in his linguistic inventiveness, which is in Heimann's view hardly second to Thomas's.[70] As with Thomas, Fried's fascination with and choice of Sylvia Plath for translation was motivated by admiration for her forms, style and themes, with all of which he shared affinities. Some of her poetry comes close to what he described in 1952 in the letter quoted above as 'Assoziationsgedichte', in which free word association is used as a means of tapping into the personal and collective unconscious. But it does not seem likely that Plath's poetry actually influenced his writing any more than that of E. E. Cummings, whom Fried presented in translations to German readers in *Texte und Zeichen* in 1957.

Thematic influences from English literature are less tangible than formal ones. Kaukoreit has gleaned interesting sidelights on Fried's preoccupation with Anglo-American literature in the 'fifties from the essay 'Englische Streiflichter', articles in the *Englische Rundschau*, and in the house programme journal of the BBC German Service *Hier spricht London*. Radio features on Auden, Graves, Thomas, and Eliot confirm his high regard for all of these very different writers. On the one hand, Fried valued the politically committed 'Pylon Poets' of the late 'twenties and 'thirties (Auden, Day Lewis, MacNeice, Spender), who employed emphatically contemporary imagery. But he also admired Eliot's classical modernism, and 'irrational' poets such as Thomas, David Gascoyne and Kathleen Raine. Robert Graves's association of poetry with religion and mystical striving in *The White Goddess* and Eliot's cultural criticism and preoccupation with identity and death are echoed in many of Fried's poems in the 'fifties. Lawrie points to features of Dylan Thomas's and Richard Hughes's radio plays, which Fried translated, recurring in his own essays in that genre in the 'sixties (pp. 208-11), and, as an example of direct adaptation of English literary material, to Fried's libretto *Arden muß sterben*, and the later theatre version *und alle seine Mörder*, which are based on the Elizabethan *Tragedie of Arden of Feversham* (pp. 330f.).

A network of orientations and influences from English writers thus took its place alongside German ones.[71] In his prose writing Fried derived aspects of modernism (the grotesque, the surreal, associative and montage techniques) from Joyce and Doderer, Woolf and Kafka, while significant English impulses in the post-war poems are derived from Owen's half rhymes, Hopkins's use of sprung rhythm, Thomas's assonance, and Eliot's self-awareness.[72] English and German influences alike fed into a 'multiperspective conception of poetry' (Kaukoreit p. 322), sustained by an underlying tension between energetic commitment and epistemological scepticism. The impact of English literature on Fried's writing waned as his contacts with Germany intensified in the late 'fifties and early 'sixties.

Whereas a record of Michael Hamburger's translations could be pieced together with reasonable confidence in the previous section, *String of Beginnings* only gives occasional indications of the impact the German writers Hamburger translated may have had on his own poetry, and my comments on this are necessarily more speculative than those on Fried. English poetry, on the other hand, was of decisive importance to Hamburger: his earliest poems and translations, for instance, were indebted to Thomas Gray in diction and Tennyson in tone (*SoB* pp. 44f.). Hamburger is generally critical of his poetic efforts in the 'forties, mentioning poems 'full of apocalyptic notions and fantasies which I mistook for vision' (p. 102), metaphysical speculations (p. 124), and 'hyperbolic rantings about war, death and destruction' (p. 141). Dylan Thomas, of whom he became a regular drinking companion for a time after meeting him in Oxford in 1941, is described as 'one of a succession of models for the derivative verse I was writing in those days' (*SoB* p. 85). In the first section of Hamburger's *Collected Poems*[73] little of this has been retained, but the diction of several poems points to Eliot and Yeats, his principal models in the late 'forties and early 'fifties. Like Fried, Hamburger was deeply impressed by 'East Coker', which he read in 1941/2, and came to appreciate 'more than any other modern poem' (*SoB* p. 62). At the age of sixteen, Hamburger started soliciting the opinion of older writers on his poems and Hölderlin translations. John Lehmann and Stephen Spender gave fatherly advice, but it was above all the 'unapproachable, exacting and austere' Eliot who became, after his own father's death from Hodgkin's Disease in 1940, at the age of 55, his surrogate father (*SoB* p. 96).

Hamburger came to poetry through creative paraphrase and translation. 'I was trying out one stance, one identity after another', he writes of his early writing (*SoB* p. 93). Among the poems he regards as having survived the test of time best are persona poems, dedications and memorial poems on German and French writers such as 'Hölderlin', 'Rimbaud in Africa: A Lost Letter' and 'Grodek: In Memoriam Georg Trakl'. It was Hölderlin, the 'modern' poet of the classical period, torn, tortured, lonely, and misunderstood by his contemporaries, with whose 'einsame Rede' and ambivalent feelings towards Germany the young émigré particularly identified. The continuing importance of Hölderlin as a source of creative inspiration is illustrated by the radio play 'Struck by Apollo', a dramatised biography he wrote together with his wife Anne Beresford in 1965.

Though the living poets who were the young Hamburger's models or heroes were English, many of them were mediators of German culture in Britain. Stephen Spender, John Lehmann and David Gascoyne, Herbert Read, Vernon Watkins and Edwin Muir all acted in varying degrees as mentors. A detailed examination of Hamburger's poetry is necessary before the various stylistic and thematic influences can be identified with any certainty. But, though Hamburger has remarked that many of Hölderlin's cadences and motifs became second nature to him, he does not seem to have experimented with Hölderlin's classical ode forms as Vernon Watkins and W. H. Auden did. Indeed, looking back in 1990, he rejects the anthologist Edward Lucie-Smith's classification of him under the rubric 'Influences from Abroad' in the Penguin volume *British Poetry since 1945* (1970), indicating the German influence on his poetry should not be overestimated: 'It happens [...] that my earliest poems were influenced more by French models than by German ones; and that later it was American poets, above all, that shook me out of my rhymed stanzaic forms.' (*SoB* p. 332) What links there are between German poetry and Hamburger's own writing probably lie less in poetic techniques or forms than in thematic influences.

Teenage 'pomposities, earnestness and public-school tight-lippedness' (*SoB* p. 57), the emotional numbness after his father's death (p. 58), and depressions bound up with repression of 'the encapsulated sensual man' in him (p. 95) had resulted in extreme introversion. The renewed confrontation with Berlin, the 'nursery of [his] neuroses' (*SoB* p. 183), and recognition that his childhood had been at once 'pampered and deprived', 'deprived of individual attention' (p. 8), leading him to become introverted and withdrawn, opened the way in the late 'fifties and early 'sixties to a sloughing off of 'Oxford Gothic', which he describes as having 'constipated' him both mentally and emotionally for years (p. 71). Unsettling though his brief period of writing in German in the 'sixties clearly was, it also contributed to an important reorientation, accelerating a process, which had already begun in the 'fifties, of literary liberation from the impersonality, classical rigour and ascetic spirituality of T. S. Eliot, and the metaphysical symbolism of Yeats. 'Die Erfahrung des Niemandslandes', he wrote in *Zwischen den Sprachen*, 'ist längst eine bewußte oder unbewußte Bedingung meines Schreibens.' (p. 56) Stereotyped Romantic symbolism, rhetorical structures and metrical regularity were now replaced by linguistic and epistemological scepticism, and a new concreteness and simplicity rooted in his childhood love of plants and animals.

Hamburger's emancipation from Romantic Symbolism can be traced in poems exploring his identity and reflecting on the role of the poet such as 'Palinode', 'The Dual Site', 'Travellers' and 'Conformist'. 'Branded in childhood, for thirty years he strove/ To hide the scar', he writes in 'Conformist' (1962):

> Until conformity brought its reward:
> A crested, gild-edged card. The great gate opened,
> A pair of stiff lips cracked and let him pass
> Into those halls his half-life's dreams had deepened;
> And out again... to breathe the ownerless air
> Night sky transfigured, lucent, fresh and clear
> After the ceilings puffed in emulation.

His own place found at last; his own self found -
Outside, outside - his heritage regained
By grace of exile, of expropriation. [...]
Healed now, of health, unmasked, of honesty,
In, out again he passed, [...]
Come late into the freedom his from birth,
To breathe the air, and walk the ownerless earth. (*CP* p. 89)

His vision of the 'ownerless earth' was developed in the 'sixties through precise observation of natural detail and an 'earthy' diction making subtle use of consonant clusters and vowel patterns to underline the meaning of the poem. 'Loach', written in 1966, is one of the best-known examples:

Loam, slimy loam, embodied, shaped,
Articulate in him. The strength, the softness.
His delicate eye draws light to riverbeds,
Through water draws our weather.
[...] (*CP* pp. 145f.)

Affinities with German poets – for instance Wilhelm Lehmann's 'verbiesterte Sachlichkeit' (Kurt Pinthus) and humility before nature, or Johannes Bobrowski's laconic evocations of the lost homeland — promise to reward examination. Hamburger shares Grass's and Enzensberger's critique of modern civilisation, and their view of the poet as a warner. Enzensberger's 'Ende der Eulen', which he translated in the early 'sixties, may have prompted early 'ecological' poems such as 'First Thing in Berkshire' and 'The Jackdaws' (*CP* pp. 120f., 125). Apocalyptic visions link him with Peter Huchel, and it seems likely Hamburger's critique of modern civilisation has been influenced in a general way by German anxieties rooted in awareness of the destructive bureaucratic and technocratic patterns of behaviour supremely exemplified in the holocaust. However, he was also also influenced by the English tradition of sensualism, stemming from Gerard Manley Hopkins, and by American Imagism and Objectivism (Pound, William Carlos Williams, Charles Olson). Finally, Wendell Berry's sense of place and ideal of stewardship, and Gary Snyder's Buddhistic nature spirituality, which Hamburger discovered in the 'sixties, when he spent periods in the United States as Visiting Professor, after giving up his academic career in Reading, have influenced his later writing. The poem cycles *Travelling* and *In Suffolk*, widely regarded as among his most significant poetic achievements, formulate a holist consciousness and an attitude of humility towards creation, in 'variations', or extended meditative repetitions, composed in free rhymeless rhythms making extensive use of assonance and alliteration. The resonance of these poems in Germany today, where Hamburger is the most frequently translated contemporary English poet, may have something to do with their affinities with the tradition of German nature philosophy and poetry. It seems likely, then, that, as in the case of Fried, orientations and influences from Anglo-Saxon and German culture converge in Hamburger's poetry.

Conclusion

There is no reason why the adoption of a new language, or the return from one learned in exile to the childhood language, should necessarily threaten the individual's identity. Indeed, in some instances it has been experienced as a release, as the gateway to a new identity, as Dieter Lamping has pointed out with reference to Klaus Mann and Peter Weiss. Language switching can serve as a means of cultural distancing, or trigger off a new literary orientation. 'Gerade für Exilierte', Lamping concludes, 'ist [...] der Sprachwechsel, jenseits aller Zwänge, auch ein Akt der Selbstbehauptung und der Selbstbestimmung auf ihrem eigensten Gebiet'.[74]

Fried's comments on the deterioration of German in exile and Hamburger's remarks on the negative impact on his English poetry of his attempts to write in German in the 'sixties should be seen in the context of a tradition going back to Ovid's *Tristia* and *Epistula ex Ponto*.[75] The émigré is here faced with a choice between standing by the mother tongue, and adopting a new language. The first opens up a gulf between the literary language and that of everyday communication, threatening the very continuation of writing. The second is interpreted as culminating in loss of identity. The language situation has become a symbol for the distress and hardship of exile.

As I have already indicated, Fried and Hamburger have in fact acknowledged advantages to their situation alongside the incontestable disadvantages. In his interview with Anke Winckler in 1978, Fried gave as the main disadvantage of living in another country losing touch with the development of the language: the folksong tone of many poems in *Gedichte* inevitably sounded false to German ears, because of its (at least temporary) discreditation by the Nazis. In the experience of a different culture, however, he sees a distinct advantage:

Diese Verschiedenheit [...] relativiert das Bewußtsein [...] Das war ein großer
Reichtum, eine große Bereicherung der eigenen Möglichkeiten. [...] Dazu kam für
mich in der englischen Literatur das ernste Sprachspiel, [...] dann Versexperimente.

His final assessment is therefore positive: 'Von da an aber war das
Existieren in zwei Sprachen sehr vorteilhaft.'[76] In *String of Beginnings*
Hamburger attributes the weaknesses of his early poetry to the uncritical
acceptance of conventions that the first stage in acquiring a new language
demands, leading to 'the exaggerated correctness that betrays foreigners'.
He recognises the encounter with German in the 'sixties as a prerequisite
for a more detached, critical control of English: 'For the next stage, a
more critical engagement with the idioms and sinews of the language, I had
to be at once inside it and outside it.' (pp. 291f.)

Fried's and Hamburger's careers refute the view that the linguistic
and literary predicament of exile was inevitably characterised by loss and
the threat of falling silent. Nevertheless, their success has been not least due
to their youth, flexibility and sheer energy in making the best out of the
situation. Translation, curiously absent in Dieter Lamping's reflections on
the linguistic metamorphoses of exile, has been vital to them both as a way
of establishing continuity in their lives, developing into a mediation
between the cultures which has attracted a broad public resonance. For
neither of them, however, has it been an aim in itself, but rather something
subordinate to, and inferior to, creative writing. Asked by Angelika
Heimann whether translation had ever stimulated him to write, Fried
answered his most common feeling was one of impatience, of having
wasted time in which he could have been writing poetry (p. 58). Poetry has
always taken priority over translation in principle for Hamburger too, but
it has been more important to him than to Fried both personally and
professionally. When the attempt to write in both languages in the 'sixties,
'far from mending the rift between the areas of experience or giving me
the freedom of dual nationality', left him 'feeling stateless in a no man's
land', translation, he concludes, 'was the right bridge for me' (*SoB* p.
291). Pointing out that translation involves 'innige Teilnahme am
schöpferischen Prozeß', and that writing poetry is in itself 'eine
Übersetzung in Worte von etwas, welches bis dahin nicht als Wortfolge
bestand', he claims: 'Für den Lyriker, der ja aus äußeren und inneren
Gründen seinen Beruf nie ganz berufsmäßig ausüben kann, ist es ein ganz
eigenartiges Glück, daß er oft übersetzen kann, wenn die Stimmung zu
eigenen Gedichten fehlt.' (*ZdS* p. 77)

Inevitably both Fried and Hamburger have experienced tensions between the demands of translating and creative writing. Fried's poetry was overshadowed by his translations for only a relatively brief period in the late 1950s. Not so for Hamburger. Regarding the 'oddity' of which reviewers of his books remind him 'with tedious regularity' that he is better known as a translator, he wrote in 1990 that translation had 'displaced' his own writing, but ultimately, in an ambiguous phrase, 'made up for the career the writing of poetry could not be':

> The first book I published was a translation, and one I have repeatedly enlarged and revised ever since. Ever since, too, translation has been so much part of my work that for long stretches it displaced my own writing, and I have translated far more poems than I have written poems of my own. Because most translations have a very limited lifespan, not even the possibility of 'permanent value' can be entertained for them, so that their main value must lie in their being useful; and being useful, of service, is the only good reason I know for having a career. Translating, therefore, like the critical writing that was also a form of mediation, made up for the career the writing of poetry could not be. (*SoB* p. 326)

In the last ten years Hamburger has focused increasingly on his own poetry. His growing recognition in Germany as a poet in his own right has been assisted by the advantageous conditions for his reception an émigré. But his reputation as a translator continues to eclipse the attention his poetry deserves in Britain and America.

Nonetheless, far from stifling his creative writing, translation has sharpened Hamburger's awareness of precise meanings and ambiguities of words, and as in the case of Fried, provided a training in poetic forms and techniques, and enriched his work thematically. Just as the experience of exile permitted a critical outsiderness, translation fostered an awareness of how language determines perception, and encouraged poetic reflection on language and a sophisticated use of the sounds and shapes of words. It gave access to new poetic techniques: 'Das Englische [ist] dem Deutschen gerade nahe und fern genug, seine literarischen Bewegungen und Versuche sind uns gerade fremd und verwandt genug, um nicht nur zu Manieren anzuregen, sondern uns Möglichkeiten zur Erweiterung des Sagbaren zu geben', wrote Fried in the 'Nachwort' to *Gedichte*, in 1958. 'Wörtlichkeit statt Bildlichkeit [...] eine weitreichende Verschiebung, bei der die englische Lyrik Pate stand', comments Alexander von Bormann, in one of the most significant advances in our appreciation of Fried's mature writing since the poet's death, challenging assumptions about its one-dimensionality and simplicity.[77] Both Fried's and Hamburger's poetry is rooted in the process of trans-national adaptation and appropriation.

Fried and Hamburger, who, despite the differences in background, personality and poetic practice, were linked by mutual regard over four decades, have gone beyond mere mediation between German and British culture. They have sought to make Jewish writers like David Rokeah known to German and English readers, and to prevent fellow émigrés from being forgotten by writing about them, reading and editing their work. Fried presented 'A Poet's Choice of German Poetry' on the BBC Third Programme in 1958,[78] and was involved in an editorial capacity in the English edition of Brecht's poems. Hamburger has translated Baudelaire, René Char and Philippe Jaccottet from French, and Franco Fortini from Italian. Not only has he written about both German poets (Hölderlin, Huchel) and English writers in German, and written or broadcast on English and American poets (Eliot, Muir, Thomas, Berry) in English, but he has also drawn attention to his predecessors as literary mediators. Much of the non-autobiographical part of *Zwischen den Sprachen* is concerned with cultural intermediaries such as Hofmannsthal and Edwin Muir, who were stimulated by contact with the other language and literature to their own creative writing, and served Hamburger as points of comparison for his own life and writing.

Study and translations of English literature in the decade after the war 'lieferte[n] zweifellos wichtige Impulse für Frieds literarischen Werdegang', as Kaukoreit writes (p. 195). 'Hätte ich mehr Talent oder Willen zur Assimilation an eine andere Kultur', Fried wrote somewhat tongue in cheek in 1958, 'so schriebe ich vielleicht "Englische Gedichte in deutscher Sprache", ja, vielleicht sogar in englischer Sprache; aber dort, wo in einem Menschen Dichtung entsteht, ist er nur selten anpassungsfähig oder anpassungswillig.' (*Gedichte* p. 108) His poems are a part of the 'second generation' of German poetry on English soil, a creative synthesis of traditions, 'eine Synthese deutscher und englischer Dichtungstraditionen, die vielleicht der wichtigste Beitrag zur deutschen Literatur ist, den die nach England versprengten Dichter zu leisten haben', as he had written ten years earlier.[79] Hamburger's writing, reconciling different parts of his experience, may prove the more ambitious attempt to synthesise the poetic traditions of the two countries.

Drawing on both cultures, Fried and Hamburger are examples of a phenomenon neglected because it crosses the traditional boundaries of the disciplines. Richard Dove has described the cultural dilemma of the German literary exiles as being 'caught, even posthumously, in the no man's land between two languages',[80] and this is echoed by Waltraud Strickhausen, who suggests Germans' publications in English have been ignored in Britain and at home in Germany because their 'European consciousness' was too far ahead of their time.[81] Such mediation and such consciousness remain important at a time when, as a younger translator commented in a recent article on the reception of German literature in England, 'Großbritannien und Deutschland [...] wissen sowenig voneinander wie etwa Burkina Faso und Brunei.'[82]

Notes

[1] See Horst Oppel, *Englisch-deutsche Literaturbeziehungen*, 2 vols (Berlin: Erich Schmidt, 1971), Volume II, *Von der Romantik bis zur Gegenwart*, pp.103, 151f.

[2] See Erich Fried, 'Der Flüchtling und die Furcht vor der Heimkehr', in *Autoren im Exil*, ed. by Karl Corino (Frankfurt/M.: Fischer, 1981), pp. 265-276 (p. 266); also Fried, *Höre Israel! Gedichte und Fußnoten* (Hamburg: Association, 1974), p. 9.

[3] Fried, 'Der Flüchtling', p. 273.

[4] See Steven W. Lawrie, *Erich Fried. A Writer Without a Country* (New York, etc.: Lang, 1996), pp. 2, 106.

[5] Erich Fried, *They Fight in the Dark. The Story of Austria's Youth* (London: Young Austria in Great Britain, 1944)

[6] There is of course a possibility Fried may have had help in writing *They Fight in the Dark*. (Steven Lawrie actually comments critically on German features in the language, pp. 35 and 106.) However, Fried's fluency in English a few years later is documented by a letter written to C. Busby Smith in 1950, in *Einblicke Durchblicke. Fundstücke und Werkstattberichte aus dem Nachlaß von Erich Fried*, ed. by Volker Kaukoreit (Vienna: Turia und Kant, 1993), pp. 98f.

[7] Erich Fried, *Deutschland. Gedichte* (London: Austrian P.E.N., 1944); *Österreich. Gedichte* (Zurich: Atrium, 1946). *Österreich* was in reality published in the autumn of 1945 and distributed by the Atrium Press, London.

[8] See Hanjo Kesting, 'Anläufe und Anfechtungen. Gespräch mit Erich Fried', in *Dichter ohne Vaterland. Gespräche und Aufsätze zur Literatur*, (Berlin and Bonn: Dietz, 1982), pp. 24-38 (p. 30).

[9] As Lawrie points out (pp. 313f.), Fried came to value his 'homelessness' for facilitating his role as 'Weltbürger', taking issue with events throughout the world. He appreciated London in later years as a 'place of retreat' (p. 334), where he could recuperate from political activities in Germany and Austria.

[10] Peter von [sic!] Mendelssohn, 'Writers without Language', in *Writers in Freedom. A Symposium. Based on the XVII International Congress of the P.E.N. Club held in London in September, 1941*, ed. by Hermon Ould (London, New York, Melbourne: Hutchinson, [1941]), pp. 92-98 (pp.97f.).

[11] See Sylvia Patsch, *Österreichische Schriftsteller im Exil in Großbritannien. Ein Kapitel vergessene österreichische Literatur. Romane, Autobiographien, Tatsachenberichte auf englisch und deutsch* (Vienna: Brandstätter, 1985); Waltraud Strickhausen, 'Schreiben in der Sprache des *Anderen*. – Eine Vorstudie zu den Publikationsmöglichkeiten und der Wirkung englischsprachiger Exilwerke in Großbritannien', in *Die Resonanz des Exils. Gelungene und mißlungene Rezeption deutschsprachiger Exilautoren*, ed. by Dieter Sevin (Amsterdam, Atlanta: Rodopi, 1992), pp. 369-382; Richard Dove, 'The Gift of Tongues. German-speaking Novelists writing in English', in *Between the Two Languages. German-speaking Exiles in Great Britain 1933-1945*, ed. by William Abbey et al. (Stuttgart: Hans-Dieter Heinz, 1995), pp. 95-115; J. M. Ritchie, 'Ernst Bornemann and the Face on the Cutting Room Floor', in *German Exiles. British Perspectives* (New York, etc.: Lang, 1997), pp. 237-257; Dirk Wiemann, *Exilliteratur in Großbritannien 1933-1945* (Opladen, Wiesbaden: Westdeutscher Verlag, 1998).

[12] Peter de Mendelssohn, *The Hours and the Centuries* (London: John Lane, 1942); Arthur Koestler, *Scum of the Earth* (London: Macmillan, 1941); *Arrival and Departure* (London: Macmillan, 1943), and *Darkness at Noon* (London: Jonathan Cape, 1940); Robert Neumann, *The Inquest* (London: Hutchinson, 1944).

[13] Dove, 'The Gift of Tongues', p. 95.

[14] Fried, 'Der Flüchtling', pp. 265f. Fried himself wrote (unpublished) love poetry in English (presumably under the circumstances described above), and an as yet unknown number of letters to the editors of English newspapers, though these were apparently corrected by others. See Lawrie, *Erich Fried*, pp. 331, 106 and 333.

[15] Fried, 'Der Flüchtling' p. 269.

[16] Lion Feuchtwanger, 'Arbeitsprobleme des Schriftstellers im Exil', in *Freies Deutschland* 3, no. 4 (March 1944), pp. 27f. Quoted from Wulf Köpke, 'Die Wirkung des Exils auf Sprache und Stil. Ein Vorschlag zur Forschung', in *Exilforschung. Ein Internationales Jahrbuch*, Volume III, *Gedanken an Deutschland im Exil und andere Themen*, ed. by Thomas Koebner, Wulf Köpke and Joachim Radkau (Munich: edition text und kritik, 1985), pp. 225-237 (p. 228).

[17] Fried, 'Der Flüchtling', pp. 269, 272f.

[18] Adrienne Ash, 'Lyric Poetry in Exile', in *Exile. The Writer's Experience*, ed. by J. Spalek, R. F. Bell (Chapel Hill, North Carolina: University of North Carolina Press, 1982), pp. 1-23 (p. 4).

[19] Dieter Lamping, '"Linguistische Metamorphosen". Aspekte des Sprachwechsels in der Exilliteratur', in *Germanistik und Komparatistik. DFG-Symposion 1993*, ed. by Hendrik Birus (Stuttgart and Weimar: Metzler, 1995), pp. 528-540 (pp. 528f.). I thank Richard Dove for drawing this and other articles on the subject to my attention.

[20] Richard Dove, 'Almost an English Author. Robert Neumann's English-language Novels', *German Life and Letters*, 51, 1 (January 1998), 93-105.

[21] See Strickhausen, p. 375.

[22] See the chapter 'Schreiben im englischen Exil', especially pp. 20-25.

[23] Köpke, p. 229.

[24] Ibid., p. 235.

[25] Michael Hamburger, *Zwischen den Sprachen. Essays und Gedichte* (Frankfurt/M.: Fischer, 1966), and *String of Beginnings. Intermittent Memoirs 1924-1954* (London: Skoob, 1991). The first edition of *String of Beginnings* was published under the title *A Mug's Game* in 1973, the second, 'corrected, patched up and filled in, possibly improved' edition with the new title 18 years later. Further references are given as *ZdS* and *SoB* with page number after quotations in the text.

[26] 'Ich habe eine Mischung aus Kinderdeutsch und Buchdeutsch, und das ergibt keine richtige Sprache', he maintained in a radio interview in 1986, though his contacts with Germany had by this time greatly intensified. (Matthias Müller-Wieferig, *Jenseits der Gegensätze. Die Lyrik Michael Hamburgers* (Essen: Die blaue Eule, 1991), p. 12.)

[27] These include 'Begegnung' and 'Abschied', both associated with meeting Johannes Bobrowski.

[28] Erich Fried, 'Nachwort', in *Gedichte* (Hamburg: claassen, 1958), p. 108.

[29] Interesting though they would be, neither a comparison of their translation strategies nor an assessment of the quality of their work shall be attempted. On the latter, see Klaus Reichert's critical commentary on Fried's Shakespeare translations in 'Die Herausforderung des Fremden. Erich Fried als Übersetzer', in *Erich Fried. Text und Kritik* 91 (July 1986), pp. 83-93; Ingrid Schramm, 'Erich Frieds "Shakespeare-Gallery"', in *Einblicke Durchblicke*, pp. 145-154; and Angelika Heimann's detailed account of Fried's translations of modern English poetry (especially Dylan Thomas and Sylvia Plath) in *'Bless Thee! Thou art Translated'. Erich Fried als Übersetzer moderner englischsprachiger Lyrik* (Amsterdam: Grüner, 1987). David Constantine and Andreas Gardt have written on Hamburger's translations of Hölderlin, Celan and the Expressionists in *Michael Hamburger: Dichter und Übersetzer. Beiträge des Michael-Hamburger-Symposiums am Deutsch-Amerikanischen Institut Heidelberg*, ed. by Walter Eckel and Jakob J. Kollhöfer (Frankfurt/M., Bern, etc.: Lang, 1989).

[30] Volker Kaukoreit, *Vom Exil bis zum Protest gegen den Krieg in Vietnam. Frühe Stationen des Lyrikers Erich Fried. Werk und Biographie 1938-1966* (Darmstadt: Jürgen Häusser, 1991).

[31] Lawrie, *Erich Fried*, pp. 2f.

[32] See Ralf Jeutter, 'The publications of Michael Hamburger: a bibliography', *Comparative Criticism* 10 (1988), pp. 346-376; and Uta Kreuter, *Übersetzung und Literaturkritik. Aspekte der Rezeption zeitgenössischer deutschsprachiger Literatur in Großbritannien 1960-1981* (Frankfurt/M., Bern, New York: Lang, 1985).

[33] Kesting, 'Anläufe und Anfechtungen', p. 34.

[34] According to Kaukoreit, Martin went on to become a bestselling writer in Australia after the war. Lawrie adds that Martin's real name was Ludwig Detsiny, and notes he changed name and started writing in English in 1938.

[35] See Kaukoreit, p. 122 and Lawrie, pp. 35f.

[36] See Weimann, pp. 26f.

[37] See William Abbey, "'Die Illusion genannt deutscher PEN-Club". The PEN-German Group and the English Centre, 1933-45', in *Between Two Languages,* pp. 135-153; also Axel Goodbody, 'Der englische PEN und die deutschsprachigen Schriftsteller in London: Betrachtungen anhand des Briefwechsels zwischen Eleanor Farjeon und Theodor Kramer', forthcoming in *Theodor Kramer Symposium in London* (*Zwischenwelt* 7), ed. by Jörg Thunecke.

[38] Nothing came of this proposed publication. Other plans Fried mentions in the letter are the novel he had just begun (published by claassen in 1960 as *Ein Soldat und ein Mädchen*), and 'eine Arbeit über den Schaffensprozeß des Dichters' taking Caudwell's *Illusion and Reality* as a starting point. My thanks are due to Reinhard Müller of the Archiv für die Geschichte der Soziologie in Österreich, Graz, and Franz Kostmann, the owner of the letter, for providing me with a copy, and to Fried's literary executor, Dr. Kurt Groenewold, for permitting me to quote from it.

[39] Lawrie, pp. 173f. See also Heimann, pp. 57, 113.

[40] Lawrie, pp. 178-180.

[41] See Heimann, p. 138.

[42] Sylvia Plath, *Ariel. Gedichte.* Englisch und deutsch (Frankfurt/M.: Suhrkamp, 1974).

[43] See Walter Eckel, *Von Berlin nach Suffolk. Zur Lyrik Michael Hamburgers* (Würzburg: Königshausen und Neumann, 1991), pp. 26-28.

[44] Michael Hamburger, *Poems of Hölderlin.* Editions Poetry London (London: Nicholson and Watson, 1943).

[45] Michael Hamburger, *Reason and Energy. Studies in German Literature* (London: Routledge and Kegan Paul, 1957).

[46] Michael Hamburger, *The Truth of Poetry. Tensions in Modern Poetry from Baudelaire to the 1960s* (London: Weidenfeld and Nicholson, 1969).

[47] According to Jeutter, this was only published twenty years later in the volume Georg Büchner, *Leonce und Lena. Lenz. Woyzeck* (Chicago and London: University of Chicago Press, 1972).

[48] Georg Büchner, 'Lenz' (with a short introduction by Michael Hamburger), *Mandrake*, 1, 5 (1947), 11-32.

[49] Hugo von Hofmannsthal, *Poems and Verse Plays*, with an introduction by T. S. Eliot, bilingual edition, ed. and introduced by Michael Hamburger (London: Routledge and

Kegan Paul, 1961); *Plays and Libretti*, ed. and introduced by Michael Hamburger (London: Routledge and Kegan Paul, 1963).

[50] Beethoven, *Letters, Journals and Conversations*, ed. and introduced by Michael Hamburger (London: Thames and Hudson, 1952).

[51] For further detail on this and the following see Kreuter, pp. 65f., 70f., 83, and 163-165.

[52] *Modern German Poetry 1910-1960. An Anthology with Verse Translations*, ed. with an introduction by Michael Hamburger and Christopher Middleton (London: McGibbon and Kee, 1962).

[53] *East German Poetry. An Anthology*, ed. and trans. by Michael Hamburger (Manchester: Carcanet, 1972); *German Poetry 1910-1975. An Anthology in German and English*, trans. and ed. by Michael Hamburger (Manchester: Carcanet, 1976).

[54] See Ian Galbraith, 'Michael Hamburger', in *Kritisches Lexikon der fremdsprachigen Gegenwartsliteratur* (Munich: edition text und kritik, 1996).

[55] Erich Fried, *Warngedichte* (Munich: Hanser, 1964).

[56] My own guesses as to the influence of Fried's translations of English literature on his writing, in a conference paper given before the publication of Kaukoreit's book in 1991 (subsequently published as 'Erich Fried — German, Jew, British and Socialist. The Composite Identity of an Austrian Émigré', in *From High Priests to Desecrators. Contemporary Austrian Writers*, ed. by Ricarda Schmidt and Moray McGowan (Sheffield: Sheffiled Academic Press, 1993), pp. 83-103, especially pp. 92-97), are modified here in the light of Kaukoreit's and Lawrie's findings.

[57] Erich Fried, *Von Bis nach Seit. Gedichte aus den Jahren 1945-58* (Vienna: Promedia, 1985); *Reich der Steine. Zyklische Gedichte* (Hamburg: claassen, 1963).

[58] Quoted from Lawrie, p. 151.

[59] See Kaukoreit, pp. 200-204, 239-244, and Lawrie, pp. 82f., 120-123.

[60] Second edition (Düsseldorf: claassen, 1982), pp. 43f.

[61] See Kaukoreit, pp. 118f.

[62] Fried, 'Lesen und Schreiben während des Exils. Interview mit Anke Winckler', in *Antifaschistische Literatur*, ed. by Lutz Winckler, 3 vols, Volume III, *Prosaformen* (Kronberg/Taunus: Scriptor, 1979), pp. 269-284 (p. 270).

[63] Lawrie, pp. 320f. The phrase 'almost like a person' was used by Gerhard Wilke in an interview with Lawrie. Fried himself notes more soberly: 'Ich habe versucht, im Wort einen gewissen Halt, ein Gegengewicht zu dem zu finden, was mir weltanschaulich problematisch und fragwürdig und zum Teil zum Verzweifeln schien in der Welt.' — 'Anläufe und Anfechtungen', pp. 34f.

[64] 'Lesen und Schreiben während des Exils', pp. 270f.

65 See ibid., pp. 269-272, where he refers to the line 'rasch an die Wandlung der eigenen Wendung geschrieben' from Rilke's *Sonette an Orpheus.*

66 See *Einblicke Durchblicke*, p. 40.

67 In *Stimmen der Gegenwart 1952*, ed. by Hans Weigel, (Vienna: Verlag für Jugend und Volk/Jungbrunnen, 1953), p. 73. Quoted from *Einblicke Durchblicke*, pp. 41-43.

68 The term is used for the writers represented in *The New Apocalypse: An Anthology of Criticism, Poems and Stories*, edited by J. F. Hendry in 1939, who were characterised by political scepticism and practised intense imaginative subjectivity akin to Surrealism. Dylan Thomas was the principal poet. New Apocalypse poetry finds an equivalent in the existential fear and apocalyptic motifs in Fried's poems in the 'fifties and the *Warngedichte.*

69 Fried, 'Englische Streiflichter', *Schweizer Rundschau* 54, 1954/55, 651f., quoted from Kaukoreit, p. 256.

70 See Heimann, pp. 118-120. Reichert comments similarly: 'Seine einzigartige Begabung zum Spielen mit der Sprache spricht sich eben nicht nur in den eigenen Dichtungen aus, sondern auch in den Übersetzungen, sofern dies möglich erscheint. [...] So sind die Übersetzungen immer wieder auch produktive Aneignungen, Weiterführungen nach Maßgabe des in der eigenen Sprache Angelegten.' ('Die Herausforderung', p. 87)

71 The overlapping of influences from German and British culture is illustrated by Rilke's influence on Fried, which was reinforced, if not initiated by the vogue for Rilke in England. (See Kaukoreit, pp. 118, 250). Similarly, one reason for Fried's interest in the English contemporary Sidney Keyes was that he was 'der am meisten von deutscher Dichtung des 20. Jahrhunderts beeinflußte Engländer' – 'Der Flüchtling', p. 267.

72 See 'Der Flüchtling', p. 273.

73 Michael Hamburger, *Collected Poems 1941-1994* (London: Anvil, 1995). Further references are given as *CP* with page number after quotations in the text.

74 Lamping, p. 540. See also pp. 534f., and 538. Lamping's argument corresponds to the shift in scientific attitudes towards bilingualism. It was traditionally held that bilingualism had a negative effect on the individual. In the 1920s Otto Jespersen believed neither of the two languages could be learned perfectly, and as late as the 'sixties experts warned that bilingualism could result in split personalities. Since the 'seventies, however, researchers in Canada and elsewhere have questioned this, claiming bilingualism can on the contrary lead to greater cognitive flexibility. All these views are undermined by language variety differences in monolinguals, which can be so great that a command of them approximates to bilingualism. The question whether bilingualism is a cognitive advantage or a disadvantage thus remains unresolved. See Suzanne Romaine, *Bilingualism*, second edition (Oxford: Blackwell, 1995), pp. 107-118.

75 See Lamping, p. 531.

76 'Lesen und Schreiben während des Exils', pp. 270f.

77 'Wörtlichkeit für Bildlichkeit: Erich Frieds Kritik der Naturlyrik', in *Die österreichische Literatur. Ihr Profil von der Jahrhundertwende bis zur Gegenwart (1880-1980)*, ed. by

Herbert Zeman (Graz: Akademische Druck- und Verlagsanstalt, 1989), pp. 1335-1359 (p. 1341).

[78] See Lawrie, p. 161, note 98.

[79] Quoted from Kaukoreit, p. 203.

[80] 'The Gift of Tongues', p. 115.

[81] pp. 379f.

[82] Michael Hulse, 'Ach so! Deutschsprachige Literatur in Großbritannien', in *Ansichten und Auskünfte zur deutschen Literatur nach 1945. Text und Kritik* Sonderband, ed. by H. L. Arnold (Munich: edition text und kritik 1995), pp. 136-143 (p. 141).

Ursula Seeber

Wo andere Leute wohnen. Kinder- und Jugendliteratur des österreichischen Exils in Großbritannien

Acculturation and in particular the literature written for children and adolescents are among those fields of exile studies where many questions are still open. The following contribution focuses on biographical documents and autobiographies as far as they comment on early reading experiences of young Austrian refugees and thus indicate processes of acculturation. The second part is an attempt to sketch the function of children's literature in the context of the Austrian Centre in London. In the third part some of the Austrian authors who wrote and published books for children in their British exile will be presented by foregrounding their working conditions, author-roles, preferences for certain genres, thematic concerns and their reception.

Großbritannien zählt zu den wichtigsten Zufluchtsländern des deutschsprachigen Exils. Von insgesamt 130.000 österreichischen Hitler-Flüchtlingen emigrierten rund 30.000 nach Großbritannien, ihre Zahl nahm durch freiwillige oder erzwungene Auswanderung bis Kriegsende sukzessive ab. Unter den früh ins Land Gekommenen war der Anteil an Geschäftsleuten und Unternehmern sowie Angehörigen akademischer Berufe überproportional hoch. Ein weiteres signifikantes Strukturmerkmal der deutschsprachigen Emigration nach Großbritannien ist der hohe Anteil an Frauen, weil sie eine Arbeitserlaubnis als Hausgehilfinnen und Krankenpflegerinnen erhalten konnten, und vor allem die große Zahl an Kindern und Jugendlichen. Mehr als ein Viertel der Emigranten war zum Zeitpunkt der Flucht noch nicht zwanzig Jahre alt, davon ein Drittel im Volksschulalter oder darunter.[1] Kinder und Jugendliche hatten schon vor Kriegsausbruch zu jenen Gruppen gehört, denen die britischen Behörden bevorzugt Einreisevisa erteilten im Hinblick darauf, daß ihre Transmigration in überseeische Länder leichter vorzubereiten wäre.

Viele Flüchtlingskinder konnten nicht zusammen mit ihren Eltern ausreisen. Unter dem Eindruck der *Kristallnacht* entschloß sich Großbritannien bekanntlich zu einer einmaligen Hilfsaktion. 10.000 jüdische Kinder und Jugendliche wurden von Dezember 1938 bis September 1939 mit den Kindertransporten aus Deutschland, Österreich und der Tschechoslowakei gerettet, darunter befanden sich laut einer Aufstellung der Israelitischen Kultusgemeinde in Wien bis August 1939

über 2.800 österreichische Kinder.[2] Vom 'Refugee Children's Movement'
(Kinder-Flüchtlings-Hilfe), das die heimische Bevölkerung mit Spenden
unterstützte, wurden die Kinder in Ferienheimen, Internaten und bei
Pflegeeltern untergebracht. Der größte Teil dieser Kinder blieb nach dem
Krieg im Land. Durch die Kindertransporte ist Großbritannien als jenes
Land in die Geschichte des Exils eingegangen, das bei weitem die größte
Anzahl von jüdischen Kindern aufnahm, die 1933 bis 1945 vor den
Nationalsozialisten flüchten mußten.

   1989 fand in Harrow aus Anlaß des 50. Jahrestages der
Kindertransporte ein Treffen statt. Viele ehemalige Kinderflüchtlinge
entschlossen sich in der Folge, den bis dahin fest versperrten 'Schrank'[3]
der Vergangenheit zu öffnen und die Erinnerungen an ihre Kindheit im
britischen Exil aufzuschreiben.

   Diese lebensgeschichtlichen Dokumentationen bilden zusammen mit
einschlägigen Autobiografien und Tagebüchern die Quellen zu Literatur
und Leseverhalten der exilierten Kinder und Jugendlichen. Sie werden
herangezogen, um ihren Prozeß der Akkulturation in Großbritannien zu
beschreiben. Dieser und die Focussierung auf den Bereich Kind bzw.
Kinder- und Jugendbuch zählen zu Arbeitsgebieten der Exilforschung, auf
denen noch viele Fragestellungen offen sind.[4] In einem zweiten Abschnitt
soll den Spuren der Kinder- und Jugendliteratur im Kontext der größten
österreichischen Exilorganisation in Großbritannien, des Austrian Centre,
gefolgt werden. Ein dritter beschäftigt sich exemplarisch mit Autorinnen
und Autoren österreichischer Herkunft, die Kinder- und Jugendliteratur
verfaßten, mit ihren Berufsbildern und Arbeitsbedingungen, den
bevorzugten Genres und Themen sowie der Rezeption dieser Texte und
ihrer Wechselwirkungen mit der Literatur des Gastlandes.

   Kaum ein Ereignis hat Kindheit und Jugend als geschützte
Entwicklungsräume so in Frage gestellt wie der Nationalsozialismus:

   My experience under *Anschluss* and emigration made a fundamental difference in
   my life. I had grown up much more rapidly than I would have otherwise, more
   ambitious and more desirous of overcoming my early obstacles, self reliant in some
   respects and distrustful and unsure of the world around me in others.[5]

Wie für den späteren Rechtsanwalt Frank Grad, der vierzehnjährig mit
einem Kindertransport aus Wien flüchtete, war die Exilerfahrung vieler
Kinder bestimmt von der Unkenntnis ihrer genauen Ursachen, vom
traumatischen Gefühl der Entfremdung und Enteignung. Nicht nur hatten
die in Großbritannien Gelandeten ein Ambiente mit unvertrauten

Lebensgewohnheiten und nicht geübten Verhaltensregeln ohne die
Begleitung der Eltern zu bewältigen, es stand auch plötzlich auf dem Spiel,
was bisher die selbstverständlichen Markierungen der Person in der Welt
ausgemacht hatte: der Vorname, der aus bürokratischen Gründen oft
anglisiert wurde, und die Muttersprache. Die Behörden hatten die
Pflegeeltern in eigenen Broschüren angewiesen, die Kinder zum
Englischlernen anzuhalten und sie weder Deutsch sprechen noch lesen zu
lassen.[6] Die Erfahrung dieser 'linguistic dispossession'[7] wurde als Schock
erlebt, und zu entsprechend radikalen Mechanismen seiner Verdrängung
griffen die Betroffenen. Wie in den von Bertha Leverton gesammelten
Berichten nachzulesen ist, sprachen Kinder oft wenige Wochen nach der
Ankunft kein Deutsch mehr, hatten in kurzer Zeit die Muttersprache
verlernt.[8] Hingegen ist in Erinnerungen von Kindern, die später als
Autorinnen oder Lehrende hervortraten, etwa Martha Blend oder Doris
Orgel,[9] der Abschied vom Deutschen wie das Erlernen und akzentfreie
Sprechen des Englischen Gegenstand positiv konnotierter oder zumindest
wertfreier Reflexion. Ein Jahr nach ihrer Ankunft beschrieb eine Lehrerin
ihre aus Wien stammende Schülerin als 'neat and tidy worker. [...]
Elisabeth shows a quick understanding of both play [am Lehrplan stand
Shakespeares *Much Ado About Nothing*] and essays',[10] und sie selbst kann
angesichts ihrer Tagebucheintragungen von 1940 feststellen: 'I am no
longer able to express myself in idiomatic German.'[11]

Den Sprachwechsel nicht als dramatischen Bruch, sondern als einen
Prozeß, der mit dem Erfahrungshorizont von Kindern mit ostjüdischem
oder jüdisch-religiösem Hintergrund harmonisiert haben mag, beschreibt
die im Londoner East End lebende Martha Blend:

> Ich setzte alles daran, schnell Englisch zu lernen, denn es mißfiel mir gewaltig, daß
> ich nicht verstand, was um mich herum vorging. Es erschien mir
> selbstverständlich, mehr als eine Sprache zu sprechen, da meine Eltern sowohl
> Polnisch als auch Deutsch konnten, mein Vater auf Hebräisch betete und meine
> Zieheltern Polnisch, Jiddisch und Englisch sprachen.[12]

Trotzdem handelt es sich nicht um Doppelsprachigkeit mit
gleichwertigen Parametern, sondern um einen 'subtractice bilingualism'[13]
genannten Spracherwerb, bei dem die Muttersprache aus verschiedenen
Gründen zugunsten der in der dominierenden Kultur gesprochenen Sprache
vergessen wird.

'And there was reading, all I wanted!'[14] Die vorliegenden
autobiografischen Aufzeichnungen dokumentieren, wie die jugendlichen

Flüchtlinge durch Sprechen kommunizieren lernten und sich in der neuen Kultur beheimateten. Sprachkenntnis wird nicht mehr nur als Hilfe zur Bewältigung des Alltags erlebt, sondern gestattet dem Flüchtling, seine kulturellen Bedürfnisse zu befriedigen. In der Literatur des Gastlandes repräsentiert sich die neue Lebenswelt, und mit der wachsenden Sprachkompetenz stellt sich die Beziehung zu ihr her und schafft Identifikation.

Bücher mögen im Reisegepäck der Kinderflüchtlinge vorhanden gewesen sein, nach der Ankunft, z. B. im Lager Dovercourt, hatten Primärbedürfnisse Vorrang: 'Nur sehr wenige lesen, teils weil es zu schwierig ist, sich nach all den Aufregungen zu konzentrieren, teils weil es fast nur englische Bücher im Lager gibt.'[15] Um sie abzulenken, brachten die Betreuer den Kindern als kulturelles Entree ins Gastland englische Volkslieder bei. Als sich ein annähernd normalisierter Alltag in Großbritannien eingespielt hatte, empfingen die Kinder starke Eindrücke der englischen Literatur zunächst nicht durch eigene Lektüre, sondern durch Vorlesen in der Schule. Offensichtlich vermittelten Gedichte mit ihrer strengen Struktur den sprachlichen Anfängern Sicherheit und versprach rasches Verstehen:

> Having poetry read aloud to us must also have formed part of the daily routine, since I remember that the rhythm and imagery of Blake's 'The Tyger' had appealed to me so much that I wanted to copy this poem into my booklet without noticing that actually I already knew it by heart.[16]

Als Schullektüre der Zehn- bis Vierzehnjährigen rufen sich die Autorinnen Milton, Shakespeare-Dramen und -Sonette und Jane Austen sowie Lyrik von Gray und Wordsworth, weiters Charles Dickens' *Pickwick Papers* in Erinnerung. Mit Ausnahme von Joel Chandler Harris' 'Geschichten von Brer Rabbit, die uns unser Lehrer vorlas',[17] ist kein Jugendbuch im engeren Sinn unter den Werken des didaktischen Kanons. Ebenfalls nicht auf kindliche Lesegewohnheiten zugeschnitten war der Lesestoff, der der religiösen Erziehung dienen sollte. Berichtet wird etwa von der Aktion des Oberrabbiners von England, der bei seinem ersten Besuch in Dovercourt sein Buch *Gedanken über das Judentum* verteilte, überliefert ist Bibellektüre und katholische Autobiografik.

Zu eigenen Büchern kamen die Flüchtlingskinder, wenn sie ihnen von ihren Gastgebern geschenkt wurden: Elisabeth Orsten etwa bekam 1940 'a very large and beautifully illustrated copy of *Alice in Wonderland*',[18] Ingrid Jacoby *Black Beauty* und *The Oxford Song Book*.[19]

Vor allem aber entwickelten sich die Kinder zu enthusiastischen
Bibliotheksbenützern. Leihbibliotheken nicht nur in großen Städten wie
London oder Manchester, sondern auch auf dem Land werden als gut
sortiert (mit umfangreichen Kinderbuch-Sektionen), als leicht und vor
allem kostenlos benützbar beschrieben.

Aus den Lektüreberichten läßt sich der Schluß ziehen, daß viele
Flüchtlingskinder mit der populären Kinder- und Jugendlektüre des
englischen Mittelstands ihrer Zeit aufwuchsen. Sie verschlangen die
Ritterromane von Sir Walter Scott und die Dschungelbücher Kiplings. Sie
lasen Mädchenbücher der viktorianischen Zeit wie *Little Women* von
Louisa May Alcott, *Anne of Green Gables* von Lucy Maud Montgomery
und die Romane von Angela Brazil, der bis in die Zwischenkriegjahre
einflußreichen Mädchenbuchautorin. *Water Babies* von Charles Kingsley
und George MacDonalds *The Princess and the Goblin*, fantastisch-
allegorische Märchen, waren ebenso beliebt wie Anna Sewells
anthropomorphisierte Pferdebiografie *Black Beauty* oder R. D. Black-
mores *Lorna Doone*. Fast alle dieser Werke englischsprachiger Autoren
aus Großbritannien und Nordamerika datieren zwischen 1860 und 1920,
sind also Produkte des 'first golden age of children's books',[20] wo das
Kinderbuch als didaktisch-moralisches Hilfsmittel vom Kinderbuch als
Unterhaltungsmedium abgelöst wurde, in dem Fantasie und eine auf die
Rezipienten zugeschnittene Erlebniswelt Vorrang hatten. Leser waren im
allgemeinen Kinder 'of the more leisured home'.[21]

Anders als in Exilgebieten wie Palästina oder Lateinamerika, die
keine gewachsene Kinderbuchszene vorzuweisen hatten, durften die Kinder
in Großbritannien auf ihrem Weg in die Kultur des Gastlandes an eine
etablierte Geschichte heimischer Kinder- und Jugendliteratur anknüpfen,
und viele Autoren und Bücher mögen ihnen nicht unvorbereitet begegnen
sein. Aufgrund der alten anglophilen Tradition in Deutschland und
Österreich war die englische Literatur vor dem Zweiten Weltkrieg in der
bürgerlichen Mittelschicht sehr verbreitet gewesen, ebenso die englische
Kinder- und Jugendliteratur aller Genres: Gestalten wie Robinson Crusoe
und Ivanhoe, Pu der Bär und Peter Pan, der Hund von Baskerville und die
drei Gerechten hatten bereits die Kinderzimmer auf dem Kontinent
bevölkert.[22]

Wenn nicht über Bücher, dann hatten die emigrierten Kinder Zugang
zur Unterhaltungsliteratur über die neuen Medien. Auf die 1937 gestartete
Comics-Serie mit den Abenteuern von 'Desperate Dan' war etwa Martha

Blend abonniert, auch war sie mit Sicherheit kein Einzelfall, wenn sie regelmäßig die Children's Hour der BBC hörte, vor allem *Tales of Toytown* von S. G. Hulme Beaman, die seit 1928 am Programm standen, und *Uncle Mac*.[23]

Ebenfalls auf spielerische Weise durfte Englisch im Kino gelernt werden, *dem* Unterhaltungsmedium der dreißiger Jahre. Kinos gab es überall, auch auf dem Land, und sie spielen in der Akkulturation der Kinder und Jugendlichen vom Kontinent eine wichtige Rolle. Zu den ersten Gesten der heimischen Bevölkerung für die ankommenden Flüchtlinge in Harwich hatte gehört, daß sie Freikarten für das Kino von Harwich bekamen, wo der erste abendfüllende Zeichentrickfim von Walt Disney *Snow White and the Seven Dwarfs* (1937) lief. An Slapsticks mit Laurel und Hardy und die Komödien mit Will Hay erinnern sich altersgemäß die Jüngeren, bei den zeitgenössischen Spielfilmen aus Hollywood kamen die Jugendlichen um Jahre früher als ihre Altersgenossen im Deutschen Reich mit der amerikanisierten Populärkultur der Erwachsenen in Berührung. *Der Glöckner von Notre Dame* mit Charles Laughton, *Vom Winde verweht*, *Rebecca* und das Lebensgefühl, das heroische und idealisierbare Figuren wie Tyrone Power, Bette Davis, Joan Crawford und Rita Hayworth vermittelten, riefen die Sehnsucht wach, 'mit einer Welt Kontakt aufzunehmen, von der ich jetzt vollkommen abgeschnitten war'.[24]

Als ganz abgeschnitten erlebten sich die Kinder und Jugendlichen in Großbritannien jetzt von der deutschen Kultur. Indem die Bücher hintengelassen wurden, verabschiedeten sich die meisten für immer von der deutschen Sprache und der Buchkultur ihrer mitteleuropäischen Kindheit, die bedeutet hatte: Grimmsche, orientalische und Andersens Märchen, griechische und nordische Sagen, Karl May, Astrid Lindgren, Selma Lagerlöf, Felix Saltens *Bambi*, Else Uris *Nesthäkchen* und Franz Karl Ginzkeys *Hatschi Bratschis Luftballon*, allen voran die Romane von Erich Kästner.[25] Wenn sie später die Gelegenheit eines sekundären Erwerbs der deutschen Sprache hatten, griffen die Jugendlichen ihrer Erinnerung nach übereinstimmend auf das nichtkompromittierte Erbe des 18. und 19. Jahrhunderts zurück: Goethe, Schiller, Gottfried Keller.

Je jünger das Kind bei seiner Emigration gewesen war, desto weniger wurde die Last der Doppelexistenz zur Kenntnis genommen, desto schneller glückte die Anglisierung und verwischten sich die Spuren der 'Continental legacy'.[26] Eine zeitgenössische Jungleserin wie Doris Orgel beschreibt ihre kulturelle Assimilierung als dynamische psychologische

Strategie, indem alles, auch defizitär Scheinendes wie mangelhafte
Sprachkompetenz und fehlendes Kontextwissen positiv umgedeutet wird:

> 'Look up words you don't understand', my mother suggested. So I took a
> dictionary along with *Alice in Wonderland* to Hampstead Heath, sat on a bench,
> looked up words like 'mimbly' that weren't in the dictionary, and was bewildered.
> But that was all right. Since Alice was bewildered too, it brought me closer to her. I
> put the dictionary down, skipped over words I did not know and just read on.[27]

Als man der Grundschülerin eine mit Fotos berühmter englischer
Schauspieler illustrierte Ausgabe von Shakespeares Gesammelten Werken
schenkt, entscheidet sie sich spontan für *ihr* Stück — die Charaktere des
Sommernachtstraums verwandeln sich zu Figuren ihrer kindlichen
Vorstellungswelt:

> Fairies were my main interest. I was astonished and intrigued to find so many of
> them included in a grown-up play. My parents went out that evening. I sprawled on
> their bed feeling as though I'd been given a magic key and read clear through *A
> Midsummer's Night Dream.*[28]

Die fremdsprachige Umgebung und ihr kultureller Kanon entwickelten
nicht nur bei der Kindergeneration ihre normative Kraft durch das Lesen.
Hilde Spiel etwa, die sich im Exil als Schriftstellerin für den
Sprachentausch entschied, beschreibt diesen Prozeß so, daß man sich in die
neue Sprache nur einlesen, sie aber nicht schreibend erobern konnte. Ein
entscheidender Impuls zum Verständnis der englischen Literatur erreichte
sie jenseits der Lektüre zeitgenössischer Autoren, indem sie nämlich die
sehr präsente nationale Kinderliteratur kennenlernte:

> Noch fehlte uns freilich das gesamte Umfeld, der Boden, dem diese eigenartige
> Phantasie, diese Bildkraft und Bilderwelt, diese Gleichnisse und Analogien, diese
> Denkmuster entsprangen. Sie waren offenbar in den frühen Jahren der Schriftsteller
> zu suchen. Erst als wir Kinder hatten, die in England aufwuchsen, holten wir die
> versäumte englische Kindheit nach und gewannen aus den Reimen und Liedern,
> den skurrilen und spaßigen Geschichten und Gedichten von Lewis Carroll und
> Edward Lear, von A. A. Milne und Beatrix Potter jene Kenntnis, an der es uns
> gemangelt hatte, um all diese Hinweise und Anspielungen, die den
> Inselbewohnern, aber nicht uns einsichtig waren, zu verstehen.[29]

'Environment scored its final triumph over heredity.'[30] Was hier als
Pragmatik des Akkulturationsprozesses bei der jüngeren Generation
beschrieben wird, funktioniert im besonderen Kontext österreichischer
Exilkulturpolitik in Großbritannien als Schlagwort in die umgekehrte
Richtung: das 'österreichische Kulturerbe zu erhalten, zu verteidigen und

zu propagieren, muß eine der Aufgaben der Österreicher in der Emigration sein'.[31] Die Politik des 'Austrian Centre', der größten und bedeutendsten Exilorganisation der österreichischen Emigration, und der 1941 gegründeten Dachorganisation 'Free Austrian Movement' (FAM) orientierte sich stark an Kulturpolitik und an der Jugendarbeit, beide Gebiete waren vom Konzept her weit gefaßt und sollten zugleich miteinander korrespondieren. Das 'gesamte Erziehungswesen. Die Erziehung von Kindern und Jugendlichen. Jugendorganisationen'[32] sah ein Vordenker wie Albert Fuchs als einen von drei Sektoren nicht nur der Kulturpolitik des Exils, sondern auch der im befreiten Österreich.

Die große Zahl der jungen Flüchtlinge, die zum Teil getrennt von ihren Familien und in alle Landesteile verstreut, mit den Problemen des Exils wie Armut, schlechten Arbeits- und Wohnbedingungen zu kämpfen hatten, fand in der 1939 gegründeten Jugendorganisation 'Young Austria' (Junges Österreich) mit ihren verschiedenen regionalen Gruppen ein soziales, politisches und kulturelles Forum für alle vor, die Anschluß an Gleichaltrige und Gleichgesinnte aus der Heimat suchten. 'Young Austria' betrieb eine betont österreichpatriotische kulturelle und Propaganda-tätigkeit sowohl innerhalb der Emigration als auch in der britischen Öffentlichkeit, die über Zeitschriften, Publikationen, Vorträge und über popularisierte Formen wie Ausstellungen, Theater, Kabarett, Volkstanz-gruppe und Chor umgesetzt wurde.[33] Mitglieder von 'Young Austria' durften nicht älter als fünfundzwanzig Jahre sein, rund die Hälfte (52 Prozent) war Anfang der vierziger Jahre über zwanzig Jahre alt und schon mehr als ein Jahr in diesem Jugendverband.[34] Ein Großteil arbeitete in der Kriegsindustrie.

Jüngere und Kinder treten in den benützten Quellen zu 'Young Austria' und 'Austrian Centre' nur marginal in Erscheinung.[35] Ihnen kam soziale Fürsorge zu, für sie suchte man mit kulturellen Aktivitäten wie Kinder-Theater oder sogar einem 'Wiener Kinderkabarett' den Schutzraum eines *normalen* Alltags im Exil anzudeuten.[36] Die 1940 rund 2.700 Bände umfassende Leihbibliothek des 'Austrian Centre' etwa enthielt nach einem Bericht ihres Bibliothekars Erich Fried Bücher 'von schwer zu beschreibender Vielfalt. Neben einigen in Leder gebundenen Bänden aus dem 18. Jahrhundert gab es mehr oder minder abgegriffene Taschenbücher aus der Weimarer Republik, dann wieder prachtvolle, aber sehr oft un-vollständige Klassikerausgaben; Jugendstilbücher, Kunstbücher, historische Romane, philosophische Abhandlungen, Essays, Kinderbücher, Gedicht-

anthologien, dazwischen alte Reiseführer und Schulbücher.'[37] Darunter
waren zwei Drittel in deutscher, ein knappes Drittel in englischer Sprache.

Den Jugendlichen kam eine aktive Rolle im politischen Kampf gegen
den Nationalsozialismus zu, was sich auch in Schreibstil und Zuschnitt der
Publikationen von Young Austria niederschlägt. Ihre Zeitschriften wie
'Junges Österreich/Young Austria' oder 'Jugend voran'[38] dienten darüber
hinaus der Kommunikation zwischen den geografisch verstreuten Altersgenossen und der Solidarisierung mit den jungen österreichischen Soldaten
in der britischen Armee und den Kriegsgefangenen. Als Jugendzeitschriften
im engeren Sinn sind sie nicht rezipierbar, lediglich über die Illustrationen
und Textsorten wie Sportberichte, Rätsel- und Witzecken läßt sich eine
Referenz auf das Alter der Zielgruppe herstellen.

Kinder galten in politischen Kontext des Exils nicht als relevante
Ansprechpartner, aber in einem künftigen: 'Bisher haben wir uns noch viel
zu wenig mit dem Schicksal unserer kleinen Brueder und Schwestern
beschaeftigt. Es ist aber unsere Pflicht[,] jenen 12-14jaehrigen Buben und
Maedels, die in Kuerze vor dem Problem der Berufserlernung stehen, zu
helfen.'[39] In Zusammenarbeit mit dem Freien Deutschen Kulturbund, der
eine Kinderkommission eingerichtet hatte, veröffentlichte 'Junges
Österreich' im Mai 1940 einen Aufruf zur Bildung von Kindergruppen,
'welche alle deutschsprachigen Kinder zusammenfassen und Choere,
Bastel[-] und Turngruppen schaffen will'. Auch eine eigene Kinderzeitung
nach dem Muster der Periodika des Jugendverbands wird angekündigt.

Bereits im Oktober 1939 war in Glasgow eine solche
Kinderzeitschrift erschienen, herausgegeben von den regionalen Gruppen
der 'Austrian Youth in Great Britain' und des 'Austrian Centre', redigiert
von Vally Rotschild: 'Der kleine Österreicher'.[40] Die hektografierte
Nummer umfaßt drei Seiten mit einer Art Editorial von Vally Rothschild
'Liebe Buben und Mädels!', in dem der Überfall Hitlers auf Polen und die
Kriegserklärung vom September 1939 an Deutschland mit einfachen
Worten erklärt wird, nicht ohne 'gerechte Hoffnungen auf ein Ende des
Nationalsozialismus' zu wecken und die Widerstandskraft des
österreichischen Volkes zu beschwören und eine Heimkehr 'zu unseren
herrlichen Bergen und Wäldern' in Aussicht zu stellen.[41] Der zweite
Abschnitt ist magazinartig gestaltet; die Redaktion kündigt einen
Aufsatzwettbewerb an, bringt Vorschläge für Spiele, Witze und eine
Kolumne Wissenswertes, sie bittet um Beiträge und Werbung für den
'Kleinen Österreicher' unter anderen Emigrantenkindern.

Daß im 'Kleinen Österreicher' das künftige Österreich andeutungsweise über seine Naturschönheiten und nicht über seine Staatsform definiert wird, kommt nicht zufällig zustande. Das Bild spiegelt sozusagen en miniature das Konzept der Mutterorganisation, nach dem man vor allem in der österreichischen Kunst und Landschaft geeignete Traditionsbezüge für die Entwicklung eines neuen Nationalbewußtseins finden könne.

'Austrian Centre', 'Young Austria' und das 'Free Austrian Movement' betrieben bekanntlich eigene Verlage und gaben miteinander etwa 150 politische und literarische Publikationen heraus. Von Hermynia Zur Mühlen, Vorstandsmitglied des Austrian Centre und Mitarbeiterin des *Zeitspiegel*, erschienen Ende 1944 *Kleine Geschichten von grossen Dichtern*,[42] zehn Prosaminiaturen über österreichische Dichterinnen und Dichter der älteren Zeit: Oswald von Wolkenstein, Ferdinand Sauter, Franz Grillparzer, Ferdinand Raimund, Adalbert Stifter, Anastasius Grün, Ferdinand von Saar, Ludwig Anzengruber, Jakob Julius David und Marie von Ebner-Eschenbach. Sie erzählen in schlichten Worten und bisweilen in österreichisch konnotierter Mundart Episoden aus dem Leben und vom Wirken dieser Schriftsteller aus der Heimat. Der Legendenton und das retardierende Verfahren, den Leser sozusagen daraufkommen zu lassen, um wen es sich bei der jeweiligen Episode handelt (Kenntnis der Literaturgeschichte beschleunigt den Prozeß), prädestinieren den Text zum Jugendbuch, wenn er auch eine nostalgische Wirkung auf Erwachsene entfaltete: das Buch bringe ein Wiedersehen mit 'alte[n] Freunde[n]'.[43] *Kleine Geschichten von grossen Dichtern* setzt das Konzept des FAM von Kulturarbeit als Methode der antifaschistischen Aktion literarisch um. Nicht umsonst zeigt das Eingangsszenario 'Kleiner Ritter' den jugendlichen Sänger Oswald von Wolkenstein in einem nächtlichen Kampf gegen die 'Feinde, die heidnischen Preussen'.[44] Die Silhouetten drohender Gegner, die ihm bei Nebel und Irrlicht erschienen waren, erweisen sich im klaren Mondschein als Weidenstrünke: die Nazis — ein Schattengeflacker. Und die als Kronzeugen aufgebotenen Schriftsteller des 19. Jahrhunderts vom Volkspoeten über den Vormärzlyriker bis zur bürgerlichen Realistin sollen nicht vergessen lassen, daß es eine eigenständige österreichische Literatur gibt, die weder von der deutschnationalen Geschichtsschreibung der Ersten Republik noch von den Nationalsozialisten selbst desavouiert werden konnte und daß dieses spezifisch Österreichische sich aus einer ehrwürdigen liberalen Tradition herleitet.[45]

Während ihrer Exilzeit in London hat Hermynia Zur Mühlen noch ein zweites Kinderbuch publiziert, die Sammlung *Little Allies*.[46] In einer Rahmenhandlung entwirft Zur Mühlen das Szenario, daß Kinder aus alliierten Nationen auf einem englischen Schloß zusammenkommen und einander ihre Märchen und Sagen erzählen, 'not only a record of the Youth of Europe but a most entertaining book expressing the variety of the National Idea as well as appreciation of the old sources of their legend and folklore'.[47] Der Band ist für eine Kriegsproduktion auffallend anspruchsvoll aufgemacht und illustriert, und er enthält auch die von einem österreichischen Mädchen erzählte Geschichte 'The Story of the Wise Judge'.[48] Um der Leserschaft das politisch nichtexistente Österreich im Kreis der Verbündeten plausibel zu machen, entschließt sich die Erzählerin zu einem Kunstgriff: '"Darling," I said, "the Danes and the Austrians are not Allies." Mummy laughed, "Oh John, don't be silly. Their countries were invaded, such tiny countries. What were they to do?"'.[49] Österreich als Opfer nationalsozialistischer Aggressionspolitik hat zwar seine staatliche Eigenständigkeit eingebüßt, nicht aber seine nationale Identität. Für die Anerkennung dieser Identität wird in *Little Allies* unter einem jungen Lesepublikum geworben. Das friedliche kosmopolitische Miteinander der Kinder, das sich im Erzählen - durch Literatur - realisiert, bringt darüber hinaus den Gedanken des Internationalismus und der Völkerfreundschaft zum Ausdruck. *Little Allies* ist die vorbildliche Umsetzung eines kulturpolitisch-propagandistischen Konzepts,[50] zugeschnitten auf jugendliche Rezipienten,

> die ein aktives Verhaeltnis dazu [zum Lesen] haben, eines, das sich an den Problemen beteiligt, wie zu einer Waffe und nicht zu einem Schlafmittel. Die Jugend in den befreiten Laendern wird sicher mit den Vorurteilen aufraeumen, dass Lernen und Vergnuegen, dass Lesen und Aktion saeuberlich getrennte Gebiete sind. Und das wird fuer Lernen, Vergnuegen und Aktion einen Aufschwung bedeuten.[51]

Hermynia Zur Mühlen befindet sich in der Gesellschaft anderer Österreicherinnen und Österreicher, die in Großbritannien im Genre Kinder- und Jugendliteratur als Autoren und Theatermacher, Illustratoren, Übersetzer oder Verleger hervortraten, darunter Oswald O. Dutch, Bettina Ehrlich, Friedrich Feld, Lisbeth Gombrich, Anna Maria Jokl, Marie und Otto Neurath, Amalia Serkin und Wolf Suschitzky.[52] Bei aller Vielfalt der Konzepte, Ideologien und Themen haben die exilierten Kinder- und Jugendbuchautoren gemeinsam, daß sie gegen Nationalismus, Rassismus und Militarismus menschenrechtliche, humanistische und kosmopolitische Ideen setzten. Besonders auf dem Gebiet des Kindersachbuchs wirkte sich der von den Emigranten geleistete kreative Transfer aus Österreich nach Großbritannien besonders innovativ aus.

Geografische, intellektuelle und sprachliche Unbehaustheit, der Kampf um die Rettung der eigenen Produktivkraft sind Erfahrungen, die alle Schriftsteller und Künstler des Exils teilen: 'In London war ich Regisseurin geworden, völlig ungeplant. Kommt man entwurzelt in ein neues Land, dann ist die Vergangenheit wie ausgelöscht, der Weg abgebrochen. Man muß sich neu sammeln, definieren, konstituieren. Das braucht lange Zeit.'[53] Der Genrewechsel zum Kinderbuch nach 1933 erfolgte bei manchen Autoren wie beim Journalisten und Filmkritiker Friedrich Feld oder bei der Dramaturgin und Drehbuchautorin Anna Maria Jokl programmatisch: weil sie 'Sinn suchte in der demoralisierenden "Vorläufigkeit" der Emigration. Ich wollte [...] für die einzige Leserschaft schreiben, die ich vertrauenswürdig fand in dem Chaos, das ich vorahnte: Kinder.'[54] Seit 1939 in Großbritannien, arbeitete sie zunächst in einem Heim für Emigrantenkinder. Sie schrieb und inszenierte das in Deutsch, Englisch und Tschechisch verfaßte Kinderstück *Where do you come from?*, mit dem die Gruppe auch in der Londoner Canterbury Hall gastierte, und realisierte in der Folge eine in London vielbeachtete Theaterarbeit für 'Young Czechoslovakia'.

In anderen Fällen ergab sich das neue Berufsbild nicht programmatisch, sondern praktisch. Journalismus, Populärwissenschaft, Übersetzung und eben Kinderliteratur waren die Möglichkeiten, einen Lebensunterhalt zu verdienen und den allmählichen Zugang zum britischen Kulturbetrieb zu gewinnen. Den Flüchtlingen war in Großbritannien bekanntlich bezahlte oder unbezahlte Erwerbstätigkeit, außer es handelte sich um hochqualifizierte Mangelberufe, untersagt. Gestattet wurde hingegen, Bücher an britische Verlage zu verkaufen. Autoren, die sich zum professionellen Sprachentausch entschlossen, hatten mehr Chancen, das gilt auch für das Kinderbuch. Vom Wirtschaftsjournalisten Oswald O. Dutch erschien etwa 1944 bei Walker & Sons das erste einer geplanten Reihe pädagogischer Kindersachbücher *Brainy Books*. Grete Fischer publizierte unter dem Pseudonym Margaret Fisher 1944 bis 1946 bei Collins vier Titel der Reihe *How Things are Made*, in der Vorschulkindern die Herstellung von Dingen ihrer Umwelt wie Essen und Kleidung erklärt wird.[55] Sie sind bereits mit Farbfotografien illustriert, eine neue Technik der

Buchgestaltung, an deren Entwicklung das Adprint Studio des Wieners Wolfgang Voges maßgeblich beteiligt war. Bei Collins publizierte auch Lisbeth Gombrich, Schwester von Ernst Gombrich. Die gelernte Juristin war im Exil zunächst als Übersetzerin von wissenschaftlichen Werken zur Kunstgeschichte und Biologie hervorgetreten, ab 1943 (*The Story of Hansel and Gretel*) veröffentlichte sie englische Nachdichtungen von orientalischen und Märchen der Gebrüder Grimm. Die Puppen, die auf den Farbfotos zur Illustration 'in naturalistic settings' nachgestellt waren, stammen von der Wiener Kunsthandwerkerin Amalia Serkin.

Der Fotograf und Kamermann Wolfgang Suschitzky hatte 1937 als unbezahlter Kameraassistent bei einer Filmproduktion von Paul Rotha zum ersten Mal Kontakt mit professioneller Tierfotografie: 'I got quite a reputation because my animal pictures were not strictly the standard record of the animal - showing all four legs and the tail. They were more like animal portraits, which was rather unusual then.'[56] In der Folge erschien mehr als ein halbes Dutzend für Kinder adaptierte Fotobücher mit seinen modernen Tierporträts, zum Teil auch als humoristische Bildergeschichte angelegt wie Roland Collins' *The Flying Poodle* (1941).

Die vom Soziologen Otto Neurath und dem Grafiker Gerd Arntz Anfang der dreißiger Jahre in Wien entwickelte Methode der Bildstatistik 'Isotype' konnte im Exil mit der Gründung des Isotype Institute in London vor allem von Marie Neurath für das Kinder- und Jugendbuch produktiv angewandt werden. Von 1947 bis Anfang der siebziger Jahre entstanden zahlreiche Serien, die den anschaulichen, stringenten 'picture-text-style' in Sachbuchserien über Geschichte ('They lived like this'), Technologie ('Wonders of the modern world') oder Naturwissenschaft umsetzten.

Anläßlich der Dritten Jahresausstellung österreichischer Künstler in den Räumen der Austrian Women's Voluntary Workers in London 1943 war im *Zeitspiegel* zu lesen: 'Unter den Ausstellern seien noch besonders erwähnt: Bettina Bauer-Ehrlichs Märchenbilder (Illustrationen zu zwei Kinderbüchern, die bereits mit großem Erfolg erschienen sind).'[57] Im britischen Exil konnte die Malerin und Grafikerin Bettina Ehrlich ihren Berufsweg ohne große Einbrüche fortsetzen, indem sie die angewandte Kunst zum Brotberuf machte: Kunstgewerbe und Kinderbuch. 1943 veröffentlichte sie bei Chatto & Windus das erste von ihr geschriebene und illustrierte Kinderbuch *Poo-Tse, the Water Tortoise* und dürfte für ihren Verlag auch anderweitig als Buchgestalterin gearbeitet haben. An die mit ihr befreundete Psychologin Elisabeth Löbl schrieb sie:

Ursula Seeber

Hab ich Dir schon erzählt, daß die Probedrucke von Cocolo (Eserl-Buch) fabelhaft geworden sind. Aber ob das Buch bis Weihnachten fertig wird[,] ist immer noch sehr fraglich. Chatto & Windus haben 2 Entwürfe von mir für Einbandpapier gekauft u. eine Textilfirma 4 für Cloqué.[58]

Mehr als ein Dutzend weitere Kinderbücher, darunter die Tier-Serie *Cocolo*, in englischen und amerikanischen Verlagen folgten. Die Protagonisten treten nicht als Mitglieder von Gruppen auf, sondern agieren als Individuen oder als Freundespaare. Ihre Geschichten werden aus der Kinderperspektive erzählt und dürfen im Schutzraum ihrer arkadischen Schauplätze immer gut ausgehen: 'I believe that tragic episodes do not upset children provided the story has a happy end and does not undermine the child's belief that grief passes, tears are dried and love is victorious.'[59] Bettina Ehrlich läßt ihre Helden in dekorativ aquarellierten, lichten Ambientes auftreten: 'I make many serious studies for my illustrations and believe that children should be given pictures based on the love and observation of nature. Any endeavor to draw like a child is, I think, horrible and insincere.'[60] Einzig die Auswanderergeschichte *Cocolo comes to America* von 1949 reflektiert von ferne den historischen Kontext. Die Heimat des Esels und seines kindlichen Herrn erscheint nur vordergründig mediterran-heiter: sie ist ein Kriegsschauplatz. Kind und Esel gehen zum Geldverdienen nach Amerika, um den bedrohten Eltern die Ausreise ermöglichen zu können.

Bettina Ehrlich wurde nach 1945 als Kinderbuchautorin in Österreich so gut wie nicht rezipiert. In deutscher Übersetzung erschien die Geschichte eines österreichischen Hüterbuben *Toni, der Ziegenhirt* 1966 bei Ueberreuter in Wien. Als eine späte Geste der Eingemeindung erfolgte Anfang 1999 die Umbettung ihres Sarges in ein Ehrengrab der Stadt Wien.

Eine Rückkehr zu Lebzeiten kam auch für Friedrich Feld, der Österreich keine Erneuerungskraft gegen Antisemitismus und Faschismus zutraute, nicht in Frage. Er blieb allerdings in der deutschen Sprache daheim und wurde in der Nachkriegszeit mit seinen kunstvollen Märchennovellen, in denen es um soziales Handeln, Gerechtigkeit und Solidarität geht, zu einem der produktivsten Autoren des Jungbrunnen Verlags. Dieser und der kommunistische Globus Verlag, in dem etwa Hermynia Zur Mühlen und Anna Maria Jokl publizieren konnten, waren die einzigen österreichischen Verlage nach 1945, die programmatisch beim 'Abtragen der faschistischen Denkweise, bei der Errichtung einer neuen Ideen- und Gefühlswelt'[61] durch das Kinderbuch aktiv waren. In geografischer Entferung vom deutschen Sprachraum und als Person nicht

eingebunden in den österreichischen Kulturbetrieb wie etwa Mira Lobe, die
früh aus dem Exil in Palästina zurückkam, geriet Friedrich Feld jedoch
trotz der geschäftlichen Erfolge ins Abseits, das Leben zwischen den
Sprachen und Kulturen blieb ein Dauerzustand. Als Anfang der achtziger
Jahre ein Schweizer Verlag seinen Roman *Die Goldene Galeere* von 1930
wiederauflegte, führte man ihn in den Registern als verstorben. An die
Lektorin des Jungbrunnen Verlags schrieb er: 'Ich bin nun 83 Jahre alt und
nehme die Welt nicht mehr so ernst, wie einstmals. Ich werde also auch
über diese Neuentdeckung über mich selbst hinwegkommen.'[62]

Anmerkungen

[1] Wolfgang Muchitsch, *Mit Spaten, Waffen und Worten: die Einbindung österreichischer
Flüchtlinge in die britischen Kriegsanstrengungen 1939-1945*, Ludwig Boltzmann Institut
für Geschichte der Arbeiterbewegung: Materialien zur Arbeiterbewegung, 61 (Wien und
Zürich: Europa, 1992), S. 5-10.

[2] *Österreicher im Exil in Großbritannien 1938-1945: eine Dokumentation*, hg. v.
Dokumentationsarchiv des österreichischen Widerstandes (Wien: Österreichischer
Bundesverlag, 1992), S. 11, 42-49.

[3] Martha Blend, *Ich kam als Kind: Erinnerungen*, übers. v. Karin Hanta, Österreichische
Exilbibliothek (Wien: Picus, 1998), S. 106.

[4] Waltraud Strickhausen, 'Großbritannien', in *Handbuch der deutschsprachigen
Emigration 1933-1945*, hg. v. Claus-Dieter Crohn u.a. (Darmstadt: Wissenschaftliche
Buchgesellschaft, 1998), S. 251-79 (S. 266); *Mit den Augen eines Kindes: Children in the
Holocaust, Children in Exile, Children under Fascism*, hg. v. Viktoria Hertling,
Amsterdamer Publikationen zur Sprache und Literatur, 134 (Amsterdam und Atlanta, GA:
Rodopi, 1998).

[5] Frank P. Grad, 'Following my Father's Footsteps', in: *Emigration N.Y.: die Geschichte
einer Vertreibung, ein Film von Egon Humer* (Wien: der Autor [Programmheft], [1995]),
S. 25.

[6] Barry Turner, *Kindertransport: eine beispiellose Rettungsaktion*, übers. v. Anna Kaiser
(Gerlingen: Bleicher, 1994), S. 93. Im fiktiven Tagebuch eines Kindertransport-
Flüchtlings bei Doris Orgel, *A Certain Magic* (New York: Dial Press, 1976), S. 16, wird
darauf Bezug genommen.

[7] Gillian Lathey, 'A Child's View of Exile: Language and Identity in the Autobiographical
Writings of Judith Kerr and Charles Hannam', in *Keine Klage über England? Deutsche
und österreichische Exilerfahrungen in Großbritannien 1933-1945*, hg. v. Charmian
Brinson u.a., Publications of the Institute of Germanic Studies, 72 (München: iudicium,
1998), S. 190-99 (S. 198).

[8] Siehe *Ich kam allein: die Rettung von zehntausend jüdischen Kindern nach England 1938/39*, hg. v. Rebekka Göpfert, übers. v. Susanne Röckel, dtv 1690 (München: Deutscher Taschenbuch Verlag, 1994), S. 135, 148.

[9] Benützt wurden Hanna Behrend, 'An Austrian Refugee in Wartime Manchester', in *This Working World: Women's Lives and Culture(s) in Britain 1910-1945*, hg. v. Sybil Oldfield (London: Taylor & Francis, 1994), S. 133-37; Blend (Anm. 3); Gitta Deutsch, *Böcklinstraßenelegie: Erinnerungen* (Wien: Picus, 1993); Ingrid Jacoby, *My Darling Diary: a Wartime Journal - Vienna 1937-39, Falmouth 1939-44* (Cornwall: United Writers, 1998); 'Doris Orgel', *Something about the Author*, Bd. 19, [o.J.], S. 193-209; Elisabeth M. Orsten, *From Anschluss to Albion: Memoirs of a Refugee Girl 1939-1940* (Cambridge: Acorn 1998); Lore Segal, *Other People's Houses* (New York: Harcourt, Brace, 1964); in diesem Zusammenhang unergiebig ist Annette Saville, *Little Grass-Orphan Annie: a Book for Children* ([o.O.]: die Autorin, [o.J.]).

[10] Orsten (Anm. 9), S. 89.

[11] Ebd., S. 109.

[12] Blend (Anm. 3), S. 104.

[13] Lathey (Anm. 7), S. 192.

[14] Orgel (Anm. 9), S. 199.

[15] Turner (Anm. 6), S. 80.

[16] Orsten (Anm. 9), S. 68. Lektüreerfahrungen mit Gedichten von Rudyard Kipling bei Blend und Jacoby (Anm. 9), S. 129, 246.

[17] Blend (Anm. 3), S. 105.

[18] Orsten (Anm. 9), S. 93.

[19] Jacoby (Anm. 9), S. 51.

[20] Peter Hunt, *An Introduction to Children's Literature*, Opus Books (Oxford und New York: Oxford University Press, 1994), S. 59.

[21] Gillian Avery, 'British Children's Books to World War II', in *Children's Books and their Creators*, hg. v. Anita Silvey (Boston und New York: Houghton Mifflin, 1995), S. 85-88 (S. 86).

[22] Walter Scherf, 'The Influence of Great Britain on German Children's Literature', in *Sub tua platano: Festgabe für Alexander Beinlich* (Emsdetten: Lechte, 1981), S. 255-65.

[23] Blend (Anm. 3), S. 104.

[24] Ebd., S. 120.

25 *Kleine Verbündete, Little Allies: vertriebene österreichische Kinder- und Jugendliteratur, Austrian Children's and Juvenile Literature in Exile*, hg. v. Ursula Seeber u.a. (Wien: Picus, 1998), S. 22.

26 Eric Sheldon, 'The Younger Generation', in *Britain's New Citizens: the Story of the Refugees from Germany and Austria*, Tenth Anniversary Publication of the Association of Jewish Refugees in Great Britain (London: Association of Jewish Refugees, 1951), S. 70-71 (S. 71).

27 Orgel (Anm. 9), S. 199.

28 Ebd.

29 Hilde Spiel, *Die hellen und die finsteren Zeiten: Erinnerungen 1911-1946* (München: List, 1989), S. 157.

30 Sheldon (Anm. 26), S. 71.

31 Jenö Kostmann, 'Österreichische Kulturarbeit: eine Kampfaufgabe' [1942], Teilabdruck in *Österreicher im Exil in Großbritannien* (Anm. 2), S. 385-86 (S. 385). Zur Kulturpolitik von Austrian Centre und FAM see Wolfgang Muchitsch: 'Cultural Policy of Refugee Organisations in Britain', in *Austrian Exodus: The Creative Achievements of Refugees from National Socialism*, hg. v. Edward Timms und Ritchie Robertson, Austrian Studies 6 (Edinburgh: Edinburgh University Press, 1995), S. 22-40 (S. 28-31).

32 Albert Fuchs, 'Österreich und die deutsche Kultur: Grundlinien künftiger Kulturpolitik' [1944], Teilabdruck in *Österreicher im Exil in Großbritannien* (Anm. 2), S. 390-91 (S. 390).

33 Benützt wurden die Chronologie und die Bibliografien in '*Fluchtpunkt England': Spuren der österreichischen Emigration in Großbritannien 1938 bis 1945, Katalog zur Ausstellung an der Universitätsbibliothek Graz*, hg. v. Reinhard Müller (Graz: Universitätsbibliothek, 1996); ein britisches Forschungsprojekt zum Austrian Centre steht vor dem Abschluß: Richard Dove, 'The Austrian Centre' [Projektbericht], *Zirkular* 30 (1997), S.4-5; vgl. Bericht von Richard Dove in diesem Jahrbuch.

34 Volker Kaukoreit, *Vom Exil bis zum Protest gegen den Krieg in Vietnam: frühe Stationen des Lyrikers Erich Fried, Werk und Biographie 1938-1966* (Darmstadt: Häusser, 1991), S. 46.

35 Die EDV-Bibliografie des Projekts 'Dokumentation, Datenbank und Handbuch österreichischer Exilzeitschriften 1933/34 bis 1945' am Institut für Publizistik der Universität Wien dokumentierte mit Stand Herbst 1995 für Periodika des Exilzentrums London zum Schlagwort *Kind* 159 Einträge, d.h. ein Prozent der Gesamteinträge.

36 Eva Kolmer, *Das Austrian Centre: 7 Jahre oesterreichische Gemeinschaftsarbeit* (London: Austrian Centre, [August 1946], S. 18-19, über den 1942 eröffneten, international besetzten Kindergarten (Austrian Day Nursery); siehe *Kleine Verbündete* (Anm. 25), S. 24-8.

37 Erich Fried, *Mitunter sogar Lachen: Erinnerungen*, Wagenbachs Taschenbücher (Berlin: Wagenbach, 1992), S. 105-06.

[38] *Kinder- und Jugendliteratur im Exil 1933-1950: mit einem Anhang Jüdische Kinder- und Jugendliteratur in Deutschland 1933-1938, eine Ausstellung der Sammlung Exil-Literatur der Deutschen Bücherei Leipzig* (Leipzig u.a.: Die Deutsche Bibliothek, 1995), S. 20-22 (zur Publizistik für Kinder und Jugendliche im Exil).

[39] 'Wir schaffen Kindergruppen', *Junges Österreich* 2 (Mai 1940), Nr. 6, S.4.

[40] *Der kleine Österreicher: Zeitung der Kinder in England*, hg. v. Austrian Youth, Group Glasgow, Austrian Centre (Anfang Oktober 1939), [Nr. 1]. Ich danke Reinhard Müller (Anm. 33) für den Hinweis auf diese Zeitschrift.

[41] Ebd., S. 1.

[42] Hermynia Zur Mühlen, *Kleine Geschichten von grossen Dichtern: Miniaturen* (London: Free Austrian Books, [1944]); Manfred Altner, *Hermynia Zur Mühlen: eine Biographie* (Bern: Lang, 1997), S. 182-84.

[43] Leserbrief von B. I. Morse (Universität Cardiff), *Zeitspiegel* 2 (27. Januar 1945), S. 7.

[44] *Kleine Geschichten* (Anm. 42), S. 6.

[45] Ulrich Weinzierl, 'Österreich als Wille und Vorstellung', in *Deutsche Exilliteratur: Studien zu ihrer Bestimmung im Kontext der Epoche 1930 bis 1960*, hg. v. Wulf Koepke und Michael Winkler, Studien zur Literatur der Moderne, 12 (Bonn: Bouvier, 1984), S. 242-59 (S. 253).

[46] *Little Allies: Fairy and Folk Tales of Fourteen Nations*, adapt. and told by Countess Hermynia Zur Mühlen, ill. by N. Nadel (London: Alliance Press, [1944]).

[47] Ebd., Klappentext.

[48] Ebd., S. 73-7.

[49] Ebd., S.7.

[50] Helene Maimann, *Politik im Wartesaal: österreichische Exilpolitik in Großbritannien 1938-1945*, Veröffentlichungen der Kommission für neuere Geschichte Österreichs, 62 (Wien u.a.: Böhlau, 1975), S. 209.

[51] [Stefan Kaufmann], *Wie liest man Bücher? Wie halte ich ein Referat?*, Jugendführerschule des Jungen Österreich (London: Jugend voran, [1945]), S. 1-3 (S. 3).

[52] Siehe Bio-Bibliografien in *Kleine Verbündete* (Anm. 25), S. 111-172.

[53] Anna Maria Jokl, *Die Reise nach London: Wiederbegegnungen* (Frankfurt/M.: Jüdischer Verlag, 1999), S. 66.

[54] Ebd., S. 67.

55 Jennifer Taylor, "'Die Kultur haben wir Ihnen aufgehoben, sie wurde nur nicht abgeholt'", in *Keine Klage über England?* (Anm. 7), S. 175-89 (S. 183, über die unbefriedigenden Verträge für die Kinderbücher).

56 Wolf Suschitzky, 'A Mirror to Life', *Visual Art* 97 (Frühling 1997), S. 6-28 (S. 22).

57 'Oesterreichische Kuenstler stellen aus', *Zeitspiegel* 21 (19. Juni 1943), S. 9.

58 Brief Bettina Ehrlich an Elisabeth Löbl, 3 November 1944 (unpubliziert). Aus dem Teilnachlaß Löbl, Antiquariat Wilfried Magnet, Klagenfurt, eingesehen 1996.

59 'Bettina Ehrlich', *Something about the Author*, Bd. 1 ([o.J.]), S. 84.

60 Ebd.

61 Alice Lederer, 'Probleme der Kinderliteratur', *Österreichisches Tagebuch* 27 (5. Oktober 1944), S. 12.

62 Brief Friedrich Feld an Ellen Weigel, 6. Dezember 1985. Unpubliziert im Archiv des Jungbrunnen Verlags, Wien. Mit freundlicher Genehmigung des Verlags.

Charmian Brinson and Richard Dove

Free Austrian Books: The Austrian Centre and its Publications 1939-1946

This article deals with a forgotten chapter of Austrian exile in Britain during the Second World War: the publications of the Austrian Centre, under the imprint Free Austrian Books, of its youth arm Young Austria, and of the 'Kulturelle Schriftenreihe des Free Austrian Movement'. It considers how far these publications may be regarded as political/cultural statements of Austrian identity and aspiration in exile, seeking to win British public opinion for the restoration of an independent Austria, to keep alive its memory in the minds of émigrés, and ultimately to engage with the political discourse of an emerging post-war Austria.

When the Austrian Centre opened in London on 16 March 1939 with an inaugural concert, few could have foreseen its rapid development. In the months immediately preceding the outbreak of war, it established itself in two adjacent terraced houses in Westbourne Terrace, rapidly becoming the main organisation representing Austrian refugees in Britain. A booklet published in May 1944 marking five years of the Centre's existence,[1] recorded that it had 3,500 members, a turnover (in 1943) of £46,000 and a staff of over 70 to run the organisation's various activities — the restaurant and coffee-house, the library and reading-room, the hostel for soldiers, the weekly newspaper *Zeitspiegel*, and the publishing enterprise Free Austrian Books.

The booklet summarised the aims of the Austrian Centre under four headings:
- to organise the Austrians in the fight against Hitler
- to promote friendship between the British and the Austrian people
- to foster the cultural life of the Austrians in this country
- to provide help, support and advice for Austrians.

The Centre's series of publications was intended to help achieve these aims — and to realise the political agenda which underpinned them.

Outwardly the Austrian Centre was a non-party organisation, seeking to represent a broad spectrum of Austrian refugees and to act as a social and cultural focal point. In fact, although it remained a broad-based organisation, it ultimately came to assume a political role, in which the dominant tone was given by the Austrian Communists.[2] When members of

the Austrian Communist Party (KPÖ) arrived in London in 1938-39, they
came with political objectives which broadly coincided with those of other
Austrian exile organisations (with the notable exception of the Social
Democrats). These were to raise awareness of the plight of Austria
amongst the British public and to propagate the restoration of a free and
independent Austrian state. Political activity by refugees was generally
frowned on by the British authorities, and the KPÖ group which formed in
London in 1938-39 was not publicly constituted, preferring to work
clandestinely. This proved to be a prudent tactic in the light of subsequent
political developments, notably the Nazi-Soviet Non-Aggression Pact of
August 1939.

In pursuit of its political objectives, the KPÖ in London sought to
create 'mass' organisations which would bring together Austrian refugees
across the anti-Fascist political spectrum: an extension of the Popular Front
policy, which followed the Conference of the Communist International in
1935, to the conditions of exile. The two largest and most influential
Austrian refugee organisations in Britain during the war years, the
Austrian Centre and the Free Austrian Movement (whose activities were
from the first closely related), were both the product of this policy. In this
context the publications of the Austrian Centre, issued firstly under its own
name and subsequently under the imprint Free Austrian Books, were to
assume a key role in promoting the party's political objectives.

The booklet *Five Years of the Austrian Centre* was one of a growing
number of publications intended to make the political voice of Austrian
exiles in Britain more widely heard. At first sight these publications seem a
disparate and even random list, including literary works (verse anthologies,
short prose, autobiography), political pamphlets concerned with
contemporary issues regarding Austria, and more general publications
which reviewed Austrian culture and history. On closer examination they
are revealed as a conscious and roughly continuous exposition, providing a
political and cultural statement of Austrian identity and aspiration during
the second world war.

These were published in German or English, the English-language
texts aiming broadly to raise British awareness of Austria's specific
cultural and political identity, while the German-language publications
were (until 1944-45) largely literary or cultural texts, intended to foster
Austrian national consciousness, particularly amongst younger Austrians.
However, the distinction between English-language and German-language

publications was not always clear-cut, at least as regards readership: English-language pamphlets, for example, were at one point apparently widely read by young Austrians serving in the British forces. Texts in either language were intended to serve the overriding political purpose: the post-war re-establishment of an independent Austria.

The very first publication of the Austrian Centre was its first annual report, issued in March 1940. Comprising some thirty pages, the report was published in English, both to comply with censorship requirements and to make it accessible to British supporters. Though primarily a functional document, it was also intended to raise awareness of the Austrian Centre, and hence Austria, amongst British sympathisers. To this end, it contains messages of support from prominent British patrons, such as D. N. Pritt, Eleanor Rathbone and the Bishop of Chichester, which preface the detailed report on the Centre's first year of activity. The report itself is unsigned, its authorship unconfirmed, but to the latter-day reader its most striking feature is its political neutrality.[3]

This first publication by the Austrian Centre was also its last for nearly two years, during which it confined itself to the production of the weekly newspaper *Zeitspiegel*. Even this was produced only as a duplicated information sheet, offering a digest of news from the British press for readers who spoke little English. Not until September 1941, in the wake of Germany's invasion of the Soviet Union, did *Zeitspiegel* emerge as a printed newspaper with its own editorial staff and policy.

The reasons for this studied reticence during 1940-41 were both political and practical. Although the Communists had played an important role in establishing the Austrian Centre and occupied leading positions within it, the Nazi-Soviet Pact of August 1939 had imposed considerable tactical constraints on them. War-time conditions precluded public support for the official line propagated by the Comintern that this was a war between rival imperialist powers which Communists had a duty to oppose; public opposition to the policy of the British government would have meant rapid internment. These difficulties were further exacerbated by internal political developments in Britain. The mass internment of 'enemy aliens' ordered by the British authorities in May 1940 forced the Austrian Centre to concentrate on immediate practical tasks, and its dealings with the British authorities in 1940-41 were therefore limited almost entirely to the question of internment and related problems of accommodation and employment which arose after internees were released.[4] Conversely, the publication programme which the Austrian Centre launched at the beginning of 1942 was a result of its new-found tactical freedom after the entry into the war of the Soviet Union.

The first book publication with which the Austrian Centre was associated was the verse anthology *Die Vertriebenen. Dichtung der Emigration*, published late in 1941 in collaboration with the Free German League of Culture and Young Czechoslovakia. Claiming to be 'the first book published in the German language in this country since the war began', this slim volume contains a selection of poems by refugee authors, aiming 'to give the British public an insight into the intellectual strivings of the refugees'. The ideological thrust of the publication is implicit in the sub-title: '37 German Poems — but not written by our enemies.' As a collaborative venture, it sought to represent all German-speaking exiles, avoiding any assertion of a specific Austrian cultural identity. However, the Austrian Centre seems to have played a leading role in this publication. The two major contributors (numerically), Eva Priester (with five poems) and Erich Fried (with four poems), were both closely connected with the Centre.[5] The cover design was by Wolfgang Schlosser, and the poems were selected by Albert Fuchs, both leading members of the Centre, while the publication address was that of the Centre's premises at 126 Westbourne Terrace.

Political conditions for Austrian exiles were transformed in December 1941 with the founding of the Free Austrian Movement (FAM), an umbrella organisation to which all the main Austrian exile groups were affiliated (with the exception of one group of Social Democrats).[6] The emergence of the FAM signalled the introduction of an overt political agenda, pursuing the aim of the post-war re-establishment of an independent Austrian state and profiling Austrian cultural achievements as an assertion of a separate Austrian identity. Shortly after, in the spring of 1942, the Austrian Centre finally launched a publishing programme which was gradually to gather momentum throughout the rest of the war.[7] By the end of the year the Centre had published five booklets encompassing various aspects of its political agenda. This agenda is most explicitly enunciated in three pamphlets entitled *Zurück oder nicht zurück?* (April 1942), *Restive Austria* (May 1942), and *The Austrian Ally* (October 1942).[8]

Zurück oder nicht zurück? reprints the text of an address given at the Austrian Centre by its President, F. C. West.[9] In a speech originally given under the title 'Zurück oder nicht zurück — das ist keine Frage', West made a strong appeal for total commitment by Austrian refugees to the British war effort, arguing that only the defeat of Hitler could create a situation in which the question posed in the pamphlet's title had any real meaning. While this text was clearly intended for West's Austrian compatriots, the next two pamphlets were equally clearly aimed at actual or potential 'British friends'. *Restive Austria* was the first of several pamphlets which sought to challenge the prevailing perception of Austria in Britain. British public opinion had hitherto made little distinction between Austria and Germany, an attitude reinforced by the British government's diplomatic recognition of the *fait accompli* of Nazi annexation of Austria in 1938. Diplomatic recognition had been endorsed by bureaucratic anomaly: Austrians who had entered Britain after September 1938 had been admitted with German passports and therefore registered with the Aliens Department as Germans.

Restive Austria is intended to modify this perception. The programmatic preface (again by F. C. West) seeks to establish Austria as the first victim of Nazi aggression: 'Austria too belongs to occupied Europe' (p. 2). The actual text, written by Jenö Kostmann, the editor-in-chief of *Zeitspiegel*, claims 'to give a report of the Austrian powder-barrel', i.e. to document the Austrian struggle for freedom. It paints a picture of a country oppressed and exploited by its Nazi occupiers, and reports growing passive resistance and acts of sabotage: a picture probably coloured by political optimism. The pamphlet's reports of incipient Austrian resistance were to be repeated and embellished in later publications, becoming a common-place of KPÖ war propaganda, intended both to bolster morale amongst Austrian refugees and to influence Allied attitudes towards Austria. That the Communists were also influenced by their own propaganda seems probable — and may help to explain the bitter disillusionment they suffered on their return to Austria after the war.

The Austrian Ally, published later that year, sought to make the case for Allied recognition of Austria as an occupied country and therefore as an ally. More specifically, it aimed 'to achieve a better understanding of the forces operating inside Austria [...] and a proper comprehension of the position of the Austrians in Great Britain, worthy allies as they are'. It consequently deals in turn with 'Austria Within' ('Guerrilla warfare has at last reached Austria', p. 3) and 'Austrians in Britain', telling 'the story of the participation of Austrian refugees in the war effort of this country' (p.

9). The pamphlet bears eloquent testimony to the need Austrian émigrés felt to explain themselves to the British: equating themselves with the anti-Nazi opposition within Austria itself. The concluding page of the pamphlet contains notes intended for Austrian readers, confirming that it was not aimed exclusively at a British audience. Kostmann's essay in the booklet ends by invoking the example of Andreas Hofer, leader of the Tyrolean struggle for freedom against Napoleon (p. 8). The reference to Hofer undoubtedly rested on the assumption that his name would be known to British readers from the sonnets of William Wordsworth.[10] However, this overt reference to an icon of Austrian patriotism suggests an ideological ambiguity which can also be detected in other publications.

It is perhaps most striking in the booklet *This is Austria*. Published shortly before Christmas 1942, and 'dedicated to all British friends of Austria by the two largest Austrian organisations in this country', the booklet was produced as an inexpensive Christmas present for Austrians to give British friends. It was intended to promote the concept of an Austria which was historically, culturally and politically independent of Germany. Subtitled 'The Story of a Beautiful Country', the booklet offers a tourist's eye view of Austria as a small country of outstanding natural beauty and cultural achievement. Consisting of text and pictures, it seeks to challenge the Nazi view of a German 'Ostmark' by tracing the historical antecedents of a separate Austrian identity. In so doing, it appropriates much of the iconography of Austrian nationalism, presenting a conception of Austria similar to that propagated by the 'Ständestaat' (corporate state) of Schuschnigg.[11] The front cover shows a mountain village in winter, the back cover a country girl in traditional dress, framed by fruit blossom. This tourist's eye view of Austria is completed by views of mountains and lakes, and above all by pictures of Salzburg, the festival town which had come to symbolise Austrian high culture. There are also attempts to convey a different tradition (that of 'Red Vienna') through illustrations of the ambitious municipal housing projects in Vienna, such as Karl-Marx Hof or the Matteoti Hof, but even these are undercut by the accompanying text, which emphasises the emergence of the patriotic front of Catholics, Socialists and Communists in Vienna immediately prior to the *Anschluß*.

The presentation of such images was not of course arbitrary. The primary political reason, as stated above, was that the Austrian Centre itself represented a broad patriotic front. However, this was a booklet intended for British readers, and the images of Austria presented were calculated to confirm current British preconceptions, reinforcing a view of Austria derived from the cinema and musical theatre. Probably the best-known Austrian living in Britain in the 1930s was Richard Tauber, whose films such as *Blossom Time* and *Land without Music* had helped to create a perception of Austria as a country of scenic beauty and song: a natural backdrop for operetta. It is no accident that one of the photos in the booklet is of the original White Horse Inn (p. 15) — the operetta of the same name having achieved enormous popularity in London in 1931-32.[12] There were undoubtedly also practical explanations for the choice of images, not least the limited supply of available photographs. Certainly, tourist photographs could be obtained more easily — and more cheaply — than news agency pictures. The overall effect, however, remains culturally regressive.

Austria, produced a year later (November 1943), is both tourist brochure and political tract. A page of photographs, captioned 'Tourists' Paradise', are juxtaposed with an essay ('Britain's Friends in the Alps') which describes the Austrian Freedom Conference held in autumn 1942. The essay concludes that 'as the first victim of Nazi aggression, it is absolutely vital for Austria that she be recognised by the Allies as an associate' (p. 14), and raises the political demand for the foundation of a Free Austrian Fighting Force. Elsewhere, the contents include essays on Mozart, Beethoven and the Salzburg Festivals, confirming the booklet's cultural conservatism.

The crucial place assigned to culture in the political discourse of Austrian exiles, and above all of the Austrian Centre, is illustrated by the Austrian 'Kulturkonferenz' held in London on 29-30 August 1942. Convened by the Free Austrian PEN, and chaired by its President Robert Neumann, the 'Kulturkonferenz' was attended by representatives of all the main Austrian exile organisations. The keynote address was given by Albert Fuchs, a leading member of the Austrian Centre. Reporting the conference in *Zeitspiegel*, Jenö Kostmann asserted 'daß die Pflege des österreichischen Kulturguts eine Waffe im Kampf gegen die Naziherrschaft ist'.[13] Fuchs's speech, published later that year as *Über österreichische Kultur*, gave a more subtle, if no less Marxist, analysis of Austrian culture, offering a dialectical reading of cultural development.

Refuting the Nazi claim that Austria was an artificial creation, 'bereit zur Heimkehr ins Reich', Fuchs reviews the 'main stages' of Austria's history, emphasising precisely the points at which it diverges from Germany's. Within this historical perspective, he seeks to delineate a distinct Austrian culture (and thereby an Austrian cultural identity). 'Wir wollen die Eigenart des österreichischen Geistes uns und anderen zur Anschauung bringen. Nichts weiter.' The course of Austrian culture is both the product of social change and the harbinger of political revolution. Thus the cultural achievements of the early nineteenth century record the economic rise of the 'aufstrebenden Mittelklassen' — and presage the political revolution of 1848:

> *Ein* Unterschied ist freilich unverkennbar: die höfische Gedankenrichtung ist fort. Schubert, Strauß sen., ebenso Waldmüller, ebenso Raimund, Nestroy, ja selbst Grillparzer wurzeln in der Vorstadt, empfangen von dorther die Impulse ihrer Arbeit. Vielfach spiegelt sich in ihren Werken der Kleinkrieg gegen das feudale Regime (p. 10).

Fuchs does not fail to mention the brilliant flowering of Austrian culture around 1900, nor the social achievements of the First Republic — 'das waren neue Ausdrucksformen des österreichischen Geistes, des Geistes der fortschrittlichen Klasse in Österreich' (p. 13).

1942 ended with the publication of the verse anthology *Zwischen gestern und morgen*, which represents something of a milestone in Austrian Centre publications. The volume is subtitled 'Neue österreichische Gedichte', though the unsigned foreword (written in fact by Georg Knepler)[14] clearly defines 'Austrian' in cultural, not ethnic terms: 'Nicht alle ihre Autoren sind in Österreich geboren; alle haben dort entscheidende Jahre verbracht; und den meisten hat Österreich den Stoff — und vielleicht einiges mehr gegeben — österreichische Autoren' (p. 2). Ten poets are represented, ranging from established writers such as Berthold Viertel, Franz Werfel and Theodor Kramer, to younger poets like Erich Fried and Jura Soyfer. While the quality of the poems is uneven, the volume itself is significant as the first anthology of Austrian verse to be published in Britain during the war.

In March 1943 the Austrian Centre launched its imprint Free Austrian Books with the booklet *Kleines Magazin*, a miscellany of poems, short stories, and political essays. The introduction of the new imprint heralded a sharp increase in publishing activity. By far the greatest number of Austrian Centre publications is concentrated in the years 1943-45, a progression reflecting a growing sense of political urgency. Most of the pamphlets published in this period are concerned with topical political events. *The House of Lords on Austria* (February 1943) reprinted speeches made in the Lords debate (2 February 1943); *Ein Weg ins Leben*

(February 1943) is a discussion of the Jewish question, taking up the appeal made by British bishops to 'make room' for Jewish refugees. It was the duty of the civilised nations 'Neutraler oder Alliierter, [...] die äußersten Anstrengungen zu machen, eine Zufluchtstätte für diese Opfer zu finden' (p. 3). The pamphlet's author was Willi Scholz, the General Secretary of the Austrian Centre, who — as a non-Jew and (more importantly) a Communist — took a strong anti-Zionist line.

According to Georg Knepler, the two most widely-read pamphlets of the Austrian Centre were *Austria: Gateway to Germany* (September 1943) and *Moscow on Austria* (December 1943).[15] The former, written by the poet and journalist Eva Priester, and aimed at 'the British friends of the Austrian cause', sought to emphasise the key strategic and military importance of Austria in the wake of the Allied invasion of Italy. It also reported growing Austrian resistance to German rule, illustrated by the formation of the Austrian Freedom Front. *Moscow on Austria* reproduces the text of the Allies' Moscow Declaration in November 1943, which represented the achievement of a major political aim of exiled Austrians. The Declaration pronounced the *Anschluß* 'null and void' and for the first time included the re-establishment of an independent Austria as an allied war aim; Austria was, however, reminded that 'account will inevitably be taken of her own contribution to her liberation'. *Moscow on Austria* is therefore at pains to stress the role of the Austrian Freedom Front, calling on Austrians abroad to support it, and raising the political demand for the formation of an Austrian National Committee in exile. Though both pamphlets were aimed primarily at British readers, they had an important subsidiary readership among young Austrians serving in the British forces.

The outstanding literary publication by Free Austrian Books, published at Christmas 1943, was *Ein Sohn aus gutem Hause*, a short volume of autobiography by Albert Fuchs. Fuchs's memoirs of his middle-class childhood in Vienna's 9th district were the evocation of a long-vanished world, all the more poignant for its contrast with war-time London. Moreover, it was a world which lived on in the minds of many of Fuchs's fellow-exiles, who shared his well-to-do Viennese Jewish background. *Ein Sohn aus gutem Hause* is more than a charming memoir. Fuchs goes on to record his conversion to the cause of Communism in 1934-35, lending his text the structure of a 'Bildungsnovelle'.

When Georg Knepler came to write *Five Years of the Austrian Centre* (May 1944), he could therefore look back, *inter alia*, on two years of successful publication. The subtext of his account was of course that the Austrians had escaped from their stigmatisation as enemy aliens, and were now free to state their case and even to exercise political influence. During these two years, he reported, the Centre had published eight booklets in English with an aggregate sale of 50,000 copies; the equivalent figure for German-language booklets and pamphlets was 'just under 19,000'. The evident emphasis on English-language publishing confirms that during 1942-43 the primary purpose of publication was the exposition of a political agenda, which sought to influence British public opinion (and government policy) in its favour.

The period up to 1943 had seen a gradual extension of Communist influence within the Austrian Centre. Given the crucial importance which the Party assigned to political education, it is unsurprising that Communist activists should dominate the Centre's publication programme. All of the eight pamphlets cited by Knepler were written by leading functionaries of the Austrian Centre — all of whom were, like Knepler himself, also leading cadres of the KPÖ. They included F. C. West, the President of the Austrian Centre (*House of Lords on Austria*), the General Secretary Willi Scholz (*Ein Weg ins Leben* and *Moscow on Austria*), and the leading cultural spokesman Albert Fuchs (*Über österreichische Kultur*); the editorial team of *Zeitspiegel* — Jenö Kostmann (*Restive Austria* and *The Austrian Ally*), Hilde Mareiner (*The Austrian Ally*) and Eva Priester (*Austria: Gateway to Germany*); and Anna Hornik (*This is Austria*), a veteran KPÖ member.

The increasingly visible profile of the KPÖ is demonstrated above all by the publication of several pamphlets by Ernst Fischer, the party's leading cultural theorist, who had spent the war in Moscow. The most notable of these was *The Rebirth of my Country*, consisting of a series of broadcasts on Austria which Fischer had made over Moscow Radio. *Zeitspiegel* recommended the pamphlet as eminently suitable for the information of British friends.[16] In fact, during 1944-45 the Austrian Centre shifted its emphasis significantly from English-language to German-language publications, reflecting the progress of the war and the changing political priorities it imposed. These shifting priorities can be clearly read in the titles of such pamphlets as *The Rebirth of my Country* (September 1944), *Die österreichischen Flüchtlinge und ihre Zukunft* (November 1944), *Was bringt der Friede?* (April 1945) and *Die Heimat ruft!* (July 1945). The last of these, advertised as 'eine reichlich illustrierte

Broschüre', was in fact a calculated mixture of pictorial nostalgia and political education, in which pictures of the Stefansdom and Altaussee were juxtaposed with extracts from the newly-established (Communist) newspaper in Vienna *Neues Österreich*, in a clear attempt to win the hearts and minds of Austrian émigrés.

The last recorded publication by Free Austrian Books engages even more directly with the political discourse of post-war Austria. It is a short pamphlet, containing a speech given by Ernst Fischer at the re-opened University of Vienna in autumn 1945, under the title *Für Freiheit und Vernunft*. Fischer was by then a prominent public figure, having already become 'Staatssekretär für Kultus und Unterricht' in a provisional government. Although the pamphlet was printed in London, the place of publication was given as Wien-London, further confirming the reorientation of the Austrian Centre towards a liberated homeland, to which all its leading activists were committed to return.

The prospect of an imminent return to Austria also determined a greater emphasis on political education, the need for which was particularly urgent in the case of young Austrians, who had spent crucially formative years in Britain and whose memories of their native country were growing increasingly distant. The youth arm of the Austrian Centre, Young Austria, which had its headquarters in a third Westbourne Terrace house (number 132), had been founded in March 1939 and proved extremely successful; by 1943 it had a total membership of around 1300 and was running groups throughout Britain.[17] It, too, like the Austrian Centre itself, issued numerous publications during the 1939 to 1946 period, initially under the imprint Young Austria in Great Britain, and from 1943, for the most part, under that of Jugend voran.[18] In all, including the joint publishing projects in which it was involved, Young Austria produced some 60 publications, both German and English-language, amounting to a total print run of the order of 300,000,[19] an extraordinary achievement for a youth press operating in a foreign country in wartime. In general, Young Austria publications catered for a more narrowly defined readership than those of the Austrian Centre, being written principally with youth and youth leaders in mind. A further distinction lay in the fact that the majority of these were in German, thus targeted largely at an Austrian readership, although British friends were not entirely neglected, as will be seen below. However, Young Austria publications followed — if frequently more crudely — a very similar political agenda to that of Free Austrian Books.

In 1945, Herbert Steiner, who played a pivotal role in the running of
Jugend voran, defined its chief aims as being to produce publications
particularly suitable for young people, to provide a forum for matters
relating to youth and education, and to offer young writers the possibility
of publishing their work. The guiding principle that lay behind all of this
was: 'größeres Wissen über unsere Heimat zu verbreiten.'[20]

The earliest Young Austria publications were almost certainly two
song books, *Österreichische Jugend singt*, which reportedly appeared in
1939,[21] and *Unser Lied*, published in May 1940, that were intended for use
at group meetings. *Unser Lied*, so its preface stated, was to serve as
'Freund und Begleiter [...] in allen frohen und trüben Tagen, die noch vor
uns liegen' and to afford 'Kraft und Zuversicht für das bessere Morgen,
das kommen wird'. In 1940, too, an eight-page report on Young Austria's
national conference appeared, *Unsere Konferenz*, that outlined the
organisation's mission and aims. A similar pamphlet was published the
following year while a further early Young Austria publication,
Funktionärschule des Jungen Österreich 1941, was a direct product of its
training programme for youth leaders. Though such pamphlets would have
been intended principally for internal consumption, an early English-
language publication, *Austria and Britain*, clearly had both an Austrian and
a British readership in mind and was indeed 'dedicated to the friendship
between the Austrian and British Youth', being published to mark the
'Austrians for Britain' campaign of August and September 1942. It
portrayed an Austrian people desperate for liberation from Nazi
oppression; and, at 'the decisive moment of our lives', Austrian youth in
exile, standing shoulder to shoulder with British youth in the fight against
Fascism.

Young Austria's publishing programme, while growing from modest
beginnings, greatly increased in scope from 1943 onwards. In September
of that year, the periodical *Young Austria* announced that the newly
instituted Verlag Jugend voran 'arbeitet mit Volldampf', and revealed some
of its plans for the future: apart from the poetry anthology *Mut* that was
then in press, it was preparing:

> Ein Kalender für 1944, Ansichtskarten von Österreich, eine kleine Broschüre von
> Fritz Walter über die Lage der Jugend in Österreich [...] ein Liederbuch und eine
> kleine Serie von sechs Büchern (Egon Erwin Kisch, aus dem neuen Buch:
> Marktplatz der Sensationen, Dr. E. Buschbeck: Österreichische Wirtschafts-
> geschichte, Ernst Fischer: Grillparzer, eine kleine Auswahl von Karl Kraus, eine

Sammlung österreichischer Gedichte aus acht Jahrhunderten und eine Broschüre
von Fritz Walter: Das neue Österreich und die Jugend). Ein Sammelband von Jura
Soyfer ist gleichfalls geplant.[22]

Mut, like the earlier *Zwischen gestern und morgen*, was a collection of
Austrian verse, this time by younger poets 'who were born or spent the
greater part of their youth in the Austrian Republic'. Opening with a poem
by Jura Soyfer, who had died in Buchenwald in 1939 and was one of
Young Austria's heroes, it proceeded to bring together the poetry of twelve
exiled Austrians, ranging in age from 18 to 29, including Erich Fried,
Arthur Rosenthal, Willy Verkauf and Hans Schmeier (who, in the
pressured atmosphere of refugee politics, had recently been driven to take
his own life). Though the volume was nominally edited by Young Austria's
chairman Fritz Walter, the selection was actually undertaken by Herbert
Steiner and by Fried himself.[23] In a foreword, the English poet John
Lehmann registered the young Austrian poets' determination 'with our
help, to build a new Austria on stronger and more hopeful foundations';
moreover their participation in the fight against Hitler served as a
reminder 'that there has always been a spirit in their homeland — which
we can revive by just and timely action — the very opposite of the barbaric
and intolerant militarism with which Prussia has sought to dominate the
world' (p. 3). Yet while the anti-Nazi struggle and the Austrian liberation
of the future are of course central concerns in the poems, it is notable that,
despite the poets' youth, nostalgia for the Austria of the past remains the
overriding theme of this collection.[24]

Soon afterwards, reportedly in a large edition,[25] Young Austria also
published an English-language pamphlet by Fried which recounted the
efforts of young Austrian patriots attempting to resist the German
occupation (Jugend voran publications, like those of Free Austrian Books,
tended to be unduly optimistic on this score). In keeping with Steiner's
belief that reading matter for young people should be amply illustrated,[26]
They Fight in the Dark contains much pictorial material; however, at least
one of the illustrations, 'People weeping in Vienna when the Germans
marched in, March 1938', an example of Jugend voran's propaganda at its
most implausible, would have struck a false note with a readership well
aware of the general welcome that the Germans received.[27]

Even while concerning itself with the current situation in Austria,
Jugend voran — again, like Free Austrian Books — increasingly looked
ahead to the difficulties to be faced there after the forthcoming defeat: thus
Vivian Ogilvie's foreword to Emmi Walter's *Die soziale und*

wirtschaftliche Lage der österreichischen Jugend unter der deutschen Fremdherrschaft, 1944, already predicted that, as a result of the National Socialist legacy, 'of all the problems of liberated Europe perhaps the most difficult will be the problem of youth' (p. 1). A further forward-looking pamphlet to appear that same year, in fact the result of a conference on education, addressed *Probleme der Jugenderziehung im neuen demokratischen und unabhängigen Österreich*. And soon after the end of the war, Georg Breuer's *Forging the Future: Austrian Youth after Liberation*, though recognising that as part of the heritage of Fascism 'destruction and demoralisation' were 'particularly serious in Austria' (p. 5), could nevertheless emphasise the work being done on behalf of and by Austrian youth and end on a highly optimistic pictorial note: a picture of the Vienna parliament (symbol of newly regained democracy) and a drawing of a train proceeding up a mountain track (an image redolent of 'traditional Austrian values') are accompanied by the slogan 'Welcome to Austria'. While the two earlier pamphlets addressed themselves principally to Austrian youth leaders, thus to a specialist readership, the Breuer publication, written in English, served once again to provide information for British friends. In addition, however, and this was undoubtedly a still more important function, it set out to reach the many young Austrians in Britain who had by then lost much of their German. Thus *Forging the Future* formed part of Young Austria's propaganda campaign to attract its young people back home to take part in Austrian reconstruction, quoting from an appeal from the newly founded Freie Österreichische Jugend in Austria as follows: 'We hope that you will soon return home. We are waiting for your hearts and for your hands. Our country needs all its sons and daughters who are devoted to its well-being' (p. 15).

The danger of young Austrians progressively losing touch with their own history and culture had been recognised for some time and a number of publications were produced in an attempt to rectify the situation. Ernst Fischer's Grillparzer pamphlet, for example, can be viewed in this light as can Hans Tietze's *Abriß einer österreichischen Kunstgeschichte* and Paul Reim's *Probleme und Gestalten der österreichischen Literatur*, all three of which stress the separateness of the Austrian, as opposed to the German, tradition. Though the writing of a specifically Austrian literary history was still in its infancy, Reim contended, Austrian youth was impatient and wanted at least 'einen kurzen Leitfaden, der ihr die wichtigsten Erscheinungen der österreichischen Literatur erläutert' (p. 1).

As already evident, an increasingly important part of Young Austria's work, and that of *Jugend voran*, was the preparation of youth leaders for the reeducation work that would be necessary in post-war Austria. From the autumn of 1944, Young Austria's 'Jugendführerschule', which in all trained around 300 functionaries,[28] put out a special series of pamphlets under the *Jugend voran* imprint as an aid to youth leaders. Among these were the highly practical *Erste Hilfe bei Unglücksfällen und plötzlichen Erkrankungen*, useful *Ratschläge für Redner und Referenten* and, based upon Young Austria's years of experience in British exile, Herbert Steiner's *Die Organisation einer Jugendbewegung*. Pamphlets that would be particularly helpful for youth leaders in the new Austria in their task of countering the years of Nazi ideology included Erich Schindel's *Über Sexualerziehung* and Walter Hollitscher's *Rassentheorie*. The contents of Paul Frischauer's *Heimbeschäftigung*, it was claimed, would also be useful for functionaries 'mitzuhelfen beim Aufbau von starken, geeinten und demokratischen Jugendbewegungen in unserer Heimat, wenn dieser Krieg zu Ende ist' (p. 9). The ambitions of Young Austria towards Austrian youth, both on the political and social level, are encapsulated in the very title of Jaro Brezik's late 1945 contribution to the series, *Für eine freie und gesunde Jugend im neuen Österreich*.

Even as Free Austrian Books and *Jugend voran* publications increasingly focussed on political and indeed practical matters at the close of the war and after, cultural issues were not neglected. Since 1942, the Austrian Centre had been producing a duplicated monthly magazine, *Österreichische Kulturblätter*, which had reflected both its own and Young Austria's cultural activities, had published carefully selected literary texts and had provided its speakers and dramatic groups with material from Austrian literature and history for cultural propaganda work. It was out of this, at the beginning of 1944, that the *Kulturblätter des FAM* developed (later that year renamed *Kulturelle Schriftenreihe des Free Austrian Movement*). These were edited by the lawyer and music critic Dr Hermann Ullrich, a leading activist in the Austrian Centre and in the Free Austrian Movement who, as well as contributing regularly to *Zeitspiegel* on cultural matters, had reportedly also played a part in producing the earlier *Österreichische Kulturblätter*.[29]

The new journal, however, which like other publications of the Free Austrian Movement was produced from the FAM's offices in Holborn, represented a radical departure from the loosely-structured and heterogeneous *Österreichische Kulturblätter*, with Ullrich choosing both to raise the level of cultural debate by a significant degree and to focus in each issue on a single cultural field: music, art, science, history, historiography, humour, the contribution of women, the great cities of Vienna and Salzburg, and literature (with one number devoted exclusively to Hugo von Hofmannsthal and another to Franz Grillparzer). Unlike Free Austrian Books and Jugend voran, which set out in varying degrees to shape both exiled Austrian and British opinion, the *Kulturblätter des FAM/Kulturelle Schriftenreihe des Free Austrian Movement* were directed at a very largely Austrian readership,[30] with Ullrich later defining his aims thus:

> Den in einer weitverzweigten, bald in einer weltumspannenden Organisation zusammengefaßten Österreichern gedachte ich die Größe und die imposante Struktur ihrer Kultur zu zeigen, jener Kultur, die zu vernachlässigen unvollständige und allzu oft unverständige Schulbildung sie veranlaßt, und die zu verfälschen, ja zu unterdrücken, die Fremdherrschaft in der Heimat allzu erfolgreich unternommen hätte.[31]

At the end of 1943, in fact, Ullrich had already tested out his new concept for the *Kulturblätter* with a preliminary number dedicated entirely to Stefan Zweig. In what would become a regular pattern, the issue was made up of a variety of articles on the late writer, introduced, compared and drawn together by a foreword from Ullrich himself. In marked contrast to the more rigid editorial policies of Free Austrian Books and Jugend voran, it is notable that the articles, by Felix Braun, Victor Fleischer, Alfred Rosenzweig, Siegmund Warburg and Richard Friedenthal, were selected for personal and cultural reasons rather than on ideological grounds (the writers, all formerly close friends of Zweig's, were of diverse political persuasions). Indeed, ideological pluralism remained a feature of the *Kulturelle Schriftenreihe* throughout its existence, a policy that Ullrich, a liberal himself,[32] sometimes felt it necessary to defend, as in his preface to *Österreicher, die Geschichte machten*:

> Vielleicht wird die Person des einen oder anderen Autors auf Widerspruch stoßen. Das gilt vor allem von Srbik, der zweifellos ein Anhänger nationalsozialistischer Ideen war. Allein sein Buch über Metternich ist ein Standardwerk, an dem niemand vorübergehen kann, der sich mit der Figur des österreichischen Staatskanzlers befaßt (p. iii).[33]

Shortly after the publication of the Zweig number, the first of the four *Kulturblätter des FAM* — 16 more were to follow in the *Kulturelle Schriftenreihe* — would appear, in January 1944, entitled *Wien im Spiegel der Jahrhunderte*. This consisted of a wide selection of poetry and prose extracts designed to illustrate 'Urteile und Vorurteile aus sieben Jahrhunderten' — wide enough, indeed, to include even an extract from *Mein Kampf*. In his introduction, Ullrich is unflinching in his juxtaposition of Vienna's glorious past with its wretched present; yet he also calls to mind the earlier occasions on which Vienna succeeded in throwing off a foreign yoke, adding for good measure: 'Auch die Tage der Naziherrschaft sind, wenn die Zeichen nicht trügen, gezählt und wieder einmal wird Österreich In ORBE ULTIMA sein' (p. i). As Ullrich subsequently commented of his intention here: 'Den Zweiflern und Kleinmütigen — und wie viele gab es damals! — sollte ein bekenntnisfreudiges CREDO zugerufen werden.'34

'Der Glaube hat sich bewährt' — thus Ullrich would introduce his later *Wien und die Welt*, a revised and expanded version of *Wien im Spiegel der Jahrhunderte*. Yet while the heroic tone had been entirely appropriate in January 1944 when the earlier issue had appeared, a more sober note was in keeping with the Austrian realities of late 1945:

> Eine wesentliche Änderung in Zielsetzung, Aufbau und Auswahl des Stoffes war allerdings nötig geworden. Alles Polemische, durch den Befreiungskampf Zeitbedingte mußte ausgeschieden, und Wiens Bedeutung in der Welt und für die Welt im Wandel der Zeiten [...] in das klare Licht objektiver Betrachtung gerückt werden [...] Auch die Fehler und Schwächen der Stadt und ihrer Bewohner durften nicht übergangen werden (p. i).

New voices to add to the old, therefore, included the Frenchman Marc Henry, who had criticised the decadence and indifference of Vienna prior to 1914, and the Englishman Edward Crankshaw who had diagnosed a state of terminal decline in Vienna in the inter-war years. Characteristically, though, even in the rigours of the immediate post-war period, Ullrich still chose to reassure his readership as to Vienna's present and future:

> Auch aus dieser Krise, vielleicht der schwersten in seiner Geschichte, wird Wien stärker und schöner hervorgehen, ernster und gealtert aber auch menschlicher und reifer geworden durch die Tiefe seines Leides (p. ix).

From the combined issues of the *Kulturblätter des FAM/Kulturelle Schriftenreihe des FAM*, it is evident that the Austrian culture with which Hermann Ullrich was most conversant and which he felt to be most appropriate to his cultural propaganda purposes was very much the high culture of past centuries. In later numbers of the *Kulturelle Schriftenreihe*, it is true, he attempted to broaden the range, as in *Die Frau in der Österreichischen Kultur*. He himself, however, in a lengthy preface, admitted to feelings of hesitancy in such an area; and it was left to the ex-Social Democratic deputy Marie Köstler, in a plain and practical foreword, positively to endorse the issue's subject-matter as well as to express her conviction that, as in the past, so women would play a full part in Austria's national life in the future. Ullrich's cultural perspective may also explain why not only the number entitled *Österreichische Wissenschaft* but also the two issues on *Österreichische Schriftsteller im Exil*, which appeared near the end of the *Kulturelle Schriftenreihe*'s life in 1946 and which obviously consisted entirely of contemporary literature, contained no contribution from their editor.

Be that as it may, Ullrich's achievement under war-time and immediately post-war conditions in bringing out a wide-ranging and high-level cultural journal — what he himself has termed a 'bibliophiles Unikum'[35] — that both fostered the Austrian cultural tradition and promoted new work by exiled Austrian writers and scholars, should not be underestimated. As Ullrich would write in the final issue, in his 'Abschied vom Leser':

> Es überstieg die Kraft und die Möglichkeiten eines Einzelnen, alle Facetten dieses Juwels zu zeigen. Und ein Einzelner blieb ich während dieser drei Jahre, ungeachtet der nie genug zu dankenden Hilfe so vieler ausgezeichneter Österreicher in der freien Welt.

Chief among the difficulties he experienced were those in obtaining the material he required: 'Ich kann nur darauf verweisen,' he wrote in his preface to *Wien im Spiegel der Jahrhunderte*, 'daß viele Werke selbst in dem ungeheueren Reservoir menschlichen Wissens, das "Britisches Museum" heißt, unter den gegenwärtigen Verhältnissen unerreichbar waren' (p. i). Moreover, until the end of 1945, quite apart from the problems associated with the war-time paper restrictions, circulation was limited by the duplicating process by which — 'der Not der Zeit gemäß' — the journal had to be produced.[36] Yet despite Ullrich's essentially lone position in this venture, he could, as he himself conceded, call on the services of a wide range of experts from among his fellow exiles to assist with selection and to write for the journal. A flyer advertising the *Kulturelle Schriftenreihe* in mid-1945 included on a list of contributors the writers Felix Braun, Albert Fuchs, Mela Hartwig, Eva Priester and Martina Wied; the artists Georg Ehrlich and Oskar Kokoschka; the musicians Hans Gál, Bruno Walter and Egon Wellesz; as well as others active in science and medicine.[37]

For its last four numbers, from the beginning of 1946, the *Kulturelle Schriftenreihe* was able to appear as the 'Literarisch-kulturelle Beilage des *Zeitspiegel*', published for the FAM by Free Austrian Books at the Austrian Centre, and thus managed to achieve higher circulation figures. 'Damit wurde ihnen,' so Ullrich would ruefully maintain, 'leider sehr spät, endlich jene Publizität gegeben, die nur das gedruckte Wort verleiht.'[38] It was in this, its final printed form, that the *Kulturelle Schriftenreihe* was to become permitted reading for Austrian prisoners in the British Prisoner of War camps. In addition, copies were at last being sent into Austria — although without much success, to judge from Ullrich's lament to Viktor Matejka of 21 February 1946: 'Schade, daß die zahlreichen Hefte der *Kulturellen Schriftenreihe*, die wir seit der Befreiung ins Land gesendet haben, offenbar verloren gegangen sind.'[39]

For the redoubtable Marie Köstler, the value of the *Kulturelle Schriftenreihe* lay in the fact 'daß sie uns in jeder Ausgabe ein Stück Heimat nahe bringen und aufzeigen, daß wir Grund haben, stolz auf unser Land und auf unsere Nation zu sein'.[40] Ullrich himself defined as his motivating force the conviction 'daß die Heimat und vor allem die durch acht Jahre Exil oder Fremdherrschaft entwurzelte, geistig unterernährte Jugend ein Anrecht auf unsere Arbeit besitze'; 'Österreich zu dienen' had been his task.[41] The issue in which his valedictory piece appeared, in June 1946, was devoted to Franz Grillparzer, 'dem größten Dichter Österreichs', a choice which in Ullrich's view bore the greatest relevance to the current Austrian situation:

> Wie aktuell ist Grillparzer doch, wie viele seiner Bemerkungen sind auch für unsere Tage giltig und wie wenig hat sich doch in Österreich im Grund seither geändert! Er, der kein Deutscher sein wollte, sondern ein Österreicher, ein Nieder-Österreicher sogar, ja vor allem ein Wiener, würde sich im heutigen Österreich bald zurechtfinden. Und so ist die Aufgabe dieses Heftes zur Beschäftigung mit dem Dichter anzuregen, nicht *zurück* zu Grillparzer zu führen, sondern *vorwärts* zu ihm.

It was on this forward-looking note that Hermann Ullrich took leave of his readers. The time had come, so he wrote, for him and many others to return to the 'Heimat'; others, who had decided to remain in their country of exile, would now strive to assume the culture of their new land.

'Nicht länger bedarf es darum einer Revue, die, aus der Not der Zeit entstanden, mit ihr gereift ist und nun die Zeit erfüllt sieht.' It was on much the same note, too, that Eva Kolmer concluded her 1946 'Erinnerungsbroschüre', *Das Austrian Centre. 7 Jahre österreichische Gemeinschaftsarbeit*, entitling her final chapter 'Die ersten Heimkehrer nehmen Abschied'. Kolmer herself, of course, as one of the Austrian Centre's leading political activists, was among those most anxious to return to Austria, though she envisaged that the Centre would continue to exist as the 'Club[s] der österreichischen Kolonie in Großbritannien' (p. 35), in other words to cater for those Austrians who chose to remain.

In fact, the Austrian Centre closed down not long after, at the beginning of 1947, having been badly affected both from a financial and an organisational point of view by members' departures. Its publications, as is evident from the Kolmer booklet, were of course only a single aspect, though an important one, of the work of the Austrian Centre in organising Austrians in exile and in alerting the British to the existence of the 'other Austria'. As Jenö Desser, the Centre's last President, wrote in his unpublished memoirs: 'Die Tätigkeit und die Leistungen des 'Austrian Centre' während der Kriegsjahre in London waren, meiner Ansicht nach, wirklich einmalig.' And further: 'Es wäre wert, die Geschichte des Austrian Centre zu schreiben.'[42] For 50 years this history has remained unwritten. Only now are there plans to remedy this deficiency by writing a full-length study, of which this essay is merely the first token.[43]

Notes

The authors would like to thank a number of people who have helped in the compilation of this article, including staff of the British Library, the Wiener Library, London, the Institute of Germanic Studies (School of Advanced Study, University of London), the Deutsche Bücherei, Leipzig, and the Dokumentationsarchiv des österreichischen Widerstandes, Vienna (especially Siegwart Ganglmair). We are particularly grateful to Georg Knepler, Ursula Seeber (Österreichische Exilbibliothek im Literaturhaus, Vienna) and Reinhard Müller (Archiv für die Geschichte der Soziologie in Österreich, Karl-Franzens-Universität, Graz).

[1] Georg Knepler, *Five Years of the Austrian Centre* (London: Free Austrian Books, 1944). Full details of all the publications cited in this essay are listed in the concluding bibliography, which includes all Austrian Centre publications we have been able to find and consult. We have also included items which were certainly published (e.g. which were advertised as available in *Zeitspiegel* or elsewhere) but of which we have been unable to find copies.

2 A detailed account of the political situation of Austrian refugees in Great Britain can be found in Helene Maimann, *Politik im Wartesaal. Österreichische Exilpolitik in Großbritannien* (Vienna/Cologne/Graz: Hermann Böhlaus Nachf., 1975) and Wolfgang Muchitsch, ed., *Österreicher im Exil. Großbritannien 1938-45. Eine Dokumentation* (Vienna: Österreichischer Bundesverlag, 1992).

3 The report on the first year of activities was probably written by Eva Kolmer, who sent a draft copy to Friedrich Otto Hertz in February 1940. (cf. Nachlaß Friedrich Otto Hertz, Archiv für die Geschichte der Soziologie in Österreich, Karl-Franzens-Universität, Graz).

4 See Eva Kolmer, *Das Austrian Centre. 7 Jahre österreichische Gemeinschaftsarbeit* (London: Austrian Centre, [August 1946]), pp. 4-7. Cf. also *Zeitspiegel*, III, 3, 25 January 1941.

5 Among the other contributors were: Kuba (i.e. Kurt Barthel) (3 poems), Max Zimmering (2), Max Herrmann-Neiße (2), Rudolf Fuchs (2), and Rolf Anders (4).

6 The Free Austrian Movement, founded 3 December 1941, was formed largely at the instigation of the Austrian Centre. The founding declaration of the FAM, signed by eleven Austrian exile organisations, is reprinted in Muchitsch, op.cit., pp. 283-84. The only major organisation which declined to affiliate was the 'London Büro der österreichischen Sozialisten' which refused to endorse the FAM's support for an independent post-war Austria.

7 Eva Kolmer's list of publications in her *Erinnerungsbroschüre* starts in 1942. The early publications appeared under the imprint Austrian Centre or Austrian Centre/Young Austria; from March 1943 most appeared under the imprint Free Austrian Books.

8 In her pamphlet (see note 4 above), Eva Kolmer suggests that *Restive Austria* was published in April and *Zurück oder nicht zurück?* in May 1942, but a contemporary diary of Austrian Centre activities confirms that they actually appeared in the opposite order. See Muchitsch, op.cit., p. 292.

9 F. C. West's speech, due to be held at Klub Paddington (i.e. 124-126 Westbourne Terrace) on 31 March, was advertised in the weekly *Zeitspiegel*, IV, 13, 28 March 1942.

10 William Wordsworth, 'Hofer', from: 'Poems dedicated to National Independence and Liberty.' See *The Poetical Works of William Wordsworth*, Vol. 3, ed. by E. de Selincourt and H. Darbishire (Oxford: Clarendon Press, 1954), p. 129. Cf. the translation of this poem by Eva Priester, under the title 'Andreas Hofer', in *Zeitspiegel*, V, 9, 13 March 1943.

11 For a comprehensive discussion of the iconography of Austrian exile publications, see Ursula Seeber-Weyrer, '"Ergötze dich am längst nicht mehr Vorhandenen": Österreich-Bilder des Exils', in Ursula Prutsch and Manfred Lechner, eds., *Das ist Österreich. Innensichten und Außensichten* (Vienna: Döcker, 1997), pp. 123-40.

12 *The White Horse Inn*, described as 'a musical spectacular', was given 651 performances at the Coliseum Theatre between 8 April 1931 and 23 April 1932.

13 *Zeitspiegel*, IV, 36, 5 September 1942.

14 According to Knepler himself (letter to the authors, 9 April 1998).

15 Georg Knepler, *Five Years of the Austrian Centre*, p. 5.

16 '... eignet sich vorzüglich für die Information britischer Freunde', *Zeitspiegel*, VI, 39, 30 September 1944.

17 See 'Sieben Jahre "Junges Österreich"', *Jung-Österreich*, VIII, 17, 28 August 1946.

18 *Jugend voran* was also the title of a periodical for Austrian youth in Great Britain as well as that of the journal of the Österreichische Weltjugendbewegung.

19 'Sieben Jahre "Junges Österreich"'.

20 Herbert Steiner, *Die Organisation einer Jugendbewegung. Organisationsformen und Erfahrungen des 'Jungen Österreich in Großbritannien'* (London: Jugend voran [Jugendführerschule des Jungen Österreich], [1945]), p. 10.

21 According to the preface of *Unser Lied*.

22 'Der Verlag der österreichischen Weltjugendbewegung', *Young Austria*, V, 20, 25 September 1943. All these plans were realised with the exception of the Jura Soyfer volume.

23 See Herbert Steiner, 'Mein Freund Erich Fried', in Volker Kaukoreit and Heinz Lünzer, eds., *Erich Fried und Österreich: Bausteine zu einer Beziehung: Eine Ausstellung der Dokumentationsstelle für neuere österreichische Literatur und der Internationalen Erich-Fried-Gesellschaft für Literatur und Sprache im Literaturhaus, Zirkular*, Sondernummer 33, November 1992, p. 10.

24 For a discussion of *Mut*, see Jörg Thunecke, '"Doch wer den Mut verliert ist besser tot!": Young Austria and the Problem of Political Poetry', in Edward Timms and Ritchie Robertson, eds., *Austrian Exodus: The Creative Achievements of Refugees from National Socialism (Austrian Studies* VI) (Edinburgh: Edinburgh University Press, 1995), pp. 41-58.

25 According to Steiner, 'Mein Freund Erich Fried', p. 10.

26 Steiner, *Die Organisation einer Jugendbewegung*, p. 10.

27 The picture had previously appeared in *Five Years Hitler over Austria*, a special edition of *Austrian News* marking the fifth anniversary of the *Anschluss*.

28 'Sieben Jahre "Junges Österreich"'.

29 See Maimann, op.cit., p. 73.

30 Nevertheless, see Ullrich's report in *Der Turm: Monatsschrift für Österreichische Kultur*, I, July 1946, p. 408, in which he claimed that the *Kulturelle Schriftenreihe* also served the purpose 'den deutschsprechenden englischen Freunden zu zeigen, daß es eine große bewußt österreichische Kulturbewegung gibt'.

31 Hermann Ullrich, 'Abschied vom Leser', in *Kulturelle Schriftenreihe des Free Austrian Movement: Grillparzer*, June 1946, p. 2.

32 According to Georg Knepler, Ullrich 'beschrieb sich als Liberaler, österreichischer Patriot, Antifaschist, als einer, der Verständnis für den Sozialismus hat, ohne selbst Sozialist zu sein' (letter of 9 April 1998).

33 It is notable that the inclusion of Srbik did not find favour with J.K. [Jenö Kostmann], for instance, in *Zeitspiegel* who termed it 'ein arger Mißgriff', maintaining further: 'Kein Wort von ihm kann in einer Anthologie von Essays, aus denen der Österreicher von heute Belehrung schöpfen soll, Unterschlupf finden' (VII, 41, 12 October 1945).

34 Hermann Ullrich, preface to *Kulturelle Schriftenreihe des Free Austrian Movement: Wien und die Welt. Urteile und Vorurteile in Berichten, Briefen, Dokumenten und Beschreibungen aus acht Jahrhunderten*, [1945], p. i.

35 See Hermann Ullrich to Herbert Steiner, 29 April 1968, in Sammlung Steiner, Österreichische Exilbibliothek im Literaturhaus, Vienna.

36 Ullrich, 'Abschied vom Leser'.

37 Flyer reproduced in Muchitsch, op.cit., p. 398.

38 Ullrich, 'Abschied vom Leser'.

39 Hermann Ullrich to Viktor Matejka, 21 February 1946, Dokumentationsarchiv des österreichischen Widerstandes, Vienna, DÖW 18 861/147.

40 Köstler, 'Vorwort', in *Kulturelle Schriftenreihe des Free Austrian Movement: Die Frau in der österreichischen Kultur. Literatur, Kunst, Frauenbewegung, Staat und Politik*, ed. Hermann Ullrich, [1945], p. ii.

41 Ullrich, 'Abschied vom Leser'.

42 Jenö Desser, 'Mein Lebenslauf: 8. März 1904-8. März 1984. Anläßlich des achtzigsten Geburtstages', p. 92. In private possession of Hans Desser, Vienna.

43 Members of the Research Centre for German and Austrian Exile Studies, Institute of Germanic Studies (University of London), including the authors of the present article, are currently engaged in a study of the Austrian Centre.

Bibliography

The following bibliography comprises only publications of the Austrian Centre, and thus excludes publications simply distributed by the Centre, such as those of the Free Austrian Movement which, though closely associated with the Austrian Centre, was a separate organisation, with its own publishing programme. An exception has been made, however, for the series *Kulturblätter des FAM/Kulturelle Schriftenreihe des Free Austrian Movement*, which were not only closely linked to the Austrian Centre at their inception, but whose final four issues were actually published by Free Austrian Books.

The bibliography does not claim to be an exhaustive list of all Austrian Centre publications. It includes all those we have been able to locate and verify, many of which are cited in the preceding essay. We have also included items we have not been able to locate, but whose publication can be verified with some certainty from the Austrian exile press, particularly *Zeitspiegel* and *Jugend voran*. (These are marked *.) Many of them appeared without a year of publication and are dated on the basis of the text and/or on advertisements and other references in the exile press.

The only previous bibliography of Austrian Centre publications appeared in Eva Kolmer's pamphlet *Das Austrian Centre. 7 Jahre österreichische Gemeinschaftsarbeit*. It is, however, very incomplete and contains numerous errors in titles, dates etc. The first systematic attempt to record all Austrian exile publications is Herbert Steiner's *Bibliographie zur Geschichte der österreichischen Arbeiterbewegung*, Bd. 3: *1933-1945*, Vienna, 1970. However, it is not specific to the Austrian Centre, and is in some respects incomplete and even inaccurate. We have also drawn on Donal McLaughlin's 'Bibliography of German-language Publications in Great Britain (1933-45)' in *Zwischenwelt 4: Literatur und Kultur des Exils in Großbritannien*, ed. Siglinde Bolbecher, Konstantin Kaiser, Donal McLaughlin, J. M. Ritchie (Vienna: Theodor Kramer Gesellschaft, 1995). The most comprehensive listing to date of publications by Austrian refugee organisations in Great Britain is the catalogue for the exhibition *Fluchtpunkt England* (shown at the Karl-Franzens-Universität, Graz, May-October 1996 and at the Austrian Cultural Institute, London, in March 1999), compiled by Reinhard Müller, to whom we are greatly indebted.

Free Austrian Books [FAB]

Austria (London: FAB, [November 1943])

Austrian Martyrs and Heroes (London: FAB, [April 1945])

Austrians in Great Britain (London: Austrian Centre, [1943])

Austria's Tribute to Russia (Glasgow: Austrian Centre and Young Austria, [1942])

First Annual Report of the Austrian Centre (London: Council of Austrians in Great Britain at the Austrian Centre, 1940)

Fischer, Ernst, *Für Freiheit und Vernunft*, Schriftenreihe *Neues Österreich*, 1. Heft (Vienna-London: FAB, [September] 1945)

Fischer, Ernst, *Nationale Probleme des Jahres 1848 in Österreich* (London: FAB, [December 1944])

Fischer, Ernst, *Der österreichische Volkscharakter* (London: FAB, [March 1944])

Fischer, Ernst, *The Rebirth of my Country* (London: FAB, [September 1944])

Fuchs, Albert, *Ein Sohn aus gutem Hause* (London: FAB, Christmas 1943)

Fuchs, Albert, *Über österreichische Kultur. Vortrag gehalten auf der Kulturkonferenz des PEN, London, 1942* (London: Austrian Centre, [1942])

Fuchs, Albert, ed., *Die Vertriebenen. Dichtung der Emigration* (London: Free German League of Culture/Austrian Centre/Young Czechoslovakia, 1941)

Die Heimat ruft! (London: FAB, [July 1945])

Herman, Jury, *Viel Glück. Aus dem Tagebuch einer Soviet W.A.A.F.*, trans. by Eva Priester (London: FAB, [May 1943])

Hornik, Anna, *This is Austria. The Story of a Beautiful Country* (London: Austrian Centre/Young Austria, 1942)

The House of Lords on Austria. Parliamentary Debates (London: FAB, [February 1943])

Kaufmann, Stefan, *Was bringt der Friede?* (London: FAB, [April 1945])

Kleines Magazin (London: FAB, [March] 1943)

Knepler, Georg, *Five Years of the Austrian Centre* (London: FAB, [May 1944])

Kolmer, Eva, *Das Austrian Centre. 7 Jahre österreichische Gemeinschafts-arbeit* (London: Austrian Centre, [August 1946])

[Kostmann, Jenö], *The Battle for Vienna* (London: [FAB], [June 1945])

Kostmann, Jenö, *Restive Austria* (London: Austrian Centre/Young Austria, [May 1942])

Kostmann, Jenö, and Hilde Mareiner, *The Austrian Ally* (London: Austrian Centre/Young Austria, [1942])

Zur Mühlen, Hermynia, *Kleine Geschichten von großen Dichtern* (London: FAB, [December 1944])

Priester, Eva, *Aus Krieg und Nachkrieg. Gedichte und Übersetzungen* (London: Austrian Centre, [1945])

Priester, Eva, *Austria — Gateway to Germany* (London: FAB, [1943])

Scholz, Wilhelm, *Moscow on Austria. For a national Committee* (London: FAB, [December 1943])

Scholz, Wilhelm, *Ein Weg ins Leben. Das neue Österreich und die Judenfrage* (London: FAB, 1943)

Spira, Leopold, *We Are Not Alone*, ed. by Austrian Centre and Young Austria Glasgow (London: FAB, [1943])

West, F. C., *Zurück oder nicht zurück?* (London: FAB, [April 1942])

Zwischen Gestern und Morgen. Neue österreichische Gedichte (London: Austrian Centre/Young Austria, [December] 1942)

Young Austria/Jugend voran

Austria and Britain (London: Young Austria in Great Britain, [1942])

Austrian Youth Looking Ahead. An Austrian Youth Programme and Suggestions for Immediate Post-War Relief Measures for Austrian Youth (London: Young Austria in Great Britain, [1943])

Breuer, Georg, *Forging the Future. Austrian Youth after Liberation* (London: Jugend voran, [1945])

Breuer, Georg, ed., *Unser Nachbar — Jugoslawien. Aufsätze, Erzählungen, Gedichte und Dokumente*, foreword by Tone Fajfar (London: Jugend voran, [1945])

Brezik, Jaro, *Für eine freie und gesunde Jugend im neuen Österreich. Referat* (London: Jugend voran [Jugendführerschule des Jungen Österreich], 1945)

Buschbeck, E., *Abriß einer österreichischen Wirtschaftsgeschichte. Von der Entstehung der Ostmark bis zum Ausbruch des Ersten Weltkrieges* (London: Jugend voran, 1944)

Churchill, Winston, *Marlborough und Prinz Eugen. Zeitgenössische Dokumente und Auszüge aus 'Marlborough, sein Leben und seine Zeit'*, compiled by Georg Porges (London: Jugend voran [Schriftenreihe Berühmte Österreicher], [1945?])

Erziehung in Österreich (London: Jugend voran, [1944])

Fischer, Ernst, *Grillparzer. Ein großer österreichischer Dichter* (London: Jugend voran [Schriftenreihe Berühmte Österreicher)], [1945])

[Fischer, Ernst], *Der Miesmacher. Politische Spottgedichte aus Österreich* (London: Jugend voran, [1943])

Fischer, Klara, *Hygiene* (London: Jugend voran [Jugendführerschule des Jungen Österreich], [1945])

For Austria and Our Future (London: Jugend voran, [1944])

Das freie Österreich und seine Jugend! Bericht über die österreichische Jugendkonferenz, 9. und 10. Juni 1945, London, einberufen durch die Exekutive der Österreichischen Weltjugendbewegung, Junges Österreich und Verband österreichischer Studenten (London: Jugend voran, [1945])

Der Freiheitskampf des österreichischen Volkes 1938-45 (London: Young Austria in Great Britain, [1945?])

[Fried, Erich], *They Fight in the Dark. The Story of Austria's Youth* (London: Young Austria in Great Britain, [1944])

Frischauer, Paul, *Heimbeschäftigung. Referat* (London: Jugend voran [Jugendführerschule des Jungen Österreich], [1945])

Funktionärschule des Jungen Österreich, 1941 (London: Junges Österreich, [1941])

Graber, Felix, ed., *Unser Lied*, foreword by Fritz Walter (London: Jugend voran, 1944)

*A Guide for the Austrian War Worker (London: Jugend voran, 1944)

*Hammerschlag, W., ed., *Unser Spielbuch* (London: Jugend voran, [1945])

*Der Heimat entgegen ... Den jungen österreichischen Soldaten in den britischen Streitkräften und Kämpfern der 'österreichischen Freiheitsfront' (London: Freie österreichische Weltbewegung/Junges Österreich, 1944)

Hollitscher, Walter, *Rassentheorie? 6 Lehrbriefe an österreichische Biologie-Lehrer* (London: Jugend voran [Jugendführerschule des Jungen Österreich], 1944)

Inside Austria. Austrian Freedom Front Calls Austrian Youth. Latest Broadcasts of the Underground Austrian Freedom Station (London: Young Austria, [1944])

[Kaufmann, Stefan], *Wie liest man Bucher?/Ratschläge für Redner und Referenten* (London: Jugend voran [Jugendführerschule des Jungen Österreich], [1945])

Kisch, Egon Erwin, *Vom Marktplatz der Sensationen* (London: Jugend voran, 1943)

Kontrollfragen für die Themen der J.F.S. — schriftlich und mündlich (London: Jugend voran [Jugendführerschule des Jungen Österreich], [1945?])

[Kostmann, Jenö], *Kurze österreichische Staatsbürgerkunde* (London: Jugend voran [Jugendführerschule des Jungen Österreich], [1944])

*Kraus, Karl, *Kleine Auswahl aus seinen Schriften* (London: Jugend voran, [1943])

Mut: Gedichte junger Österreicher (London: Jugend voran, 1943)

*Österreichische Jugend singt (London: [Young Austria (?), 1939])

Probleme der Jugenderziehung im neuen demokratischen und unabhängigen Österreich. Bericht über die Erziehungskonferenz des 'Jungen Österreich in Großbritannien' (London: Jugend voran, 1944)

Reim [i.e. Reimann], Paul, *Probleme und Gestalten der österreichischen Literatur* (London: Jugend voran, 1945)

Schindel, Erich, *Über Sexualerziehung. Referat* (London: Jugend voran [Jugendführerschule des Jungen Österreich], [1945])

Spira, Leopold, *Aus der Geographie Österreichs* (London: Jugend voran [Jugendführerschule des Jungen Österreich], 1944)

Steiner, Herbert, *Die Organisation einer Jugendbewegung. Organisationsformen und Erfahrungen des 'Jungen Österreich in Großbritannien'* (London: Jugend voran [Jugendführerschule des Jungen Österreich], [1945])

Steiner, Herbert, *Wohin führt dein Weg? Die jungen Österreicher im Ausland und in der Heimat* (London: [Young Austria, 1945])

[Tessarek, Anton], *Erste Hilfe bei Unglücksfällen und plötzlichen Erkrankungen* (London: Jugend voran [Jugendführerschule des Jungen Österreich], [1945])

Tietze, Hans, *Abriß einer österreichischen Kunstgeschichte*, foreword by Oskar Kokoschka (London: Jugend voran, 1945)

Unsere Konferenz. 'Junges Österreich' — Aufgaben und Ziel unserer Organisation. Bericht über die Landeskonferenz des 'J.Ö.' vom 17./18.und 24./25. Feb. 1940 (London: Young Austria, [1940])

Unser Lied (London: Young Austria, May 1940)

*Vorwärts für unsere Zukunft (London: Jugend voran, [1946])

Walter, Emmi [i.e. Berta Brichacek], *Die soziale und wirtschaftliche Lage der österreichischen Jugend unter der deutschen Fremdherrschaft. Ein Referat auf der Fürsorge-Konferenz des Free Austrian Movement im März 1944*, foreword by Vivian Ogilvie (London: Jugend voran, 1944)

**Walter, Fritz [i.e. Otto Brichacek], *Das neue Österreich und die Jugend* (London: Jugend voran, [1943])

Walter, Fritz, *Österreichs Jugend unter der deutschen Fremdherrschaft. Material und Berichte über die Lage der österreichischen Jugend*, foreword by F. C. West (London: Jugend voran, [1943])

Walter, Fritz, *Unsere österreichische Jugendführerschule. Einleitung zu den Materialien der Jugendführerschule* (London: Jugend voran [Jugendführerschule des Jungen Österreich], [1945])

Walter, Fritz, *Youth in the Reconstruction of Liberated Europe. Report on Youth Activities in France, Belgium, Holland, Italy, Yugoslavia, Poland, Greece, Bulgaria* (London: Jugend voran, 1945)

*Wien sprach zu mir. Österreichische Gedichte aus 8 Jahrhunderten (London: Jugend voran, [1943])

2. Landeskonferenz des J. Ö., London 27.-28. Dezember, 1941 (London: Young Austria in Great Britain, [1941])

Kulturblätter des FAM/Kulturelle Schriftenreihe des Free Austrian Movement
(These items, all of which were edited by Hermann Ullrich, are listed in chronological order.)

Stefan Zweig. Eine Sonderpublikation der 'Funktionärblätter' aus Anlaß des 62. Geburtstages des Dichters (London: Free Austrian Movement, [1943])

Kulturblätter des FAM: Wien im Spiegel der Jahrhunderte. Urteile und Vorurteile aus sieben Jahrhunderten, January 1944

Kulturblätter des FAM, February 1944. (Contains articles on 'Tirol unter bayrischer Fremdherrschaft', Grillparzer and Schickaneder.)

Kulturblätter des FAM: Österreichischer Humor von Neithart von Reuental bis Alfred Polgar, March 1944

Kulturblätter des FAM: Österreichisches Pantheon, April 1944

Kulturblätter des FAM: Wiener Kleinkunst im Exil, May 1944

Kulturelle Schriftenreihe des Free Austrian Movement: Österreich vor hundert Jahren. Landschaft, Städte, Menschen; aus Briefen, Tagebüchern, Memoiren von Zeitgenossen, [June 1944]

Kulturelle Schriftenreihe des Free Austrian Movement: Österreichische Seele, [1944]

Kulturelle Schriftenreihe des Free Austrian Movement: Das Wien unserer Großeltern. Essays, [1944]

Kulturelle Schriftenreihe des Free Austrian Movement: Die Berühmten und die Vergessenen. Österreichische Dichter 1830-1930, [November 1944]

Kulturelle Schriftenreihe des Free Austrian Movement: Hugo von Hofmannsthal (1874-1929). Zum 70. Geburtstag des Dichters, [December 1944]

Kulturelle Schriftenreihe des Free Austrian Movement: Salzburg. Bildnis einer Stadt. Essays, Briefe und Dokumente, [January 1945]

Kulturelle Schriftenreihe des Free Austrian Movement: Zweihundert Jahre Österreichischer Musik. Briefe, Essays und Erinnerungen, [February 1945]

Kulturelle Schriftenreihe des Free Austrian Movement: Die Frau in der österreichischen Kultur. Literatur, Kunst, Frauenbewegung, Staat und Politik, [1945]

Kulturelle Schriftenreihe des Free Austrian Movement: Österreichische Wissenschaft. Essays, Biographien, Betrachtungen, [1945]

Kulturelle Schriftenreihe des Free Austrian Movement: Bildende Kunst in Österreich. Rückblick und Ausblick, [1945]

Kulturelle Schriftenreihe des Free Austrian Movement: Österreicher, die Geschichte machten. Essays, Betrachtungen, Kapitel aus Monographien, [1945]

Kulturelle Schriftenreihe des Free Austrian Movement: Wien und die Welt. Urteile und Vorurteile in Berichten, Briefen, Dokumenten und Beschreibungen aus acht Jahrhunderten, [1945]

Kulturelle Schriftenreihe des Free Austrian Movement (Literarisch-kulturelle Beilage des Zeitspiegel): Beethoven. Zum Gedächtnis seines 175. Geburtstages, January 1946

Kulturelle Schriftenreihe des Free Austrian Movement (Literarisch-kulturelle Beilage des Zeitspiegel): Österreichische Schriftsteller im Exil, February 1946

Kulturelle Schriftenreihe des Free Austrian Movement (Literarisch-kulturelle Beilage des Zeitspiegel): Österreichische Schriftsteller im Exil. Neue Folge, April 1946

Kulturelle Schriftenreihe des Free Austrian Movement (Literarisch-kulturelle Beilage des Zeitspiegel): Grillparzer, June 1946

William Abbey

"Mit freundlichen Grüßen aus der Ferne": Exile Holdings at the Institute of Germanic Studies

When the University of London set up the Institute of Germanic Studies in 1950, exile was not a subject studied in British departments of German. Within its library, however, the Institute (known briefly as the Institute of Germanic Languages and Literatures before adopting its present name) introduced an acquisitions policy that included, or would include, as the subject began to take shape, exile literature along with all other aspects of literature in German from the beginnings to the present. It is a policy that is still in force today and in essence concentrates whatever library resources are available on certain types of publication rather than on specific subject areas within the field: on primary texts by literary authors (and 'texts' here embraces letters, diaries and autobiographies as well as novels, poems and plays), on journals, and on reference works of all kinds. Fashions and trends in scholarship are never ignored and emphases may sometimes shift, but in general the policy is maintained independently of the needs of any individual department or researcher.

There are clearly gaps in the Institute's coverage: it has never had the resources, for example, to be more than highly selective in its purchase of secondary literature; nor have its forays into the secondhand or antiquarian market ever been more than occasional. Nevertheless, it has built up substantial collections of critical and biographical material, and its holdings of pre-1950 titles — works published prior to its foundation — are extensive. By far the greater part of this material results from a series of donations and bequests that the Institute has attracted since 1950, and is still attracting as it approaches its fiftieth anniversary. Along with many other areas of the library, the exile collections have profited from this established combination of a consistent acquisitions policy supplemented by material acquired from a variety of individual and organizational sources, and it is the object of this brief essay to give some indication of the Institute's holdings in this field (though perhaps only a full-scale bibliography could really do them justice).

As a result of the priority given from the outset to the acquisition of primary texts, the Institute has acquired collected editions of all major and many minor exile authors published since 1950, from Thomas Mann,

Bertolt Brecht, and Stefan Zweig down to, more recently, Max Herrmann-Neiße and Theodor Kramer. Attempts were also made to get as many as possible of the relevant editions published (notably by Aufbau) in the German Democratic Republic — of Anna Seghers, Arnold Zweig, Lion Feuchtwanger, J. R. Becher and so on — though some gaps in the sets remain. As resources have allowed, smaller collections and individual texts (sometimes reissues, often exile works published for the first time) have been acquired regularly. There are too many to list here but as an example, the most cursory of searches for autobiographies with some British connection alone turned up the names of Richard Friedenthal, Robert Neumann, Grete Fischer, Fritz Beer, Gabriele Tergit, Elisabeth Castonier, Gertrude Elias, Ruth David, Hermann Sinsheimer, Alice Zadek, Ludwig Berger, Lilli Palmer, Jürgen Kuczynski, George Weidenfeld, Lily Pincus, Otto Zarek, Herbert Freeden and Keith Spalding, and there is no reason to think this list exhaustive. The Institute's own efforts have been topped up by, for example, the presentation by his daughter of all reissues of Ludwig Winder's novels, and the Ida Herz Bequest included editions and translations of many works by various members of the Mann family.

Under this same bequest the Institute also received a large collection of secondary material relating to Thomas, Heinrich, Klaus and Erika Mann. Interesting material about exile in Switzerland and the important work of the 'Schauspielhaus' in Zürich between 1933 and 1945 has come from the 'Kulturstiftung Pro Helvetia', and over the years the Austrian Institute (now the Austrian Cultural Institute), as well as giving texts, has donated secondary material relating to Elias Canetti, Erich Fried, Hilde Spiel, Theodor Kramer and many others. However, full coverage of secondary literature, on exile in general, on exile in particular countries, and on individual authors, remains a distant target. Early works such as Walter Berendsohn's pioneering *Die humanistische Front* (Zurich: Europa, 1946) and W. K. Pfeiler, *German litera-ture in exile* (Lincoln: University of Nebraska Press, 1957) were acquired, but of the flood of publications that have appeared in the last two decades only a handful can be purchased each year, preference normally, but by no means exclusively, being given to titles dealing with exile in Britain.

Secondary material in journal form is a different matter: periodicals have always been an Institute priority, whether they are devoted to exile in general — *Exil, Exiljahrbuch* — or to individual figures: *Brecht Yearbook/Jahrbuch*, *Argonautenschiff* (on Anna Seghers), *Peter Weiss*

Jahrbuch, Zuckmayer-Jahrbuch (formerly the *Blätter der Carl Zuckmayer Gesellschaft*), *Walter-Hasenclever-Gesellschaft Jahrbuch* and *Zwischenwelt* being among the better known. Attempts are made, not always successfully, to obtain even such shortlived titles as *Horváth Blätter* or the *Internationale Erich Fried Gesellschaft Jahrbuch*.

Similarly, reference works are a permanent priority and the Institute has an outstanding collection of exile bibliographies, handbooks, and biographical dictionaries, from the first edition of Wilhelm Sternfeld and Eva Tiedemann, *Deutsche Exil-Literatur 1933-1945* (Heidelberg: Lambert Schneider, 1962) and Günther Soffke's *Deutsches Schrifttum im Exil (1933-1950)* (Bonn: Bouvier, 1965) onwards. Early lists from the GDR include Horst Halfmann, *Zeitschriften und Zeitungen des Exils, 1933-1945: Bestandsverzeichnis der Deutschen Bücherei* (Leipzig: Deutsche Bücherei, 1969), *Die Sammlung der Exil-Literatur 1933 bis 1945 der Deutschen Bücherei* (Leipzig: Deutsche Bücherei, 1973) by the same author, with Helmut Lohse, and the important *Verzeichnis der Schriften, die 1933-1945 nicht angezeigt werden durften*, also produced by the Deutsche Bücherei as a supplement to the *Deutsche Nationalbibliographie* (Leipzig: Verlag des Börsenvereins der deutschen Buchhändler, 1949). Standard works such as the *Biographisches Handbuch der deutschsprachigen Emigration nach 1933* (Munich: Saur, 1980-83), John Spalek's *Guide to the archival materials of the German-speaking emigration to the United States after 1933* (various imprints, 1978-1997) and the Deutsche Bibliothek's *Deutsches Exilarchiv 1933-1945: Katalog der Bücher und Broschüren* (Stuttgart: Metzler, 1989) are all held, as are several major exhibition catalogues.

Add to this the many titles by exiles who went on to make careers, in Britain and elsewhere, as academics in the field of German language and literature and whose works the Institute collects both for their own value and as contributions to the history of German studies, and it is clear that the overall holdings of exile-related material as described so far are extensive without being distinctive: it is a collection that any academic library with an interest in German exile and adequate funding could have built up. As exile studies grew, though, in the 'eighties in particular, and demands on the Institute's resources became more specific, it became necessary to examine in more detail exactly what was available within the library. It soon became evident that if the basic research material was the cake, then its icing was an outstanding collection of works published during the period between 1933 and 1945 outside Germany and Austria, a collection that had grown together, almost unnoticed, from the various donations and bequests. Some of the smaller items and pamphlets had either not been adequately recorded or never catalogued at all: they lay hidden and unrecognized in pamphlet boxes. Other works were there on the bookshelves but were often so slim and unprepossessing in appearance that only opening them to examine the imprint revealed their significance. There are undoubtedly more such items to be found. The addition, in 1995, of Professor Hamish Ritchie's personal library to the Institute's holdings enhanced the overall collection considerably, filling gaps and proving to be the icing on the icing.

Unsurprisingly, few titles from outside Europe have been found: perhaps the surprising thing is that there are any at all. Only a handful of works have found their way back across the Atlantic. From the USA, there are three Aurora publications: *Morgenröte*, the anthology with introductions by Heinrich Mann (New York, 1947), Berthold Viertel, *Der Lebenslauf* (New York, 1945) and Brecht's *Furcht und Elend des III. Reiches* (New York, 1945), one of very few published plays in the entire collection; other well-known titles include Hermann Broch, *Der Tod des Vergil* (Pantheon, 1945), and Johannes Urzidil's *Der Trauermantel* (Krause, 1945, one of a hundred signed copies), both published in New York, but Mascha Kaleko's *Verse für Zeitgenossen* (Cambridge, Mass.: Schoenhof, 1945) is perhaps less familiar. West coast titles include two works published in Los Angeles, Franz Werfel's *Gedichte aus den Jahren 1908-1945,* and Thomas Mann, *Leiden an Deutschland* (both Privatdruck der Pazifischen Presse, 1946). Rilke and Beer-Hofmann titles published by the Verlag der Johannespresse from 1944 onwards are not strictly exile works, though Otto Kallir, who set up the company, was himself an exile and was continuing the work of his earlier Vienna-based Johannespresse. One relevant journal title is a facsimile reprint of Klaus Mann's *Decision: a Review of Free Culture* (Nendeln: Kraus, 1969), originally published 1941-42.

The pickings from Latin America are even slimmer, though this again is hardly unexpected: Günther Ballin's *Zwischen gestern und morgen* (Buenos Aires: Editorial Cosmopolita, 1945) and two works by Paul Zech, certainly one of the better known authors to end up in this part of the world: *Neue Welt: Verse der Emigration* (Buenos Aires: Quadriga, 1939), with a handwritten dedication dated February 1940 to 'Mr [i.e. Jethro] Bithell', and *bäume am rio de la plata* (Buenos Aires: Transmare, 1935), with the signed inscription 'mit freundlichen Grüßen aus der Ferne', one of 250 copies printed. A later work, though clearly pertinent to exile, is Walter Jacob's *Theater 1940-1950: zehn Jahre Freie Deutsche Bühne in Buenos Aires* (Buenos Aires: Jupiter, 1950). Erwin Walter Palm's *Requiem für die Toten Europas* is unusual for its imprint alone: 'Insel Hispaniola: Privatdruck, 1944'. Many of Palm's other writings, chiefly on Spanish and South American art and architecture, are held in the Warburg Institute. A letter to Professor August in the Institute's archives indicates that Palm was, however briefly, in exile in Bristol. Disappointingly, no original titles published in Mexico City by El Libro Libre, one of the most significant and active exile organizations, have yet been traced, though a facsimile reprint of the journal *Freies Deutschland/Alemania libre* (Nendeln: Kraus, 1975), originally published 1941-46 is held, as is *Deutsche Blätter* (Nendeln: Kraus, 1970, originally Santiago, Chile: Imprenta Universitaria, 1943-46). North and South America, it is clear, have not contributed a great deal to the Institute's holdings.

The same is true of Palestine, Czechoslovakia and the Soviet Union: so far, only two books published by Junge Dichtung in Jerusalem during the war years, both written by Manfred Vogel, have been found: *Herzfloetensolo* (1940) and *Spiegelsterne* (1941). There are three titles from the Soviet Union, all published in Moscow, two, unsurprisingly, by Johannes R. Becher, *Der Glücksucher und die sieben Lasten* (Verlagsgenossenschaft ausländischer Arbeiter in der UdSSR, 1938) and *Gewißheit des Sieges und Sicht auf große Tage* (Das internationale Buch, 1939), the third by Willi Bredel, *Der Sonderführer* (Verlag für fremdsprachige Literatur, 1944). The only work from Czechoslovakia that the Institute has is Fritz Wielek's anthology *Verse der Emigration* (Karlsbad: 'Graphia', 1935). Once again, journals enhance the picture: an original set of *Das Wort*, edited by Brecht, Bredel and Feuchtwanger (Moscow: Jourgaz; Verlag Meshdunarodnaja Kniga, 1936-39), and reprints of Arnold Zweig and Wolfgang Yourgrau's *Orient* (Hildesheim: Gerstenberg, 1982, originally Haifa: Orient, 1942-43), *Der Gegen-Angriff* (Leipzig: Zentralantiquariat der DDR; Nendeln: Kraus, 1982, originally Prague, 1933-36), and *Neue deutsche Blätter*, edited by Oskar Maria Graf, Wieland Herzfelde and Anna Seghers (Berlin: Rütten und Loening, 1974, originally Prague: Faust, 1933-35).

The modest number of works from France is disappointing, though some of the titles are important: Alfred Kerr's *Melodien* (Paris: Editions

Nouvelles Internationales, 1938) and two non-fiction items: Rudolf Olden, *Hindenburg* (Paris: Europäischer Merkur, 1935) and *Naziführer sehen Dich an* (Paris: Editions du Carrefour, 1934), published anonymously but attributed to Walter Mehring. Of particular interest are a 'Bühnenmanuskript' of Walter Hasenclever's *Münchhausen*, which has no imprint but the author's return address is given as the Grand Hôtel du Mont Boron, Nice (Alpes Maritimes), and a handwritten dedication to Gerald Cooper is dated London, 20th February 1936, and a complete run (a total of eight rather flimsy issues) of *Das Buch: Zeitschrift für die unabhängige Literatur* (Paris: Editions Nouvelles Internationales, 1938-40).

Holdings of works from Sweden, Switzerland and the Netherlands are extensive, and it is quite possible there are more waiting to be discovered; titles range from the notorious — Klaus Mann's *Mephisto* (Amsterdam: Querido, 1936) — to the unfamiliar: Adrienne Thomas, *Dreiviertel Neugier* (Amsterdam: Allert de Lange, 1934) and *Katrin! Die Welt brennt!* (Amsterdam: Allert de Lange, 1936). But it was these countries, after all, in which the most important German-language publishing houses such as Oprecht (Zurich), Bermann-Fischer (Stockholm) and Allert de Lange and Querido (Amsterdam) operated, publishing most of the major exiled authors and many of the minor ones, and it is their output that would best be served by a full bibliography of the Institute's holdings: there are simply too many to be covered in a survey such as this. Mention should be made of two original journals: Klaus Mann's *Sammlung* (Amsterdam: Querido, 1933-1935) and *Mass und Wert*, edited by Thomas Mann and Konrad Falke (Zurich: Oprecht, 1937-1940). *Über die Grenzen: von Flüchtlingen — für Flüchtlinge* is present as an original (Wallisellen; Zurich: s.n., 1944-45) but only the facsimile reprint (Leipzig: Zentralantiquariat der DDR, 1988) has the accompanying 'Schriftenreihe'.

Britain had no obviously comparable German-language publisher. Throughout the 'thirties, several of the major firms issued translations, continuing programmes that in many cases had started in the previous decade: exile authors *are* represented but so are writers such as Kolbenheyer and Fallada. Only with the outbreak of war do the non-exiles disappear and the exiles (and a handful of classics) predominate. Again, there are too many titles to list individually but among the important publishers, in the literary field at least, are Cape, Cassell, Hamish Hamilton, Hutchinson and Secker. It is noticeable, though, that non-literary titles also feature in their output both before and during the war, examples being Rudolf Olden, *Hitler the Pawn* (London: Gollancz, 1936) and Karl Otten's *A Combine of Aggression* (London: George Allen and Unwin, 1942), translated from a then unpublished German manuscript. Works published by Lindsay Drummond, a company that placed particular emphasis on German themes, included Erika Mann, *School for Barbarians* (London, 1939), Heinrich Fraenkel, *The Other Germany* (London, 1942) and *After Nazism — Democracy*, edited by Kurt Hiller (London, 1945).

The war years also witnessed Hamish Hamilton's series of German-language publications, represented in the Institute's collections by Lion Feuchtwanger, *Die Brüder Lautensack* (London, 1944), Franz Werfel, *Das Lied von Bernadette* and Zweig's *Die Welt von Gestern* (both London, 1941). Other German-language works were published by smaller firms or, as we shall see, by the many exile organizations. Of the former, Max Herrmann-Neiße's *Letzte Gedichte* (London, 1941) and *Mir bleibt mein Lied* (London, 1942) were published by Barmerlea, for many years one of the Institute's principal book suppliers; the Grey Walls Press issued bilingual editions of Fred Marnau, *Der Tod der Kathedrale* (London, 1946) and *Die Wunden der Apostel* (London, 1944); Jakob Hegner, himself an exile, published Richard Friedenthal's *Brot und Salz* and Toni Sussmann, *Theodor Däubler: ein Requiem* (both London, 1943); and Georg Rapp's *Das Narrenspiel* appeared with Barnard and Westwood (London, 1942). One somewhat unusual example was the publication by Lincolns-Prager of both the German original of Dosio Koffler's *Die deutsche Walpurgisnacht* (London, 1941, another rare drama) *and* the English translation, *The German Witches' Sabbath*, a year later.

If there is one group of works that must be singled out, it is the original novels written in *English* by authors whose first language was German: holdings are modest so far but include Peter de Mendelssohn, *Across the Dark River* (London: Hutchinson, 1939) and *The Hours and the Centuries* (London: John Lane/Bodley Head, 1944; the US edition *Fortress in the Skies*, New York: Doubleday, 1943, is also held), and Robert Neumann, *The Inquest* (London, 1944) and *Scene in Passing* (London, 1945), both with Hutchinson. Evidence of other exiles' efforts to carve out a life and earn a living in Britain is perhaps provided by such works as *Modern German Verse*, edited by A. Weiner and Fritz Gross (London: Gregg, 1936), Else Johannsen and Albert Malte Wagner's *Die Abenteuer von Paula und Peter: Ten Broadcast Dialogues in German* (London:

University of London Press, 1937) and Carl Brinitzer's *Cassell's War and Postwar German Dictionary* (London: Cassell, 1945).

Many of these titles are now rare and difficult to get hold of but they are still essentially mainstream publications. They are complemented by a growing collection of pamphlets issued by the various exile organizations based in London. The Institute's core interest in literature is reflected in several important anthologies, all of them published in London, among them the poetry collections *Mut* (Jugend voran, 1943), *Stimmen aus Böhmen* (Verlag der Einheit, 1944), *'Und sie bewegt sich doch!'* ('Free German Youth', 1943, with its distinctive John Heartfield cover), *Die Vertriebenen* (Free German League of Culture; Austrian Centre; Young Czechoslovakia, 1941), and *Zwischen gestern und morgen* (Austrian Centre, Young Austria, 1942). Works by individual poets, again all published in London, include Erich Fried, *Deutschland* (Austrian P.E.N., 1944), Rudolf Fuchs, *Ein wissender Soldat* (Verlag der 'Einheit', 1943), Theodor Kramer, *Verbannt aus Österreich* (Austrian P.E.N., 1943) and Max Zimmering, *Der Keim des Neuen* (Freier Deutscher Kulturbund, 1944). There is also a large number of historical, political and economic pamphlets by writers such as Curt Geyer, Jürgen Kuczynski, Otto Lehmann-Russbueldt, Paul Reimann and Otto Strasser. Admittedly, their content may now be of little interest other than to specialists but the pamphlets themselves, with their addresses, lists of publications, and announcements of forthcoming events, can be a mine of information about the activities of their parent organizations. Even the advertisements can be revealing. This type of work also underlines the fact that exile is one of the few areas where the Institute has moved, albeit in very modest fashion, beyond its traditional emphasis on language and literature. The single journal from the exile community in Britain that the Institute has is a broken run (1942-1945) of *Einheit*, the journal of the Sudeten Germans in London.

While works by German-speaking exiles remain at the heart of the Institute's holdings, a number of other contemporary titles have come its way that broaden the picture: two discussions addressed to a British audience, for example: *You and the refugee: the morals and economics of the problem*, by Sir Norman Angell and D. F. Buxton (Harmondsworth: Penguin, 1939) and the pamphlet *Are refugees an asset?* (London: Europa, 1944); and two conferences held by PEN in 1941 and 1944 respectively, *Writers in Freedom* and *Freedom of Expression* (published by Hutchinson in those years), at the earlier of which Alfred Kerr, Erika Mann, Peter de Mendelssohn and Robert Neumann all spoke. Other titles of interest include *War Poetry from Occupied Holland* (Bristol: Arrowsmith, 1945) and *Lidice: a Tribute by Members of the International PEN* (London: Allen and Unwin for the Czechoslovak PEN, 1944).

The Institute's exile collection is continually expanding: new pamphlets added during the academic year 1998/1999 include Berthold Jacob, *Warum schweigt die Welt* (Paris: Editions du Phénix, 1936), two titles published by Free Austrian Books in London: Ernst Fischer's *Nationale Probleme des Jahres 1848 in Oesterreich* (1945) and Wilhelm Scholz, *Moscow on Austria* (1943), and two by I.N.G. (i.e. Inside Nazi Germany): Heinz Schmidt's *Goebbels and the 2nd Front* (London, 1943) and the anonymous *I Escaped from Nazi Germany: a French Deportee's Report* (1944). Three titles from Hutchinson's series of 'Fight for Freedom Publications' were acquired: K. F. Bieligk's *Stresemann* (London, 1944) and two by Bernhard Menne: *Armistice and Germany's Food Supply 1918-19* (1944) and *The Case of Dr Bruening* (1943). Other political pamphlets obtained were Ernst Fischer (again), *From People's Front to National Front* (London: Communist Party of Great Britain, 1941), *England and the Last Free Germans*, by Wenzel Jaksch and Walter Kolarz (London: Lincolns-Prager, 1941), Heinrich Fraenkel's *Vansittart's Gift for Goebbels* (London: Fabian Society, 1941), his reply to Robert Vansittart's *Black Record* (London: Hamish Hamilton, 1941), not itself an exile work but also in the Institute's collection, Leopold Spira's *We are not alone* (Glasgow: Young Austria; Austrian Centre, 1943?), one of the very few British works found so far that was not published in London, and from Switzerland *Die Bewegung 'Freies Deutschland' und ihre Ziele* (Zurich: Oprecht, 1945) by Wolfgang Langhoff.

New reference works added to stock have been the *Handbuch der deutschsprachigen Emigration 1933-1945*, edited by Claus-Dieter Krohn and others (Darmstadt: Wissenschaftliche Buchgesellschaft, 1998) and the three-volume *Handbuch des deutschsprachigen Exiltheaters 1933-1945*, edited by Frithjof Trapp and others (Munich: Saur, 1999). Of recent autobiographies, Elisabeth Orsten's *From Anschluss to Albion* (Cambridge: Acorn, 1998) and Arnold Höllriegel (i.e. Richard A. Bermann), *Die Fahrt auf dem Katarakt* (Vienna: Picus, 1998) should be mentioned, as should Höllriegel's *In 80 Zeilen durch die Welt* (Berlin: Transit, 1998) and two other collections: Alfred Kantorowicz,

Nachtbücher: Aufzeichnungen im französischen Exil 1935 bis 1939, edited by Ursula Büttner and Angelika Voß (Hamburg: Christians, 1995) and Georg Schirmer's edition of Walter Mehring, *Das Mitternachtstagebuch: Texte des Exils 1933-1939* (Mannheim: Persona, 1996). Gerhard Schaub's *Kurt Schwitters und die 'andere' Schweiz: unveröffentlichte Briefe aus dem Exil* (Berlin: Fannei und Walz, 1998) is of interest, and Jost Hermand and Wigand Lange's *"Wollt ihr Thomas Mann wiederhaben?" Deutschland und die Emigranten* (Hamburg: Europäische Verlagsanstalt, 1999) is a fascinating look at post-war German attitudes to the exiles. Secondary literature has again been acquired sparingly: somewhat belatedly the Institute obtained Peter Heumos's *Die Emigration aus der Tschechoslowakei nach Westeuropa [...]* (Munich: Oldenbourg, 1989), and biographies added included Gwendolen Webster's *Kurt Merz Schwitters* (Cardiff: University of Wales Press, 1997) and Ingrid Marchlewitz, *Irmgard Keun: Leben und Werk* (Würzburg: Königshausen und Neumann, 1999). And this brief survey of recent works should not end without a mention of the Institute's own *Keine Klage über England: deutsche und österreichische Exilerfahrungen in Großbritannien, 1933-1945,* edited by Charmian Brinson et al. (Munich: Iudicium, 1998).

Because the Institute's prime concern has always been the acquisition of texts of all periods, it has never really needed to define 'exile' or to separate it off from other areas of the library. The exile generation has its roots in the literature of expressionism and the Weimar Republic, where the Institute's holdings are extensive. Its holdings of post-war 'exile' literature, however defined, are just as substantial, taking in not only the works of authors who returned to Germany, east and west, or Austria, but also those of writers who stayed on in Britain or other host countries, or who arrived after the war had ended; they embrace those who never stopped writing, those who resumed writing after a long interval and those who published for the first time, both the well known — Erich Fried, Elias Canetti, H. G. Adler, Stella Rotenberg, Arno Reinfrank, Henriette Hardenberg — and the many others: Rudolf Majut, Hans Cohn, Heinz Priebatsch, Hedwig Katscher, Else Dormitzer, Lotte Pagel ... Exile refuses to be bound by the years 1933 to 1945 and the Institute's policy will continue to reflect this.

The Research Centre for German and Austrian Exile Studies

The Research Centre for German and Austrian Exile Studies was established at the Institute of Germanic Studies, University of London, in 1995 when the Institute offered a home to this new organisation, which combined the former London Research Group for German Exile Studies and the Research Centre for Germans and Austrians in Great Britain, previously at the University of Aberdeen. Professor J. M. Ritchie, Emeritus Professor of German at Aberdeen, who donated the Ritchie collection of books on exile, was nominated Honorary Research Fellow of the Institute and serves as Chairman of the Centre.

The work of the Centre focuses on the history of those German-speaking émigrés who found refuge in Great Britain, on their personal recollections and experiences, their reception in British society, and their enrichment of the life of their new country of residence in such varied spheres as the professions, industry and commerce, literature, art and culture, politics, publishing, the media, and the world of entertainment and leisure. The concept of German-speaking exiles extends to those who came from the then Czechoslovakia, Hungary, Poland and other European countries, as well as from Germany and Austria. The main focus of the Centre has so far been on the émigrés who came to Britain in the 1930s and 1940s, but the Centre intends also to embrace the important groups of émigrés who arrived in the nineteenth century, and earlier.

The Centre has been responsible for organising some of the first symposia on exile in Great Britain and for publishing the proceedings. Examples are *Between Two Languages: German-speaking Exiles in Great Britain 1933-45*, ed. by William Abbey et al. (Stuttgart: Heintz, 1995); *'England? Aber wo liegt es?' Deutsche und österreichische Emigranten in Großbritannien 1933-45*, ed. by Richard Dove at al. (Munich: Iudicium, 1996); *Keine Klage über England? Deutsche und österreichische Exilerfahrungen in Großbritannien 1933-1945*, ed. Charmian Brinson et al. Publications of the Institute of Germanic Studies, 72 (Munich: Iudicium, 1998). The Centre aims to promote research in exile studies and, with the Institute of Germanic Studies, to establish postgraduate scholarships and research fellowship to allow scholars, especially younger scholars, to pursue research in the field. In addition to the books held in the Institute's Library, the Centre is building up an archive of taped interviews and documents as a historical record of exile life in Great Britain.

J. M. Ritchie

The Austrian Centre: Politics and Culture in Exile 1933-47

The Research Centre is currently conducting a study of the London-based Austrian Centre as a social, cultural and political organisation. While the project is a discrete piece of research, it is also part of the Research Centre's overall work of recording and analysing aspects of German-speaking exile in Britain.

The project is jointly supported by the University of Greenwich and the Institute of Germanic Studies and has recently received a Major Research Grant from the British Academy.

The project team consists of Richard Dove, Marietta Bearman, Charmian Brinson, Anthony Grenville, Jennifer Taylor and Marian Malet.

Project outline

The Austrian Centre in London is very much a paradigm of Austrian exile in Britain. Founded in March 1939, at a time when the stream of Austrian refugees arriving in Britain was reaching its peak, it was wound up in January 1947, as many of its activists were returning to Austria, while others chose to remain and assimilate into British society.

Founded to represent the interests of Austrian refugees in Britain, the Centre quickly developed into a comprehensive social, cultural and political organisation. During the early years of its existence, its activities focused primarily on relief work. In 1940 it campaigned against the internment of 'enemy aliens', making determined efforts to secure the release of detainees. With the entry of the Soviet Union into the war in June 1941, the Centre was able to pursue a more overtly political agenda, playing an influential role in moves to establish the Free Austrian Movement (FAM), which campaigned for the post-war restoration of a democratic and independent Austrian state.

The Austrian Centre continued to devote itself to social and cultural tasks, though pursuing, through its newspaper and its cultural activities, a political agenda which was consistent with the aims of the FAM.

By 1941 the Austrian Centre had three centres in London and one in Glasgow, as well as several provincial branches, developing a comprehensive social and cultural programme which made it the most successful of all refugee organisations in wartime London. The Centre at Westbourne Terrace ran a restaurant, a library and a reading-room. It also promoted a wide range of cultural activities, both directly and through its affiliated youth organisations. It produced a weekly newspaper, *Zeitspiegel*, with a circulation of some 3,000, and also published a wide range of books and pamphlets under several imprints ('Free Austrian Books', 'Jugend voran' etc.). The club premises at 69 Eton Avenue housed a theatre, the Laterndl, which from June 1941 to June 1945 regularly produced plays and revues, featuring well-known actors and directors. The Centre also sponsored a regular musical programme comprising concerts and choral performances. The aim of these cultural activities was not only to satisfy the cultural aspirations of Austrian refugees but also to establish a specific Austrian cultural identity: a conscious correlative to the political agenda pursued more overtly through other organisations.

A major focus of interest will be the political offshoots of the Centre (notably the Free Austrian Movement) and the Centre's relations with other cultural organisations (e.g. Austrian PEN). Further aspects of proposed research (hitherto completely unresearched) are: the publications of the Austrian Centre, its collaboration with other exile groups (e.g Czechs and Poles), and its relations with Britain and the British authorities. Research will also investigate the hopes for an Austrian National Committee in exile and the various proposals for post-war Austria.

Sources

No complete archive of the Austrian Centre now exists, its records and documents having been widely dispersed. There are, however, important collections of documents and/ or publications in London, Frankfurt, Graz and above all, Vienna. In addition to consulting documents and publications, it is intended to interview surviving 'Zeitzeugen' now living in Austria, Germany and Britain.

Research objectives

It is intended to record and evaluate the full range of the Centre's activities (newspapers and other publications, theatre, music and art) showing their relationship to the Centre's political agenda. The main objective of the proposed research will therefore be to investigate the interaction of politics and culture in the situation of exile in Britain.

Some early results of the research are contained in this Yearbook in the article "Free Austrian Books". As research proceeds, it is hoped to published other preliminary findings, where appropriate, in scholarly journals — particularly in Britain and Austria, but also in Germany. However, the ultimate objective is to publish a full-length study of the Austrian Centre.

Richard Dove

The Oral History Project

Since 1994 members of the Research Centre have been engaged in interviewing ex-refugees from Germany, Austria and Czechoslovakia, both Jewish and non-Jewish, with the twin aims of preserving their experiences and of building an archive for research purposes.

Project members have used the interviews processed to date as the basis of a study, entitled 'Home from Home?', which is nearing completion. It is intended to publish the study in the near future.

The text consists of a series of essays on various aspects of the background and lives of the interviewees whose ages at emigration ranged from eight to thirty-four. The approach chosen was part chronological, part thematic, as this seemed to best do justice both to the wealth and diversity of the material and to the process of exile itself. Thus the groundwork is laid with chapters on the context from which the ex-refugees came and the place they and their families occupied within it, and this is followed by an analysis of the actual circumstances of emigration and the reasons for the choice of Britain as a destination. Pre-war, wartime and post-war aspects of everyday life in Britain as experienced by the interviewees are then explored. The themes of education, internment, language, relationship to Judaism (where applicable) and relation with the country of origin are examined in further essays. Through this in-depth analysis of a small group we seek to go beyond the stereotypical to demonstrate what the processes of acculturation and assimilation actually mean in concrete terms at the level of individual experience.

* * *

The archive currently consists of 35 interviews, most of which have been transcribed with generous financial support from *German Life and Letters* and the Association of Jewish Refugees, and this has recently been swelled by the gift of eleven interviews with members of Club 43 which were kindly donated by Jens Brüning. Members of the Centre hope to continue to record interviews to add to the corpus in due course.

Marian Malet

Index

Abbey, William 261
Abraham a Sancta Clara 182
Adams, Walter 34f.
Adler, Bruno 34, 43-59
Adler, H. G. 149, 173, 178, 260
Adler-Rudel, S. 3
Adorno, Theodor W. 34
Aesop 108
Alcott, Louisa May 203
Alexander, Kurt 4
Altmann, Berthold 34
Andersen, Hans C. 204
Angell, Sir Norman 258
Antal, F. 34
Anzengruber, Ludwig 208
Arden, John 175
Arendt, Hannah 86f.
Arnheimer, Raoul 68
Arntz, Gerd 211
Aronsfeld, C. C. 14
Ash, Adrienne 167
Astor, David 77
Auden, W. H. 183-5
Augst, Peter 157
Austen, Jane 202

Bacharach, Jacques 61
Bachmann, Ilse 179
Baeck, Leo 17
Baker, Philip Noel 123
Ballin, Günter 254
Baltrusaitis, Jurgis 37
Barb, Alfons 34
Baring, Arnulf 77
Barker, Sir Ernest 11
Baron, Hans 34

Barthel, Kurt (see Kuba) 97
Bartmann, Marion 34
Bartov, Omer 81
Baudelaire, Charles 177, 191
Beaman, S. G. Hulme 204
Bearman, Marietta 262
Becher, Johannes R. 44, 252, 255
Beckett, Samuel 167
Beer, Arthur 34
Beer, Fritz 252
Beer-Hofmann, Richard 254
Beethoven, Ludwig van 178, 249
Behrens, Käthe 70
Benjamin, Walter 64
Benn, Gottfried 101, 179
Berendsohn, Walter A. 60f., 69,
    96, 252
Beresford, Anne 185
Bergenthal, Max 135
Berger, Klaus 34
Berger, Ludwig 252
Berghahn, Marion 2f., 12
Bergner, Elisabeth 65
Berman, Richard A. (see Höllriegel,
    Arnold) 259
Berry, Wendell 187, 191
Berlin, Isaiah 37
Bichsel, Peter 179
Bieligk, K. F. 259
Bing, Gertrud 26, 30f., 33, 36, 39
Birn, Ruth 79
Bismarck, Otto von 77-9, 81
Bithell, Jethro 254
Blackmore, R. D. 203
Blake, William 202
Blend, Martha 201, 207f.

Blixen, Karen 167
Bloch, Ernst 100
Blunt, Anthony 37f.
Bluth, Karl Theodor 64
Bobrowski, Johannes 170, 187
Böll, Heinrich 157
Börne, Ludwig 167
Bohrs, Niels 37
Bolbecher, Siglinde 242
Bormann, Alexander von 190
Bornemann, Ernst 147
Botticelli, Sandro 26
Bradt, Eva 34
Braun, Felix 178, 234, 237
Brazil, Angela 203
Brecht, Bertolt 60, 62, 67, 70, 100,
    147, 179, 191, 251f., 254f.
Bredel, Willi 255
Brehm, Eugen 66, 129-32
Breitenbach, Edgar 34f.
Brendel, Otto 34, 37
Breuer, Georg 232, 245
Brezik, Jaro 233, 245
Brinitzer, Carl 46, 257
Brinson, Charmian 260-2
Broch, Hermann 179, 254
Brod, Max 100
Brodetsky, Selig 20
Bruckner, Ferdinand 70
Bruening, Heinrich 259
Brüning, Jens 264
Buchthal, Hugo 35f.
Büchner, Georg 163, 177f.
Büttner, Ursula 259
Burschell, Friedrich 60f., 63, 66,
    71, 127
Buschbeck, Ernst H. 35, 230, 245
Butler, E. M. 107f.

Buxton, D. F. 258

Calef, Guido 35
Calman, Hans 35
Cameron, Norman 45
Canetti, Elias 167, 252, 260
Carossa, Hans 32
Carroll, Lewis 205
Cassirer, Ernst 30, 37
Cassirer, Heinrich W. 34
Castonier, Elisabeth 72, 252
Caudwell, Christopher 173
Cecil, Lord David 118, 123f., 126
Celan, Paul 178f.
Chalmers, Martin 146
Chamberlain, Neville 126
Chamisso, Adelbert von 167
Char, René 191
Chichester, Bishop of 127, 221
Churchill, Winston 54, 70, 119,
    245
Claassen, Eugen 150, 174, 180
Clutton, George 37
Cohn, E. J. 128
Cohn, Hans Werner 173, 178, 182,
    260
Cohn, Joachim Werner 61, 69
Collins, Roland 211
Comfort, Alex 173f.
Conrad, Joseph 167
Constable, W. G. 29, 37
Cooper, Duff 76
Cooper, Gerald 255
Cooper, Ray 37
Courtauld, Samuel 30
Crankshaw, Edward 235
Csokor, Franz Theodor 173
Crawford, Joan 204

Cummings, E. E. 183

Däubler, Theodor 257
David, Jakob Julius 208
David, Ruth 252
Davis, Bette 204
Demel, Paul 70
Demus, Otto 35
Demuth, Fritz 131
Desser, Jenö 238
Deutsch, Ernst 68
Deutscher, Isaac 77
Diamant-Almas, Josef 61, 69
Dickens, Charles 202
Dieterle, Wilhelm 66
Dietrich, Marlene 66
Diringer, David 35
Doberer, Kurt 66f.
Döblin, Alfred 64, 66
Döry, Heinz 35
Döry, Iwan 35
Doderer, Heimito von 184
Donne, John 150, 174
Dormitzer, Else 260
Dove, Richard 166f., 192, 261f.
Duden, Anne 149
Duschinsky, Richard 67
Dutch, Oswald O. 209f.
Dutschke, Rudi 149

Ebeling, Hans 127
Ebner-Eschenbach, Marie von 208
Eckardt, Eva von 31
Ede, Chuter 5
Edelman, Maurice 19
Ehrenburg, Ilya 108f.
Ehrenzweig, Albert 35

Ehrenzweig, Robert (see Lucas, Robt.)
Ehrlich, Bettina (Bauer-) 209, 211f.
Ehrlich, Georg 237
Eich, Günter 179
Eichler, Willi 123, 131f.
Eichmann, Adolf 81, 86
Eichner, Hans 173
Einstein, Albert 63, 118
Einstein, Carl 34, 64
Eisenstadt, Mussia 35
Elias, Gertrude 252
Eliot, T. S. 150, 168, 173-5, 178,
    183-6, 191
Enzensberger, Hans Magnus 179, 187
Eppelsheimer, Hanns 72
Ernst, Alois 131f., 135
Esslin. Martin 43
Ettlinger, Dora 35
Ettlinger, Leopold 36

Fabian, Dora 119, 121f., 125
Fabian, Hans-Erich 16f.
Fajfar, Tone 245
Falke, Konrad 256
Fallada, Hans 32, 256
Feddersen, Martin 35
Fein, Otto 31
Feld, Friedrich 209f., 213
Feuchtwanger, Lion 32, 60, 64, 147
    149, 156, 166, 252, 255, 257
Feuchtwanger, Ludwig 35
Fischer, Alfred Joachim 61f.
Fischer, Ernst 228-30, 232, 243,
    245, 258f.
Fischer, Grete 104, 210, 252
Fischer, Heinrich 71
Fischer, Klara 245

Fisher, Margaret (see Fischer, Grete)
Fleischer, Victor 234
Flesch-Brunningen, Hans 147, 149, 165
Flower, Robin E. W. 30
Focillon, Henri 37
Fortini, Franco 191
Fraenkel, Heinrich 135, 256, 259
Fränkel, Hermann 34
Frank, Bruno 68
Frank, Leonhard 64
Frankel, Liselotte 35
Freeden, Herbert 2f., 18, 252
Frei, Bruno 100
Freiligrath, Ferdinand 96
Freyhan, Robert 34
Fried, Erich 104, 145-98, 206, 222, 226, 231, 245, 252f., 258, 260
Fried-Boswell, Catherine 149
Friedenthal, Herbert (see Freeden, Herbert)
Friedenthal, Richard 71, 234, 252, 257
Friedlaender, Walter 38
Friedmann, Hermann 133
Frischauer, Paul 233, 246
von Fritz 34
Fuchs, Albert 206, 222, 225-8, 237, 243
Fuchs, Rudolf 67, 70, 258
Fuerst, Helmut 35

Gál, Hans 68, 237
Gascoyne, David 184f.
Gellner, Julius 70
George, Stefan 168
Geyer, Curt 132, 258
Gibson, C. S. 29
Ginzkey, Franz Karl 204

Gloag, John 11
Globocnik, Odilo 81
Gmeyner, Anna (see Reiner, Anna) 70
Goes, Albrecht 179
Goethe, Wolfgang von 26, 163, 179, 204
Goldhagen, Daniel J. 75-93
Goldschmidt, Adolph 30
Goldschmidt, Günther 35
Goldschmidt, Werner 35
Goll, Yvan 168
Gombrich, Ernst H. 25, 35-8, 211
Gombrich, Lisbeth 209, 211
Gooch, G. P. 120, 123
Gorky, Maxim 104
Gottfurcht, Fritz 70, 149
Gottfurcht, Hans 127
Graber, Felix 246
Grad, Frank 200
Graf, Oskar Maria 148, 255
Gramberg, Werner 35
Grass, Günter 179, 187
Graves, Robert 183f.
Gray, Thomas 184, 202
Grebly, Martin (see Ilberg, Werner) 100
Greene, Graham 174f.
Grenville, Anthony 262
Grillparzer, Franz 208, 226, 230, 232, 234, 237, 245, 248, 250
Grimm Brothers 204, 211
Gross, Fritz 121f., 126, 257
Grün, Anastasius 208
Grünebaum, Gustav von 35
Grunberger, Richard 2
Gutmann, Julius 70

Haffner, Sebastian (see Pretzel, Raimund) 75-93
Halfmann, Horst 253
Hallo, Gertrud 35
Hamburger, Michael 148, 163-98
Hardenberg, Henriette 260
Hardtmuth, Paul 70
Hardy, Oliver 204
Hardy, Thomas 151
Harris, Joel Chandler 202
Hartwig, Mela 237
Hasek, Jaroslav 51
Hasenclever, Walter 64, 252, 255
Hauptmann, Gerhart 32, 51
Hausdorff, Rita 104
Hay, Will 204
Hayworth, Rita 204
Heartfield, John 63, 257
Heckscher, H. P. 35
Hegner, Jakob 257
Heimann, Adelheid 34-6
Heimann, Angelika 175, 183, 189
Heine, Heinrich 96, 109f., 177
Heise, Carl Georg 29
Heißenbüttel, Helmut 179
Heller, Otto 109
Hellmer, Arthur 70
Henried, Paul 65
Henry, Marc 235
Herman, Jury 243
Hermand, Jost 259
Herrmann-Neiße, Max 69, 251, 257
Hertz, Mary 27
Herz, Carl 130f., 136
Herz, Ida 35, 252
Herzfelde, Helmut (see Heartfield, John)
Herzfelde, Wieland 100, 255

Hess, Jacob 35
Hesse, Hermann 32, 177
Heumos, Peter 259
Heydenreich, Heinrich 35
Hiller, Kurt 62, 67, 71, 132, 256
Himmler, Heinrich 85
Hindenburg, Paul von 33, 255
Hindus, Maurice 69
Hinks, Roger 30, 37
Hirsch, Erika 75f.
Hitler, Adolf 1f., 7, 12f., 16, 19ff., 38, 43-5, 47, 50, 52f., 67, 75, 77-81, 84f., 127f., 130, 132, 148, 150, 157, 207, 219, 223, 231
Höfer, Werner 76
Höfler, Peter Karl (see Thoor, Jesse)
Hölderlin, Friedrich 163, 176-9, 185, 191
Höllering, Franz 64
Höllriegel, Arnold (see Berman, Richard A.) 259
Höltermann, Karl 135
Hofer, Andreas 224
Hofmann, Paul 35
Hofmannsthal, Hugo von 55, 163, 170, 176, 178-80, 191, 234
Hohenzollern, Friedrich Georg Wilhelm Christoph (see Mansfield, George)
Holborn, Hajo 33
Hollitscher, Walter 233, 246
Hood, Stuart 146, 148f.
Hopkins, Gerard Manley 182-4, 187
Horb, Felix 35
Hornbostel, Frau von 35
Hornik, Anna 228, 243
Horvath, Ödön von 253
Huchel, Peter 179, 187, 191

Hübner, Kurt 175
Hugenholtz, J. B. 119-21, 125, 135
Hughes, Richard 184
Huizinga, Johan 37
Huxley, Julian 11

Ihle, Peter (see Illing, Peter)
Ilberg, Klara 99
Ilberg, Werner (see Grebly, Martin) 67, 95-115
Illing, Peter 46

Jaccottet, Philippe 191
Jacob, Berthold (see Rollin, Marcel and Salomon, Berthold Jacob) 68, 124-6, 128, 132, 258
Jacob, Walter 254
Jacobs, Monty 71
Jacoby, Ingrid 202
Jaeger, Hans 67, 131f., 135
Jaffé, Elsbeth 36

Jaksch, Wenzel 259
Jameson, Margaret Storm 173
Jastrow, Elisabeth 35
Jeutter, Ralf 172
Johannsen, Else 257
Johst, Hanns 32
Jokl, Anna Maria 71, 209f., 212
Joos, Kurt 127
Joyce, James 181-4

Kästner, Erich 71, 208
Kafka, Franz 176, 179, 184
Kaiser, Erich 64
Kaiser, Georg 69, 72
Kaiser, Konstantin 242
Kaleko, Mascha 254

Kallir, Otto 254
Kalmer, Joseph 172-4
Kaltenbrunner, Ernst 81
Kamnitzer, Heinz 103
Kantorowicz, Alfred 259
Kaplan, Chaim 87
Kapp, Ernst 35
Katscher, Hedwig 260
Kaufmann, Emil 35
Kaufmann, Stefan 243, 246
Kaukoreit, Volker 172, 180f., 183f., 191
Keller, Gottfried 204
Kellermann, Bernhard 96
Kerr, Alfred 70-2, 255, 258
Keun, Irmgard 64, 259
Keyes, Sidney 174
Kimche, Jon 77
Kingsley, Charles 203
Kipling, Rudyard 203
Kirkpatrick, Ivonne 131
Kisch, Egon Erwin 230, 246
Klapeter, Harry 68
Kleist, Heinrich von 177f.
Klemperer, Victor 35, 79, 157
Klibansky, Raymond 37
Klibansky, Sonja 35
Klopstock, Friedrich Gottlieb 26
Knepler, Georg 226-8, 244
Koch, Bernhard 61f.
Koenen, Emmy 97
Koenen, Wilhelm 97
Köpke, Wulf 168
Körner, Theodor 176
Koestler, Arthur 77, 165, 173
Köstler, Marie 236f.
Koffler, Dosio 67, 257
Kohut, Adolph 14

Kokoschka, Oskar 60, 237
Kolarz, Walter 259
Kolb, Annette 32
Kolbenheyer, Guido 256
Kolmer, Eva 238, 242, 244
Koplowitz, Jan 97, 103f.
Korda, Alexander 68
Kormis, Fritz 35
Kortner, Fritz 69
Koseleff, Olga 35
Kostmann, Jenö 223-5, 228,
    244, 246
Koyré, Alexander 37
Kozak, Jan Blahoslav 60
Kramer, Theodor 167, 180,
    226, 252, 258
Kraus, Karl 46f., 71, 230, 246
Kraus, Paul 34
Kreuter, Uta 172
Kris, Ernst 35, 37
Kristeller, Paul Oskar 35
Krohn, Claus-Dieter 259
Kuba (see Barthel, Kurt) 97, 127
Kuczynski, Jürgen 97, 252, 258
Küster, Fritz 124, 135
Kuhn, Helmuth 34f.
Kunert, Günter 179
Kunze, Reiner 179
Kurella, Alfred 101
Kurth, Betty 35
Kurz, Otto 35f.

Labowsky, Lotte 34
Ladner, Gerhard 35
Lagerlöf, Selma 204
Lamping, Dieter 167f., 188f.
Lange, Wigand 259
Langgässer, Elisabeth 174

Langhoff, Wolfgang 259
Langstadt, Erich 35
Lania, Leo 64, 70
Larsen, Egon (see Lehrburger,
    Egon) 67
Laughton, Charles 204
Laurel, Stan 204
Law, John 71
Lawrie, Steven 172, 174f., 180f.,
    184
Lear, Edward 181, 205
Lechner, Ruzena (Rosi) 99, 101f.
Lehmann, Jeanette (née Saphir) 129,
    133, 136
Lehmann, John 185, 231
Lehmann, Lucia 121-3
Lehmann, Wilhelm 179, 187
Lehmann-Russbueldt, Otto 117-144,
    258
Lehrburger, Egon (see Larsen,
    Egon) 70
Lenyi, Dr. 63
Leonhardt, Rudolf Walter 175
Lerski, Helmar 35
Leslie, Vera 176f.
Lessing, Gotthold Ephraim 26
Leverton, Bertha 201
Lewitt, Paul 70
Lichtenberg, Georg 96
Lichnowsky, Fürst 118
Liebeschütz, Hans 35
Liebreich, Aenne 35
Liebknecht, Karl 118
Lind, Jakov 147
Lindgren, Astrid 204
Lindsay, Jack 172f.
Litten, Hans 124
Lobe, Mira 213

Loeb, Walter 131f.
Löbl, Elisabeth 211
Löwenstein, Hubertus zu 121
Löwenschuss, Fräulein 133
Löwenthal, Ernst 4
Lohse, Helmut 253
Lorenz, Konrad 37
Lorre, Peter 68
Lothar, Hans 76
Lowes, E. A. 37
Lucas, Robert 43-59
Ludwig, Emil 32, 72
Lytton, Lord 127

MacDonald, George 203
MacNeice, Louis 184
McLaughlin, Donal 242
Majut, Rudolf 260
Malet, Marian 262
Manasse, Ernst Moritz 35
Mandowsky, Erna 36
Manifold, John 174
Mann, Erika 63, 65, 70f., 252,
    256, 258
Mann, Klaus 67, 147, 153, 167,
    188, 252, 254, 256
Mann, Heinrich 59f., 64, 66,
    252, 254
Mann, Monika 63
Mann, Thomas 59-73, 78, 102, 134,
    179, 251f., 254, 256, 259
Mansfield, George (see Hohenzollern,
    Friedrich Georg Wilhelm
    Christoph) 8
Marchlewitz, Ingrid 259
Marchwitza, Hans 96
Marck, S. 35
Marcks, Erich 33

Marcuse, Ludwig 66
Mareiner, Hilde 228
Margital, Peter 61
Marinetti, Filippo Tommaso 168
Marnau, Alfred 178, 257
Martin, David 172
Martin, Kingsley 11
Marlé, Arnold 70
Masaryk, Thomas 122
Masefield, John 174
Masur, Gerhard 33
Matejka, Viktor 237
Maugham, Somerset 174
May, Karl 204
Meckel, Christoph 179
Mehring, Walter 255, 259
Meier, Hans 31, 33, 36
Meinecke, Friedrich 33
Meinhoff, Ulrike 76
Mendelssohn, Peter de 147, 155, 165,
    257f.
Menne, Bernhard 61, 69, 71f., 132,
    259
Messersmith, George 30
Metternich 234
Meyer, Ludwig 107
Meyer-Udewald, Johanna 35
Michaelis, A. P. 3
Middeldorf, Ulrich 34
Milch, Werner 182
Milne, A. A. 205
Milton, John 151, 174, 202
Moering, Ernst 34
Molnar, Lilli 70
Montgomery, Lucy Maud 203
Morrison, Herbert 5
Mühlen, Hermynia Zur 72, 165,
    208f., 212, 244

Mühsam, Erich 117, 125
Müller, Reinhard 242
Münz, Ludwig 35f.
Münzenberg, Willy 64, 69
Muir, Edwin 179, 185, 191
Murner, Thomas 182
Musil, Robert 71

Nabokov, Vladimir 167
Napoleon 224
Natonek, Hans 68, 72
Necker, Wilhelm 67, 127
Neher, Carola 70
Nestroy, Johann Nepomuk 226
Neufeld, Gunther 34
Neumann, Robert 127, 146f., 165-7,
    225, 252, 257f., 260
Neumann-Tönniessen, Mrs. 35
Neurath, Marie 209, 211
Neurath, Otto 209, 211
Nielsen, Fritz Walter (see
    Wallensteiner, Friedrich)
Noel-Buxton, Lord 118, 125
Novalis (Friedr. v. Hardenberg) 177

O'Flaherty, Liam 174
Ogilvie, Vivian 231, 247
Olden, Ika 63
Olden, Rudolf 33, 63, 96, 102, 127,
    134, 255f.
Olson, Charles 187
Orgel, Doris 201, 204
Orsten, Elisabeth 202, 259
Orwell, George 77
Ossietzky, Carl von 117, 124, 126, 133f.
Otten, Karl 256
Ould, Hermon 173
Ovid 26, 188

Owen, Wilfred 155, 182-4
Pabst, E. W. 65
Pächt, Otto 35-7
Pagel, Lotte 260
Palm, Erwin Walter 254f.
Palmer, Lilli 252
Panofsky, Erwin 30
Patsch, Sylvia 165
Pauli, Herta 64, 68
Pessoa, Fernando 168
Petersen, Jan 97, 100
Petrarca 179
Pfeiler, W. K. 252
Pfemfert, Franz 66
Pincus, Lily 252
Pine, Kurt 68
Pinthus, Kurt 187
Piscator, Erwin 66, 68
Plath, Sylvia 163, 175f., 183
Pol, Heinz 64
Polgar, Alfred 64, 66, 248
Pollatschek, Stefan 71
Polotsky, Hans 34
Pommer, Erich 65
Pont, Peter (= Kosta, Oskar) 71
Porges, Georg 245
Potter, Beatrix 205
Pound, Ezra 187
Poussin, Nicolas 38
Power, Tyrone 204
Praz, Mario 37
Pretzel, Raimund (see Haffner,
    Sebastian) 75
Priebatsch, Heinz 169, 177f., 260
Priester, Eva 222, 227f., 236, 244
Priestley, J. B. 68, 165
Prinz, Rabbi Joachim 4
Pritt, D. N. 221

Raimund, Ferdinand 208, 226
Raine, Kathleen 184
Rakhmanov, L. 104
Raphael, Kurt 68
Rapp, Franz 35
Rapp, Georg 145f., 173, 257
Rathbone, Eleanor 127, 221
Rauch, Georg von 157
Read, Herbert 185
Reading, Lord 9
Rechnitz, Wilhelm 35
Regler, Gustav 64
Rehfisch, Hans José 127, 133
Reichenbach, Bernhard 126, 130
Reichert, Klaus 175
Reich-Ranicki, Marcel 158
Reim, Paul (see Reimann, Paul) 232,
   247, 258
Reimann, Paul (see Reim, Paul)
Reiner, Anna (see Gmeyner, Anna) 70
Reinfrank, Arno 260
Retzlaff-Kresse, Bruno 110
Retzlaw, Karl 125f., 130f., 135
Reuental, Neithart von 248
Reuter, Ernst 118, 136
Richter, Friedrich 70
Riepl, Hans 61f.
Rilke, Rainer Maria 168, 174, 176,
   178-80, 182, 254
Rimbaud, Arthur 180, 185
Ritchie, J. M. (Hamish) 242, 254, 261
Robertson, E. Arnot 11
Röhl, Klaus Rainer 76
Rokeah, David 191
Rolland, Romain 96, 106f.
Rollin, Marcel (see Jacob, Berthold
   and Salomon, Berthold Jacob) 125

Roosevelt, Franklin D. 54, 66
Rosenberg, Alfred 33
Rosenstock, Werner 2, 15f.
Rosenthal, Arthur 231
Rosenthal, Franz 35
Rosenthal, Otto 34
Rosenzweig, Alfred 234
Rosenzweig, Wilhelm 67
Ross, Sir Dennison 29
Rotenberg, Stella 260
Rotha, Paul 211
Rothfeld, Hans 35
Rothschild, Vally 207
Rotzoll, Christa 76
Rushdie, Salman 167

Saar, Ferdinand von 208
Sachs, Nelly 179
Salomon, Berthold Jacob (see Jacob,
   Berthold and Rollin, Marcel) 128
Salomon, Richard 30, 34f.
Salten, Felix 204
Sandmann, Manfred 34
Sargent, Malcolm 11
Sauter, Ferdinand 208
Saxl, Fritz 28-31, 34-6, 39
Saxl, Gertrud 35
Scève, Maurice 177
Schaffner, Jakob 32
Schaub, Gerhard 259
Schikaneder, Emanuel 248
Schiff, Edgar 35
Schiff, Victor 125
Schiller, Friedrich 26, 106, 204
Schindel, Erich 233, 247
Schirmer, Georg 259
Schlegel, August Wilhelm von 175,
   179

Schlosser, Wolfgang 222
Schmeier, Hans 231
Schmidl, Marianne 35
Schmidt, Heinz H. 101, 258
Schönberger, Guido 35
Scholz, Wilhelm (Willi) 227f., 244, 258
Schoyer, Adolf 15
Schrade, Leo 35
Schrecker, Paul 37
Schröder, Rudolf Alexander 32
Schubart, Marianna 35
Schubert, Franz 226
Schultz, Walter D. 61f., 69
Schuschnigg, Kurt 224
Schwarzschild, Leopold 64, 69
Schwitters, Kurt 259
Scott, Sir Walter 203
Seghers, Anna 64, 68, 252, 255
Seidmann, Maks 35
Senghor, Leopold 167
Serkin, Amalia 209, 211
Sewell, Anna 203
Seznec, Jean 30, 38
Shakespeare, William 147, 163, 175, 181, 202, 205
Simon, K. E. 35
Simpson, Esther 31, 33, 35, 37
Sinsheimer, Hermann 252
Sitwell, Edith 175
Smalley, Beryl 37
Snyder, Gary 187
Soffke, Günter 253
Solmitz, Walter 35
Sommer, Clemens 35
Sommer, Ernst 71
Soyfer, Jura 226, 231
Spalding, Keith 252

Spalek, John 253
Spender, Stephen 172, 174, 178, 184f.
Spiel, Hilde 146f., 153, 165, 205, 252
Spira, Leopold 244, 247, 259
Spitz, Rudolf 70
Srbik, Heinrich 234
Stahl, Ernst Ludwig 33
Stalin, Joseph 54
Stechow, Wolfgang 34
Steed, Violet 118
Steed, Wickham 118, 120, 122f., 128, 131
Stehr, Hermann 32
Stein, Otto 35
Stein, W. F. 125
Steiner, Franz Baermann 149, 169, 173, 178, 182
Steiner, Herbert 230f., 233, 242, 247
Steinfeld, Justin 61f., 70
Sternfeld, Ernst 35
Sternfeld, Willy 61, 69, 74, 96, 103, 124, 129, 133f., 253
St. Goar, Miss 35
Stifter, Adelbert 208
Stollberg, Graf 33
Stolle, Walter 100
Strasser, Otto 258
Strauss, Emil 32
Strauss, Ernst 35
Strauss, Johann 226
Stresemann, Gustav 259
Strich-Rohne, Lili 70
Strickhausen, Waltraud 167, 192
Stross, Friedrich 35
Stuebs, Albin 61f., 69, 71
Suschitzky, Wolf 209, 211

Sussmann, Toni 257
Swinburne, Algernon Charles 168
Swift, Jonathan 62
Synge, John Millington 175

Tauber, Richard 225
Taylor, Jennifer 133, 262
Tennyson, Alfred Lord 184
Tergit, Gabriele 252
Tessarek, Anton 247
Teufel, Fritz 149
Théry, Gabriel 30
Thomas, Adrienne 64, 256
Thomas, Dylan 149, 151, 163, 174f.,
    182-4, 191
Thoor, Jesse 66, 70, 169, 178
Thuerk/Thürk, Werner (see
    Tuerk, Werner)
Tieck, Ludwig 175, 179
Tiedemann, Eva 253
Tietze, Erica 35
Tietze, Hans 35, 232, 247
Toller, Ernst 99, 134, 173
Torberg, Friedrich 64
Trakl, Georg 178-80, 185
Trapp, Frithjof 259
Tritsch, Hans 35
Tuerk, Werner 61f., 69
Turek, Ludwig 96

Ullrich, Hermann 233-37, 248
Ungaretti, Giuseppe 168
Unruh, Fritz von 64
Urbach, Franz 34
Uri, Else 204
Urzidil, Johannes 69, 254

Van Gogh, Vincent 71

Vansittart, Robert 107f., 130-2, 135,
    259
Veidt, Conrad 65
Vengerov, Semen Afanasevich 106
Verkauf, Willy 231
Viertel, Berthold 68, 226, 254
Vogel, Alexander 61
Vogel, Hans 125
Vogel, Julius 66
Vogel, Manfred 255
Vogelweide, Walter von 177
Voges, Wolfgang 211
Voß, Angelika 259

Wachsmann, Klaus 35
Wagner, Albert Malte 257
Waismann, Friedrich 34
Walbrook, Anton (see Wohlbrück,
    Adolf) 8
Waldmüller, Ferdinand Georg 226
Wallensteiner, Friedrich (see
    Nielsen, Fritz Walter) 61
Walter, Bruno 237
Walter, Emmi (= Berta Brichacek)
    231, 247
Walter, Fritz (= Otto Brichacek)
    230f., 246-8
Walter, Hans-Albert 96
Walzer, Richard 34
Warburg, Aby 25-43
Warburg, Charlotte, née Oppenheim
    25
Warburg, Erich 30
Warburg, Max Moritz 26, 30
Warburg, Moritz 25
Warburg, Siegmund 234
Warschauer, Frank 63
Watkins, Vernon 185

Webster, Gwendolen 259
Weidenfeld, George 252
Weigel, Hans 182
Weinberger, Martin 34f.
Weiner, A. 257
Weinert, Erich 43f.
Weiss, Ernst 66
Weiss, Peter 167, 179, 188, 252
Weißbecker, Thomas 157
Weizmann, Chaim 18f.
Wellesz, Egon 237
Wells, H. G. 174
Wells, Yvonne (née Lehmann) 118,
    121-3, 126, 131, 137
Weltmann, Lutz 18
Weltsch, Robert 20f.
Wendhausen, Fritz 46
Werfel, Franz 32, 66, 226, 254, 257
Wescher, Paul 34f.
Wesemann, Hans 68, 120, 124
Wesker, Arnold 175
West, F. C. 222f., 228, 244
Whiting, John 175
Wiechert, Ernst 106
Wied, Martina 237
Wielek, Fritz 255
Wiemann, Dirk 167
Williams, William Carlos 187
Winckler, Anke 188
Wind, Edgar 29f., 31, 36f.
Winder, Ludwig 252
Wistrich, Robert 81
Wittenberg, Ilse 35
Wittkower, Rudolf 37
Wohlbrück, Adolf 8
Wohlwill, Fritz 34
Wolf, Friedrich 43-5, 47, 54f., 66
Wolff, Karl 106

Wolfgang, Otto 61
Wolkenstein, Oswald von 208
Wolske, Ingeborg (née Lehmann)
    117, 135
Woolf, Virginia 165, 184
Wordsworth, William 202, 224
Wormald, Francis 37
Wurm, Mathilde 122, 125

Yates, Frances 37
Yeats, W. B. 185f.
Yourgrau, Wolfgang 255

Zadek, Alice 252
Zadek, Peter 175
Zarek, Otto 252
Zech, Paul 254
Zeitlin, Leon 71
Zimmering, Max 61f., 69, 97, 258
Zondeck, Theodor 35
Zuckmayer, Carl 69, 252
Zweig, Arnold 60, 99, 109, 252, 255
Zweig, Stefan 32, 65, 234f., 248,
    251, 257

RESEARCH CENTRE FOR GERMAN AND AUSTRIAN EXILE STUDIES

The second volume of the Yearbook will appear in 2000. Edited by Anthony Grenville, it will contain the following contributions:

Andrea Hammel (Sussex): The Sexual Politics in Anna Gmeyner's Exile Novels

Gillian Lathey (Roehampton Institute): A Journey in Children's Literature: The Hiatus in Childhood Reading Caused by Exile to Great Britain from Germany and Austria 1933-45

Kay Schiller (SSEES): The Predicament of a German-Jewish Historian: Hans Baron and the Society for the Protection of Science and Learning

Esther Schneider-Handschin (Birmingham/Basel): Berlin in 'Saus und Braus': Peter de Mendelssohns und Hilde Spiels Kulturaufbau im Dienst des britischen Re-educationprogramms

Waltraud Strickhausen (Marburg): Ein 'Spätjakobiner' im englischen Exil: Exilerfahrung und Englandbild am Beispiel des Schriftstellers, Berufsrevolutionärs und Exilanten Harro Harring (1789-1870) im Vergleich mit der politischen Emigration des 20. Jahrhunderts

Ulrike Walton-Jordan (Sussex): The Contribution of German Lawyers in Exile to British Post-war Planning, 1942-49

Frank Baron (University of Kansas): Rudolf Vrba, the Auschwitz Report, and the Problem of Rescue in Hungary

Marion Hamm (Tübingen): Continental Refugees from Nazism in British Bed-sitting Rooms and Boarding-Houses: Threshold People in Liminal Spaces?

Monica Lowenberg (Sussex): The Education of the Cologne Jawne Gymnasium Children and the Berlin ORT School Boys in Germany and England

Stefan Wolff (Munich): Emigrierte Physiker im Vereinigten Königreich: Eine gelungene Integration?

Wilfried Weinke (Hamburg), '... im Herzen Australiens, wo die Savanne aufhört und die Wüste beginnt. Deutsch-jüdische Emigranten, aus Deutschland geflohen, in Australien interniert

Jennifer Taylor (London): The German Social Democrats and the British Labour Party 1940-1941

Marian Malet (London): Hans Litten: The British Campaign

Charmian Brinson (Imperial College): Eva Kolmer and the Austrian Emigration in Britain, 1938-1946

Deborah Vietor-Engländer (Darmstadt): Die Pein der Wissenden, aber zum Stummsein Verurteilten - im fremden Land: Alfred Kerr's Exile in London